LEADING MIND

Critical Understandings in the Mastering of Life

Peter Hey

BALBOA.
PRESS

A DIVISION OF HAY HOUSE

Balboa Press books may be ordered through booksellers or by contacting:

Balboa Press
A Division of Hay House
1663 Liberty Drive
Bloomington, IN 47403
www.balboapress.com
1 (877) 407-4847

Print information available on the last page.

ISBN: 978-1-9822-2024-2 (sc)
ISBN: 978-1-9822-2026-6 (hc)
ISBN: 978-1-9822-2025-9 (e)

Library of Congress Control Number: 2019900841

Balboa Press rev. date: 2/13/2019

I dedicate this book to all the people who have the courage to confront their inner dark shadow, which we all carry inside of us, and transform it into light. The state of our civilization is, simply put, a reflection of our unwillingness to deal with this inner darkness.

Table of Contents

Part 3: Mind Transformations 309

Table of Figures

Table for Cases

Acknowledgments

First, I would like to express my love and gratitude to my parents. You provided us with all the comforts that every human should have access to, as well as an environment of rich historical and cultural contrasts that taught us to see life with wider horizons. To my sisters, Susana and Sabina, thanks for being my constant companions in this journey. I love you deeply. Susi, thanks for all our conversations during my travels, you were my constant virtual travel companion. Thanks also for your amazing shamanic journeys, what an astonishing ability you have!

To Tim Simmerman, director of the Hypnotherapy Academy of America, for offering a great learning environment for personal transformation. Your attention to the individual personalities of your students was crucial for someone like me, analytical and in need to be in control all the time, so that I could start to overcome my inner hurdles. Thanks for the safe and constructive guidance that you provided and that I know you continue to provide to your students.

To Patrick Singleton, one of my teachers at the academy, and with whom I did weekly sessions for nine months. Patrick, you enabled my emotional rebirth in this life. Your knowledge in the fields of personal transformation, your sincerity and transparency, and your work from the heart is inspiring and a warm light to this world. Love and gratitude to you always.

To the AHEFT (Asociación Hispana de EFT), and Liana Brailowsky in particular, for their active role in spreading the use of Emotional Freedom Techniques through their training and certification programs. The world needs them.

To all my clients, who gave me the permission to publish the cases that I present in this book. Thanks for your trust, and thanks for helping this world become a better place not only because of your own transformation but also because you're allowing me to share your experiences.

To all the people who gave me their permission (due to the special circumstances of their sources of information) to publish their cases or information. They are, in order of appearance, David Rock, Juan José Lopez Martinez, Roberto Goltzman, Ruben García, Karen Joy, Ann Barham, Christian Fleche, Angeles Wolder, and Jean Guillaume Salles. Also thanks to footprintnetwork.org and uplift.tv. You embody what I believe is the next step in our evolution: constructive cooperation.

Words cannot express the gratitude that I feel toward Diane Kennedy; Sergio Estrada; my wife, Martha; and my mother, Ines, for the effort and time that they dedicated to reading the original manuscript. The book was reshaped and reorganized into a more coherent and logical body of expression thanks to your input. May I be able to give back to you the generosity that you offered me. I also want to express my appreciation to Mónica Bitar and Dhyanprem Waltman for the additional comments that they provided. Thanks to you all!

Francois and Valerie, your generosity and trust in letting me use your pop-up camper gave me the experience of a lifetime. And it was life-changing! A major chapter of my life has been marked by the travels that I did with your camper and, later on, with my own one. Thanks, my friends!

To Tom: thanks for the stimulating conversations about our human nature. You introduced me to the concept of emotional batteries, which I extensively use in this book as part of my model of the mind. I hope to visit again that small but extraordinary town of Mount Shasta.

Thanks to Mauricio Arnal for the valuable feedback that he provided about the cover design. Your input provided new perspectives that lead to the beautiful and effective final result.

Thanks to all the staff at Balboa who helped this dream become a reality. Thanks to the editors and in particular to Mary Oxley for her effective interface to all my questions and requests.

Finally, to my beloved, Martha. Thanks for your company, and thanks for your teachings and patience. Life is warm in your company. I know that our connection has roots that go well beyond this life. I love you!

Introduction

A Glamorous Life

Family Life as a Child

I was born June 15, 1959, in Medellín, the second largest city of Colombia, in South America. My father, born in Szeged, Hungary, in 1909, emigrated from Europe after the Second World War. He survived the Nazi concentration camps but had lost his family, and Hungary was occupied by the communists. He found no reasons to stay there. Eventually, through different contacts, he got a job offer in a tannery (leather factory) in Colombia, which gave him the opportunity to restart his life, essentially from a blank slate. He emigrated with the few personal belongings he had in his luggage. Through hard work and a spirit of entrepreneurship, he later started his own companies (shoes, plastics).

I remember growing up in an environment of financial security, where thinking about our livelihood was not an issue. My two younger sisters and I went to private schools with high academic standards. We were members of a private country club, where we spent our weekends enjoying the pool, the tennis courts, and the social life that it entailed. Our vacations frequently took us to the United States and Europe, among other places. My mother, born in Bremen, Germany, in 1934, lived through World War II separated from her parents. Because the German cities were under constant bombardment from the Allies, in order to protect the youth against the raids, Hitler ordered to have the children sent to the countryside. My mother and her two sisters were sent to a small town called Neustadt an der Orla, where they lived in separate homes. They saw each other in the local school where they had to continue their education. After the war, her family was reunited. Besides the trauma of the separation of the family, the education during Nazi Germany emphasized a strict discipline (my mother, as a child, had to pass tests like staying in water for forty-five minutes without touching the walls of the pool), where feelings and personal desires where out of the question.

Excelling

Both my dad and mom were swimmers, and so it was logical that when I turned four, Dad started coaching me until about seven years old, when

I continued my training with the country club's swimming team. This became the main extracurricular activity that would stay with me well into my university years. Later, as the department[1] created an official swimming league, we would go every year to national championships. I won many medals, including golds, in a successful sports career. At the same time, in my studies, I was always at the top of my class throughout my primary and secondary school years. At university, while studying electronic engineering, I won several scholarships for having the best grades. Once I finished my undergraduate studies in Colombia, I went on to Stanford (California) to do a master's in computer design, where I graduated in 1985. Taking advantage of the practical training my visa allowed, I took a job with a company that later sponsored me for my permanent residency in the United States. From there, I went on to do the "classic" Silicon Valley path: startups. I was part of the first team in two of them and did lots of intense, hard work that eventually led to the successful sale of the companies. At the first one, the first day on the job consisted of renting a moving truck to pick up our work desks. From that day one to the moment that the company was acquired, we went from a team of seven to more than one hundred employees. From wearing all the different hats that you have to wear in a small working group, we saw the company flourish into a structured, professional organization with the well-defined departments that you find in other established companies. It was not a straightforward path though. The markets kept changing, and so we were forced to change course in our product development. What we thought would be a couple of years of intense work ended up being more like six, but in the end we were rewarded for our efforts. It was an exhilarating experience. The satisfaction of knowing that we had created a brand-new product and a company from ground zero was great. Going through the challenges of not only the technological aspects of the product, but also of working with a team in which the personality differences get amplified by the intense pressures that these types of jobs imply, was quite a memorable chapter in my life.

The Shadows Behind ...

Behind this wonderful picture that I have painted about my journey—a wonderful facet indeed—cracks started to appear in that canvas.

---

[1] Departments, in the centralized government that Colombia has, are the equivalent to the states in a federal government.

Bullying

In a twisted way, while growing up, one of my best friends became a bully. There was nothing specific that triggered it. It was a dynamic that started slowly, in which he realized that because I never directly confronted him back, he could keep at it with me. I tried to passively dodge his attacks (like acting in pain more than it actually felt when he would hit me), with no success. Years went by with a dynamic in which we would be best friends mixed with the random bullying that would come out of him. Most of the time, it was right in front of our swimming teammates. Some of them laughed at the situation, and others wondering why I did not do anything about his behavior. My last resort, and the only way I knew how to confront (as you will understand later in the book), was to break that friendship by not talking to him anymore, even though we were still on the same sports team and had the same classes at school.

Academic Drama

During my first year at the university in Colombia, I was almost expelled because I failed two key courses. One more, and that would have been the end of that career. I remember this surreal experience when, just before a test, I explained how to solve a specific exercise to a classmate. That exact exercise showed up in the exam. It should have been a breeze, but my mind suddenly blanked out, and I was not able to solve it. After the exam, my classmate thanked me, but I was left with a frustration beyond description. That was one of the courses I failed. Later, at Stanford, I had to repeatedly cancel several courses because the normal course load was simply too much for me. The system was very different from what I was used to, and I had problems adjusting. It took me five quarters to finish the degree, instead of the usual three that it took the others. There was a tension in my life that was starting to take its toll on me.

Loud Insecurities

In my first job, the first years became an everyday battle against my inner voices that were constantly screaming, "I am too slow in your assignments. Will I be able to do this? What if I cannot solve this job? I do not understand what I need to do. How am I going to come out of this?… These were not subtle voices—they were full-blown emotional messages coming from a perfectionist, brutally critical inner judge that I had to deal with every day.

It got to the point that my boss noticed my insecurities and staged, as I later realized, a mock-up conversation with another supervisor relatively close to where I was working, so that I could hear their exchange. In the conversation, he told the guy how well I was doing my job. My gratitude to him. It is still so amazing to me, and I can so clearly remember that in spite of hearing what they were talking about, it did nothing to change my attitude. Right there, as I listened, I brushed those comments off and continued trying to solve whatever it was that I was working on at that moment. I suffered years of very painful emotional turmoil. Through sheer will, persistence, and hard work (and lots of stress), I was able to start seeing through my dark emotional clouds and realize that, yes, I was able to do my job.

Academics over Relationships

In my personal life, my relationships were short-lived. Relationships were not encouraged at home. I remember when I was in my late teens, my father commented that we were too young for relationships. Our parents wanted us focused on academics. Social life took a backseat. Still, as part of what I saw as how to be in this world, I had it clear that I was going to marry and stay married to my partner for the rest of my life; divorce was not an option. When, after three years into my first marriage the relationship collapsed, the foundations under which I was guiding my life started to seriously shake. I remember telling the marriage counselor at the end of my first appointment (without my then-wife in that particular session) that my goal was to solve our issues so that we could move with our lives together. She replied, "I can help you with the issues, however I cannot promise that you will remain together." I was surprised by such a statement, but in my mind, I had it very clear about my personal view of my desired outcome. She helped us with our issues, and out of our sessions came out the beginning of a profound questioning about all the reasons behind everything that I was doing in my life. We divorced.

The Son of a Holocaust Survivor

As I started to pay attention to how my mind worked, I noticed its tendency to turn trivialities into big emotional drama. I could be walking in the street, and for who knows what reason, my mind perceived that a person passed by a little too close to me. Soon, in my head I was involved in a huge fight with that person. I remember walking on the sidewalk, and a car drove on the road with a little girl who had her arm extended, enjoying the wind. All of a sudden, I had to stop myself as I noticed how upset I was because, in my mind, I was in a lawsuit because she hit me with her arm. If I saw a biker on the street, moments later in my mind, I would be in a fight with him. This occurred with any inconsequential happenings in my daily life. The more I started seeing this inner behavior, the more I had to become aware of my thoughts so that I could catch myself before going too deep into whatever inner drama I had created at the moment. This went on all day long. Yes, it is important to become aware of your thoughts, but it's exhausting when you live in the mode of constantly putting out inner emotional fires. As you will see, in my case this has to do with being the son of a holocaust survivor.

The Curse of Realization

At work, once I got the hang of it, I was able to truly enjoy my first year at the first startup, where we sprung to life a brand-new telecommunications switch. Nevertheless, as time passed and the company grew, new responsibilities showed up. I was very focused on doing the specifics of my job, but I was not self-motivated to study and expand on what I knew. As dedicated as I was to my job, work was work, and as soon as I was done with it, I did not want to have anything more with it. Life felt like a constant pressure, full of obligations. It was in December 1993 when I was reading the book *Do What You Love, Money Will Follow*[2] by Marsha Sinetar, which I had picked by pure coincidence when I saw it on a stand next to the checkout line of a store. I remember the night when I read about the concept that you want to do what you enjoy. It turned my world upside down. It was like having a big bucket of ice cold water dumped on me, and I was shocked. That night I had problems falling asleep. Not only was the concept so radical to me, but it also became so logical and obvious that I kept saying in mind, *What have I been thinking and doing all these years?* Then I also remembered when, talking about what career to choose, my father told me to make sure I would do a "real" career like law, engineering, or medicine. No art, music, or the like. Under that directive, and because I really did not know what career to go for, my logic went like this: *Because I like music a lot, and with that sound systems, let's go for electronics.* That is how I chose my career.

---

[2] Marsha Sinetar, *Do What You Love, The Money Will Follow: Discovering Your Right Livelihood*, Sinetar & Associates, 1987.

After finishing Sinetar's book, I set out to find what it is that I really liked to do. I went to bookstores searching through all the different topics, I went to a career center, and I did psychological exams. As much as I was trying to do my homework, the job in my startups was so intense that it did not leave the necessary space for introspection that one needs in such a search. Life went on, but now that I'd realized that I did not enjoy my job, it became like a curse. It was getting more and more difficult to deal with it.

The Last Straw

At the beginning of 2000, already in the second startup, I had an intense dispute with my bosses. These things happen sometimes, and normally people make amends and move on. To me, that was it. With all the "golden handcuffs" that we had (salaries, stock options), I did not care anymore. By the middle of the year, I handed them my resignation.

I had no idea what I was going to do with my life. Family and close friends freaked out about my decision. My friends told me to seek counseling. I didn't want to do that. To begin with, I needed time to breathe. Life felt overwhelming. The good thing was I did have some money in the bank to back me up in the "crazy" action that I was taking. With this, at the age of forty-one, I was closing what would be the first chapter in my life.

Life Reset

Nature's Beauty

As a young boy in Colombia, I was fascinated by a series of books that we had at home about our planet. I can't tell how many times I went through their pages over and over again. Many of the places that they depicted were national parks here in the United States. I always loved nature. Now that I really had time for myself (notice what happens when we create space in our lives), ideas started to brew up about taking my car and a tent and visiting all these places. When I mentioned this to friends of mine, a couple, they offered me their pop-up camper; she was pregnant at that time, and therefore they were not going to use it during the coming months. I accepted their offer. What I thought was going to be a one-month trip extended to three months. What an adventure! A new chapter in my life started. I was so excited with this experience that, upon arriving back to the Bay Area, I remember how clearly this realization came to me about being done with my life in Silicon

Valley. There was nothing else to do there. I put my house for sale, sold all my belongings, bought a new pop-up camper, and left for what would be six years living in a van and visiting the national parks, hiking, taking pictures (twenty-five thousand of them), and devouring books about the mind.

Inner Quest

As I mentioned earlier, my family was financially well off, and we did not have any worries with respect to money. I remember as a little child, maybe six years old, I was walking and holding hands with my father in the streets of Medellin, where we lived. As we were walking, we would pass beggars in the streets asking for money. Within me, I had this weird feeling about what I was seeing. There was something in me questioning how come I was so lucky to have been born in a family that had money. And how come the others did not? What did they do? What did I do to deserve my life status? This did not come from conversations with my parents or friends, certainly not at that age. It was coming directly from within me. That reality did not make sense to me. The same questioning went on for all the dramas that I started to notice in life (including illnesses). I have always had this inner questioning for as long as I can remember.[3] I started to read books about the mystics, parapsychology, and more. My parents always commented about the "weird" books I read: "Why can't you just read a novel?" This search and study continued throughout my growing years and my career as an engineer.

Now that I had the freedom and joy of visiting beautiful places, I went deeper and more intensely into that need to understand myself, my inner conflicts, what life was about, and what it was that I wanted to do with mine. Besides books, I went to different teachers and gurus, studied their philosophies, did workshops, and kept looking for answers. What became clear from all that was that I needed to go deeper inside of me. I needed more powerful tools. That was when I decided to check out hypnosis. In what would be another story in itself, I ended up in Santa Fe, New Mexico. There, I saw that a local hypnotherapy academy, the Hypnotherapy Academy of America, was having an open house, where they were going to talk about hypnosis and their certification program. I signed up for the whole course right then.

Tim Simmerman, the director of the academy, noticed my struggles to open up emotionally and recommended private sessions with another

---

[3] Whose origins I will explain later in the book, in the section of transpersonal components.

one of the academy's teachers, Patrick Singleton. After finishing with the certification, I continued for another nine months (emotionally rebirthing, one could say) doing private sessions with Patrick. In the beginning, it was a lot of difficult work to simply be able to break through the protective walls that my mind had built so that I could live life carrying my inner turmoil. I remember the first time Patrick helped me open up. In the middle of the session, I was expressing in a very civilized manner my displeasure about a certain event. He saw very clearly what was behind those good manners. He grabbed a pillow, put it in my lap, and told me to start punching it while expressing what I felt. I could not do that. It felt pointless and out of place. It felt ridiculous, I did not want to be another one of those "touchy-feely whiners." I thought, *Life is tough, and so you need to be tough too.* Seeing my internal struggle, he grabbed my fists and literally punched the pillow while holding them, commanding me to say what I really felt. Commanding, not suggesting, because he knew that that was the way to get to my unconscious mind.[4] In the beginning, he was the only one expressing what he knew I truly had inside. And it took him a while. Finally the shell cracked open, and out came the very strong emotions that he knew were there, repressed for so many years. That was just the beginning. In the sessions that followed, there would be much more punching and crying.

Second Opportunities

In the string of "coincidences" that I have had in my life, while studying for the certification, I got back in contact with a woman who had been my girlfriend at the university in Colombia. After I broke up with her, it was not too long before I realized that I'd made a mistake. Part of these emotional shadows. Nevertheless, the circumstances in my life at that time (I was already leaving to go and study at Stanford) dictated separate paths for the two of us. Every once in a while, I asked my sister, who lived in Colombia, whether she knew anything about her. I heard nothing about her until one night, by pure chance, my sister went to a restaurant with her partner to celebrate her birthday. They were actually going somewhere else, however traffic was so terrible that they decided to go to this place instead. Martha was there, at a different table with a group of friends. She recognized my sister and said hi to her.

We started writing long e-mails almost every day, catching up on thirty years of experiences. After three months, we decided to meet. We chose

---

[4] A part of our minds that I will explain soon.

Miami, the middle point between Santa Fe and Bogotá. One can imagine the excitement, and also the nervousness, on the way to our first reunion. We faced the challenges of a long-distance relationship. After I finished my certification, she was offered a job in Spain, and then another one in Mexico. I had no other personal commitments, and so I decided to go with her. We became full-time partners. We married when we came back to the United States. As much as I do feel regrets about my decision to finish the relationship back then, I also know that it is was exactly as it had to be so that I could get to a point where I could face and resolve the issues that always come up in a close relationship. I was not ready then. Now, we've been married for almost three years and have been together for around seven—the gift of a second chance after very deep emotional work.

New Career Directions

We thought Mexico would be a one-year chapter before coming together to the United States. Nevertheless, once there, it soon became obvious that this was not going to happen in that time frame. I had my certification in hypnotherapy, and people started to ask me whether I could do sessions on them. I had done the certification as a personal work, not really with the intention of becoming a professional practitioner. Even so, because I had nothing else to do, I began to do one-on-one sessions free of charge. As more people kept asking me to do sessions with them, I decided to open my own consulting practice. This is how my professional life took the long trajectory change (about twelve years), from high technology to the fields of the mind.

One thing that I started to notice with my clients was an implicit questioning about, "Why me? Where did this behavior come from, these negative feelings?" Their inquiries led me to create a small presentation that I would give to all my new clients on their first session. What I thought would be a half-hour explanation became a full-day seminar. I started to present it, and from the positive feedback that people gave me, I had the idea to write a book so that these ideas and concepts would reach a wider audience. In 2015 we resettled in the United States, and my first order of business was to write the book that you now have in your hands.

About This Book

This book presents a model of the human mind and its mechanisms based on what we observe in the fields of the transformation of the mind.

This book sprung from the need to understand my life. The personal challenges and sufferings that I went through demanded an explanation because otherwise life simply did not make sense. Traditional religions and their explanations did not satisfy my inquiries. Same with the models of traditional science and psychology. Intuitively speaking, it has always been very clear to me that there is a transpersonal nature in us. By transpersonal, I mean aspects in us that go beyond our present physical reality. Psychology cannot address these aspects because its commitment to being science based. Unfortunately, as of today, science has no way to address these facets in us. I wanted to have as complete as possible a picture of the nature of our reality as human beings. Equally important, I wanted a direction about what to do with my limiting behaviors. What I am presenting to you here is the result of this personal quest. It started with my inner questionings early in life, which led to a lifetime of search and study. It continued with my certifications in hypnotherapy, neurolinguistic programming, and Emotional Freedom Techniques (EFT)[5]—while studying others on my own as well, adding my own experiences of personal transformation, and working with clients. After a little more than three years of professional practice, I was able to put together a picture of how the mind works, its structures and components. I do not pretend that this is the "all your questions answered" book, but I do believe that it will help many of you in your own personal inquiries. There will always be more questions, and we continue to be a mystery ourselves.

Intentions

My main intentions for writing this book are as follows.

- **Share with you what I have learned about the mind:** This is intellectually as well as experientially. To understand how your mind works (its mechanisms), why you became who you are, and why you react the way you do during the daily events in your life.
- **Suggest to you actions to improve the quality of your life:** Having all that knowledge would not be very useful if you were condemned to be who you are. By understanding the mechanisms of the mind, it becomes clear what we need to do to change our behavior.

---

[5] These are different methodologies, beside many others, that we can use to transform our negative, limiting behaviors in our lives.

- **Give you a sense of the far-reaching implications of who you are:** The fate of humanity is not really decided by the politicians or those in power, as we may want to think. The fate of humanity is being decided by the thoughts and decisions that each of us is making right now (which is how politicians get into power). As insignificant as you may feel, your thoughts, decisions, and actions have a ripple and summing effect that affects everybody. This book is about leading your life, as well as that of humanity and that of this planet as well. To show this, this book, which is aimed to be very personal in nature, will reach to topics that go far beyond the individual. I will touch on a lot of social[6] and even environmental issues. It may seem that I diverge from my purpose here, but it is very intentional. I want to show how you, as an individual, are affecting the outcomes of this civilization.
- **Suggest to you a sense of your core:** From the fields of the transformation of the mind, the observations strongly suggest that we are nonphysical entities. This sense is emphasized not just in one section but throughout the whole book.
- **Suggest to you a sense of your body:** The body is an instrument used by your (nonphysical) Essence in order to interact with the physical world. It is a gateway that allows your Essence to access this universe. As an instrument, it is under the control of the mind (as I will define soon).
- **Present to you a bigger scheme of why you are here:** The whole purpose of our experiences is to master the physical dimension with this instrument that we call our bodies. You become a master of this dimension when you become the full expression of the Essence that you are within: unconditional love. That will happen when you become a transparent vehicle of expression of your core. Right now, we cloud the light within.

There are other important points about the book.

- I want to make sure that the information that I explain here is easily understood by anyone. Because of that, I will start with very basic concepts and build upon them. Do not let this initial simplicity trick you

---

[6] I want to emphasize that my message here is social, humanistic, and based on what we observe while working with the mind. Even though the material may naturally have ramifications into political thinking, that is beyond the scope of this book.

about the deeper aspects of this book. As you advance in your reading, there will be some complexity in the concepts that I present to you, but I believe that this material is still relatively easy to grasp and understand. The contents are structured in such a way that they build on their own. The first very basic concepts are fundamental to understand the following ones. Thus, at least the first time that you read this book, you must read it in sequential order, one chapter after another. Because of the great number of concepts that I introduce in this material, you will find at the end of the book a glossary of the most important definitions, as well as an appendix with the most important figures, for easier reference.

• As I mentioned above, the beauty of all the information that I am about to give you in this book is that you can change your limiting behaviors. In order to do that, you have to follow special procedures for reasons that will be very clear to you. Traditionally, these special procedures have fallen under the generic name of therapy. Unfortunately, this concept still carries the stigma that the person doing therapy "has problems." After reading this book, it will be very clear to you that there is no human being on this planet who does not need therapy. I am including here all the people who are socially functional, like most of us. We all have limiting behaviors. It is that simple. You may be a multimillionaire or a leader in your professional field. It does not matter. In our current state of evolution, all[7] of us have conflicting patterns of behavior that we need to change if we want to reach harmony in our lives and on our planet. At our current level of consciousness, that is not possible. We need to change. Because this stigma is a barrier for positive change, I am going to introduce new terminology here, in the hope that people will see this from a different perspective. Instead of talking about therapy, I will be talking about a mind transformation process, or MTP for short. My point in this book is that just as it is very well accepted that you should do physical exercise to promote health in your body, you need to do MTPs to promote your emotional health as well. It is an exact parallel. We have

---

[7] There may be some very advanced individuals in certain regions of the planet (India is a typical example) who are already at the level of "permanent cosmic consciousness connection" (or whatever similar description). Even though I have not personally met them, I have no reason to believe that they do not exist. These enlightened individuals generally live isolated, secluded lives. For the purpose of this book, when I say all of us, I mean to say all who are active participants of this civilization as we know it.

emotional bodies that we have neglected with disastrous results, at the individual level as well as at the humanity level. Following on the new nomenclature, instead of therapist I will talk about practitioner, mind practitioner, or mind transformation guide (MTG).

Instead of talking about patients, I talk about clients. My clients are not "people with problems." They are human beings who are aware of their limiting behaviors and want to transform them to live more fulfilling lives. In fact, these are the individuals that are the most self-aware. They are the leaders in the change that humanity needs.[8]

- I give numerous real-life examples to support what I explain. I intertwine my own experiences, cases with my clients, and also cases from other scientists and professionals in the field of the mind. The purpose is to show you that my own experiences doing sessions with my clients are not just some strange, isolated, or "weird" cases. The experiences with my clients are consistent with those of my peers. They are universally human.

  Important: Understand that all the conclusions and opinions in this book are my own. I am solely responsible for how I interpret the cases and examples. My conclusions come from a lifetime of self-study, academic certification, and direct observation. Other scientists or peer practitioners may or may not agree with what I have to say in this book, including those whose cases I include to support my explanations.

  Disclaimer: As of the time of writing this book, I do not have any financial interests of any kind with any of the authors, practitioners, or organizations that I mention. I have chosen them simply because I believe (based on my own studies and research) that they represent credible, reliable sources that validate what I explain.

- I will need to go into the inner recesses of our minds. This means that I will need to touch on a lot of sensitive material to many of you. This includes your own beliefs and particular life circumstances because they are an integral part of your behavior. I do this always with all my respect and always with the intention to create a better life for all of us. Please understand this if you find yourself reading material that is triggering you, emotionally speaking. I am looking forward to your experiences and

---

[8] Notice that the term *therapy* can still be used to differentiate the processes used to help individuals who cannot function by themselves in society due to the severity of their mental dysfunction (severe cases of schizophrenia, severe bipolar disorders, hallucinations, etc.). In this case, it is appropriate to talk about therapy, and about patients instead of clients.

opinions. Let this be the initial platform for constructive dialogue about our differences.

- I will extensively talk about parents and parenting. I will speak of the traditional family of a father, a mother, and their children simply because of convenience and because it is still the most prevalent model today. However, everything that I write about parents simply refers to the primary caretakers of the child. Whether it is a single parent of either gender, a same-gender couple, a foster parent, or a foster caretaker in an orphanage, it all applies to them as well and in equal terms.

- This book intends to present a paradigm for us with relation to this physical world. This paradigm is mainly based on what we observe across thousands and thousands of sessions that practitioners do with their clients. As such, this book is not intended to be religious, spiritual, or scientific. I do talk about us being nonphysical entities, which of course you are free to interpret as a spiritual concept. All that I talk about, I present it here simply as part of a bigger reality that I suggest that science needs to more seriously consider. To me, there is no separation between science and spirituality. *It is a total reality that we need to explore and understand.* The book is based on what we observe in sessions of mind transformation, and so it is not scientific. When clients go to practitioners to receive guidance and resolution to their personal problems, they are on very intimate quests to improve the quality of their lives. By the very nature of this interaction, this is not a scientific process. But due to the immense collection of experiences, as reported by practitioners all over the world, I believe that the observations deserve a very serious consideration for the understanding of our nature as human beings.

This book is not about becoming rich or successful in the traditional sense that Western civilization intends to convince us. There's nothing wrong with money and great careers. Still, there is more to life than that. This book is about you living your life—the life that you did intend to live before embarking in this physical experience—and how it affects the rest of this planet. Whatever shape it was, *you* decided. This is not about easy schemes; this is about deeper schemes. Only you will know what your deeper scheme is, and when you have the courage to follow it, then you will have the experience of feeling truly successful.

Part 1

The Mechanisms of the Personality

Our Inner Universe

Case 1: Phobia to Lizards

A woman in her twenties tells me about the panic she feels about lizards. Just looking at a photograph of one causes her to jump back in terror. I explain to her that contrary to what one would expect, usually these phobias are easy to clear because they originate from a single event. She agrees to do a couple of sessions with me to see where they take us.

I use with her the Emotional Freedom Technique[9] (EFT) as a mind-transformation process, also known more informally as tapping. She quickly goes back to the event that originated the phobia.

She is two years old and blissfully sitting in a high chair in her home. Her older brother, as the typical boy his age, decides to do a little prank on her. He throws a live lizard at her. Just imagine the scene. Here is this little, happy girl when, all of a sudden, this "monster" comes flying at her. It's total panic! Of course, maybe her brother was scolded by their parents, and maybe she was consoled after that scare. Nevertheless, it is from that event that she cannot get anywhere close to anything that resembles a lizard—all the way to her adult life.

As we continue to do the tapping, her anxiety comes down. It is easy to measure her anxiety level because just by showing her a picture on my computer, she is able to tell me how she feels.

After she is able to stay calm at seeing just a picture, we now go through videos of lizards. Her anxiety shoots up, and so we go through more rounds of tapping. In the end, she stays calm. A couple of days later, she e-mails me a picture of her next to a lizard in a pet store.

I am quite sure you have heard of phobias, and you may even know someone who suffers from that condition. They are not uncommon; we accept them as part of the human experience. What is really amazing is how we seem to have two minds, each working completely on its own. Think about it. It was obvious to this woman that the lizard in the picture was not a threat, yet she couldn't help but to jump back in terror.

---

[9] More on this process in section 3 of this book.

What you need to understand is that she was truly in terror. She felt the fear as if she had a lion in her face ready to attack. How can we behave so irrationally? What is going on inside her head? And from this come some questions to consider seriously: How objective are we? How can we really trust the way we interpret reality?

Case 2: Childhood Guilt

My new client is a successful professional woman with a great sense of humor. She makes herself comfortable in the reclining chair in my office. She explains that she is coming to me because she has already had previous surgeries (because of other physical conditions), and now the doctor is saying that she may need another one to alleviate her trigeminal neuralgia pain. This pain is caused by a nerve that runs along the side of the face. She is desperate, not only for the excruciating pain in her face but also for the prospect of yet another surgery. For the moment, she is medicated with the hope that the pills will be able to contain and eventually reduce the pain. The doctor's prognosis is that the treatment will take at least several years.

She participated in my seminars in which I talk about the emotion-illness connection,[10] and she tells me that she wants to give it a shot. She has nothing to lose at this point. She will try whatever she can do to try to avoid yet another surgery.

After I make sure she understands that she is to follow the doctor's orders and treatment while we work together, we start doing sessions. Among others, guilt is one of the major emotional factors related to neuralgia. As we revisit her past experiences, it becomes obvious how much guilt she has accumulated along her life.

The main event occurs when she was around seven. One of her older brothers came into the room where she and her younger sister (then age five) were sleeping. He molested her sister. As all this happened, she lay in her bed paralyzed and confused, trying to understand a situation she did not know anything about. But she could clearly feel that it was not right.

In the mind of this seven-year-old girl, she became responsible for this event (and the subsequent ones that took place) because she was not able to stop that from occurring. She did not protect her younger sister as she should have. This is just one major guilt, among others, that she has been carrying

---

[10] The concept that illnesses are interrelated to our emotional states.

along all of her life. What makes this even worse is that she has kept it as a secret. She does not dare to share this with anyone. She says, "It was my fault. What are the others going to think about me?"

As we work through each of the events, transforming guilt into understanding, her pain starts to subside. And after three months of sessions, the pain disappears. She no longer needs to take medication.

As I mentioned above, in my seminars I explain the connection between emotions and illnesses. This is becoming more and more obvious not only in the fields of mind transformation but also to many medical doctors. So why does the mind do that? Does it want to hurt us or punish us? Obviously not.

There is a tight mind-body interrelationship that explains why things such as illnesses happen to us. The specifics go beyond the scope of this book. I am illustrating this case as another example of all the different facets that we have in our minds as human beings.

Case 3: Regressing to a Past Life

I have been working with this client already for several months, so I know her life story very well. In this particular session, she tells me how, when she first wakes up in the morning, she feels this deep dread and anxiety. As she tells me that, something tells me to use hypnosis directly. (As any professional of the mind will tell you, with experience, intuition becomes an essential tool in your practice.) I am already familiar with how her mind works and connects with her inner world, and so I know that she will regress without any problems. I guide her into a deep relaxation.

Once I see that she is in that deeper state, I direct her to go back to the event that originated this sensation of dread, after I count to three. I do the count, and with a snap of my fingers, I ask her to tell me what she sees. She says,

> It's in the 1800s, it's dark at night, I am in a forest next to my village, and I am a boy. The village has been attacked by men with helmets. They have killed all adults, including my parents. I am hiding behind the trees with other kids. Nevertheless, we are caught. They round us up and start excavating. Once the holes are deep enough, they put each of us in wooden boxes and bury us alive. I can see myself in

the box. I know I will asphyxiate. I can only wait, with dread and panic, until I see myself floating away from my body.

I want to emphasize that I did not tell my client to go to a past life. In fact, I had no way of knowing that her morning dread is because of an event that occurred in a different lifetime. I do not do past-life regressions just for the sake of curiosity. As I am illustrating with this case, I work with my client on a given issue, and if the process takes us to a past life, then so be it. Even more, in her case, she had never had a past-life regression before and was not sure what to think about that topic.

What happened in that session took her completely by surprise. She was not remotely expecting this outcome. Ultimately, from my point of view as her guide, my goal is to provide healing through understanding. That is what we accomplished in the sessions, with her mind giving us the information that we needed to do that.

Is this proof of reincarnation? Not really. It might be a construct of our minds to help us live in spite of traumatic events that we went through. For now, I want to convey to you that this type of phenomenon occurs spontaneously, if the practitioner allows it. All the resistance to this topic that I see in people is so interesting to me. I have had clients tell me as a matter of fact that they did not believe in reincarnation and were completely caught by surprise when we ended in a "past life."

I'll talk more about this later. For now, simply understand that this phenomenon occurs independently of whether the person believes in it or not. It is part of the inner mind.

Case 4: Decisions in Our Lives (Part A)

He is an avid proponent of adoption. When you hear him talk about it, you can feel how solid is his standing in this regard. "Adoption is a best option that can happen for couples or single people who want to have children, as well as babies or children who don't have parents for one reason or another," my friend asserts. He is intelligent, well educated, and living a healthy and well-balanced life. When you hear him expressing his opinions about any particular type of events, you can sense his depth and discernment in the topic. In his first marriage, he and his wife were trying to have children, unsuccessfully. They tried all possible methods available from medical science at that time, still unsuccessfully. In the end, it came down to adoption. As he tells me in his story, even before getting to the point of considering that option, he always had it very clear in him that, with respect to adoption, his answer would always be a no. Understand here that he did want to have children, and otherwise, there were no financial difficulties or any other practical reasons for not choosing it as the solution.

So then, how could such an obvious incongruence between thinking and behavior exist in someone who, from any other point of view, one would right away characterize as a solid person? Of course, he is not alone. We see this every day in our lives, like when people say that they want to lose weight and then proceed to eat that calorie-rich dessert that they know so well is going to add more dreaded pounds. I include my friend's story because I want to make sure you understand that these behaviors happen to the best of us—in fact, to all of us. I will complete his story and finish the explanations of this case after I have explained the mechanisms behind these behaviors. It will be yet another clear example of how our minds work. For now, I simply want you to ponder at the ways in which we behave. Everybody wants peace and harmony in life. If we are so in agreement in this respect, how come our actions don't reflect these basic inner wishes? What is going on inside of us? With respect to my friend's story, let me close here by saying that his marriage ended in divorce, and even though this aspect may not have been the main reason, it certainly was a significant factor in the end result of their relationship.

Case 5: NDEs

Michael Sabom, in his book *Recollections of Death*,[11] talks about the phenomena of near-death experiences, or NDEs. As a cardiologist, he recounts in his book about how, before he did this type of research, when someone mentioned to him the work of Raymond Moody (the pioneer in this field), he simply said, "I don't believe it." Circumstances in life (which he describes in his book) led him to finally decide to conduct a scientific study (he "easily" found in his hospital people who had had this type of experiences). It was scientific as much as it is possible, given the simple fact that science has not advanced enough to deal with this type of phenomenon. As of now, science has no grasp on what it is what we call consciousness. As much as neurologists

---

[11] Michael Sabom, *Recollections of Death, A Medical Investigation*, New York: Harper & Row Publishers, 1982.

talk about how the brain works, it is a complete mystery how consciousness can spring from neurons firing impulses. It does not make sense. In the book, as is typical of other books in this field, Dr. Sabom gives numerous cases as examples. In one of them, he describes the experience of a forty-four-year-old man who had suffered a massive heart attack.[12]

> His resuscitation required multiple electric shocks to the chest. From his vantage point detached from his physical body, he was able to observe carefully and then later to recall, among other things, the movement of the needles on the face of the machine (defibrillator) that delivered the electric shock to his chest. He had never seen a defibrillator in use before.

> It was almost like I was detached, standing off to the side and watching it all going on, not being a participant at all but being an uninterested observer … The first thing they did was to put an injection into the IV, the rubber gasket they have there for pushes … Then they lifted me up and moved me onto the plywood. That's when Dr. A began to do the pounding on the chest … They had oxygen on me before, one of those little nose tubes, and they took that off and put on a face mask which covers your mouth and nose. It was a type of pressure thing … sort of a soft plastic mask, light green color … I remember them pulling over the cart, the defibrillator, the thing with the paddles on it … It had a meter on the face … It was square and had two needles on there, one fixed and one which moved … [The needle] seemed to come up rather slowly, really. It didn't just pop up like an ammeter or a voltmeter or something registering … The first time it went between 1/3 and 1/2 scale. And then they did it again, and this time it went up over 1/2 scale, and the third time it was about 3/4 … The fixed needle moved each time they punched the thing and somebody was messing with it. And I think they moved the fixed needle and it stayed still while the other one moved up …

---

12 Ibid., 28–29.

[The defibrillator] had a bunch of dials on it. It was on wheels with a little railing around the thing, and they had stuff on it. And they had the two paddle affairs with wires attached … like a round disk with handles on them … They held one in each hand and they put it across my chest … I think it was like a handle with little buttons on it … I could see myself jolt.

In the book, Sabom goes over the different possible explanations to these events. He talks about effects of drugs, endorphin release, depersonalization, and more. And one after another, it becomes very obvious that they are not good enough at explaining what he has observed. NDEs occur in spite of whatever interpretation one may want to give them. It is a universal phenomenon, irrespective of race, social class, or education. Simply because science has no satisfactory way of explaining them is no reason to deny their occurrence. As I talked about this in the previous case, and as I will explain more in this book, in the fields of the mind, there are other experiences that are congruent with NDEs. Under deep states of trance, an experienced practitioner can regress an individual to the point where the person will be able to recall what happened before she or he inserted into the present body—independently of whether the person believes in this type of stuff, and independently of the cultural background. People talk about the time in between "physical insertions." People also talk about past lives with as many details as a patient who, while experiencing an NDE, can see what the doctors are doing to his or her body, while trying to revive it. As much as science cannot explain this yet, these phenomena suggest that consciousness is separate from the brain and the body. I cannot go into the details of NDEs here. I strongly encourage that you, as a necessary component about understanding the human mind, read this type of material. It is an indispensable piece in the understanding of the human puzzle.

There are also the behaviors that we hear or maybe even see and experience in our daily lives, like parents abusing their children. The love that parents can feel and express toward their children is probably the closest example of unconditional love in humans. How can then something like that happen? It's such an aberration in human behavior. On the other hand, all the extraordinary acts of heroism, altruism, and more that we are capable of doing. Then again, the horrors of the wars that we impose on each other. And then the extraordinary beauty that we can create through art and music. How come human beings display such extremes in behavior? Most of all, how is it possible that we do so much harm to each other? Why is it so difficult for us to remain in a continuous harmonious state of living? We are so much more than what we perceive with our physical senses. Our behavior points very clearly to the fact that we are complex creatures, and if we want to create a better life for all of us, it is indispensable that we begin to understand ourselves better.

Let's Start with a Model ...

Conceptual Models in Science

While studying to become an electrical engineer, I had to go to the laboratory to do experiments that would confirm the theory that we students learned in the classroom. This is essentially how science operates. It creates theoretical models about the phenomenon being observed. Then, in order to see whether the model is correct or not, it recreates its conditions in the laboratory to see whether the outcomes match what the model predicts. If the results confirm the model's predictions, then it is assumed that it is correct, and therefore it is an accurate representation of that aspect of our universe being studied. It becomes "truth." Now, what you need to understand is that it is still just a model. It is an interpretation—it is not reality. As an example, take electricity. We have built a whole civilization based on machines that make extensive use of electricity. We have very sophisticated theoretical models that allow us to build devices (computers, cellular phones, TVs, etc.) that give us the comforts that we enjoy in our daily lives. Nevertheless, what is electricity, really? We don't know; it is a mystery to science. That is how science works. And if at one moment in time, we observe that there are new outcomes to the phenomenon, then the model will need to be revised and retested. If it does not work with the new outcomes, it will need to be changed or even discarded for a new one. The history of science is a history of self-corrections.

The same applies to the study of the mind, and to the phenomenon of consciousness. They are still a mystery. We don't understand them at their core. However, we do clearly observe their effects. And based on what we see, we create models. As long as the models remain valid, we take that knowledge and apply it, hopefully for our own benefit.

What I will do here is present a model of the human consciousness. I will use it throughout the book to explain the information that I want to share with you. In turn, that information becomes the basis for having the model as I present it.

A Model of Human Consciousness

The model, graphically, is as follows.

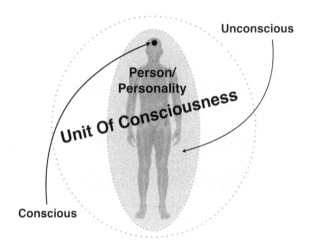

The model depicts a Unit of Consciousness. The material presented in this book is intended for anyone who is interested in making more sense of who we are, independently of any religious or spiritual beliefs. Because of that, and even though one could trace similarities between the concepts of soul or spirit and what I refer to as the inner core, I will rather refer to it as:

- Essence
- Individualized Consciousness
- Unit of Consciousness (UC)

All of these terms are equally interchangeable and capitalized throughout this book to emphasize that I specifically use these names to refer to our inner core. I use all these terms because depending on the particular context that I am explaining, it makes a better fit using one name rather than the other. Again, they are all the same. As you will see shortly, even if you don't believe in anything beyond this material universe, the fields related to the transformation of the mind force us to look at this concept of our inner core.

One of the points that I intend to show in this book is that at our core, we are not physical entities. This is who you really are. This assumption is based on the phenomena that we observe in the fields of the mind and also in the medical fields.[13] They strongly suggest that there is "something else" in a human being that transcends its physicality, because consciousness does seem to exist independently of the human body. Interesting enough, in the medical field, very often these observations have come from skeptical doctors that started their investigations with the intention of clearing once and for all that "weird talk" that they heard from patients in their clinics. In this book, I will talk about what we see in the fields of the transformation of the mind, to corroborate this model.

I am creating this model based on study and observation. At this point in time, strict science does not present models that give us satisfactory explanations about consciousness (quantum physics is getting closer). Still, we can observe its effects, as with electricity. In contrast to electricity, which can be easily measured and tested, consciousness evades detection from our scientific devices. This is the reason for the hypothesis that it belongs to a yet undetected dimension, that I simply refer to as nonphysical. These are universal, observable effects that occur over and over again.

As shown in the figure, you are a nonphysical Unit of Consciousness inserted into a physical body. If you observe the figure carefully, you will see that I depict the boundary of the UC with a dotted line instead of a continuous one. This is intentional. Phenomena like distance healing, telepathy, and clairvoyance point to the concept that somehow, the Individualized Consciousness seems to have the ability to create connections that transcend space and time. My intention is to expand on this in a future book. In this one, I will focus on the internal mechanisms of the mind that operate in what we commonly call the personality. More precise definitions about these concepts are coming. Also, from the figure, there is a dotted line between the unconscious and the UC. This boundary is subtle, but it can be established in general terms, as I will show here. Then there is the (very small) conscious. I will talk extensively about the conscious and the unconscious in this book.

Notice that I present this model as a *human* consciousness model. What I want to point out here is that given the premise that we are not physical entities, and that the human body is just an instrument that we use to interact with the environment on this planet, there is nothing to preclude the possibility that we could very well decide to experience the environment of a different planet somewhere else in the universe. In fact, that is what we

---

[13] Such as the NDEs, which I mentioned earlier.

"observe" in the fields of the transformation of the mind.[14] If that were the case, the instrument that we would use there would probably be very different from our human bodies. As a speculative example, it could be that on such a planet, there would not be a need for an unconscious when, say, using the particular type of body appropriate to that physical environment. Thus, a different model of consciousness would have to be used in that case. Still, it would include the Unit of Consciousness. This Essence that we are transcends the physicality of our universe. This is important to understand:

This model applies only to Units of Consciousness that insert into a human body on planet Earth.

The model is for a Unit of Consciousness already inserted into the human body.

Characteristics of the Units of Consciousness

In this model, as pure consciousness we are:

- Nonphysical
- Unconditional love
- Limitless creativity and power

Notice that at least the first two points, are quite different from what you would generally qualify to human beings. I have already mentioned about us being nonphysical entities, a topic that I will come back to many times in this book. Unconditional love is a rarity among all of us. In small instances, parents may show us a glimpse of that. I know that this may cause some stir, but think about it: parents get, on a frequent basis, frustrated and mad at their children. I know that does not mean that they don't love them. They do. That love is as close to unconditional love as we get. Ultimately, unconditional love is unwavering. And how many internal conflicts and crises arise between parents and their sons and daughters, all the way to their adulthood? To the point where they break their relationships, or may even intentionally hurt each other? You see, as long as people comply with our expectations, we can love them. When they challenge us in opposing directions, then the relationships

---

[14] As Dr. Michael Newton shows in his work. I will talk about his work later in the book.

become more and more challenging, even between parents and their children. So you would say that, in spite of their frustrations, their love is there, deep in their hearts. Indeed, it is. I contend that in fact, that is equally valid to all of us humans. We all crave love and connection with everyone else. We can only crave what we love. And this is what we[15] see when we do sessions with our clients.

Let me give you a generic example. Let's say that a client comes to me to do sessions because he can become explosive and irrational with people (which may include his family). From the outside, that person's behavior would be easily judged as bad. Most certainly, very few people would subscribe to the notion that at his core, this person is unconditional love. Even so, what sessions do is uncover the reason for that behavior. As I will explain in great detail, that behavior came from a negative, limiting program that her unconscious mind had to create in response to a previously experienced event. Once that program has been successfully processed in the session, the person will no longer exhibit that behavior. And because that negative program has been deactivated, now that person is closer, even if by a small step, to becoming an example of unconditional love. When a person transforms a negative behavior into a positive one, what she is doing is peeling away, one by one, the negative layers that obscure the inner light within all of us. This applies to all human beings, including the most horrific examples that we know of. I know that this is a very difficult thing to accept, especially if you or someone you loved have been affected by a person who caused immense pain. Keep reading. Understanding is part of the healing. Following with all this that I have said so far, the reason why it seems so inconceivable that we are unconditional love at our core is because we have accumulated an enormous amount of personal and collective negativity through the millennia of our history, generation after generation. From the models and mechanisms of the mind that I will present to you, I hope to show you that we all are responsible for this result. As such, we all are equally responsible to clean up our act. This is all part of an enormous process of evolution in which we are all active participants. The same way that we fell so many times before we learned to walk, we go through our pains to gain wisdom until we learn to fully express what we truly are, at our core. You can see how difficult it is to express unconditional love. It's very difficult to not judge a sexual predator, an assassin, or a corrupt government figure. Nevertheless, the reasons for every single one of those behaviors can be uncovered (and changed) if such a

---

[15] We, meaning practitioners in the fields of the transformation of the mind.

person were to willingly and honestly go through such a transformative process. Unfortunately, precisely because of that negative programming, most of the time these individuals are not willing to change their behavior on their own. They are caught up in a self-destructive loop of behavior. Now, I am talking here about more extreme cases. Still, make no mistake: we all have limiting and/or sabotaging behaviors that we keep repeating over and over. The mechanism is the same, as I will show you soon.

With respect to limitless creativity and power, I hope you agree that this is an intuitive concept to grasp. Do you see us human beings ever running out of new ideas? Or coming to a point where we don't know any more what to create, what to invent? I think it is self-evident that this is not going to happen. On the contrary, it seems that the possibilities grow as we expand on our knowledge.

The Human Body: Our Interface to the Physical World

Because this model asserts that our Essence is not physical, it needs to have an instrument that it can use to interact with the physical universe. An instrument that allows it to bridge the gap between its dimension and this physical dimension. That instrument is what we call the human body. That is all that our body is. If you look at your arms or legs, or any part of your body, what you are seeing is a whole bunch of different atoms and molecules. And that physical machine is the corpse left behind when your nonphysical Essence leaves it. Here are some important points about this concept.

1. There could also be other intermediary, nonphysical dimensions that form part of the complete instrument. In related literature, you will find about them as the etheric body, the astral body, and more. For the purposes of this book, we do not need to concern ourselves with the existence of these layers, simply because we currently know too little about them and how they impact our behavior. What is relevant right now is that we do observe, in the fields of the mind transformation, that there is a permanent, nonphysical core in us and that it uses an instrument that includes a physical component to interact with this universe. The physical component of the instrument is the human body.

2. As a friend of mine read these statements, she commented that it gave her the impression that they gave permission to abuse and rape the body, because it is just molecules. Two points to address this perspective:

a. It's exactly the opposite. The body is literally your home in this physical world, in its most intimate definition. It is the vehicle that will gift you with the experiences of this dimension. As such, it only makes sense that you truly care for it. Abusing it in any way will only impair the quality of experiences that it will give to you. You will be directly affected by how you treat it. It is your responsibility to provide it with the best materials (what we call food), as well as a lifestyle (sleep, exercise, rest, etc.) that contributes to its optimal needed daily regeneration.

b. One of the main premises of this book is that we are nonphysical entities who use bodies in our path of personal evolution. To do physical harm to another individual is to harm the vehicle that that Unit of Consciousness is using to evolve. Viewed from this perspective, there is a deeper understanding about the importance of mutual respect (physical, emotional, etc.) among all of us.

It is an amazingly complex, versatile, and sophisticated machine. The body is alive from conception, from the energy of the mother. It remains alive, as an independent entity, when a Unit of Consciousness inserts itself in it and "injects" it with its own life force. How this happens is still a mystery.

An aside here, in the interest of opening our minds to possibilities: On this planet, our bodies are built based on carbon molecules. It doesn't have to be like that. One day we will have robots that are sophisticated enough to make it worthwhile to a Unit of Consciousness to insert itself into one of them. As you read this book, you will see that this idea is not as far-fetched as it sounds. Our computers today pale in comparison to our bodies. Our robots can only provide an extremely limited interaction with the physical world, compared to what our bodies do. It is not worth it to a Unit of Consciousness to waste its time with such a primitive vehicle, when it can use this other one (the human body) that is superior. So right now, the only practical choice to interact in earth's environment is through our carbon-based bodies. There is no reason to think that this body is the only possible instrument in this universe that the Unit of Consciousness can use to interact. In the same way that a Unit of Consciousness injects life into a carbon-based machine, a Unit of Consciousness can inject life into a metal- or silicon- based machine. There is not even the need to go that far. We already see this today: as medicine and technology progress, more and more parts of our bodies are being replaced for better ones. (Of course, we haven't yet come close to replace parts of the brain, the ultra-sophisticated main organ to interface consciousness, which goes back to my earlier point at the beginning of this paragraph.) As long as the functionality remains the same or better, the Unit of Consciousness can make use of the modified body.

Continuing with the explanation of the model, when a Unit of Consciousness decides that it wants to interact with the physical world, it will have to insert itself into a human body. In the case of the human species, there are two basic models to choose from, so to speak. There is a male model and a female model. Thus, your nonphysical Essence will have to decide whether it wants to experience the physical world through the perspective of a male body or the perspective of a female body. This is part of the richness of the experiences that this particular planet gives us. Notice the case that I presented earlier about the woman who went to a past life and found herself being a boy. Under this perspective, it becomes clear how absurd it is to discriminate between men and women. We all have been one or another throughout our process of physical insertions. Sexuality is not intrinsic to the UC. Sexuality is a characteristic of this particular instrument that we use, the human body. On other planets, most likely there will be different instruments, and there may or may not be a sexual aspect to them. There could also be more than two sexual modalities; there are no reasons why this could not be.

I invite you to open your mind to greater paradigms. By accepting greater points of view and greater panoramas, we take a more realistic view about our position in this universe and how little sense it makes to keep hurting ourselves the way we do, from the personal level all the way to the violence and wars that this planet has seen. We are just one more species on this small but beautiful planet that we call Earth, which is moving in the far outskirts of one of the millions and millions of galaxies of this known universe.

Requirements for a Successful Insertion

Whether male or female, in order for this insertion to work as intended, there are three basic requirements that have to be met.

1. The Individualized Consciousness has to be able to manage the internal functionality of the instrument that it is using. Because of the enormous complexity of the human body, simply taking care of this requirement is an extraordinary feat. This is under the supervision of the unconscious

part of our mind, and the implied enormous power required to do this task has big implications on our behavior.

2. Because the human body is the interface to the physical world, part of its functionality is to provide data about the surroundings in which it is. The Unit of Consciousness must be able to process that data. Some of this data comes through our senses (smell, taste, vision, etc.). And as we will see, there is also a lot of data that comes through other parts of the mind and body.

3. Because what we want to do is interact with the physical world, the Individualized Consciousness must be able to actuate the body so that it performs actions and responds to its physical environment. We don't want to be passive receptors of data; we want to be active participants in this universe. We want to create, change, and express!

Definitions

I want to use this section to give you my own definitions of the main terms that I will be using throughout the book. This is because you may find different definitions somewhere else to some of the concepts used here. It is not about which is right or wrong; it is more about setting the context for their use.

In order to be able to meet the requirements mentioned above, when the Unit of Consciousness inserts itself into the body, it assigns a part of itself (for a lack of a better description) to be in charge of the physical experience. The part of the Unit of Consciousness that is now in charge of all the experiences while in the body becomes your mind. Notice what is implied here: only a *part* of your nonphysical Essence inserts into your body. The rest remains in its nonphysical dimension. This is how I illustrate it in the figure of the model, where the Unit of Consciousness extends beyond the body. This makes sense because by not being totally sucked in into the body, your Essence can keep giving you guidance from that higher, more encompassing dimension. Think of it as you being inside a forest, and a friend is hovering above it, giving you directions about where to go. You are surrounded by trees everywhere, with no indication about what direction to take. In contrast, your friend can see your destination from above and direct you to it.

The human mind refers to the internal, nonphysical processes that result from consciousness manifesting through a human body.

There are several things to notice in this definition. First, notice the term *human mind*. Even on our own planet, we talk about the mind of other species of animals, like chimpanzees, horses, and dogs. In a similar fashion, continuing with our open-minded discussion, beings on other planets will most likely have different minds, compared to our own. For the purposes of this book, when I refer to mind, I will be referring to the human mind unless otherwise noted.

The next thing to notice in the definition is my reference to "internal, nonphysical processes." The mind is the result of pure consciousness interacting with the corresponding structures of the body, in particular with the brain, which is the main organ in charge of our behavior.

The personality is the external manifestation of the mind working in conjunction with the physical structures of the body.

From this perspective, personality is the total sum of all your behaviors. They are also determined by the physical design of the body, as I will explain. Personality is what we see from you when you interact with the environment. We talk about someone being shy, introverted, extroverted, talkative, or impulsive. These external behaviors are the result of the mind of the individual and the inner workings of its different components.

Components of the Mind

These are the basic elements that make the mind what it is. Mind is the result of the interaction of all these components in each of us. Think of them as the bricks of the mind.

- Intrapersonal
    - Memories
    - Thoughts
    - Emotions
- Transpersonal
    - Memories
    - Thoughts
    - Emotions
- Unit of Consciousness Related
    - Awareness
    - Intuition

- o Telepathy
- o Clairvoyance
- o Clairaudience
- o Compassion
- o Empathy
- o Inspiration
- o Etc.

Intrapersonal components refer to the memories, thoughts, and emotions generated and expressed during the present life, from conception to adulthood and all the way to death. Each physical insertion has its particular set of these components generated in that lifetime. Transpersonal components are those that come from events that transcend the experiences that the individual has had in this life. I will expand on this later, but for now, understand that you have memories, thoughts, and emotions that did not come from your personal experiences during this lifetime (as our work with the mind suggests). Intuition, telepathy, and more are phenomena that clearly go beyond the normal awareness of the individual. The individual somehow experiences them. In my model, these are the result of the person being a sophisticated enough channel to allow expression of these aspects, which are intrinsic to your Essence. So are compassion, empathy, and inspiration in their pure form. I say pure form because they can be influenced and tainted with emotions. An individual expresses compassion, for example, but there might be also a hidden unconscious emotion motivating that behavior. An extreme example: Hitler felt "inspired" to create a superior race. In principle, this could be interpreted as healthier, emotionally balanced, intellectually, and transcendentally developed individuals. We all want that. Nevertheless, because of the way he executed that "inspiration," it is easy to see that it came from very negative personal emotions. That inspiration was not generated from his Essence because it clearly goes directly against what It is (unconditional love).

In general, memories, thoughts, and emotions are the predominant components of our minds in our current state of evolution. By far, they control most of our behavior. The present state of our civilization (which can be vastly improved, to say the least) is the result of two facts related to how we use all the different components of our minds.

1. For all[16] human beings on this planet, our emotions and thoughts run wild and uncontrolled. Our behavior is at the mercy of these two components. In our current present state as human beings, we are predominantly a reactive species.
2. There is minimal communication with our nonphysical Essence, which would bring a more positive behavior on our part. We are an emotional and rational civilization. As I will explain shortly, this makes us extremely near sighted in our decision-making process. Deeper states of consciousness and awareness, like intuition and those attained in mindfulness practices, bring a wiser knowingness that allows us to make decisions which are more congruent with beneficial, long-term solutions.

Notice that I consider emotions an integral aspect of the mind. Some people think of the mind as the intellectual part in us, and they think of emotions as a separate aspect. As I will show, thoughts and emotions are completely interrelated. They work hand in hand in determining your behavior.

Continuing with the definition of the human mind, I refer to it as nonphysical. From my observations and studies, I believe that the core mechanisms of our mind are nonphysical. I will explain why I say this. What is critical to understand here is that precisely because the body is the interface to this world, it must provide physical structures and processes that support the expression of the mind. In a conversation that I was having with a medical doctor, he stated how, just by touching certain parts of the brain, doctors can make the individual feel a certain emotion. That was his argument in favor of reducing us to being nothing more than physical entities. However, that does not necessarily mean that the physical layer is all there is to it. We can observe those processes already, very clearly in our labs. The body, via its main interface organ, the brain, translates the (nonphysical) mind actions into detectable emotions, thoughts, and gut feelings. So thoughts, at the physical layer, correspond to the firing of neurons that scientists observe in an FMRI,[17] for example. Emotions correspond to the release of specific molecules associated with each of them, as well as the firing of associated circuits of neurons. In mainstream science, and understandably so, consciousness is reduced to these mechanisms. Even though, for instance, it is a total mystery

---

[16] All, as qualified previously.
[17] Functional magnetic resonance imaging.

how consciousness could possibly spring from molecules jumping across the spaces that exist where neurons connect with each other (synaptic clefts). What we observe in the fields of the mind suggests the existence of higher level mechanisms not yet undetected but whose effects are observable.

Next definition:

A person is that particular combination of mind and body.

This combination of your mind and your body creates the uniqueness that you are, your persona. *Persona* comes from Latin, and it refers to the character that an actor performs in a play. That is what you are as a person, for a particular insertion into the physical world. From what we see in the fields of the mind, every time the nonphysical Essence inserts into the earth's environment, it does so as a different person, with the implicit consequence of each person exhibiting a different personality. Your Essence, for a particular insertion, takes on a particular body with which it will play a particular role. After the insertion has been completed, that body is left behind (that person/persona/personality), and the UC takes with it all the new learnings and experiences gained as part of its path of evolution.

This scheme could give people the impression that:

1. **We, as individuals, are insignificant, irrelevant in a cosmic contex**t: Even though it may seem a logical conclusion, there is more to this point of view. From the personality perspective, it sure is a yes. Precisely because it has a very limited perspective, it does not see beyond the physical experience that it is having. What you must understand, though, is that every single insertion is an essential, irreplaceable, indispensable part of the Unit of Consciousness' path of evolution. If you were to take away any particular insertion, it would make that path look totally different from what it has become. So you as a person are as important and relevant as anything else in the cosmological, Unit of Consciousness' path.

2. **We are just puppets of the Unit of Consciousness:** The issue here is our disconnection with our Essence. Because of that, events in life seem like accidents in which we are just victims, with no control or say in what we experience. And then, under this model, accidents and events come from the UC, and we are at its mercy. You see, you need to understand that, paradoxically, you are the Individualized Consciousness. You are its expression in this present insertion. That consciousness that you are is the

one who decided the type of life and experiences that you would have—ultimately, because of your own choice. This can be a very challenging concept to assimilate, especially with all the great suffering that we all have gone through at one point or another. This is precisely because we are living our lives dissociated from what we really are. We need to connect and become transparent vehicles to our Essence (as an example, via mind transformation processes). Accidents and victimization will disappear then, and you will be the master of your experiences.

The particular body that you have influences your nonphysical mind processes, and vice versa. It is fairly obvious to see how our minds affect our bodies. All the different thoughts and emotions make our bodies react one way or another. Anger, happiness, excitement—we notice how they affect us physically. For example, you may be feeling depressed. Still, you decide to go out for a run. And because of that physical activity, now your depression is gone and you feel great. The body changed the dynamic of the inner workings of the mind. There is a tightly coupled feedback loop between the mind and the body—your uniqueness.

To close the explanations on the definition of the human mind, notice that in my model, I differentiate consciousness from mind. In this model, the human mind is the phenomenon that occurs when consciousness uses the human body. Consciousness in its pure form does not have a mind. It is awareness, and simply put, it's a mystery.

Types of Mind

The human body is an extremely complex instrument. It demands precise control to be able to function properly. At the same time, despite that inner complexity that needs to be managed, what we really want to be able to do is focus on *interacting* with the physical world. Interacting with this world is what we came here to do. It's not particularly interesting to take on the responsibility of deciding when it is that the heart needs to beat again, especially during a whole lifetime! As we say, we have better things to do. Nevertheless, if we want to be able to interact with the outside world, someone had better take care of the heart's beats. Obviously, there is someone. That someone is the unconscious, and it does that while the conscious you is deciding whether to go to the grocery store or finish that dissertation. I will be talking about these two minds for the rest of the book.

A clarification here: I just want to point out that besides the unconscious and conscious, there are also the concepts of subconscious and preconscious minds. They can be quite confusing, and for instance, in some places, unconscious and subconscious are used interchangeably, whereas in others they are differentiated. Unconscious is for the deepest memories, and subconscious is for data that you are not normally aware but could recall on demand, like a phone number (this last example also used to refer to preconscious mind). For the purposes of this book, there is no need to delve into the precise meanings of these terms. I will be talking about the mechanisms of our behavior that operate below our everyday awareness, in what I simply will call the unconscious mind. In the same way that you are not aware of your heart beating, you are not aware of the processes behind every decision that you make in life. You are aware of the decisions that you make, though, and that is the conscious mind. Their interaction is the key to your behavior. More precise definitions and explanations next.

The Unconscious

The unconscious is the part of the mind that provides all the necessary mechanisms for the survival and interaction of the human body with the physical world. These mechanisms function below our everyday awareness—hence the name unconscious. This includes, as I mentioned earlier, taking care of the internal functionality of the body, which is an extraordinary task in itself. It also includes the mechanisms that dictate our behavior in the environment in which we are, to maximize our chances of survival. This is what is going to become critical in understanding why we behave the way we do not only as individuals but also as a species. We think we are in control of the decisions in our lives. Not so, really. Your unconscious is dictating your behavior much more than you think it does. On the physical layer in the human body, for the most part the unconscious mind uses the structures of the midbrain and the hind brain. They handle all the autonomous processes that keep the body alive, as well as the regulation of emotions. Now, because emotions are associated with thoughts, there is interaction with the cerebral cortex (which is a separate structure in the brain from the other two I just mentioned), and thus the separation of physical areas versus types of minds is not a simple black-and-white definition. Notice also that in the graphic of my model of the human consciousness, I draw the unconscious extending beyond the physical boundaries of the body. This is my graphical representation of my argument that we are not physical entities.

A simple, direct experience that we all have about this is when we meet someone for the first time. This is the famous first impression that we all talk about. You get an impression of the person, even before starting to talk to her. It could be that the other person did not say anything wrong in particular, but you could not help but feel uncomfortable with her. You don't know why, nevertheless the feeling is clear. That impression is something that comes from your unconscious which, somehow[18] interacts with the other person's unconscious. As I hope to explain in a future book, our relationships with others are determined by the interaction of our unconscious minds. Precisely because the unconscious is so key to understanding our behavior, I will leave this section as simply an introduction to it, as part of the mind model that I am explaining here. This book will greatly expand on it in the following chapters.

The Conscious

To use an analogy, the conscious is the skin of the mind. It is the outer layer of the mind with which we are aware of the interaction with the environment. It is the part of the mind that we explicitly use to interact, create, and participate with purpose in this physical world. At the physical layer, it is associated with the cerebral cortex and, particularly in us humans, the prefrontal cortex that generates the higher functions that differentiates us from the rest of the species of this planet. That is how I show it in the graphic of the model. In your daily conversations, when you talk about "I" or "me," you are referring to your conscious. From the perspective of the topics that we are interested in, in this book, its main characteristics are as follows.

- It uses the senses
- It is where the faculty of reasoning resides
- It makes decisions
- It is where willpower resides

---

[18] I say "somehow" because we don't know what the mechanism or the medium of transmission is. Electromagnetism, which is what science can offer us as an explanation, does not seem to be the way our unconscious minds communicate, as suggested by experiments done in different labs around the globe. Check the experiments of Dean Radin, a pioneer in this field.

The senses are giving you feedback about the environment in which you are. You process that information (with the help of the unconscious), and based on your perceptions, you make decisions and interact.

From this list comes a key point that will be crucial to understand our behavior:

The faculty of reasoning resides in the conscious.

It does *not* operate in the unconscious. This will start to make sense of events like failed New Year's resolutions, failed diets, and more. Only the conscious reasons. Based on reasoning, it makes decisions. The problem comes when the conscious makes a decision that is not in agreement with the unconscious. Let me explain. Go back to Figure 1. Notice how the conscious is so much smaller than the unconscious. In fact, if I were to draw that figure to scale, the conscious would be so small that you would not be able to see it. This is an important fact that I want you to take away from this book:

The conscious is infinitesimal compared with the unconscious.

As a corollary, or even more to the point:

The power of the conscious is infinitesimal compared to the power of the unconscious.

David Rock travels around the world giving talks about leadership, under the perspective of how our brains work. He received his professional doctorate from Middlesex University and is the director of the NeuroLeadership Institute. While at Google,[19] on November 12, 2009, he gave this analogy that I think illustrates very well what I am talking about here. The part of the brain that performs the key functions of the conscious, as I described above, is the prefrontal cortex. The analogy that David gave then was that if you represent the amount of information that the prefrontal cortex holds as a one cubic foot space, the rest of the information that the brain holds would be the size of the Milky Way! Even though you could argue that this does not map exactly to conscious/unconscious boundaries, it is still a very good approximation.

---

[19] David Rock, *our Brain at Work*. YouTube, GoogleTechTalks, December 2, 2009, https://www.youtube.com/watch?v=XeJSXfXep4M. Accessed December 10, 2018. Around the 3:30 mark.

It also illustrates beautifully the vast difference of information processing between the conscious and the unconscious. This is a big surprise to a lot of people. You think that you (the conscious) are the master of your life, that you are making decisions of your own free will. It's not that simple. Later, when talking about the power of the unconscious, I will give you very clear examples that illustrate this difference in processing power. So if the conscious made a decision (like starting a diet, for instance), but the unconscious does not agree with it, who do you think will win? The unconscious, of course. I hope that these first points are already giving you more understanding about why you don't seem to be able to finish goals that you honestly want to accomplish. This is also where the topic of willpower comes into play.

The American Psychological Association (APA) defines willpower as "the ability to resist short-term temptations in order to meet long-term goals."[20] *Merriam-Webster's Dictionary* defines it as "energetic determination"[21] (energetic as in strong). Whatever definition you find, it is very obvious that willpower refers to a faculty that implies some sort of effort from our part. The faculty of willpower works in conjunction with the faculty of reasoning. By using the faculty of reasoning, we reach decisions that require an action from us. If these goals present obstacles to reach them, we will use willpower to overcome them. As you can see, we are talking about two faculties that reside in the conscious. As such, willpower is very limited in its reach (read the APA article I just mentioned; it will give you a very good idea about this aspect of our minds). I want to make an important distinction at this point.

Willpower is different from inspired action.

Willpower is just effort, and so it automatically implies that your decision is not congruent (i.e., in agreement) with the structures of your unconscious. Therefore, you are putting yourself at risk of failing in your endeavor if you do not manage this faculty correctly, because the unconscious is so much more powerful than the conscious. All the failed diets and New Year's resolutions

---

[20] Kirsten Weir, "What You Need to Know about Willpower: The Psychological Science of Self-Control." *American Psychological Association,* American Psychological Association, 2012, http://www.apa.org/helpcenter/willpower.aspx. Accessed December 10, 2018.

[21] Merriam-Webster, *Merriam-Webster,* https://www.merriam-webster.com/dictionary/willpower. Accessed December 10, 2018.

are a testament to the limited power of willpower. This faculty must be used very carefully. In fact:

Minimize the use of willpower while maximizing inspired action in your life.

Inspired action comes from true inner passion. This force comes directly from your nonphysical Essence, through your unconscious. Thus, you are working with an unlimited source of power. When you are using willpower, you face problems. When you are inspired, you face challenges. These are completely different attitudes and as such give you very different experiences in your life. For example, if, while using willpower, you require the participation of other people, and they fail to meet your expectations, you will start to resent them. When inspired, you will feel motivated to rally them behind your goal, or else simply find another way of getting there. Using willpower depletes your mind energies. Inspiration does not. And quite often, as a result of an unkept resolution, the person ends up feeling worse about herself, now adding self-esteem issues to the problem. When willpower starts to fail or, simply put, feels like too much effort, you need to revisit the real motivation behind that goal. Yes, it is healthier for you to quit smoking, but if you attempt to do it just because of the rationale of it (conscious decision) instead of truly feeling ready for a healthier change in your life, then your unconscious will prevent you from getting there. It is not sufficient that your partner, family members, or friends convinced you to do it. You want the action to fully come from within. Then it becomes inspired action, and your chances of succeeding will grow exponentially.

Having said that, do understand that willpower is a valuable faculty. Life moments are not lived at 100 percent inspiration. This faculty helps us accomplish goals in spite of less than ideal circumstances at a given moment. Simply be aware about how you are using it, and be prepared to make changes in your life if it feels like a constant effort. With the information that I will present to you, you will be able to fully understand the interactions between your conscious and unconscious. This will help you not only to avoid falling into the trap of failed resolutions but also to improve the overall quality of your life experiences.

I gave you the basic model of the human consciousness. I have explained to you how, once the nonphysical Essence inserts into a human body, its consciousness becomes the mind that we use in our daily experiences. All these models and their definitions are simply academic. As human beings, we are a holistic entity where all these aspects and components work together as one. Our different definitions are simply for our easier understanding of the concepts that we want to grasp. I explained the main characteristics of the conscious. I just touched on the unconscious. Let's expand on it now. It is there where the biggest answers are.

Introduction to the Unconscious

Prime Directive of the Unconscious

The unconscious provides all the necessary mechanisms for the survival and interaction of the body with the physical world. The reason I explicitly include the term *survival* in the definition is because of its relevance. Let me put it very clearly like this:

> *The objective of your unconscious is, first and foremost, your survival in this physical world.*

This has an impeccable logic. What good is it to you to be thinking about your happiness, for example, if you then carelessly cross the street and get run over by a car? Think about it from the perspective of the Unit of Consciousness. Look at the insertion process into the human body and the long time it takes to develop into maturity (compared to most other animals on this planet). It would be very wasteful of time and energy to insert into a body that would be easily lost to the environment in which it lives. The nonphysical entity would have to try again and again until finally, by chance in that particular insertion, it would have been able to reach maturity and have some meaningful experiences. That is inefficient. That is why the unconscious was created with core mechanisms that maximize the body's chances of survival.

This explains to you a human behavior, as much as it seems so logical and not needing explanation. Take a homeless person or a beggar in the street. Why do you think (as a generalization) that the person is not interested in the arts, philosophy, mathematics, or any other "higher" intellectual activities? You could say that it is because these people don't have the money or the education. It is actually more than that. Their unconscious will not let them go there. That person has not resolved the basic issue of "when and how I am going to get my next meal." That is survival. And until that person resolves that issue, the unconscious will not let him focus on anything else. This is another example of the unconscious controlling our behavior.

Understand that this implies that to your unconscious, survival is way more important than peace, happiness, and harmony. Any of those things that we yearn for and desire are actually lower priority in its to-do list. Any decision that you make in your life will go first and foremost through its survival assessment mechanisms. Any threat that it may perceive about any decision that you are considering will affect its outcome. You will think that you made the decision. Not so. By definition, the unconscious is working without you noticing it. This is the reason that I emphasize so much about the power of the unconscious. If you couple this concept of survival with the power it has, you start getting an idea of what is really behind all your decisions in life.

Some Basic Characteristics

The unconscious is a subject for endless study material. As I did with the conscious, I will talk about its characteristics that are relevant to us in this book. These characteristics are:

- The unconscious controls the inner functionality of the body
- The unconscious has stored everything that has happened to you
- The unconscious is a machine
- The unconscious stores everything associatively
- The unconscious generates and stores our emotions
- The unconscious stores all the programs to dictate our behavior
  Let's go over each one of them.

The Unconscious controls the Inner Functionality of the Body

My intention here is to show you how enormous the power of the unconscious is. You may already know about the information that I am going to give you next. If you don't, then great—it's something new you will learn. Otherwise, the reason I am going to take you through this material is because I want you to view it from a different perspective. I have already been telling you that the unconscious dictates your behavior, and I will soon show you how. That is why it is crucial that you understand the magnitude of the power that we are talking about.

The human body is an organization of human cells that work together to be able to give you the functionality that allows you to live your life. In order to accomplish that, the cells are organized into structures called organs. Organs, in turn, are organized into systems. Thus, you have the digestive system, the circulatory system, the lymphatic system, and more. All the cells, systems, and structures in your body need to be working in an organized manner so that there is a coherent result in its overall functionality. Someone must be orchestrating everything so that this coherence is maintained. That someone is the unconscious. Think about this: you don't have to worry about when your heart needs to beat again, or how fast it needs to do that to cover the oxygen needs of the body as it changes activities. You do not need to worry about when to breathe or, when you eat, about how that food is going to be digested. It is the unconscious that is directing all this activity for you. This is so that you, the conscious part of the personality, can concentrate on living your life, so that you can concentrate on interacting with the physical world.

Cells, Cells, Cells …

If you search the Internet, you will find out that the body has around forty trillion cells. The number can change quite a bit depending on the sources and how you compute it (I have seen numbers from ten trillion to one hundred trillion cells), but the average will be around there. That is forty million-million cells! Think about the task of coordinating each one of those cells so that they work in harmony to produce the magnificent functionality that your body has. Your unconscious is doing that, and it is a staggering organizational feat. The number is so big that it is difficult to visualize. Let me give you a bigger number that may ironically make this more palpable. Fritz-Albert Popp is a German biophysicist known for his research on biophotons. According to him,[22] in each one of those cells, around one hundred thousand chemical reactions occur every second. So as you are reading this, every second your body is doing something like four million trillion chemical reactions. This may sound silly, but try to pronounce that number every second. You'll barely be able to keep up! That is the number of chemical reactions that your body is doing every second. For the critics of these numbers, what we are talking about is so big that even errors in one or more orders of magnitude do not change the point of what I am trying to show you. Every single one of those reactions needs to be done at the right time and place. They cannot happen at random; this is simply common sense. Otherwise, your body would not function. There has to be an organized series of events to obtain the functionality that we get out of our bodies. In other words, it is the unconscious that is orchestrating all these chemical reactions. All the

---

[22] Science & Spirituality: Living Light: Biophotons and the Human Body—Part 1. Supreme Master Television, November 5, 2007, https://www.youtube.com/watch?v=2STCpAJtSRw. Accessed December 10, 2018. At around the 9:30 mark.

appropriate chemical reactions are happening simultaneously in each of our cells. The processing capacity of our unconscious is so big that it is simply difficult to grasp. As an electrical engineer who designed computing machines in Silicon Valley, I can tell you that there is nothing close in our current technology to this. It's not even close, as much as any documentary may want to portray how advanced our technology is. This is the power that is behind our behavior, our unconscious.

Something as Simple as Just Moving …

Another example is the muscular system. The body has more than six hundred muscles. Let's say you want to grab a glass of water that is on the table where you are reading. You extend your arm, grab the glass, move it toward your mouth, and proceed to drink. You, the conscious, decided to drink. Now, who was the one who actually executed that decision? The unconscious. Think about something this simple that we constantly execute in our daily lives. Did you have to think about how to actuate the different muscles in your arm and hand? At every instant along that movement, some muscles need to be contracted while others are relaxed, and all in the right degree, so that the movement happens in the smooth, familiar way we do it.

Now view it from this angle. If you, the conscious, would have to be in charge of each of the muscles involved, how long do you think it would take you to accomplish that task? Most of us don't even know how many muscles we have in our arms and hands. Let's say there are thirty. (It is actually more, and much more if you consider muscles in the shoulder and face that you also need to do this.) How long do you think it would take you to coordinate, one by one, thirty muscles in each instance to accomplish that task? I would speculate hours, and just to grab a glass of water. The conscious simply does not have the processing power to do this. You would not be able to even get out of your bed to start your day (because to do that, you would have to, at any given instant, adjust, one by one, the over six hundred muscles in your body). Ponder about it. How many things can you truly do simultaneously at one given instant? If you wanted to argue that jugglers, as an example, are doing simultaneous tasks, you are right. Nevertheless they are actually being performed by their unconscious, not the conscious. That is why they need to practice until their unconscious learns how to do it. If you try to do two things at the same time, like speaking on the phone while answering an e-mail, you might be able to do it, but your efficiency drops, and you start making more mistakes. Your conscious performs best when executing one task at a given time. It is that limited. There is an enormous gap of power between the conscious and the unconscious.

Let's Go Out for a Ride …

Are you starting to contemplate the possibility that there may be other forces behind your behavior? Here's one more example that we can use to relate this to the way we act. Let's say that I invite you to come with me on a small road trip outside the city. Once we are in a rural road with no traffic, I stop my car. From the roof rack, I take down a wooden plank and set it down across the road. The plank is two feet wide, and it is a little longer than the width of the road. Now I ask you to go to one end of it, step on it, and walk across the road on top of that plank. I think it is easy for anyone (who doesn't have a physical disability that would prevent the person to do this) to accomplish this task. Very well. I take the plank and put it back on the roof of the car, and once secured, we continue our drive.

Now, we go to the city, where I know there happens to be two very tall buildings across the street from each other, and with the same height. We park, I grab the plank, and we take it to the roof of one building. I then place it and secure it across the two buildings. Now I ask you to do the same exercise that you did with the plank sitting on the road. We all know what is going to happen, right? As soon as you try to step out of the border of the building, your body will freeze, your knees will shake, and you will have a vertigo sensation. You will not be able to do the very simple task of walking across that plank, in contrast to how you easily did when it was on the road. What is going on here? Your unconscious detects danger. As soon as it does that, it takes control of your body. Notice that this is instantaneous, practically speaking. You will not be able to walk. And you, the conscious, won't be able to say, "I do not want to feel this vertigo right now, because I really want to cross to the other building." You, the conscious, do not have the power to override the unconscious. You cannot simply turn off those sensations. Once you feel that vertigo, until you retreat inside the inner area of the roof, you will not be able to move forward.

Let me put it to you from this other point of view. While you are walking within the periphery of the roof of the building, the unconscious does not detect danger, and therefore it allows you to do that. As soon as you get close to the border, it detects the danger and takes control of your body. In other words, in life you have "permission" to do anything you want as long as your unconscious does not detect danger. When it does, it will exert control on your behavior.

So are you free to decide anything in life? Yes, you do have choices, but you are not as free as you think you are. In fact, we are quite limited in our own choices, in our current state of evolution. However, you have the potential to become unlimited. I will explain what you need to do to accomplish that. The first step is to become aware of this. You cannot solve an issue if you are not even aware that there is an issue.

The Unconscious Has Stored Everything That Has Happened to You

As you go about your daily activities, your unconscious is capturing all kinds of data about your surroundings. Because the unconscious is so much more powerful than the conscious, the unconscious has to filter all that information to the bare minimum that the conscious can handle. Otherwise, it would overwhelm the conscious. Simply because you, the conscious, are not aware of that data, that does not mean that it is not affecting you.

In the academy where I got my certification in hypnotherapy, all of us in my class of around twenty-five people learned how to perform a process called natal regression. In this process, once you have a client in the state of hypnosis, you guide her unconscious to go back in time. In fact, you can go back all the way to when the client was in the mother's womb. The client will be able to tell you what happened all along the pregnancy. This is not something that only some gifted people can do. You can do it; anyone has that capability. And everyone has, in his or her unconscious, the memory of those in utero days.

Case 6: Unwanted Baby

This woman came to me because she felt that she had self-esteem issues. As we were doing the technical sequences of EFT,[9] she became aware that, already in the mother's womb, she was not wanted. They did not want to have another child, especially her father. For some people, this comes as an awareness; for some others, it comes as images or other sensations. What was clear to her was that this was true. This was not speculation. This becomes as fact as any event you would describe that happened in your day. In the case of my client, this reality fit perfectly well with her issues. Think about it: "If not even my parents wanted me, then who else in this world?" Or, "There has to be something wrong with me, if not even my parents want me." That was the perception that was engraved in her mind, already before even being born. And even though she did not become aware of that until that day in our session, this perception colored everything that she did in her life. Her actions and responses were affected by that point of view of herself.

I also want to point out something you may not have caught. When she regressed to her mom's womb, she realized (as the unborn baby inside of her) that both her mom and her dad did not want another child. How could that baby know about what her father was feeling for her? The mom we can understand; the physical connection is there. But her dad? That's the unconscious and its power.

Case 7: Surgery Room Memories

Juan José Lopez Martinez is a medical doctor who graduated from the University of Murcia (Spain). Besides other degrees in his career as a medical doctor, he also became a regression therapist, using hypnosis. He practices medicine as well as regression therapy, with more than six thousand documented regressions.[23] Besides the books that he has written (which I will refer to later), you can find videos of his conferences in the Internet (unfortunately, they are only in Spanish). In one of them, entitled "Juan Jose Lopez, Charla 2 de 2,"[24] he talks about the case where another doctor had performed a gallbladder surgery on a woman. That doctor then referred her to José to do regression therapy because of a different issue. In one of the sessions, while in trance, this woman was able to recall the conversations that the doctors were having while performing the surgery—not only the conversations but also who was doing what part of the surgery. José carefully wrote down her story. The doctor who'd performed the surgery on her worked at the hospital where José worked as a medical doctor, and so it was easy to get a hold of him and ask about her recall. José's colleague was astonished that she could recall in such detail what had happened in the surgery room.

If you attribute this to insufficient anesthesia, it may be in some cases. But it's definitely not in all cases.11 Whatever the circumstance, the fact

---

[23] Per our e-mail correspondence.

[24] Juan Jose Lopez Martinez, *Terapia Regresiva*. YouTube, Asociación Jumillana de Reiki, November 9, 2013. https://www.youtube.com/watch?v=9PnjdMYL99U. Accessed December 10, 2018. The event is at around the 37:10 mark.

is that the patient did not remember the events that were later recalled via trance. More and more doctors are becoming aware that the unconscious of the patients is active and paying attention to what is going on, even while under general anesthesia. The relevance of this is that the conversations in the surgical room can have a negative impact in the patient. It is very clear to me, as a practitioner, that doctors refrain from any negative conversations in general and particularly about the patient. This is especially true when they make comments about findings during the surgical procedure. Comments like "His liver looks bad; he is going to have problems later on in his life" are not a good idea. The patient may recover perfectly well from that particular surgery but also be left with an inexplicable anxiety.

These are sample cases of events that are quite common during hypnotic regressions. As you can see, many of them have been corroborated afterward, and so they cannot be reduced to simple imagination. In some cases, that may be, but not all of them. The unconscious has a reach (physically and figuratively) that extends far beyond that of the conscious. The data that it compiles without your awareness is affecting your behavior in your everyday activities.

The Unconscious Is a Machine

As simple as it sounds, this is the most important concept you need to know about the unconscious. It's why we keep having the same thoughts over and over. It's why we keep repeating behaviors again and again, even though we are very clear that they do not serve us. Often we see how we hurt other people, many times our loved ones, because the way we behave. Somehow, we can't stop ourselves when we get triggered. That is our unconscious. As soon as it detects something in the environment that triggers it, it reacts according to its programming.

The big contrast (besides the difference in power) between unconscious and conscious is this key point:

The conscious reasons. The unconscious does not *reason.*

The best analogy that I can give you is that your unconscious works like a computer. The computer just executes the programs you downloaded to it. It does not judge. There are computers in military equipment that will be used to guide weapons to kill millions of people. There are computers controlling irrigation systems to maximize the growth of plants that we use for food. They don't judge; they simply execute the programs they have. So does your unconscious. This explains to you why you repeat the limiting behaviors that you have. It does not matter that you, the conscious, do not want to do them again. Because the unconscious is so much more powerful than the conscious, it will win, and you will act once more that undesired pattern. That limiting behavior is a program. I will show you its structure and how it works.

The Unconscious Stores Everything Associatively

You already saw that the unconscious has stored all the data it has accumulated throughout your life. How does it organize it? By association. To illustrate this clearly, I am going to use an analogy with an old library filing cabinet. For those of you who are young enough to have never seen one, all that you need to know is that it is a cabinet with a whole bunch of little drawers. For our analogy, each drawer will represent a quality that the unconscious uses to describe anything.

Start with an Apple

Let's start simple. Let's assume that you have never seen an apple before. I am with you, and I show you an apple and invite you to taste it. You like it. Out of this experience, what does your unconscious do? Using our metaphor here, the unconscious takes a piece of paper, writes the concept of apple on it, and puts it in the drawer that contains all the cards that represent the foods that taste good to you.

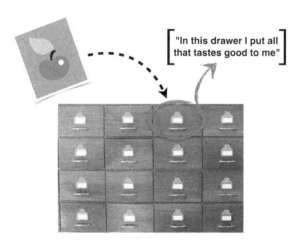

"In this drawer I put all that tastes good to me"

Now notice this. Because you already had that experience with the apple, and your unconscious did that classification, you no longer will need me to know what to do when you see an apple the next time. The unconscious created a program that will determine your behavior when confronted with that object or concept. In our example, the next time you see an apple, your unconscious will search through all the drawers it has (millions of them!) to see where *apple* has been classified. When it finds it in the drawer of "things that taste good to me," if you are hungry, you will feel a desire to eat the apple. Take the time to think about this process. How many millions of objects and concepts have you experienced in your life? Even so, as soon as you see that apple, you recognize it and know what to do with it. I say this because you know that you can eat an apple, whereas you can't eat a chair. That is also another classification that takes part of that first experience that you had with the apple. That happens with its color, size, texture, and everything related to the concept of apple. This process is happening continuously with all the objects as you move in your daily life. You instantly recognize the things that surround you. This also applies to abstract concepts like war, poverty, health, and more. It's an astonishing information-processing power.

Now Go to a Cave

Let's go to a more sophisticated example. When I ask you to think about a cave, it is very likely that you will see it as a relatively dark place underground. That is what most of us experienced the first time we entered one of them. We had to use lights (or there were already lights installed). You can see, then, how you have this association. Your unconscious, at that first time, took a card, wrote *cave* on it, and put it in the drawer where all things associated with darkness are. It is stored as such in your mind.

Now let's take an example of a boy who is around five years old and is playing with his friends in his home. As it turns out, there is a cave nearby. They decide to go there and explore. As they go in, they go into its tunnels. Our boy goes into an opening that turned out to be too tight. Even though he managed to get halfway through, he is stuck. He cannot get out. He calls his friends for help. They try but are unable to free him. He is getting nervous and is scared. Because his friends were not able to free him, they decide to go and call the parents. For this example, let's say that they all left this boy alone in the darkness of the cave. He is stuck, he is scared, and he is even in a panic. Eventually, though, his friends come back with his parents, and they free him. He is safe! In the end, nothing else happened. Even though he is a little bit shaken, after a little time, he regains his energy and ends the day playing with his friends like any other child. Thinking logically (faculty of reasoning), he should be fine.

However, out of this experience, what happened in his mind? Remember that the unconscious wants to ensure your survival in this physical world. The experience that this boy had was quite a scary one. To his unconscious, this translated as danger. It will want to make sure it does not happen again. What it does, then, is take note of the characteristics of that event and stores them in the drawer labeled *dangerous*. It will create an association. The concept of cave will now go into the dangerous drawer. And it will also do it to the characteristic of darkness, which will also be labeled as dangerous. Anything significantly related to that event will be classified as such.

Our boy is ready to go to bed. Aside from the panic in the cave, he had a great day in company of his friends. He knows that he is safe at home, and he goes to sleep in his room, as he has done countless of previous nights before. He turns off the light. The room goes dark. As far as the conscious is concerned, he is ready to go to sleep. Nevertheless, his unconscious does not rest. After all, your heart does keep beating while you are asleep. The unconscious is always checking the environment in which it is, comparing it with the data it has obtained from previous experiences. What it finds now that was not there the previous nights is that darkness is in the drawer labeled dangerous. The fact that he is now safe in his bed at home is irrelevant. The unconscious will turn on the alarm. The boy will now feel the fear of being in darkness. Depending on how traumatic the experience was, he may not be able to sleep just this one night, or maybe it's a couple of nights. It could happen that from this day on, he will suffer from restless sleep because of that association in his unconscious.

In his mind, the concept of cave is in the dangerous drawer, and he will also experience fear whenever he goes into one. If this fear is so intense that it becomes panic, the boy now feels claustrophobic in caves. It could also become a generalized claustrophobia if his unconscious also put the concept of tight spaces into the dangerous drawer.

Case 8: My Own Fear of Darkness

When I was one year old, my parents were in Germany visiting relatives. My grandparents lived in a multistory home in which the bedrooms were upstairs. On this particular day, they put me in bed for my afternoon nap in one of the bedrooms above. I normally slept well during my naps, and so they left me in my room alone and went downstairs to be with family and some other friends. When they went back into the bedroom, which was dark, they found me standing in the middle of the bed, crying in desperation. For how long was I there? I don't know.

Out of that experience, I developed a fear of darkness that accompanied me through my childhood years. My parents had to leave a dim light on in my room so that I could sleep. I tucked myself completely with the bedsheets, including my head and face, leaving a little opening for my nose so that I could breathe. That is what I felt could protect me from the terrors of the darkness.

Opposite Qualities

Here's one more example to show you how the unconscious does not judge one way or another. Let's take a little girl who has a loving father. As a result of her experiences with her father, her unconscious has put the concept of father into the drawer of love. On the other hand, her father happens to have a very explosive personality. As loving as he normally can be, he explodes in rages of anger for seemingly unpredictable reasons. As a result of these experiences, her unconscious will also put the concept of father in the unpredictable box (or it could go as well into the frightening drawer). So *father* is now classified under love and unpredictable. Because she will be under this father's behavior during her growing years, her perception will be that love and unpredictability are tied together. Her unconscious will now create an association of love and unpredictability. In our model, it does it by putting a card labeled love in the unpredictable drawer, and a card labeled unpredictable in the love drawer. (Remember, this is just a model; exactly how it happens in reality is a mystery.) What is the consequence? She will grow with the perception that love is unpredictable, that it is normal that the person she loves is also unpredictable in his behavior. This is how she will look at close relationships in her life. Here, you have an initial explanation of why (and I am generalizing) people who grew up in abusive environments end up in abusive environments and relationships, or why children from alcoholic parents become also alcoholics or marry alcoholics. There is more to this (I'll write a future book about relationships), but this association is a big variable in the equation that explains this type of behavior.

You are starting to get an idea about how your unconscious is regulating your behavior. I encourage you to revisit your past and reexamine it while you read this book. It will help explain a lot of things about yourself and the dynamics of your family and friends.

The Unconscious Generates and Stores Our Emotions

This concept is easy to understand. Notice that you cannot control when you are going to feel an emotion or not. Don't confuse controlling with repression. Simply because you repressed an emotion, that does not mean that you did not have it. You cannot say, "Today, I will not feel the emotion of fear." It does not work like that. You simply feel as you go through the events in your life. You, the conscious, have no control over the generation of emotions. Therefore they can only be coming from our unconscious.

What is important is that you understand that the unconscious stores emotions. As you will see, these stored emotions are going to be the ones that you will feel when you react to circumstances in your life similar to those that you have experienced before. They will control your behavior by association.

In the next section, where I go deep into the mechanisms of the unconscious, I will expand on this and the next characteristic. Thus, this is just a short introduction to them here.

The Unconscious Stores All the Programs That Dictate Our Behaviors

A program is the basic structure in the mind that the unconscious uses to determine behavior.

There are millions and millions of them. You, the conscious, may be aware of some of them. Still, they act from the unconscious. I will show now the structure of these programs and how specifically they operate.

The Programs in Our Unconscious

We humans are a species that is extremely adaptable to the different kinds of environments that this planet offers. This is because of the adaptability of our survival mechanisms. Our unconscious has the capacity to learn the rules of survival of the specific environment in which we are. This is one of the big differences that we have with respect to all the other living creatures on this planet. Because the main concern of the unconscious is survival, the mechanisms it uses need to be present and active from the beginning of our lives. It does not make sense to develop a survival mechanism that activates only when you mature, because by then you most likely would be long dead. This capacity of adaptation is already present when the baby is born (in fact, as I will show later, it is already present in the mother's womb). This is very logical. Think about it: a baby who is born in the desert is going to have very different rules of survival compared to a baby born in the arctic, or a baby born in the Amazon. A baby born in the arctic, from the perspective of survival, will not need to know about lions. That baby will need to know about polar bears and the extreme cold. That we learn in school about all the animals is simply an intellectual activity. From the point of view of survival, it is irrelevant. What is relevant is that the baby learns as soon as possible about survival skills to the particular environment in which he or she will grow. The human body has been designed with that capability.

Adapting to the Environment

How did nature design this survival mechanism in us humans so that we adapt the fastest and in the most efficient way to the environment in which we are born? To really understand this, let's start by taking a human newborn and comparing her behavior against the characteristics of the conscious.

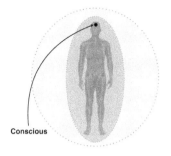

Conscious

The Conscious

- **Self awareness**

- **Uses the senses**

- **Reasoning**

- **Makes decisions**

- **Willpower**

In the figure, going bullet by bullet, observe first of all that the baby has no concept of self; there is no self-awareness.[25] With respect to the five senses, the baby has them, but she still needs to develop quite a bit. For example, a baby recognizes her parents because of the patterns she sees, however the eyes need to develop more to be able to focus better. Look at the movements a newborn makes. He needs to learn to move the arms and legs in a more coordinated fashion, and he needs to learn how to grab objects. With respect to the faculty of reasoning, a baby does not reason; a baby reacts to what he feels. If the baby is hungry, she will cry; if the baby is happy, you will get that beautiful smile that conquers our hearts when we see them. In other words, a baby does not make a decision and does not come to a conclusion. A baby is reacting to the internal and external environments. Finally, following the figure, a baby does not exert will; the willpower has not been developed. From all the explanations above:

A newborn does not have the conscious part of the mind developed.

The conscious simply does not exist in a newborn. I defined the mind as conscious plus unconscious, but in a newborn the mind is pure unconscious.

---

[25] Interesting enough, and ironically, in a way babies and kids up to around six years of age are more connected to their Essence than us adults. As you will fully understand shortly, the conscious of a child is not fully formed, and neither are the few mind programs that they have. Don't confuse connection to your Essence with self-awareness as a human being, which is what I am talking about right here.

This takes us to another big implication. Remember, when I was explaining to you about the conscious, that I said that it was the outer layer of the mind?

Because the newborn does not have a conscious, the unconscious of a newborn is in direct contact with its environment.

The conscious that in us adults sits in between the unconscious and the environment is not there in newborns. Before I get into the important implications that this has, let me first explain a little more about the development of the conscious in humans.

In contrast with most of the other animals on this planet, human beings have a very long period of development. It is well accepted today that the brain does not finish its development until about twenty-five years of age,[26] with some taking up to around twenty-eight years. If you think about it, it is an amazingly long time, yet it makes sense if you put it into the context of the complex behavior that we have. This development is not just one single, homogeneous phase that goes from 0 to 100 percent. Instead, it has phases or tonalities where certain new characteristics develop at a certain time.

Just a Touch of Piaget

Swiss psychologist Jean Piaget became very well-known for his studies in child development. Even though today there are newer models and theories, for the purposes of our discussion here, the core of his theory gives a good generic view of this development process. Very briefly, Piaget divided the development of children[27] as follows.

---

[26] You can find numerous sites about this. Here's one from the University of Rochester Medical Center, in New York: *"Understanding the Teen Brain,"* https://www.urmc. rochester.edu/encyclopedia/content.aspx?ContentTypeID=1&ContentID=3051 (Accessed December 10, 2018). Also watch the YouTube videos of Daniel Siegel, where he often talks about adolescence going all the way to around twenty-four years of age.

[27] Piaget developed his theories through many years and published several books about them ("The Origins of Intelligence of Children," "The Construction of Reality in the Child," "Play, Dreams and Imitation in Childhood," etc.). From there, numerous compilations were published (i.e., "Piaget's Theory of Intellectual Development," by Herbert Ginsburg and Sylvia Opper), and today you can easily find his general concepts on numerous websites.

1. **The sensorimotor stage:** From birth to age two, infants acquire knowledge through sensory experience and manipulation of objects.
2. **The preoperational stage:** From two years old to around seven. This is the age of imagination, when children live in their worlds and grow through this pretend play.
3. **The concrete operational stage:** From around seven to around eleven years old. Logic starts to form, but it is still quite limited. No abstraction. Children start to take on the concept of "I" versus "the others."
4. **The formal operational stage:** From age eleven on. At this point, the children begin to use the ability to reason, including abstract concepts, and they start coming to their own conclusions.

A lot has been researched and added to this model. Whether the ages are that exact number, and whether those characteristics follow exactly that pattern, is subject to discussion and ongoing study. There may be overlaps, and individual cases certainly will vary. Still, the model is valid in that it does depict very well that there are different stages that we go through in our development into full human beings. What I want you to notice is that logic and reasoning start to show up around seven years old, yet really it is more after age eleven that this faculty will start to take a more solid place within the personality. And notice that starting at seven, the child begins to have that sense of "I" (they do speak using the "I" before seven, but that is more of a mechanical or learned pattern that allows them to communicate. They still don't have that sense of self-awareness).

An Informal Correlation to EEGs

Interesting enough, these stages correspond roughly to what we see physically when we study the electrical activity of children brains at different ages. The brain works via electrochemical impulses that can be detected using an EEG.[28] The four main types of brain waves that are associated with brain activity are delta, theta, alpha, and beta. There are several others, and one of them is gamma waves, which occur in higher states of consciousness (observed in Tibetan monks in deep meditation, for example). For the purposes of the discussion in this section, we will talk about the first four. As an adult, in your normal awake state, the predominant waveform is beta. When you are relaxed, mentally speaking, your predominant brain

---

[28] Electroencephalogram.

wave will now be alpha. If you were to go into deeper states of relaxation via, say, meditation or hypnosis, your predominant brain wave pattern will be theta. And if you go to sleep or into very, very deep states of trance, delta waves will take precedence. Until the age of two, children display predominantly delta waves. Until the age of six, it's theta waves. Alpha waves take precedence after six years, and beta waves up around twelve years of age. (Again, these are approximate ages.) Notice that it roughly follows the stages of development that Piaget talked about. Also, notice then that until around six years of age, children are essentially in a state of hypnosis. You will say, "How can that be? They jump, play, and interact." The last thing one would think is that they are in hypnosis. This is, unfortunately, a huge misconception brought up by the world of movies and the media. Hypnosis is a state of single focus—that is all. Every one of us experiences states of hypnosis in our daily routines. When you watch a movie that really interests you, you are in hypnosis. It's the same when you are doing a job or project in which you are totally caught up. Has it happened to you that you were driving somewhere, and "all of a sudden you got there" while you were thinking about something else? You were in a state of hypnosis, so who did the driving? Your unconscious, which already knew how to get there (notice that this will not happen when you are searching for an address that you have not been to before). This is in contrast to our ordinary moments when our mind is wandering from one place to another. At that point, we are no longer in a state of hypnosis. Your beta waves kick in. These beta waves correlate with the noise in our minds, the continuous and repetitive thoughts that we carry all along our lives. What happens with children below six years old is that their minds are mainly in one place and do not have all the noise that we adults have. (If you are not familiar with this, try focusing on one thing and see how long you can keep that state.)

The Appearance of the Conscious

What is it that I am trying to convey to you with all this information? Two main characteristics that I mentioned about the conscious were (1) the sense of "I" and (2) it is the seat of the faculty of reasoning. From all the above, from seven to twelve years of age is when the sense of "I" and a very simple capacity of logic processing start to appear. In practical terms, the faculty of reasoning only starts to take a significant role at around eleven or twelve years of age. This leads us to this critical concept:

Our conscious only starts to play a significant role after around ten years of age.

I round to ten. Before then, the sense of "I" and the faculty of reasoning have not, *from a practical point of view,* developed enough to be main characteristics in the personality of the child. This means that what I said about the newborn's unconscious being in "direct contact" with the environment can in fact be extended to children up to around ten years of age. In other words:

In children up to around ten years of age, *the unconscious is in "direct contact" with the environment.*

The conscious is not, in a significant way, present and in between their unconscious and the external world, as in the case of babies. Let's see why this is so critical to understanding our behavior. Let me give you a hypothetical example. Let's say that someone tells me, "Everybody who steals should be executed," speaking with great conviction. To this person, that statement is a 100 percent valid statement.

Nevertheless, my response to that person would be something like, "I do not agree with you *because* (1) I don't think it is fair, and (2) I don't think it would resolve the problem of stealing." Notice that I emphasized the word *because.* That word reflects the mental process that I am doing at that moment, which is reasoning. In other words, because of my ability to reason, I rejected that idea in contrast to the other person, who holds it as valid. Therefore because of my ability to reason, that idea was not implanted in my unconscious. It did not become truth to me as it is for that other person. Thus, the next critical concept:

The faculty of reasoning is a filter that determines what goes (or not) into the unconscious.

The reasoning faculty...

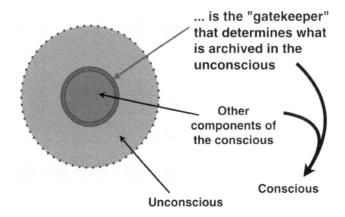

... is the "gatekeeper" that determines what is archived in the unconscious

Other components of the conscious

Conscious

Unconscious

To emphasize, in the previous figure, the ring representing the faculty of reasoning is also part of the conscious. Connecting all these concepts, we can conclude that:

Every event children experience, up to around ten years of age, gets stored and classified in their unconscious directly, simply as they perceive it.

This concept is the answer to the question about how nature implements in us that mechanism of compiling the rules of survival in the fastest and most efficient way (which I presented at the beginning of this section about adapting to the environment). In these children, the conscious, with its faculty of reasoning as intermediary to the unconscious, is not present. Therefore there are no filters that interfere with the assimilation of experiences. During these first years, our unconscious assimilates everything that we experience as is. If you experienced something as positive, that is how your unconscious will classify it (association). If you experienced something as negative, that is also how the unconscious will store it. How is this connected to our chances of survival? Very simple. These mechanisms go back to the ancestral times, when we used to live in nature and surrounded by predators. In fact, this is the reason why they were created in the first place. If you, as a child in those times, lived in a place where there was a certain predator, and you saw how your parents run to safety as soon as they saw it, that experience would have been recorded immediately in your unconscious. Once in your unconscious, you would have never forgotten about that predator and how to react to it. You learned, and thus you adapted to that environment. Automatically. In such dire situations, you needed to learn quickly. Otherwise if confronted again with that predator, and you did not know yet what to do, you would have died. That is why this is no time for reasoning. Reasoning is slow.

The Impeccable Logic and Wisdom in the Design of the Conscious

As part of giving you an understanding about yourself, I want to point out how the different aspects of our development in our early years fit and complement each other so well. Children up to around ten or twelve are essentially in absorption mode. Their minds are like sponges, taking in as much as they can from the environment. Nevertheless, don't think about this stage as a passive stage. The brain is developing and frantically creating new neural connections. It needs to develop quite a bit before the functionality of the conscious starts to become significant in the personality of the individual.[29] The creation of the conscious is, in us humans, an amazing accomplishment of nature. The conscious is the biggest differentiation that we have with respect to all other living beings on this planet, and it needs time to develop.

Notice how congruent and logical our development is during our first years of our lives.

1. During these years, all the experiences that the child is going through are being assimilated directly by the unconscious. This is the period of compilation of the rules of survival for the environment in which the child is. The assimilation is fast and efficient because there is no pondering (no reasoning) about all the different possibilities with respect to a specific event.

2. While the child is learning the rules of survival of the environment, her brain is building the extraordinary conscious and its faculty of reasoning. They will give us the unique ability to make decisions as individuals, which is the essential richness of being human.

3. At the end of the period of assimilation of the "essential rules of survival," at around ten years of age, the child has built an inner database about the environment. By this point in time, the basic blocks of the conscious have

---

[29] Interesting enough, during adolescence starting at around twelve years of age, the brain starts pruning unnecessary connections and even neurons. Thus, the biggest explosion in neural growth occurs during the first twelve years in children.

been put in place. Now the faculty of reasoning can start to play its role. Understand that in order to reason, you need to have ideas, concepts to reason about. So you see, if we would have been born with a developed conscious, it would have been sitting idle during most of those initial years because it would not have had a database to work with. Ideas build from concepts, which you gradually acquire in life. And later, as the database started to build up, it would not have allowed for a complete assimilation of the rules of the environment because it would have started to interfere with their assimilation.

It is a puzzle where all the pieces fit beautifully. That is why we develop the way we do. Nothing is capricious in the designs of Nature. We are part of it.

Structure and Operation of the Programs in the Unconscious

To explain the structures of these programs, I am going to illustrate two cases: the case of a negative event and the case of a positive event. Notice that I do not talk about good or bad. I talk about events that make you feel negative or positive emotions. There is no such a thing as a bad emotion. I will explain. I use these two cases because these are the types of events that affect your behavior. You will reject events that made you feel negative emotions. You will feel attracted to events that made you feel positive emotions. You could say, intellectually speaking, that there are neutral events. In reality, we emotionally color everything in our lives. We are constantly making decisions based on the final emotional results that they entail. That is what the programs in our unconscious do.

The Case of a Negative Event

As I already mentioned, these mechanisms were put in place since the beginning of time, when we started this adventure of interacting with the physical world. Let's go back in time and imagine the age when we lived in caves.[30] Without getting entangled about how exactly the social structures were then, let's say we have a father, a mother, and their son. The son is

---

[30] Exactly when and how this happened, we don't know. I simply put this case as a hypothetical example, for illustrative purposes.

around five years old. The parents see the need to go outside into the forest to gather fruits and vegetables for the next meal. The child goes with them. While they are exploring and gathering the food, all of a sudden, the child sees his parents frozen and completely focused on something. The child looks in that direction. At a certain distance but clearly visible is an animal. The child senses the tension and the fear of the parents while observing a creature that he has never seen before. The parents know that it is a dangerous animal. The father then grabs the child and, with the mother, runs to the cave. Once there, panting but relieved, he puts the child on the floor. The child, even though he did not quite understand what was happening, senses the relief.

What happened in the child's unconscious as a result of this experience? The child sensed the terror in the parents; he felt the danger. Using our model, his unconscious takes a card, draws this animal, and puts it in the box where all dangerous things are stored and classified. And something else happens that is critical in the understanding of our behavior. The emotion that the child felt during that experience gets stored in that drawer as well, associated with that card. I mentioned that the unconscious stores and generates emotions. Here you see it. The child's unconscious generates the fear in his body when it detects it in his parents. Then the unconscious stores this emotion along with its classification. Additionally, another thing that the unconscious will do during this event is store what to do physically, how to react. In our example, it's run. This completes the list of the necessary components to create the new program that will be stored in the child's mind. In other words, the structure of the program that he has now as the result of this experience, is:

Animal: dangerous, panic, run

General Structure of the Programs in Our Unconscious

From the example, and now generalizing, the structure of our programs in our unconscious is as follows.

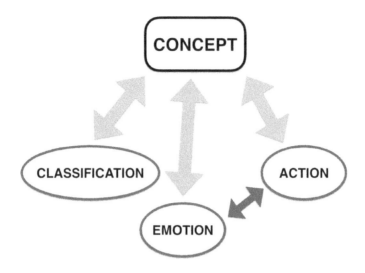

Every time the child has a new experience in his life, the unconscious will classify the event and store the experienced emotion and the action to take. Here it is in a less graphical way, using the previous format.

Concept: classification, emotion, physical action

Action refers to the internal (within the body) and external physical behaviors that result from this program. This is the structure of the programs in your unconscious. These are the structures that determine your behaviors in life.

Let's go further. Similarly to the case of the apple (which I gave you when explaining the characteristics of the unconscious), because the child has now stored this program in his mind, the next time he sees that predator, he no longer will need to have his parents at his side to know what to do. What will happen if that is the case? As soon as the child sees the predator, his unconscious will look in its archives to see where that concept is stored. In the case of the boy, because of the previous experience with his parents, his unconscious finds the card that represents the concept of that predator in the drawer labeled as dangerous. Once it finds it there, the unconscious looks for the associated emotion. In this case, it is the fear and panic that the boy felt that first time. What the unconscious does now is open the gates that confine the emotion in its storage place. The emotion rushes out. The boy feels again that panic in his body. Finally, the unconscious checks the physical action to take, which is stored as "Run!" The boy feels that urge to run. In reality and less analytically, how will the boy experience his encounter with the predator? He will feel panic and immediately run toward the cave. That is his learned behavior. Because of the immense processing power of the unconscious, he does not experience it as the series of steps that I explained above. In our perception, this is instantaneous—we feel scared and run, and that is it. Nevertheless, internally in our minds, that is the processing that is happening.

There are two important things that I want you to take note of, to emphasize what I explained earlier.

1. Because there was no reasoning involved, he learned this rule of survival immediately. He did not have to sit down and analyze the whole event to conclude that the predator is dangerous and that he needs to escape from it. The unconscious assimilated that event and created that structure in his mind, automatically.
2. This boy, because of this instantaneous learning, knows how to behave when confronted with this predator. The unconscious will take over and react accordingly. As a consequence, he has now a better chance to survive in that environment. He has adapted to it thanks to these programs.
   And from this latest illustration, we can also write the structure of the program as:

Concept: classification, emotional reaction, physical reaction

Because:

Once a program has been created by the unconscious, it will become the reference for how to react in future events that are associated in one way or another to the one that generated this structure.

Therefore in a future event, the stored emotion becomes the emotional reaction to the event, and the stored action becomes the physical reaction to this event as well.

The Effect of Negative Programs in Our Lives

Let's continue with our prehistoric family to introduce yet another crucial point. This child, before he had that first experience with the predator, knew nothing about this type of animals. Thus before that experience, whenever he went out into the surroundings, he felt great. It was a great adventure to explore. The surroundings were simply this great playground right there at the footsteps of his cave. There was a lot of space to explore and play. However, after having had that first experience, his perception of the surroundings changed. His unconscious has already installed the program that identifies predators as dangerous. It also made the association of "surroundings" and "predators" (because the encounter was in the surroundings of where they lived). Therefore, now there is an association of "surroundings" and "dangerous." So what is going to happen? Where before there was a great, fun playground, now there is a field of potential danger. Whenever he ventures out, whether with his parents or by himself, he will be alert and watchful. That is his unconscious at work. Now he is not simply going to be happily jumping and strolling wherever he goes. His behavior is more restricted and limited. You can see a critical key point to understand in our behavior:

Programs associated to negative emotions create limitations in our lives.

This is one of the most critical concepts in this book. All the negative programs that we carry in our unconscious are creating limiting behaviors in us. Today, as I will illustrate, we have so many of them that we live lives not truly, fully lived. We see this concept at work everywhere; it is the common story of this civilization. What I want to emphasize here is that we are not to blame this mechanism for our limitations. As much as there might not be predators in our cities, there still are physical dangers that the unconscious needs to protect us from. A very simple example is when you are going to cross a street. If you don't want to get run over by a car, you'd better look for incoming traffic. Notice that this program that makes us stop and look first is indeed a limiting program. If you did not have it, you would be "free" to simply cross the street—but then, you could die as a result of that "freedom." That limiting program increases your chances of survival—exactly what it was intended for since the beginning of time. The argument that one hears so much about our inner mechanisms not having evolved (or kept pace) with our civilization is simply not true. It is because of this ingenious mechanism that we survived the early days in nature, and we use it today in our societies.

Even so, as I mentioned:

We don't live our full potential because of the negative limiting programs that we implant in ourselves.

It is our own doing. It is a misuse of this mechanism. This mechanism was designed to protect us from dangers, not to make us believe, as an example, "I am not good enough," because our parents or teachers said so in our early years. I will explain this shortly when I connect all these concepts to our modern-day living.

The Case of a Positive Event

The unconscious is, from this perspective, a very simple machine. Continuing with key concepts, here is the next one:

The same type of structure is used to store an experience, whether it was a positive or a negative one.

In the case of our prehistoric child, as the result from that same experience with the predator, the child feels how his parents protect him. He feels safe. Another structure that his unconscious creates, as the result of this interaction with his parents, is:

Parents: protection, safe, relax

In other words, the concept of parents will go in the drawer under the concept of protection (that is, the drawer that has everything associated with the concept of protection). The emotion he feels in that state, feeling safe, gets stored as well. So, does its physical reaction, relaxation. That means that whenever he knows that his parents are around, he will relax because he will feel safe. And equivalent to what happened in the opposite case of stress, the unconscious will also start a series of hormonal and other physical changes within the body, but now related to the state of calm. As I will explain next, there is always a biological response to an emotion.

Of course, understand that I am keeping things simple here, for explanation purposes. He may or may not feel that relaxed with them, depending on all the other interactions that he has had with them. His final state will be the result of the unconscious assessing all the programs associated with his parents under the particular circumstances that he is in at a given time. I hope you are beginning to understand the complexity of our behaviors, because we have millions of programs stored in our unconscious—the result of all the experiences in our lifetime. That is why it is necessary to have something that has an extraordinary capacity to process information and determine a behavioral outcome in real time, as we do. In the human case, that something is our unconscious (with its associated physical counterparts in the brain).

The Effect of Positive Programs in Our Lives

Continuing with our example, it is easy to understand that when the child senses the protection from his parents, he feels valued. He feels that he is important and that he counts. In other words, his self-esteem grows stronger.

Here's a crucial point about positive programs:

Programs associated to positive emotions become psychological resources that help you grow and expand in your life.

This is in contrast to the negative programs, which create limitations in your life. The more positive programs a person has, the easier it will be for him to live the full life he wants. You can see how critical it is that a child start in a positive environment. That is why I will dedicate a whole section to parenting later in the book (relevant to you, irrespective of whether or not you are a parent).

About the Physical Action of Our Programs

I mentioned earlier that the physical action of a program refers to the internal bodily action, as well as the external behavioral action. A better way to understand this is to approach it from a different point of view. There are two components to a physical action.

1. Biological
2. Learned

The biological component is always present, whereas the learned component may or may not be present.

Biological Action

Notice that in the previous figure I drew an arrow that connects emotion to action directly. That is the biological action that will always be present when a program triggered. To better understand this aspect of the structure of our programs, let's expand:

There are two primary types of emotions: positive and negative.

This is the most basic classification that the unconscious does. Within these two are all other ones. The reason for this very basic classification is that because the main task of your unconscious is to insure your survival, the first thing that it needs to asses is whether there is danger involved or not.

Biological Actions Related to Negative Emotions

Here's the next key concept:

All negative emotions are associated with danger.

Of course, there will be degrees of danger, as well as degrees of positive emotions. Events associated to very intense emotions will elicit a correspondingly strong reactive behavior. Less intense emotions associated to an event elicit subtler reactions. Ultimately, this is how your unconscious sees these negative events. They are to be avoided!

The next key concept:

Negative emotions manifest as stress.

Every single time you feel stress, it is because you are feeling a negative emotion. When you are feeling stressed, it is because your body is, biologically speaking, in that state. So that you understand this internal physical effect in your body, let me explain to you how it manifests and why it does it that way.

Effects of Stress on the Body

Bruce Lipton, in his conference "The New Biology,"[31] describes in simple and clear terms the effects of stress in the body. The unconscious will activate all the hormones and physical reactions related to stress. These are automatic. Of course, this is not an arbitrary design of nature. On the contrary, as he explains.

---

[31] Bruce Lipton, "The New Biology." Spirit 2000, Inc. At around 1:37:00

1. Let's say that all of a sudden, you are confronted by a predator. Is it more important to finish your digestion or run away to safety? Obviously, the highest priority will be to escape that danger. What the unconscious does is redirect the blood flow from the internal organs to your extremities. Your extremities will be the main means to escape from the danger, so you might as well give them the maximum amount of oxygen and nutrients they will need for the task. The consequence of this is that as long as you are under stress, your internal organs will receive less blood, which means less oxygen and nutrients to perform their functions. Also, their metabolic waste will take more time to leave.

2. You have a cold. You are confronted with a predator. Is it more important to cure the cold or escape the predator? Yes, escape. Curing the cold is useless if you are going to be dead in the end. When the unconscious perceives danger, what it will do is turn off as much as necessary the immunologic system. Why specifically this system? Because, in order to protect the body from all the different pathogens that surround us, the system requires a lot of energy to perform this task. Therefore in order to increase your chances of survival, it is worth it for the unconscious to reduce the activity of this system so that that extra energy is now available to be directed to where it really is needed: escaping. The idea here is that the escape will be a momentary situation, after which the system can be restored to its normal levels. Still, while in stress, you are vulnerable to the attack of pathogens.

3. You are confronted with a predator. Is this the time to plan your daily activities? Of course not. This is no time for thinking. What the unconscious will do is restrict blood flow in the prefrontal cortex and send the extra blood supply to the reptilian brain, which is in charge of your reflexes. That is what you need to escape as fast as possible from the danger. This means that under stress, your IQ literally diminishes, and you don't think as clearly as you would otherwise (we all have had this experience; in my case, I gave you the example of the exercise at university). Also, if you remain stressed throughout your day, your prefrontal cortex is receiving less blood than what it needs. How healthy do you think this situation is for your brain?

After observing the explanations that I gave you about the stress condition, it is clear that the body is changing internally in order to maximize the efficiency of an associated external action (escape). In other words, there are two components to the biological action of a program:

a. Internal
b. External

Escaping is one of the predefined biological external actions of a program associated to a negative emotion. The four types of external biological reactions are the four Fs:

1. Fight
2. Flee
3. Freeze
4. Faint

These are the expanded version of the classic "fight or flight" that you hear so much about (flight meaning flee, escape).

As It Was Then, so It Is Today

Let me make explicit what I have been implying throughout all these explanations.

These early survival mechanisms are still in place today, in all of us.

These biological responses are exactly the same today as way back then in the ages of the cave boy. We continue to operate from them today. Notice once more the impeccable design in the handling of danger on the part of the unconscious. When in front of a predator, the unconscious will take all the necessary actions to maximize your chances to remain alive. It works perfectly well for this type of situations. Where it does not work well is for the sustained conditions of stress, which is how most of us live our daily routines nowadays. It's like when you are afraid that your boss is going to fire you every day that you go to work. Under these circumstances, your organs deteriorate (ulcers, heart attacks), you are vulnerable to infectious deceases (colds are the first and most common consequences), and your intellectual abilities are impaired. Here you have a direct connection between negative programs and your health. The more negative programs you have, the more stressed out you will live your life. In ancient times stress did correspond physical dangers, but today, more than anything, it is the result of *perceived danger*. This perceived danger comes from negative programs in our unconscious. I will give you more examples soon. What I want to point out right now is that we are reacting exactly in the same way today as our predecessors in the caves. When you get irritated with someone, what is it that you want to do? Insult (fight) that person? You raise your voice, and your demeanor becomes aggressive. Or maybe you want leave that place (flee); you don't want to be around that person, and you want to get out of there. We've all had these experiences. Whether it is at home, with friends, in intimate relationships, and even more so in the professional world. As civilized as we want to see ourselves, that animal, instinctual, reactive aspect is right there in all of us. It is simply the unconscious trying to protect us. When it perceives danger, it takes control of us.

Biological Actions Related to Positive Emotions

In contrast to negative emotions, positive emotions are associated with harmony, happiness, satisfaction, and more. Positive emotions also elicit biological responses like relaxation or excitement, as well as their corresponding internal bodily reactions. As with negative emotions, there will be gradations according to how strong the emotion associated to the program is. For example, when you are feeling peace, you may be feeling relaxed. That feeling of relaxation has its corresponding internal state of lower heart rate and calmer breathing. On the other side of the positive spectrum, when a little girl hears that the grandmother whom she loves so much is coming to visit, she gets excited, jumping in happiness. Her heart rate increases. Notice that nobody had to teach her to get excited. She simply does so automatically. It is a biological response to the emotion that she is feeling. This is a case of a behavior that is purely biological, without a learned component.

Notice how I have extended my explanations more with respect to negative emotions than positive ones. Whatever it is that you are doing that keeps you in a positive state, keep doing it. It is the negative states of being that affect the quality of our lives. These states come from negative programs stored in the unconscious. Thus the need to understand them very well and the greater focus that I place on them in this book.

Learned Action

Besides the biological action (internal and external) associated to a program, there might be a learned behavior. It will always be external. To illustrate this, let's say that in this group of cave dwellers, there is a very authoritarian chief. The boy sees how someone else was punished because that individual did not bow in front of the chief. From that observation, the boy quickly learns how to behave in front of the chief (plus, he'd very likely learn from his parents' explanations also). Whenever he is in front of the chief, there will be the biological reaction of fear that he will feel in his body, plus the impulse of not wanting to be there (flee), added to the learned behavior (bow) that he knows he must do to avoid being punished. The learned behavior will be associated to the concept as well. Notice that in the modern-day case that I mentioned about crossing the street, the learned behavior is to stop and look for incoming traffic. When the individual comes close to the street with the intention of crossing it, her unconscious detects danger in that situation and searches for the associated program in its database, where it finds as the action "look for incoming traffic before attempting to cross." That is how she will behave, as directed by her unconscious. It's exactly the same program structure and functionality as that of our cave boy long time ago. We can then depict the structure of the programs in a more detailed and accurate form as:

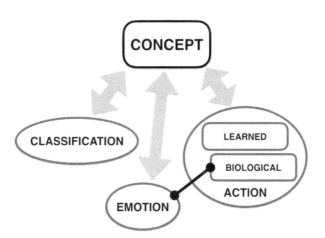

Notice the link that ties the emotion with the biological action. That will always occur. A learned response may or may not be associated with that concept. The biological action will include an internal bodily reaction, as well as an external one. If the program is associated to a negative emotion, then the external biological reaction will be fight or flight or freeze or faint. The learned action, if present, is always an external behavior. Graphically, this can be summarized as follows.

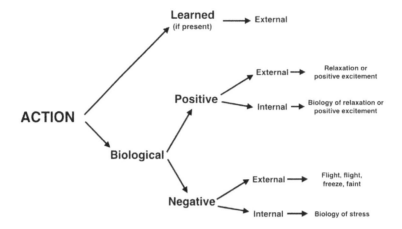

These Programs Dictate Our Behavior

Here you have it. The unconscious is a machine that assimilates events into inner structures that it will use as a reference for future similar events. At that point, these structures will determine how you behave. We can then generalize as follows:

All new experiences are assimilated in the unconscious as programs.

The unconscious operates as a machine, it does not reason. Thus:

The unconscious does not judge.

This means that the unconscious will assimilate experiences into programs without applying any value (good/bad) to what it is storing. Don't confuse labeling with judging. When you label something as bad, to the unconscious it is just another label like good or delicious. This explains the behavior of a religious militant who, in his unconscious, may have a program like "killing in the name of God is good," as well as the behavior of a person who has the program "killing is not a viable option to resolve a conflict." The concept of killing is associated to good in one case and bad in the other one. When the militant encounters someone who he considers and enemy of God, he will kill him with no regrets (assuming in this case a fanatic). His unconscious will simply execute that program. If the militant is debating whether to kill someone or not, it is not because the unconscious itself has doubts. It is because it is executing the different programs associated with the situation. This explains to you the tyrants as well as our most exemplary individuals in our history. As we live our experiences, the unconscious creates and stores the programs associated with them. Later, the unconscious will execute the programs without judgment. Whether they are positive or negative is irrelevant.[32] It simply executes what it has in its database according to the circumstances that the individual is experiencing at a given moment. To state it explicitly:

The programs in our unconscious dictate our behavior.

If a program with an associated negative emotion gets activated, you will feel that emotion and thus will want to avoid that experience. If the activated program has an associated positive emotion, you will feel attracted to that event. All and each of us are nonphysical entities inserted into this physical instrument that is in continual execution of programs whose outcome is our behavior. Ponder about it. I will talk about free will later.

Basic Example in Prehistoric Times

For the sake of completeness, and to finish illustrating how these structures allowed us to survive and adapt in all kinds of different environments, let's take a look one last time at our prehistoric boy. Let's say that the environment in which his tribe lives is such that food is difficult to get, and therefore the adults know that it is necessary to store and ration the meals accordingly. Our little boy is hungry. He sees the food stacked up in the corner of the cave. He goes there to get some; after all, he is hungry. At that moment, his mother sees him. She grabs him and tells him that he can't eat yet. Whether it is because she explains this to him or due to repetition, eventually the boy gets it: he can't simply grab from the food pile and eat. They have to manage their food stock so that they can survive if, for some reason, they go through times of scarcity. As a result of this interaction with his mom related to food, the unconscious will create a program that might be:

---

[32] I am oversimplifying here so that you get the main point in this discussion. As we will see later in the transpersonal components of the personality, the less negative programs you have, the more your nonphysical Essence will be able to express itself through you. Thus, it will become a more active factor in your behavior. To the vast majority of people today, this is still more the exception than the norm.

Food: scarce, frustration, restrain

As a result of this program, because it has a negative emotion (frustration), the unconscious will want to avoid being in that type of event ("scarce food"). This program will be the force behind the individual giving extra attention to gathering food, because he knows that if there is not enough food, he will not be able to eat as much as he wants.

From all this, in the next figure, you have a picture of the programs stored in the unconscious of the little boy.

Of course, the boy will have many more programs in his unconscious. I simply talk about these ones for illustration purposes. Still, look at the figure. Notice how these programs are effectively guiding him in the environment in which he is growing. Now he knows that he has to pay attention when he goes outside the cave. He knows that once in the cave, he is safe. He knows that his mother loves him and that she will be a source of needed affection. He knows how to behave in front of the chief of the tribe. These programs in his unconscious are dictating his behavior in that environment. He has adapted to it.

Basic Example Nowadays

Let's run through a hypothetical example, but perfectly typical in a present-day family. Of course we're oversimplifying, yet it's clear enough that you get the idea.

A Girl Loved by Her Parents

Our family has a girl under ten years of age. Both parents show their love and affection to her. As a result of that experience, she will have a program in her unconscious that associates parents with the concept of love. This, of course, is a program with a positive emotion that will make her feel loved, appreciated, and valued. This program will add to her self-esteem.

With a Hard-working Dad

On the other hand, her dad works very hard. It is not uncommon that he arrives late at night from his job. And after a long day at work, she can see very clearly that he is tired. As the result of this experience with her dad, her unconscious will create a program like, "life is hard work" or "in order to succeed, you have to work hard." This program is associated with a negative emotion. She sees how tired he arrives at home. Plus, her dad says things like, "I can't wait for the weekend," so that he can relax a little bit. That reinforces the program even more. She will grow seeing life as such: you have to work hard, life is not easy, and money is tough to get. From these experiences, all kind of different programs arise. And she will see life through these lenses. Because this program is associated with a negative emotion, it will limit her.

To give you an example, let's say someone offers her (as an adult now) a great job opportunity. It's a job where, without having to work that hard, she could make a very good living with comfortable and flexible hours. (Here, you can check yourself. How do you feel about this last sentence? Is it possible to have something like that? How easy do you think you can find yourself in such a job? Whatever the answer, that is your programming.) Because of her programming, she will be suspicious of that offer. "Sounds too good to be true." She may not even consider it and simply reject it. She will miss opportunities in her life because of that negative (limiting) program.

And Great Friends

Continuing with our little girl, she gets along very well with her friends. She is outgoing and connects well with others. You will see another very important implication of the different concepts I mentioned earlier. The unconscious is a machine, and it does not reason. It assimilates every experience as rules of behavior. There is no distinction between one type of experience or another—everything is assimilated. For this case, her unconscious will create a program (among many others) that will translate as "I connect very well with the others." Notice that something interesting is happening here. This program will determine not only how she feels with others but also, how she feels about herself. It is part of her self-image.

The programs in your unconscious form the basis of your identity.

How you see yourself is also the result of your experiences and interactions in life. They result in programs that will form the mosaic of how you see yourself. There are some other factors, which I will talk about later, that also form part of your self-image. These also translate into programs.

Mom's Comments while She Is Sick

Let me give you another instance that's a little more drastic but perfectly real about self-image. Let's say that our little girl could not go to school because she is ill. She is in her room in bed. While she is resting, her mom, just across that room, is talking to a friend of hers. The conversation revolves about her daughter's illness. The mom tells her friend how her dad (the little girl's grandfather) also had that illness, and how he suffered so much for the rest of his life as a result of that particular disease. The little girl hears that comment. Remember, she has not developed her critical thinking (reasoning). That comment will go straight into her unconscious with the implication that she will suffer the rest of her life because of the illness. "I am a sickly person" will be the program in her unconscious. If she doesn't communicate this to her mom, who has the power to change her perception, she will start seeing herself as such from then on. That becomes part of her self-image. Because it is a very limiting program, she will start avoiding any physical activities, and she will feel shy, anxious, and more. It could have been very well the case that in her grandfather's time, there were no medical treatments for that illness, whereas in her present time there are. It does not matter—now she has been programmed, and that is how she sees herself. You may think that I am exaggerating, yet this and similar events happen all the time.

She Wants to Belong to the Theater Group at School

In school, our little girl wants to become part of the theater group in her class. Unfortunately, in the end, her teacher does not pick her to be part of the group. A classmate of hers makes the comment that the teacher said she was not good enough for the part. How is she going to perceive this experience? Negatively, needless to say. "Life is unfair" could very well be the program that her unconscious installs. Or the classic "I am not good enough." This last one is present in all humans to greater or lesser degrees. It's one of the most pervasive programs we carry, with so much detriment in our lives.

She Brings the Grades from School

Here's one more case that will complete this illustration and give you a good idea about how your personality formed. The girl brings home her grades from school. It turns out that she did very well in all subjects except drawing, which was not as good as the others. It was not necessarily a bad grade, but it was not as good as the others. The parents react by saying, "What happened with drawing? Are you having problems with it? How come the grade was not as good as the others? Should we get you a tutor?"

What impression will she get from all these questions? Most likely it's "there is a problem here. This should not have happened. Otherwise, they would not keep asking so much about drawing." The impression within her easily translates as "I am not good at drawing." This is now how she sees herself. It could be very well that she is not that interested in drawing; her dreams are about becoming an Olympic athlete. Drawing is not her preference, and so it is natural that she did not perform that well in that subject. The issue with this little girl is that she created a negative self-image out of this experience because the parents created this expectation that she must perform equally well in all areas. It is very different to say, "I am not interested in drawing." That is a statement of preference. That is what differentiates all of us, what gives richness to the human life. And indeed, because she would not be very interested in drawing, she would not be performing that well doing it. That is fine; nothing wrong with that. Yet another thing is to say, "I am not good at drawing." This implies "I have a deficiency, and there is something wrong with me." The same event can be seen from very different perspectives. The difference in perspective will make the difference between high self-esteem and low self-esteem. It becomes identity. "I am not good at drawing" has a negative emotion associated with it. "I am not interested in drawing" does not. Every time you say anything about yourself with the terms "I am not good at …" it means you have a negative, limiting program in your unconscious that is affecting your self-esteem and your experiences in life.

The (Oversimplified) Picture of Our Girl's Unconscious

Our girl's unconscious now has these programs.

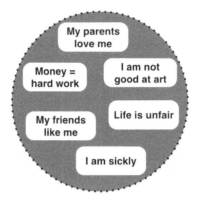

This is how the little girl will see the world, and she will start making decisions accordingly. Here's a real life example.

Case 9: I Am Not Good with Numbers

This client of mine is a young man just starting a new career at the university. He feels he doesn't finish the projects that he starts, and he is frustrated by his self-sabotage. After talking a little more, it turns out that he is studying a career that requires a lot of drawing, and he doesn't like it. After I inquire further, he says he would love to design cars; he actually would love to be an automotive engineer. He did not go that way because "he is not good with numbers." As much as he feels so much passion for that career path, he is convinced that he would fail at it because of his handicap. Then why do such a thing?

As we do our sessions, what surfaces is that some years earlier, his father, a prominent businessman, gave him the opportunity to sell some merchandise so that he could have firsthand experience about the business world. The young boy sold everything very well. Even so, after more carefully checking the numbers, he actually lost money because he did not calculate the price correctly. "How could I have done such a stupid mistake?" This is how he felt when he realized what had happened. His father was disappointed. That amplified the whole situation because he admired his father for his intelligence and business expertise. His unconscious created a program that said, "I am not good at numbers," with that huge negative emotion attached to it. That is the program that directed him to choose another career. Because "he is not good with numbers," then he'd better not choose a career that requires a lot of math. His unconscious is trying to protect him from another failure.

He feels that emotion as soon as he considers a career that requires math. It executes successfully. Nevertheless, that decision goes against what he really wants to do in life. Even though the program has a positive intention, it does not serve him well anymore. Why? Because of the mechanical response of the unconscious. It does not adapt to new circumstances. After four sessions of processing this event and some other aspects, he changes his career to what he really wants to do.

Other Current-day Examples

- On the return flight from a workshop in San Francisco, on the opposite side of the aisle sat a young couple with their baby. In the middle of the flight, the baby started to cry—classic nightmarish scenario for parents with babies in an airplane. The father, in a very sweet voice, told him, "Now, now John. We know that boys don't cry." It amazes me that to this day, I hear parents giving their young boys that type of message. Notice that I pointed out that he said it in a sweet tone of voice. Parents are doing everything the best way they know; it has always been like that. Nevertheless, we need more than best intentions. We need deeper knowledge, to start with. That sentence, irrespective of the tone of voice, implanted a new program in the child: boys don't cry. You think that a baby does not register that concept? Think again. His unconscious does, and I will give you more examples later. Also, do you think that this will be the one and only time that his father will tell him that? That message is going to be repeated again and again, every time that baby and later that boy, cries. If his father reacted to this event in the airplane that way, it is because he has that program implanted in his unconscious, which in turn likely came from his parents. This is one of the many everyday examples that illustrate how limiting beliefs are being passed from generation to generation—with devastating results. Do you think that he took a moment to ponder about what he should say or do in that type of situations? Very unlikely. His response is simply the result of a program in him being activated, and he reacts like a machine. Men, exactly the same as with women, have a need to express their emotions. Not doing that causes repression, with all the well-known damaging psychological effects. That extends to the relationships that the person will have in his life. For a successful intimate relationship to last, there needs to be emotional intimacy as well. That means that the two people involved must be willing to open up emotionally. It is going to be very difficult for a man who grew up with those types of messages to put himself in such a vulnerable place. So that you connect this event with the concepts that I just gave you, the structure implanted in the baby will be:

Cry: things/actions men don't do, scared, repress

The unconscious will put a card with the concept of cry in the drawer where all the concepts associated with "things/actions that men don't do" will be stored. The associated emotion will be scared (of being rejected by the others). If everybody rejects you, then you would end up alone in life. That means fewer chances to survive, which is danger to the unconscious. The learned action in this case is to repress the emotion. Once this program installed, it will execute every time the boy, and later the man, feels like crying.

It's similar with ideas like "girls don't laugh." Think about the fact that we have in our unconscious programs like "things/actions that boys/men don't do" and "things/actions that girls/women don't do." That is already a mental health issue in our societies. The only reason for needing to have that type of classification is because someone acted in a way that was arbitrarily decided as not appropriate for that gender. Yet by definition, if a person of a gender acts in a certain way, then it is because that way is part of the expression of that gender. It's massive social repression in our civilization. This is also an example of what I touched on earlier about us being responsible for the state of our minds in which we currently are. It is we who came up with that arbitrary classification of gender-appropriate behaviors. The mechanisms of our minds were created to protect us from the dangers of this particular planet on which we live, not to impose arbitrary limiting behaviors on ourselves. There is nothing obsolete about how our mind works.

- Everyone in the professional world experiences tensions that arise in the work environment. It is not uncommon in business meetings for people to get upset with each other. Why the irritation after a coworker said something? From the perspective of our mind programming, there are a lot of possibilities depending on the specific case. An easy hypothetical example is that you feel that the person is interfering with your job. That would mean that you will not be able to do your work. This in turn means that you will end up being fired. You will not have money to eat. You will not survive. It's danger to your unconscious. Biological reaction: attack! Therefore you become irritated and raise your voice, and the confrontation ensues. In general, that will be the scenario with a co-worker. If it is your boss, who could fire you, then the reaction will most likely be that you do what he says. In other words, in this case there is a learned program whose reaction is going to be "escape/flee," which manifests as closing your mouth and doing as he says. I have been in meetings where people got so upset that they leave the room. Here you have an example of a literal flee reaction. The emotion associated with that program is so big that it overrides (more on this later) the other programs of behavior, like "we stay in the meeting until it is finished," "we work as a team," and "we respect each other's decisions." These are clear examples of how our programs dictate our behavior. Let me point out to you that there is no free will here, just robotic responses.

- Let's say there is a meeting to decide what to do about something. This can be in the business world or anywhere else, like a family decision. A decision is reached, but as a result, someone is upset because it was not her choice of action. As always, there are many possibilities in our human behavior for what program is behind that reaction. As one illustration here, people who come from very authoritarian families, where they had to obey what their parents said and expected of them, can easily be the ones in this type of scenarios. Programs that these individuals carry may look like this.

Parents: authority, fear, obey
Expressing myself: risk of punishment, fear, repress

They always had to do what they were told to, with the implied consequence that they never had the opportunity to really express what they truly wanted. We came here to express; that is intrinsic to the human spirit. As a result of not being able to do it, first frustration and then anger will accompany the emotion of fear. The structure becomes:

Expressing myself: risk of punishment, fear
+ frustration + anger, repress

Observe what we have here: frustration and anger, with repression. Not a good combination. The person will try to contain that anger, however eventually the emotion will win and come out with a very strong expression. It's like the person in the meeting who was upset because he felt he was not listened to. His unconscious associated what happened in the meeting to his childhood years when he was equally not listened to, because his only choice was to do as told by his parents. In extreme cases, this expression will become the violent bursts that we hear so much about—for instance, in domestic violence or in school shootings. These individuals have a very painful internal struggle in their minds, forces that pull them in opposite directions (like in the program above). If you get what I am explaining here, instead of vilifying them, you will understand them (because of a dysfunctional past that they had to live through) and support them in transforming those damaging behaviors into more constructive ones.

Parents need to be very attentive to their children's expressions. Whether authoritarian or not, children who simply obey what others tell them to do are very likely carrying a program like:

me: not important, unempowered, obey

The association can be with "not important" or "I don't count" or "my opinion is not important." Or it can be all of them. That directly impacts the self-esteem of this person. As long as this program is active, the individual has no chance to live a full life.

For the sake of completeness, let's see the opposite case, an individual who has this program in her unconscious:

me: important, empowered, express

A person who has had a healthy expression knows that he counts. There is no need for external proof about it. (Don't confuse this with parents allowing children to do whatever they want to do. This leads to unbalanced expression, which results in totally self-centered individuals.) When this person experiences the situation of the meeting in which his suggestion was not taken, he will be okay with it. This program is the inner resource that grounds and supports him when things don't turn out as expected in life. And, of course, it will be a force behind him accomplishing what he sets out to do. The person with this inner resource will not take that event personally, because there is no need for outside proof that he counts. He knows and feels it. In contrast, the person with the negative program will perceive that event as yet another confirmation that his opinion is not important—thus, the anger.

And so on, with all your behaviors. Notice how as adults, we are reacting according to programs that were, by the most part, implanted in us as children. And from then on, they take control of our behavior. Again, I invite you to go back and revisit your past with this new knowledge and perspective so that you can understand why you are who you are. This is the first step to pinpointing the programs that are limiting you in life.

Characteristics of the Programs in the Unconscious

These programs are the key to understanding who we are as human beings. Let's go over their characteristics. I have been talking about some of them more or less implicitly. Because it is important that you have this clear, I will make them explicit here. There is much more, but with these, you will be able to understand your behavior very well.

- Negative programs have higher priority than positive ones.
- The programs are classified according to the perception of the event.
- The intensity of the emotion determines how much it affects our behavior.
- The programs in the unconscious are designed to be stable.

Negative Programs Have Higher Priority Than Positive Ones

Programs with negative emotions are associated with danger in one way or another—in other words, with survival. Survival is the highest priority of the unconscious, and this means:

Negative programs have higher priority than positive ones.

It has to be this way to survive with this instrument (the body) on this particular planet. On this planet, a lot of predators happen to like the components of our bodies. In the early days, that is why we needed to make sure there was not a predator behind us before we started thinking about the things we were going to do that day. In our more modern days, you need to make sure that you will be able to get food on your plate before you start thinking about buying tickets for the football game. We don't realize it, but this is what our unconscious is assessing all the time in our daily lives. If it happens that you do know when you will get your next meal, you proceed with your activities. Your unconscious gives you permission to do so. If you were not sure about your next meal, you would not be thinking about football at all. Your unconscious would force your attention to getting food on the plate.

There are different grades of intensity of emotion associated to the programs, and you could have a program with a very strong positive emotion that could very well override another one with a small negative emotion. Say you are invited to a party where you know that there will be a person whom you don't like. You will go to that party if you know that very good friends will be there too. In spite of that person whom you don't like being there, you will go. Otherwise, if your good friends are not there, most likely you won't go. Understand that you cannot create a formula like "60 percent positive overrides 40 percent negative." It is not that simple. It depends on the type of events, personal motivations, and more. There are too many variables to be able to quantify this into a formula. And there is no need to do that. The important concept that you need to get from here is that programs with negative emotions have much higher priority than programs with positive emotions, because negative emotions are associated with survival.

This explains to you why we are the way we are. We all want peace, love, and harmony. We want great, loving relationships … until a person makes a comment that really upsets us, and now we get into a fight. So much for peace and love. The program associated with the irritation (negative emotion) easily overrides the loving one (positive emotion). This is how it goes for all our relationships, including our professional ones. When heads of governments are making decisions, these mechanisms are right there behind every single decision they make, from economic policies to war decisions. And depending on their personal unconscious programs, the country will follow in their direction.

The Program Is Classified According to the Perception of the Event

In general, you cannot tell me that a specific event will always be classified in a certain way by the unconscious of an individual. It will be classified according to how the individual lived that experience, which could be very different from how you or someone else would have lived it. An example: Angie, age seven, is sitting in class with her classmates. Class is going normally. At some point, the teacher asks her a question. Caught by surprise and feeling the pressure to give an answer, she blurts one that not only was wrong but also made her whole class laugh. How do you interpret what I just described? Notice that I did not say that her classmates laughed at her. It could have been, but it also could have been that her answer just came out funny. Whatever way you interpreted my example reflects your programs. Here, you have your own personal experience about perception.

Angie could have interpreted it in two completely opposite ways. Unfortunately for most of us, we would feel that it would be very normal to expect Angie to feel ashamed of herself as the result of that experience. And indeed, that is one possibility. If this were the case, out of that experience, Angie's unconscious may create a whole bunch of different programs.

- I am stupid
- People don't like me
- I don't like … (art, math, whatever the class was about)
- How dangerous it is to make mistakes in front of others
  With those come their own associated emotions (shame, fear, etc.).

One event can generate multiple programs.

This causes unfortunate effects in the life of the person (in the case of negative programs). The program "how dangerous it is to make mistakes in front of others" is the classic program behind our fear of public speaking, for instance. It's one of the most common fears people mention. If this is what happened to Angie because of that event, she will now have a fear of public speaking. As an adult, in her job, if her boss asks her to give a presentation, she will get nervous right away. Because her unconscious is telling her, "Danger— we may get ridiculed" (which means that she will be left isolated, which means less chances to survive), her tendency, as long as that program is in her unconscious, will be to try to avoid anything related to public speaking. Negative programs create limitations in our lives. Until she transforms that program in her unconscious, she will keep feeling its effects for the rest of her life.

On the other hand, Angie could have very well interpreted that event as a positive experience. Her unconscious could have created programs like:

- I am funny
- People like me
- I love being in front of people

And, because of this event and the resulting programs, later in her life when choosing a career, she may very well decide to become a professional comedian. A totally opposite effect. Perception is everything and is personal. Now, what is it in her unconscious that makes it interpret the event one way or another? The programs that she already had in her mind at the time of the event (plus the transpersonal components of her personality, which I will talk about later). As I will show you, even a newborn already has programs. There is no such a thing as a completely blank mind or starting with a completely blank slate. So when or where does all this process start? Keep reading.

The Intensity of the Emotion Determines How Much the Program Affects Our Behavior

The stronger the emotion, the more that program will control your behavior when it gets activated. This is very intuitive. If you are going to be giving a public speech and are just a little nervous, you probably will be fine. On the other hand, if you are terrified, you may even get sick. You may not be able to do it because that emotion is so strong. To make it easier to explain the new concepts that I want to introduce to you, we can speak of emotional charge here. Remember how I explained that the unconscious stores the emotion that was felt during the event? You can visualize this as an emotional battery, similar to the electrical batteries we use in cars. Let me explain it to you this way. Let's say someone says something that irritates you. What happened? You already know: your unconscious associated whatever the person said to a program that has that emotion linked to it. What the person said makes the unconscious trigger the program. The unconscious will open the gates of the storage compartment where the emotion is, and zap! you feel that irritation. So think of every program having associated with it a special type of battery that does not store electricity (like the one in our cars) but instead emotion. It's another example of a conceptual model, as I mentioned at the beginning of the book. Every time the unconscious triggers the program, it connects the battery to your body, and you feel the emotional charge stored in it. It would look something like this.

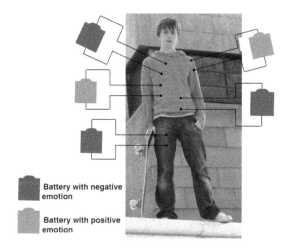

Battery with negative emotion

Battery with positive emotion

Your unconscious has thousands and thousands of different emotional batteries, each one associated to its corresponding program. Every time a program triggers, the unconscious connects its battery to your body, and you feel the emotion. The more temperamental a person is, it means that the person has a lot programs with strong emotional batteries associated to them. People with violent behavior have programs with emotional batteries that have a very big negative charge. When I talk about negative emotions, there is no judgment involved. Every negative emotion that you have is there to protect you from a perceived danger. A negative emotion is simply an emotion that you don't like to feel—that's it. How a person reacts to anything, whether it's at home or at work, reflects the charge of the emotional batteries that the person has in the unconscious. This applies to positive emotions as well as negative ones.

What determines the level of charge of the emotional battery associated to a program? There are two factors.

1. **The intensity of the event that generated it:** This is what I have explained all along up to this point. Whatever emotion you felt during the event that generated the program will be stored in the battery associated to the program—the type of emotion (irritation, fear, anger, sadness, etc.), as well as its intensity.

2. **The repetition of events that reinforce the same program:** Every time you live an event that is associated to a program, and you experience it in a similar way as the original event, the emotional charge will increase. Of course, per point one, the emotional charge will increase proportionally to the perceived intensity of the repeating event.

Point two means that if you have a program associated to a negative emotion, even if the program originally did not have a big emotional charge, then with repetition it can become big. In other words, the individual will get more and more traumatized as the repeating events happen. A typical example applies to parents and the "casual" comments they make about their children. A parent who, when showing something to the child, starts a phrase by saying, "You are doing it wrong. This is how it needs to be done." That comment of "You are doing it wrong," even if not said in an upset manner, is like a little drop of negative emotion. And every time the parent says that, it is another drop of negative emotion that keeps charging the battery associated to the program. The program will be "I do things wrong." And from this, you can have a child who, when young, was outgoing and confident but later in her adolescence is now insecure. There was no single big, traumatic event. And then the parents are left wondering what happened to their young, confident child. This can very easily happen in a family that otherwise is a loving household. Still, the negative programming takes effect. Think about it: why the need of a parent to use that language? The answer is because of his own programming (which in turn came from his parents, school teachers, etc.). If this can happen (and it happens all the time) in "normal" households, imagine children that are growing up in explicitly abusive environments, or imagine soldiers and civilians who live the atrocities of war. All these individuals are not only living events where each one is traumatic on its own, but on top of that, they go through them several times. They end up with highly negatively charged programs, which result in serious behavioral and social handicaps because of the severe limitations that these programs impose in their behavior. Additionally, the explosive reactions that result from repressing all those emotions. An example of this is PTSD,[33] a disorder that unfortunately we hear so much about these days, especially with war veterans.

As a corollary of what I am explaining in this section:

Emotion is what gives power to a program.

---

[33] Post-traumatic stress disorder.

Many people ask whether it is the emotion or the thought that determines how you are going to behave. It is the emotion. A thought without emotion has no power; it is simply a concept. The emotion may have come from a thought that you had, that triggered its associated program. Or it may have come from an event that the person is going through. Ultimately, emotion is what affects your behavior. For someone who is claustrophobic, it is incomprehensible what cave explorers do. The emotion will not let her into the cave. Cave explorers do know that there are dangers in what they do, which are as true to them as anyone else. "Yes, I know there are dangers, but I just love it!" they will tell you. That thought of "cave exploration is dangerous" does not have a significant negative emotion associated with it, and so it is just a concept that does not affect their final behavior. Whatever level of negative emotion they have associated to that concept will influence their behavior and make them take more or less precautions, accordingly.

Emotions regulate our behavior, according to their intensity.

With this understanding, let's take again the previous case of the young man with the fear of numbers. You may say that he did not necessarily feel that disappointment of the originating event when making his first (wrong) career choice. Nevertheless, the unconscious knows about the emotional charge associated to the program. It is the magnitude of the emotion that led him to make that decision. There was no need to connect the emotional battery because he had not yet acted on the decision to study engineering. If somehow he would have been forced to study engineering from the beginning, then the unconscious would have triggered the program. At that point, it would have connected the battery in order to force him to abandon that course of action already taken. Thus:

The programs in your unconscious affect all your decisions, whether or not they are triggered.

If they are in your unconscious, they affect you, and their effect will depend on the magnitude of their emotional charge.

Modes of Affecting Behavior

From what I just explained, programs and their associated emotions affect your behavior in two different ways.

1. **Explicit:** When the program triggers, you feel the emotion and react accordingly.
2. **Implicit:** Even if not triggered, the unconscious uses them every time when it is in the process of making a decision. If the concept of a program stored in the unconscious is related to the decision to be made, it will become part of the decision process. The stored emotional energy will be the weight that the program has within that decision process.

The implicit influence that programs have in our behavior is crucial to understanding the importance of transforming negative programs, whether or not they may explicitly activate in the particular circumstances of your life. Because they will affect you as long as they have an emotion associated with it, like in the previous example with the young man and his career choice. Here is where I can finish the story of my friend whom I narrated at the beginning of the book. It's a clear case of the implicit effect that a program has in your decisions.

Case 10: Decisions in Our Lives (Part B)

So that you understand his decision to not adopt, let me tell you more about his family history, starting with his paternal grandfather. He was an individual who came from humble beginnings yet, through hard work, became a very successful person. He was also very generous. He married, and from that first marriage, he had seven children. One of them was my friend's father. He married a second time, with five children from that marriage. He married one more time, but in this third relationship, they had no children, and instead they adopted a boy and a girl. My friend's father married, however because of his heavy drinking and the problems that came with that, his wife was already separated from him by the time my friend was born (he only saw his father three times, as an adult). And, because of this situation that his son created, the paternal grandfather decided to take care of his family. He became, practically and emotionally speaking, my friend's father who also provided all the financial security that they needed. My friend loved his grandfather.

At the same time, it turned out that the relationship between his grandfather and the adopted children of his third marriage became very conflicted. It ended up affecting that marriage and, to the point here, inflicted great suffering in his grandfather. My friend had to see and experience it as it was happening. He painfully saw the conflicts unfolding and how they caused so much hurt in him. Years of going through these events built up in my friend powerful, negatively charged batteries associated to adoption. Here you have also a very clear example of how the unconscious creates associations by perception of experiences. My friend knew then and now that just because that was the case with his grandfather's adopted children, it does not mean that all adoptions will go awry like this one. That is rational and correct. Nevertheless, that was not the experience he was having, and instead his unconscious recorded it as he experienced it. You cannot cheat your unconscious; it does not work. What his unconscious recorded as a program was, essentially, "adoption is a nightmare." Even though conceptually he had the best opinions about it, when it came to the point of living that option, this program in his unconscious was the one who made the decision. What looked from the outside as his decision was not his—it was this program's. Understand that when he was telling his wife that he did not want to adopt, he was not screaming as if reacting to an occurring negative event. He was as well put together as one sees him anytime. That clear sense about "his" decision was in reality the result of that negatively charged battery associated to that program, which now was part of this decision-making process.

This is how we are making decisions in our lives. It is a seamless process throughout the vast majority of our daily routine. Also, this implicit influence highlights the importance of solving our problems at the root of them, not just by covering up the symptoms that may be personally inconvenient or socially inacceptable. Take nail-biting, for example. Many of the recommendations to stop that habit include covering them with a bitter-tasting polish, chewing gum, or wearing gloves. With children, there's even punishment. Nail-biting is the result of a negative program which can't be expressed, usually anger or a stress due to an insecurity. Even if that person stops biting his nails through some of these methods, the originating program is still in his unconscious. The conflict remains inside. The person will keep making limiting decisions in his life, even though he is not biting nails anymore. And by the way, because the causing program is still intact, it will seek expression in some other ways, normally through another habit (like overeating).

Program Triggers

The program sits in standby mode as long as its associated concept is not detected by the unconscious. When the unconscious detects its concept in the environment, it activates the program by connecting its emotional battery to the body and initiating the corresponding physical reaction. You will feel it. Someone with claustrophobia will be fine at the beach. Not so when the doctor orders an MRI.[34] Lots of people feel claustrophobic when they try to get in the tube section of the scanner. In this case, when the doctor is trying to "save" you from your illness and orders that scan, your programming will stop you. What an irony—these programs were created by nature to help you survive. Here you can see a great example of the mechanical nature of the unconscious. It does not reason. The person getting the scan knows very well that there is no danger in getting into the tube. That is her conscious part. On the other hand, for that person's unconscious, cramped spaces are classified as dangerous, period. It does no care whether in a cave or at the hospital. Also, this example shows you once more how powerful the unconscious is. In many cases, even under doctor's orders, the patient will not be able to get in. I had a friend who was so horrified of getting into that machine that even after having been offered tranquilizers to help him do it, he vehemently refused them. Can you promise me that you will not ever get irritated in your life again? I don't think so. When you start to understand and respect the power of these programs, you will start having a chance to take the right actions to transcend them. They shape our civilization.

There's a key point to add in this respect:

The level of triggering for a program depends on the immediacy of the concept associated with it.

In other words, a program does not necessarily just activate or not. When it activates, the unconscious will connect the emotional battery to a level proportionate to the detected danger (in the case of negative programs) perceived around its associated concept. In the case of our prehistoric family, if they see the predator at a far distance, they will pay attention but will remain relatively calm. If the predator starts to get closer, they will become more and more alarmed. The unconscious will start increasing the level of the emotion that it connects to the body. In today's world, if you work for a company and rumors start to circulate about possible layoffs, you may get nervous—just that little bit of the total emotional charge of that program. However, if they

---

[34] Magnetic resonance imaging, a medical device traditionally shaped as a tube in which the person must go in, lying down.

hand you the pink slip, you will get the full intensity of the emotion stored in that program's battery.

The range of emotional intensity that the unconscious has at its disposal for a given program is set by the total emotional level stored in the program's battery.

This is because the maximum emotion is dictated by what is stored in the battery. The unconscious then will connect the appropriate level according to what it perceives in the environment.

The higher the emotional charge of a program's battery, the more the tendency of the unconscious to fully connect it to the body.

This is because it has such a power stored in it. Anything "small" triggers the brunt of it (i.e., is perceived as very dangerous for negative programs). Anything small becomes a big deal. It will be very difficult for that person to respond more calmly to that specific situation. These are the people with explosive responses, as a generic example.

Case 11: A Holocaust Survivor

My father. While in the concentration camps during World War II, he saw right in front of him the lines of people who were being sent to the gas chambers. In that environment, any single little mistake could cost you your life. He had to be hyper-vigilant all the time. His unconscious created programs with giant emotional batteries, like "everything is a big deal" and "any small mistake can be fatal," to ensure his survival under those conditions. In this case, these programs executed perfectly well and according to what they were intended for: his survival in a concentration camp. My father lost his family and possessions during that war and was forced to restart his life again after the war. We were his only family, and he loved us deeply. But he had a very difficult temperament. Everything to him was a big deal—a huge deal. He constantly reacted very strongly and explosively to the circumstances of life. Most of them were simply not worth getting upset at all in our post-war environment. He went through lots of suffering, as did all of us because the programs did not adapt to the new circumstances in his life. He was now reacting mechanically, under the control of programs created decades ago.

It's similar with people who get easily irritated or offended. A typical scenario for people who are easily offended is that they are expressing the repressed emotion stored when an authority figure forbade them to do what the "offending" person is doing now. They wanted to do that but couldn't. That frustration comes out as being offended, and that is how they are expressing it now (this is called projection in psychology). Most of the moral judgments related to sexuality come from this type of programming. Sexuality is part of being human and is a very strong biopsychic force. It requires programs with very big emotional batteries to repress it, as parents generally still try to do with their children nowadays. Instead of educating and teaching youngsters to be responsible for this beautiful, natural energy in all of us, we convert it into taboo and inhibition with the result of the sexual abuses, rape, and other damaging behaviors we hear so much about.

In general, the more strict and judgmental a person is, whether in terms of moral values or otherwise, the more negative, highly charged emotional batteries he or she has. This emotional rigidity goes against a basic principle in life, which is adaptation to the ever-changing circumstances that are an integral part of our evolutionary path. This does not mean that we do not hold basic universal principles. Don't confuse arbitrary moral values that we created and impose on ourselves with the universal principle of unconditional love. Unconditional love is always adaptive and valid under any circumstance.

To close this section, the unconscious will activate a program when it detects its concept, whether in physical terms or in abstract terms. An example of what I mean by abstract terms is the case where a co-worker tells you that there will be layoffs coming within the company. The simple thought of that event, which has not occurred yet and in fact may never occur, can trigger a program in your unconscious that will take you into a stress response immediately.

The Programs in the Unconscious Are Designed to Be Stable

There are two solid reasons for this.

1. **Rules for survival:** From the old days, if you just learned that a certain predator was dangerous, you'd better remembered that the next day when you woke up. You could not afford to forget these rules of survival. These structures were designed to be very resilient, which explains why it is so difficult for us to change our behaviors. We keep repeating hurtful

behaviors, inflicting pain on us and others. This is why if you want to change your behavior, you need to do special procedures that allow you access and process these programs directly in the unconscious. This is what a mind transformation process (MTP) does (see section 3 of this book). It is extremely difficult to try to change these programs via the conscious. If it is a program with a very small emotional charge, you might be able to do it. But those are, generally speaking, not the ones that call our attention. The self-sabotaging behaviors, deeper insecurities, and anger cause a bigger toll in our lives. These require an intentional intervention (via an MTP) in order to transform them into positive patterns of behavior.

2. **Identity:**

   The programs in your unconscious define your identity.

   The bulk of who you are, as an individual in your current life (and in our current state of evolution), is these programs. Even though you are a nonphysical entity and your Essence is a powerful influence (as I will explain in the transpersonal components of the personality), more than anything, these programs define you. They define how you see yourself and how you interact with the rest of the world. Can you imagine if every day you woke up, your identity changed? Every time you would be a different person. There would not be consistency in your life because every day you would have different behaviors, likings, and goals. This does not work. You are you because the core of your programs remains the same through the days, months, and years in your life.

Case 12: Too Much Change Too Quickly

As part of doing the hypnotherapy certification, we were encouraged to do sessions with our teachers. A good mind practitioner works on clearing his own limitations before intending to transform those in others. On top of that, as part of our training, we not only studied theory but also did practice exercises. These practices were essentially supervised sessions among all of us. In my case, this ended up becoming overwhelming. There were so many issues coming up that it was too much for me. It was just me; the other students were fine. The irony of this situation is that my transformation was for the better. Nevertheless, mind transformation is personality transformation. There has to be time to integrate the changes.

I knew that I had a lot of issues. I did my certification because I needed answers to so many questions about my inner demons. In the end, I took a break for that semester and finished my certification in the following one.

The stability of our programs in our unconscious provides us with the foundation that enables us to function in our lives. This stability is what allows congruency in our lives, in our behaviors, and in our goals. Let me point out that there are cases where massive program transformations may work positively. In extreme cases, they result in a nervous breakdown of the person, which prevents her from temporarily continuing with daily life. I have personally known people who went through this, and there is one well-known spiritual teacher, Eckhart Tolle, who in his book *The Power of Now*[35] writes about it. During these episodes, a great number of negative limiting programs are transformed and transcended. The person does not "forget" who he is, but a new personality emerges, a new identity. Eckhart Tolle describes this very eloquently in his book.

> I understood that the intense pressure of suffering that night must have forced my consciousness to withdraw from its identification with the unhappy and deeply fearful self, which is ultimately a fiction of the mind. This withdrawal must have been so complete that this false, suffering self immediately collapsed, just as if a plug had been pulled out of an inflatable toy.[36]

He still remembered who he was, but he also knew that he was a new person. The previous personality disappeared. It is one way to evolve. The path that most of us follow is that of a more gradual transformation. That is an individual's choice, one that actually comes more from the nonphysical Essence than the personality. (The people involved in this process do not intentionally pursue, as their goal, to have a nervous breakdown. They simply collapse, psychologically speaking, under the weight of the circumstances in their lives, to later emerge radically transformed in a positive manner.)

---

[35] Eckhart Tolle, *The Power of Now, A Guide to Spiritual Enlightenment*, 15th ed., Vancouver: Namaste Publishing, 2003.
[36] Eckhart Tolle, *The Power of Now*, 2–3.

There is an important implication that emerges from the assertion that these programs define your identity. Because most of them originated from your interactions with the environment in which you grew up, this means that the environment shaped your identity. If you would have been born in different circumstances, you would have gone through different experiences that would have led you to come to different conclusions about yourself. For example, if you would have been born in an abusive environment, your parents may have led you to belief that you are worthless. It is very unlikely that you would have come to that conclusion if you would have been born in a nurturing and supportive family. That belief that you are worthless is part of your identity. That is how you see yourself as a person. It's the result of your particular experiences for the most part. As I will show you later, there are transpersonal factors, including the fact that you are a unique Unit of Consciousness, and as such you're intrinsically unique and different from all others. Your identity as a human being will be the result of the combination of all these factors. The more limiting programs you have, the more they will hijack your behavior and what you see as your identity. The freer you are from negative programming, the more transparent you will be to the expression of your Essence, who you truly are, and unconditional love.

The Virtual Reality of Being Human

There is no such a thing as "objectivity" in our lives. There would be so much more tolerance amongst us if people truly understood this.

You are a nonphysical entity inserted in a human body. The way you experience this planet through this particular vehicle is subject to the mechanisms of its physical receptors as well as those of its mind. If you would have inserted into a body with different specifications, you would potentially be experiencing this planet in a totally different way.

Our Body's Generated Virtual Reality

The body is a biological machine designed to interpret reality in a specific way. For example, when an electromagnetic wave of the specific frequency that we call green strikes your eye, your brain will construct an inner perception that makes you see what you call the color green. Instead, the brain could have been designed to make you see black-and-white stripes whenever that same electromagnetic wave hit your eye. So whatever you see as green now, you would see as black-and-white stripes. If that were the case, you would not have any idea of what green is as you perceive it today. That reality you call green, as you perceive it now, would not exist for you. In reality, colors do not exist. The green that you see is the arbitrary translation that your brain does to that wave when it strikes your eye. The combination of eyes and brain in this instrument that we call the human body have been designed in such a way that they give you the perception of what we call colors to differentiate (an extremely narrow set of) different electromagnetic frequencies. Electromagnetic waves do not have color; they are simply waves. A lot of animals see different parts of the electromagnetic spectrum that we don't. We have no idea of how they perceive that spectrum. That reality does not exist for us. You could also have a body that, when a green electromagnetic wave hits its receptors, it interprets it as a particular sound. Instead of seeing the color green, you would be "hearing green." On the same topic, darkness is simply the interpretation of your brain when you close your eyes and it doesn't detect light waves anymore. The universe is full of all kinds of energy radiation. There is no such a thing as darkness; it is an invention (more properly said, an interpretation) of our brains. With the proper receptors, you would see the universe's background energy all the time. You cannot speak of what your body's sensors are telling you, as an objective reality. You don't even know if I see green the same way that you do. The way we perceive the physical is a completely arbitrary construction of our particular processing apparatus that we call the brain and body. Additionally, as sophisticated as our bodies and senses are, they could be giving us the wrong perception of physical reality. Two people watching a rotating radar may very well be seeing it rotating in opposite directions (with some training, you can even "make it" change the direction of rotation yourself).

The analogy here is the virtual headsets that we have available today. For those of you who have tried them, you know that whatever it is you are seeing seems totally real to you.

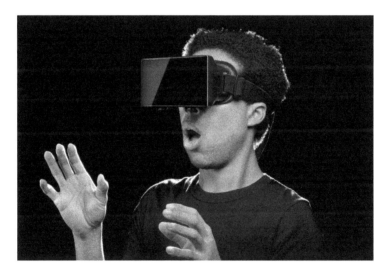

You will even move your body according to what you are seeing. In a way, it is ironic that we are so fascinated with the experience that these headsets give us because we are all wearing such headsets: our bodies. If you think that our current headsets are amazing, how do you think the experience will be when technology improves to the point of giving you the sense of touch, smell, taste, pressure, temperature, and acceleration? When technology gets there, and you insert yourself into that virtual machine, your brain will not be able to determine which reality is the real one. Maybe now it is a little easier to accept the radical concept that I mentioned at the beginning of the book, where I speculated that it might be possible in the future for Units of Consciousness to insert themselves into a machine instead of the human body.

That machine simply must have enough functional capabilities to make it attractive to the UC to experience the physical world through it. That is what our bodies do nowadays.

Our Mind Generated Virtual Reality

As the children grow and have more experiences, more and more programs are being created by their unconscious. These programs will determine how they will interact with everything in their lives. They will determine not only how they behave but also how they see themselves, the world, and life. Because we all have had unique experiences, we all have different programs—thus our unique behaviors, our individuality. We may be seven billion humans on this planet, but there are no two individuals with exactly the same view of life. The little girl in our example, as an adult with the programs "making a living is hard work" and "life is unfair," will have a tendency to stick to her current job even if she doesn't like it anymore. Because of the way that she perceives life, it's better to not take risks because she may land another job that could be much worse. Her programs paint her life with their specific colors in the same way that your programs are doing it to the way that you see life. Now, your way certainly does not have to agree with her way. Even though you both are living in the same physical world, you are actually living different inner realities. She feels that she is making that decision from her own free will. Not so. At this point, she is not thinking about the incident with the theater teacher in school. Nevertheless, that program is still in her unconscious, and it takes part of that decision, in conjunction with all other associated programs to this type of event. This is how you are making choices in life.

Our programs in the unconscious become the filters through which we look at ourselves and at the outside world.

Throughout our lives, we cannot, in our current state of evolution, simply take these filters out of our everyday living. Some people may be able to transcend them momentarily in altered states of consciousness, like in meditation or deep prayer. Those are just small instances. Our sensory organs give us information about the environment in which we are. That information first goes through the programs in our unconscious, which color it according to our own unique associations. Only then, afterward, it comes to our awareness as our perception of reality.

What you experience in your life is your continual, personal unconscious interpretation of your environment.

In neurolinguistic programming,[37] this is called your internal map of reality (also, in more colloquial terms, your mental territory). Take a lake, for example. For someone who loves the water, the lake is a symbol of fun. On the other hand, for a person with a fear of water, that lake is a nightmare. In the end, the lake is just a bunch of water molecules, which in itself is not either exciting or nightmarish. These attributes come from us, from our minds. If you put these two individuals side by side in front of this lake, they will experience completely different realities. This applies to concrete things (like the lake) as well as abstract ideas. Another very common experience that all of us have had is when you and a friend meet another person for the first time. After that encounter, you exchange opinions, and it turns out that you two ended with totally different impressions about that person. You may have thought that he was nice, but your friend may have gotten the impression that he was arrogant. It was the same physical experience, lived subjectively in two different realities. You probably have had the experience of knowing someone whom you know to be very talented at something. Ironically, there is no way to convince that person about that ability that she has. She is in a different reality from yours. What you see so clearly in her, she doesn't. What I am conveying to you here is that this is more than just a simple difference of opinions. In our minds, we look at life on this planet in completely different ways, according to how our programs color our perceptions. Coming back to Eckhart Tolle, in his extreme case of transformation, look how he describes the afterward of the event.

> I got up and walked around the room. I recognized the room, and yet I knew that I had never truly seen it before. Everything was fresh and pristine, as if it had just come into existence. I picked up things, a pencil, an empty bottle, marveling at the beauty and aliveness of it all.
>
> That day I walked around the city in utter amazement at the miracle of life on Earth, as if I had just been born into this world.[38]

---

[37] Neurolinguistic programming (NLP) is one of the many mind transformation processes in existence, like hypnotherapy and psychotherapy.
[38] Eckhart Tolle, *The Power of Now*, 2.

He describes so clearly his new way of perceiving reality. Again, this is a very extreme case, but precisely because of that, it illustrates so well what happens when you change the programs of your mind. In our more common way of doing mind transformation work, via sessions, I can guide a person who fears water to change that filter of perception so that a lake will become pleasant and enjoyable. My clients experience this change of filters after every session. They experience firsthand what it is to see reality differently. Before they came for a session, they looked at a given experience in their lives in a certain way. After the session, they see that same event under a different light. They tell me so.

Each of us lives in the personal virtual reality of our minds.

An analogy is when you wear sunglasses that have a certain color tint. After a while, you don't notice it anymore until you take them off. That is exactly how we are looking at the physical world as humans. We are all wearing our own particular sets of lenses, each with our own distinct tints. We think we see the world as is. We do not. You realize this when you change one or more of your programs (change your glasses). Then you notice that now you see life differently.

This applies to all programs because, as we saw, they all take part in your decision processes.

Even if not triggered, all programs in your mind are acting as filters through which you see reality.

The "Subjective Objectivity" Effect

There is no such thing as being objective when referring to how we see things. If you give a little bit of thought to all this, you will start to question more and more how we behave and the civilization that we have created—the way we hurt each other, the way we attack each other, the disparities that we see in our societies. We are all Units of Consciousness who insert ourselves into these extraordinary machines that we call the human body, and then we end up creating so much suffering. Life is indeed beautiful; however you cannot deny the pain that we add to it in our current state of evolution. How can this be? This information will help you understand this. The body interprets the "outer reality" subjectively and according to its own physical design. The mind also adds another layer of subjective interpretation. This process is so amazingly seamless that we do not even realize it. There are consequences to that.

1. We believe that what we see is objective. This is what I call the "subjective objectivity" effect.
2. We interpret our perception as absolute.
3. Because I know that I am right, that means that if you don't agree with me, you are wrong. (It must be that the other person missed something, or didn't get it.)
4. Because I know that you are wrong, I need to make the truth prevail (which in reality is *my* truth).

And here is the beginning of the chain of violence that goes from the personal level, our relationships with others, to the level of our civilization, with nations warring against each other because each side believes that its position is the correct position.

These are the repercussions of how our body and mind operate. The day when we all become more aware about this internal virtual reality and how it tricks us into believing that what we see is objective reality, violence on this planet will reduce drastically.

You will know that you cannot claim objectivity, and so you won't allow anyone else. Thus, the only thing that will make sense is to build bridges of communication that enable a mutual understanding that allows all involved parties to accomplish their own goals.

Of course, this is always done under principles of mutual respect.

The Faculty of Reasoning

As the youngster grows older than ten years old, the conscious starts to take a more prominent role. Implied within this is the ability to reason. The youngster is coming more and more to her own conclusions and now is on her way to become an independent entity. Contrary to what many people think, the faculty of reasoning has very little, if any, creativity in it.

The faculty of reasoning is a tool that allows for the manipulation of ideas.

This applies to existing ideas. Reasoning involves giving logic to thoughts and connecting them in a logical way. This has another consequence that is key to understanding how we behave.

The faculty of reasoning is the glue that holds together all our programs.

The faculty of reasoning is going to become the tool that your mind uses to give consistency to all the programs (experiences) that you accumulated in your life. It has to be that way; otherwise, we could not function. If our internal world were not consistent, we would go insane. This reinforces the concept that I talked about earlier about the programs designed to be stable structures. What the faculty of reasoning will do is add logic to make sense of all of them. It will "glue" them so that you see and feel reality as one logical, consistent construction. This will allow you to function within it. In your mind, the way you see things, everything has a logic, a reason. Thus, because of this:

We always have a justification for whatever we think and do in our lives.

This is how we have justified doing the most beautiful things—and also the most monstrous acts in human history. I will expand on this in the next section. For now, let's say that this includes how we see ourselves. You will give me all the reasons in the world about why you believe whatever it is about yourself. In other words, if you think that you are not good at music, you are going to give me all the reasons why you believe that. If you think you are clumsy, you will tell me why that is so. If you think life is unfair, you will explain why. Now, a person sitting next to you may think exactly the opposite and will tell me also why that is true. Both think (and "know") that they are right. This goes for everything in our lives—political views, religious beliefs, and even scientific views. Scientists, as human beings, are not exempt from this. This is the faculty of reasoning in action. It does so impeccably. We argue for our beliefs. We even argue for own limitations with as much conviction as anything else! In my seminars, when I explain with scientific examples that you are indeed the master of your reality, people argue. They are so identified with their role of victims that they are not willing to give my explanations a chance. I think we all have had the experience of giving someone robust advice (from our personal point of view, of course) about something, and the person does not follow it, leaving us baffled about her inaction and trying to understand her reasoning. There are three possible reasons behind that behavior.

1. Her faculty of reasoning makes her find her own reasoning more logical (the glue of his inner reality). If your advice is really not as robust as her own logic, there is no reason for that person to change.
2. There is a negative program that is stopping her from taking action.
3. The new way of thinking would imply a new way of how she sees himself, which means a change in identity. Change of identity is always danger because it implies "possible death" to the current one. It goes against the basic survival tenet of the unconscious. An example of this would be to ask someone to change her religious beliefs. If she truly believes in her religion, which is part of her identity, it does not matter your reasons; she will follow her faith.

The faculty of reasoning solidifies your programs, and it amplifies the subjective objectivity effect even more. Not only do you perceive something and interpret it as objective, but now you have the faculty of reasoning to back it up. You entrench in that belief. As a result, another effect comes out of this.

The "Information Filtering" Effect

Remember the example I gave you about the person telling me, "Everybody who steals should be executed"? I answered explaining why I do not agree with that opinion. What prompted me to give that answer? The programs that I have stored in my unconscious and the faculty of reasoning. My faculty of reasoning ties the related beliefs to this particular topic and then builds my answer with the corresponding logic. In this example, I rejected his idea. That idea, which is true for the other person, did not reach my unconscious because it is not congruent with my beliefs. It does not match the mental structures, the programs, stored in my mind. My mind is now filtering out anything that does not match my inner programs. This is what I call the "information filtering" effect.

The faculty of reasoning filters out the realities that do not match your internal map of reality.

It works in perfect unison with the subjective objectivity effect. This is not a capricious design from nature. Your programs took a long time to be assimilated. What nature is assuming here is that they are valid because, after all, the individual did survive to the age where his faculty of reasoning developed. There was ample time to test and make the necessary corrections if a learned behavior was not appropriate to that environment. If at this point there is something that may not match your rules of survivorship, it is more of an exception. There are always exceptions in life, but that does not mean that the learned program is necessarily invalid. Thus, our unconscious now uses the faculty of reasoning as a tool to protect its programs, in order to maintain the consistency of its internal reality.

Why We Don't Like to Be Wrong

When we realize that we were wrong about something, it means that the faculty of reasoning was not able to keep congruency within that internal reality of your mind. We don't like to be wrong about something. Why do you feel bad when that happens? What does it mean if one of the rules of survivorship (in this case, a belief) turned out to be wrong? To make it clearer for you, what if all the rules of survivorship were all wrong? What would be your chances of survival? Not very high. In other words, when you realize that you were wrong, to your unconscious, it is a confrontation with death. It is a questioning of your internal rules of survival that you take for granted in your life.

Do Old Dogs Learn New Tricks?

In the United States, there is a saying: "You can't teach an old dog new tricks." That refers to older people being so set in their ways. Where does a saying like this come from? Even though not everybody falls in that category, it is safe to generalize that there is a tendency for people to settle in their ways as they age—not only in their behaviors but also in their ideas. With respect to their ideas, it is the result of the reality filtering effect. As time passes, the mind of the person will tend to accept only what matches the structures of his mind ("You see?! I knew I was right!"). We will look for events and information that validate our beliefs. As an example, we will sympathize with the news channel that most matches with our opinions, and that is the one we will watch. Our beliefs will entrench more and more. We will tend to ignore events and information that contradict our beliefs. Increasingly, you will start to automatically reject any other views. In the end, the old dog does not learn new tricks anymore. This is not because the brain loses its capacity to learn new things, as so many people believe. The brain has the capacity to create new neural connections throughout the entire life (neuroplasticity). What keeps the individual entrenched are the mental structures. As the individual keeps filtering the information that matches a particular program in his mind, its associated emotional battery increases its charge to the point where the person feels strongly about that specific topic. It is that emotion that keeps the structure in place.

This is easily observed in a session with my clients. Before the session, they are locked into a point of view about the conflict they want to resolve. As soon as the emotion has been processed, the person can now move to a different perception of the event. It is not because of the brain. It works equally well with adults as with younger people. The brain will reconnect without any problems.

We are constantly filtering incoming information through our programs.

This is a potentially dangerous effect that explains the tendency that we have to polarize and, ultimately, radicalize.

All of us, as human beings, have this tendency. Do not put yourself above this. You are not. This being the case, what can we do about it?

It is crucial that we practice the art of maintaining an open mind, at the same time exercising discernment.

It is a life practice. This requires attention to our own reactions, questioning, knowledge, and critical thinking to be able to discern. It also requires emotional maturity because you need to have inner strength to be able to put yourself in the vulnerable position of confronting your own beliefs. Most people are not ready to see themselves in such a situation. First of all, the subjective objectivity effect makes them convinced that they are right. Second, there is the unconscious force to protect the identity built around that belief. Thus, instead we go on automatic and defend our programmed points of view. The more we feel that they are threatened, the stronger we will attack.

Polarization, unfortunately, is commonplace nowadays—a phenomenon that is so clearly seen in politics, for instance. Here in the United States, we can see it in the government. People criticize congress for bipartisan inaction. What they don't see is the polarization in themselves as well. It starts right at the bottom in each of us, when we are unwilling to work constructively with people of different political parties. The commentaries that individuals make to articles and blogs in the media, as an example, are as polarized as the top branches of government. I am aware of the fact that this may sound radical in our world of politics, but from the perspective of how the human mind works, and specifically from this information filtering effect, when you call yourself as democrat, republican, capitalist, or socialist, you are putting yourself in a very vulnerable position that easily leads to polarization. Why impose such a label on yourself? It automatically imposes restrictions in your ability to fully analyze a certain issue, because it will necessarily go through the mental filters of that label. The fewer labels you apply to yourself, the more open and flexible you are to contemplate different points of view about any topic. This statement is simply a direct result from all that I have explained to you about how the human mind works.

Part 1 Conclusions and Implications

Who You Are

Every day in your life, when you wake up in the morning, you know exactly who you are. You take it for granted, and of course it needs to be this way. Your programs keep the integrity of your personality. On the other hand, you cannot promise me that you will not get angry again in your life. That is the programs' power. They define us and control our behavior.

- The food you eat. I can (very easily, by the way) show you foods that people eat in different cultures that you would consider disgusting. Simply watching a video of them eating this type of foods could make you feel nauseated. For them, they are great delicacies. Even so, you were born in an environment in which that food was considered disgusting, and so were you programmed. Do you think that your taste is just a natural personal inclination? Think again—it is programmed taste. Yes, with individual nuances, but all within your generic cultural setting.[39] Being aware of things like this helps you understand the relativity of our experiences in this physical world and therefore makes you more tolerant of others.
- The way you dress. In our Western society, if I ask you to go out in just a loincloth (normal in other cultures), you will cringe at the thought of doing that. Your unconscious screams "Danger!" to that idea. You have been programmed to fit in your environment. Notice that this is not necessarily a negative thing (even though it still is limiting programming). This is precisely the purpose of these programs, as we saw. The problem comes when we make these rules absolute. We talk about good taste and bad taste in the way we dress. There's no such a thing, and they're totally arbitrary conventions. We judge, classify, chastise, and hurt each other because of them. Just recently, at the time of writing this book, I read

---

[39] If you want to experience firsthand the power of your cultural programming in this respect, go to YouTube and search for, as an example, "disgusting foods." Please take care of yourself. My point is not that you do this until you feel nauseated to confirm what I am saying. Simply noticing your first reactions is enough to be a clear experience of your own programming.

an article about a woman in a European country who was sent home from her job because she did not want to wear high heel shoes.[40] You say it was part of her job description. And why is that? The company did that because, indeed, wearing high heels causes "an impression" on its customers. It's a self-reinforcing circle of societal programming happening today in the "modern" twenty-first century, as it has happened throughout human history. You think that when you go to your favorite store, you are freely choosing what you like. Yes, but what you like has been programmed in you. The moment you wake up in the morning, your unconscious activates all these programs, and you start acting them so seamlessly that you feel as if you are making free decisions. Who knows what creative ways of dressing people would come up if we were to live in a society that allows freer expression? These programs are severe limitations to our expression and creativity.

- The way you behave (the point of this book). There are customs in your culture that are disrespectful in other cultures. We say, "They are the weird ones." Of course, that is exactly what they think about us. Burping after eating a meal is a sign of appreciation in some cultures. In others, it is a sign of bad manners, to the point of being disgusting. This applies even to sexuality, which one would think is purely biological.[41] Not so. We all have seen the pictures of women in tribes who do not cover their breasts. It's no big deal to them or to the men in their societies. In the United States and many other Western societies, it is a big deal because of the sexual connotation. This does not have anything to do with how "advanced" a society is. This has to do with societal programming. If we see someone not behaving as we expect, we get angry, we feel disrespected, and we feel insulted. All these reactions are the (mechanical) responses of the programs that have been implanted in our minds. Nothing more. It is amazing to me to see how much we suffer because of these abstractions that we have created. We have converted them into "heavy steel" mental structures.
- Your beliefs. This is a sensitive topic. Morals are arbitrary principles that people impose on others to classify "right" or "wrong" conduct. Don't

---

[40] BBC News, "London Receptionist Sent Home for Not Wearing Heels," May 11, 2016, http://www.bbc.com/news/uk-england-london-36264229. Accessed December 10, 2018

[41] That is why I called it earlier a psychobiological force.

confuse morals with universal principles. Universal principles remain true irrespective of time, space, or situation, like unconditional love. Many years ago, I read about the diary of a woman who was taking part in the migration to the west in the United States in the 1800s. She had a suitor. She tells the anecdote about how he once, by surprise while saying goodbye, he dared to give her a kiss on her cheek. This was totally inappropriate at that time, and she reprimanded him for doing that. (Nevertheless, in her diary she did admit to being excited about it.) Sounds cute, right? Not at that time, though. Women allowing such a behavior could very easily be cast out from their social circles. And if you were living at that time, you would have been part of that morality. You would have been judging her as anyone else. Today, under the same circumstances, where the woman does feel attracted to the man with whom she is going out, this is not considered immoral. (In fact, the opposite: she would probably feel disappointed if the man did not try to kiss her.)

In 1907, Annette Kellermann was arrested in Revere Beach, Massachusetts, for indecency—for wearing the one-piece bathing costume that you see in the picture instead of the combination of dress and pantaloons that women were expected (by law!) to wear at that time. You will find plenty of other similar cases on the Internet. Amazing, isn't it? It's hard to believe by today's moral standards. At that time, you would have been part of that morality. In what is known as the Dred Scott case, in 1857 the US Supreme Court declared that African Americans were not and could never be citizens of the United States.[42] That decision is considered one of the worst decisions ever made by the Supreme Court today. I am giving you this example because I want to show you that what we would call well-educated, sophisticated people, like these judges obviously were, are not exempt from the consequences of these programs. And these are actually mild stories with regard to behaving outside the accepted morals in our human history. A step toward eliminating violence in our societies is becoming conscious about the arbitrariness of our existing rules of behavior. We need to question more if we want to create the change for more tolerance that is needed in this civilization.

If you would have been born on another part of the planet where people practice different types of spiritual beliefs, you would be practicing those beliefs, as they do. I am not saying that you have to abandon whatever spiritual beliefs that you have. I am asking you to be conscious about how you got them—and yes, to have the courage to question them. If you don't give yourself permission to question and consider alternative points of view about your religious beliefs, it is because (1) you have been programmed too emphatically, which will put you in peril of fanaticism and intolerance, or (2) you are afraid about the consequences of doing so (God will punish you, societal rejection, etc.), which denotes limiting negative programs. Understand that these beliefs are arbitrary to the place where you were born and to the time in which you were born. The examples about the women that I gave you above also describe behaviors that were considered

---

[42] Melvin I. Urofsky, "Dred Scott decision," *Encyclopaedia Britannica*, Encyclopaedia Britannica, March 25, 2014, https://www.britannica.com/event/Dred-Scott-decision. Accessed December 10, 2018.

sinful by the religious organizations of that time. As far as I know, they would not be considered sinners today. So what moral is right? What religious principles are right? What behaviors are right? How do you think people are going to look back at today's morals one hundred years from now? We have inflicted ourselves with a lot of suffering as a result of principles that are not the creation of God but rather man.

Case 13: Marrying a Divorced Man

My client told me how happy she was the day of her marriage. As the ceremony was ready to start, a family member approached her in a private moment. This family member told her that she wants to make sure that she understood that she was marrying in sin because her husband to be was a divorced man. This family member was trying to help my client (in fact, "save her"). That was her internal map of reality. She was doing "the right thing," and her action was totally justified by her religious beliefs and reasoning. Yet she not only dropped a bucket of ice water on my client's wedding celebration, but she also left a huge guilt with her as well. Here she was with me, over thirty years later, wanting to work out this weight that she had been carrying all these years since her wedding day.

This is not an isolated case; it is still everywhere. I have great female friends who are smart, well educated, and very successful. They defend their particular religions, even though it is clear that these religions discriminate against women. Still, when I explain this to them, they give me all the reasons why they belong to them. The superb work of the faculty of reasoning, working in conjunction with powerful programs in the unconscious.

The Ultimate Question: Do We Have Free Will?

After reading all this information, our human landscape may seem pretty dark, wouldn't you say? I have been emphasizing how these programs control our behaviors. Thus, it may look as if we are doomed, and we really don't have that sacred free will that we want to believe in … or do we? Yes, actually, we do. However, in our everyday lives, as we live nowadays, we have very, very little.

Restricted to Your Mental Territory

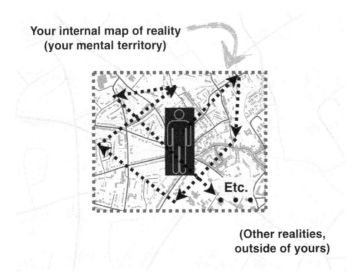

Your internal map of reality (your mental territory)

Etc.

(Other realities, outside of yours)

All of us are living our lives within the confines of our mental territories. There are two main reasons.

1. First principle:

    The programming that we have is the database that contains all that is known to us.

    You know about clothes, tables, chairs, restrooms, cars, traffic, work, and government, and how to interact with them. You know how to behave at any instant because you have a program that tells you what to do. How could you behave in a certain way or do something that is unknown to you? By definition, you can't. Meeting a new person and finding a new address are just known unknowns, with the corresponding programs in your mind. On the other hand, the mental territory of a murderer is a reality that I hope and assume is unknown to you. It is outside of your territory, the same way that you would not wear a loincloth to work or eat disgusting food. The programs in your mind keep you confined to your mental territory.

Then you ask, "Where do new inventions and ideas come from?" They come from your Essence via focused attention, intuition, or any transcendental state of mind. When you fully engage in creative activities (job, hobby, etc.), you connect to your Essence. To do that, you need to transcend the personality, your programs. More on this later. For now, understand that in your routine activities, you remain confined to the programs that tell you how to move across them.

2. The second principle, which proactively enforces this confinement:

    Anything that is outside your mental territory is, by default, considered dangerous to your unconscious.

    Let me explain this with an example. Let's say you that are walking in a forest, and you see an animal that you have never seen before in your life. Because you don't know whether the animal is dangerous or not, what do you do? Do you approach it, or do you run? You have not seen this animal before, and so your unconscious does not have anything in its database (i.e., a program) that will tell it how to react. This event is outside your internal map of reality. Your unconscious is in charge of your survival, and it will choose survival first. If you were to choose to approach the animal, it may eat you. It will not take the risk, which means it will tell you to move away. Thus, it will not let you step into that reality of interacting with that animal.

    The unconscious will do anything in its power to
    keep you within your mental territory.

    This is how you make decisions in your life with very little free will. During the vast majority of your daily routine, you are simply executing programs.

Effect of Negative Programming on Free Will

We already saw how negative programs create limitations in your life, whereas positive ones become psychological resources that enable your full potential. This is what will determine the degree of free will that you have.

The more negative programs in your mind, the less free will you have.

The more you get angry, scared, irritated, or upset about anything that is happening in your environment, the more limited in life you are. Notice that it is irrelevant whether you think that you are right or not. If you are right but irritated, that emotion is the result of a negative program taking over. And because of that type of reaction, you will see very limited ways to resolve that situation (remember the effects of stress on the body, and in this particular case, your prefrontal cortex). What matters are your reactions to the circumstances that you are living. The very first time that you have a brand-new experience, your unconscious generates a program with the emotion that you felt with it. Otherwise, your emotions are simply the result of the activation of a program. Thus, the more negative programming you have, the more you will be buffeted by the circumstances in your environment. They will constantly trigger these negative programs. You will be a victim of your environment, automatically feeling bad about the events of your life. There's little free will here.

How can you not feel bad when someone insults you? Let's say that someone calls you stupid. If I ask you how you felt when that happened, you will tell me that it upset you. And we say that it is the normal to react that way. Yes, it might be normal nowadays, nevertheless I will tell you that that response is not natural at all. The reasons why you are getting upset are (1) you have a program in your unconscious that does believe that there is a possibility about you being stupid, and/or (2) you are scared that other people will believe that person, and thus that you will be rejected by them (social isolation is danger to your unconscious: how are you going to survive alone?). These are limiting programs that are implanted in your mind. If you did not have them, you would not feel their negative emotions. That insult would not touch you. You would fully believe in yourself, and you would also understand that, as humans, we make mistakes. That does not mean that you are stupid. And if you did make a mistake, you would take responsibility for it, correct it, learn from it, and then move on with the newly acquired wisdom.

Every time you feel a negative emotion, irrespective of the external circumstance that triggered it, I urge you to explore where it actually came from inside of you.

The program about being stupid very likely came from an early experience in your life, maybe with your parents or a teacher at school. The emotion generated and stored during that experience is the one you feel now. It is a regression in time. Every time you react negatively to something (unless it is a first-time experience), you are emotionally regressing to when the originating event occurred, most likely when you were a child. People who are all the time in reactive mode have what is called low emotional intelligence, which translates into low emotional freedom.

Emotions are the internal signposts that show us where we are in our evolutionary process.

Increasing Your Free Will

Why do I say that we do have free will? Based on all that I have talked about, we have the potential and capacity to exercise it. We need to develop it. How? There are four key factors.

1. Acquiring knowledge
2. Liberating yourself from negative programming
3. Acquiring positive programming
4. Introspection

1. **Acquiring knowledge:** Knowledge is power. Knowledge with discernment (permission to question) gives you freedom. Nowadays, there is plenty of literature that explains in layman terms the implications of the deepest scientific discoveries. Having knowledge gives you more power because it gives you an intellectual backing (faculty of reasoning) to your beliefs.

2. **Liberating yourself from negative programming:** Einstein expressed it very clearly: "We cannot solve our problems with the same thinking we used when we created them."[43] To solve our existing problems, we need to go to a higher level of consciousness. Your negative programs don't let you do that. They are the enforcers that the unconscious uses to keep you within the boundaries of your mental territory. To be able to substantially change your negative programming, you need to do a mind transformation process. The default transformation tool in humans has been suffering. It is what has forced us to question and transcend (after

---

[43] Albert Einstein Quotes, *Brainy Quote*, Brainy Quote, https://www.brainyquote. com/quotes/albert_einstein_121993. Accessed December 10, 2018.

all, we do have evolved throughout our human history). Today's available mind transformation processes allow us to do it in a much less painful way, faster and with a better understanding about us, others, and life in general. It's a smarter method to evolve.

3. **Acquiring positive programming:** The more positive programming you have, the more freedom you have, because you have the psychological resources that let you know that you can achieve anything that you want in life. These psychological resources give you the power and courage to go outside of your mental territory. Free of your own boundaries, now you can start playing with bigger realities of your own true choosing. There are many ways you can acquire positive programming, but here are two generic ones to get you started.

   a. Intellectual: Read, view, and study materials that expand your consciousness. Seek materials that make you feel well and inspired. Take in materials that bring you solutions to things that you are looking for in life, that give you answers to move ahead. Seek materials that give you new ideas, new points of view that make you revisit what you believe in your life. Take courses that expand your life.

   b. Practical: Join groups with activities that help others, or activities that make you feel good. Exercise is a classic example. Eat well. Have hobbies. Even better, take up hobbies that you can share with other people. Participate in community programs. Practice gratitude, and practice seeing the positive that you have in your life. I am not saying that it is easy to do. As with physical exercise, you can slowly train your mind to get more into that mode. It is also a good way to become more conscious in your life.

   Positive programming can also be generated as part of a mind transformation process. I will talk about this later in the book.

4. **Introspection:** In order to play with bigger realities, you need to go inside. The personality does not have the scope to go beyond. For the most part, the personality is the sum of your programs. Therefore it is already defined, bounded. Thus, introspection. Whether it is meditation or any other way, it is up to you. It is inside of you that the answers reside. The inside of you is your Essence, who you really are. It's inspiration and a portal to bigger realities.

The Ego

A note in this section about the ego that you hear about in spiritual and New Age literature.[44] In this literature, the ego refers to the negative, false self-image that we have in us ("I am not good enough," "I am stupid," etc.). By giving it a convenient name, it produces several counterproductive effects.

- It hides the true nature about what this phenomenon is.
- We make it into an abstract entity, which automatically gives it more power. It is an enemy within that you have to fight against.
- It gives it more permanence: it is something that resides in us.
- It makes you a victim of this abstraction.

I do not endorse the use of this concept. The negative self-image that we have about ourselves is the result of programs in our minds that were created under the very positive intention of the unconscious to adapt us to our environment. These programs were created by us, in our current social context. Consequently, if we have the power to create this situation, that means that:

1. We have the power to change it
2. We are responsible to change it

And that is what you need to know and understand about this concept. There's no such a thing as an ego residing in us; it is simply programs in our minds.

Assassins, Tyrants, Mass Murderers, Etc.

A Proud Brother in Pakistan

At the time I was writing this book, I read in the news[45] how a man in Pakistan killed his sister because she was "bringing dishonor to the family." For most of us in a Western society, this would be considered a murderous act of bigotry. It's an act that is difficult to understand. Now, would you say that this man

---

[44] This does not include the Freudian and other psychological definitions, which refer more to the sense of self, which parallels my concept of the conscious.

[45] Juliet Perry, et al., "Brother of Pakistan's Qandeel Baloch: I'm 'proud' of strangling my sister," July 19, 2016), https://www.cnn.com/2016/07/18/asia/pakistan-qandeel-baloch-brother-confession/index.html. Accessed December 10, 2018.

was mentally ill? After reading what I have given you so far, I hope you can understand that the answer is no. In the society where he was born, he grew up with those principles, which are nothing more than programs. In the article, he expresses how proud he was because of his action. Can you see how his actions are totally congruent with his internal map of reality? It has to be like that, for him to be able to execute that behavior, those programs with very heavily charged emotional batteries created by the family and the society in which he was raised.

Hitler

Let me press you even further. Was Hitler, when he woke up every morning, feeling any regrets about what he was doing? No. Did he know that killing is not "good"? Of course he knew. Still, in his internal map of reality, what he did was totally justifiable. In fact, from his point of view, he was doing humanity a favor because he was going to create a "superior race." Those were totally congruent actions within his mind. That is what gave him the power to start a world war. If he would have had any doubts about his beliefs, he could not have done it. He would not have been able to convince the others. Look at the power of his speeches. He even wrote a book in which he explained all that he believed in (faculty of reasoning). All the atrocities well justified in his mind.

Now, where did such an internal map or reality come from? I invite you to do research on his childhood years. What you will find is that Hitler grew up with a father that routinely beat his sons with a whip. Hitler, at the age of eleven, "refused to give his father the satisfaction of crying, even after 32 lashes."[46] The repression and abuse that Hitler went through in his childhood created ultra-charged emotional batteries. The repressed emotional energy that he accumulated had to express itself in one way or another. In his case, the net result of all the programs that made up his personality resulted in the behavior that produced such an aberration in human history. You could say that all that abuse made him mentally ill. Okay, if you want to define mental illness as the result of heavy emotionally charged programs, then so be it. What I am saying is that in general,[47] our

---

[46] Stephen A. Diamond, "How Mad Was Hitler?" *Psychology Today,* December 20, 2014, https://www.psychologytoday.com/us/blog/evil-deeds/201412/how-mad-was-hitler. Accessed December 10, 2018.

[47] There are abnormal behaviors due to severe structural deficiencies in the brain, but this is not what explains conflicts in daily routines for the vast majority of human beings.

behavior is the result of these programs. And the mechanisms that were acting in Hitler's mind are the same mechanisms that make you react with irritation in your own personal life.

I will keep asking you this all along this book: Can you promise me that you will never again get irritated or angry in your life? You simply can't promise that. And I will venture to say that you consider yourself to be "a good person" in general, right? Still, you don't have the power to stop being irritated ever again. That is how Hitler's programs controlled his points of view (the virtual reality in his mind) and his behavior. The more you understand how these programs work within you, and the more you observe yourself, the more you will understand our human history—all the Hitlers, the Stalins, the Idi Amins, the street robbers and murderers, down to each of us and the hurts that we have imposed on others, including our loved ones.

The Columbine Massacre

Sue Klebold, in her book *A Mother's Reckoning*,[48] shows her excruciating pain in trying to explain the behavior of her son. He was one of the two boys who perpetrated the Columbine High School massacre in 1999. She describes all her inner search, and the outer research she did, to try to make sense of her son's actions. Just from reading her book, as a practitioner in the area of the mind, I could see all the signals that were there long before her son acted on April 20, 1999. This is not blaming her for what happened with her son. She and her husband did the best they could, in the same way as all other parents do. They did not quite see the signals, and the vast majority of today's parents don't. A big point that I will bring again later is that parents educate their children without true knowledge about how the human mind works. They simply follow the rules and regulations that they in turn learned from their parents, and they hope for the best. A big part of the anger of other parents toward her is because, deep inside, they are scared given that they know that there is no guarantee that their children will not turn out like that. They hope that it will not happen to them. Still, what occurred in Columbine has happened not just there but in many other places, and it will keep repeating until all of us understand how the mind works. Sue's son, Dylan, and his companion did what they did not because of the programming in their minds. More than anything, it was because of the huge emotional batteries that those

---

[48] Sue Klebold, *A Mother's Reckoning: Living in the Aftermath of Tragedy*, New York: Crown/Archetype, 2016.

programs had. Simply the bullying they suffered at school was reason enough to convert anyone into an emotional ticking bomb. Add to that all the rules and regulations that don't make sense and that parents force-feed into their children, and top it off with a lack of understanding about how to manage and take emotional responsibility, and you have the formula for potential disaster. As Sue writes in her book,

> His journals are filled with his struggles with conscience. And yet, at the end of his life, something overwrote the lessons we had taught him. [49]

That something was the level of the emotional batteries that stored his anger and frustration, which increased until they overrode all the other programs of behavior taught by his parents. In the end, Sue Klebold talks about brain illness and brain disorders. The events in our lives generate the programs in our minds that shape our brains, not the other way around.[50] Of course, if someone had an accident or an illness that destroyed part of the brain, it would affect that person's behavior. This is not the case with these children. It is the unconscious that controls and shapes the body.

We Are Shaped by the Environment

Are you getting the point about how our minds are shaped by the environment? The brother in Pakistan would not have killed his sister if he would not have grown in such an environment. Hitler would not have done what he did if he would have been raised in a nurturing environment. Dylan would not have perpetrated that massacre if he could have had the opportunity to truly process his internal anger and frustration, which was exponentially amplified by the bullying at school.

So is it still going to be difficult for you to understand that a politician who steals, a robber who robs, and a murderer who kills are doing these things because of the programs in their minds? In their minds, there is a justification for what they do, even if they know it is not right. We all do this at our own scale. You quickly park illegally somewhere, you drive above the speed limit, you cheat on the promotion or the return policy of a company, and so on.

---

[49] Sue Klebold, *A Mother's Reckoning*.
[50] This is already backed by science. I will come back to this later when I talk about the effects of meditation on the brain.

You think about it, and you will justify it one way or another, knowing that it is wrong. You say, "It is just small things." That is simply perspective. The politician who steals one million dollars may be okay with that because it is nothing compared to what others are stealing; that is his frame of mind, his inner map of reality. I agree that stealing public funds is very different than going files miles per hour over the speed limit. That loss of perspective is due to negative programming born from the circumstances lived in their lives. That environment is not just the parents; it includes friends, teachers, and the neighborhoods and society in which they were immersed.

We live in a civilization of our own creation, in which the vast majority of individuals grow in unnurtured and unempowered environments.

An Outdated Justice System

With the results that are right in front of all of us, what an irony that we have created a society full of destructive environments in which individuals are born, and which then punishes them if they don't behave properly. And how does it do that? By incarceration. In many societies, we even condemn people to death. Essentially, it's the same method that we have been using for thousands of years. What our system does is to put people in jail for an amount of time so that they "learn their lesson." Afterward, we open the door with the great expectation that now they are going to behave. I hope you now realize the absurdity of this way of thinking and operating. It's ignorant in all respects to how the human mind works, and to the human condition. The individual saw no other way of doing things because that is what he learned from the environment in which he grew up. And now he is punished. How is jail time going to change the programs? How are the big emotional batteries— charged with anger, frustration, impotence—going to be discharged? At the very least, the emotions need to be processed if you want to see a real change in the behavior of the individual. Instead, what ends up happening is that the punishment creates yet another program with an even bigger emotional battery. This program restrains (or so we hope) all the other programs that made the individual do the crime. The end result is an individual with an even bigger internal struggle of programs. Think of the original inner conflicts, which big enough to make them do the crimes that they did. Even if, after jail time, this person is now able to behave, this will be a tormented person for the rest of his life. And that is how our system of justice works.

The results? I am transcribing here what you find in the United States National Institute of Justice,[51] in its Recidivism page.

> Bureau of Justice Statistics studies have found high rates of recidivism among released prisoners. One study tracked 404,638 prisoners in 30 states after their release from prison in 2005. The researchers found that:
>
> - Within three years of release, about two-thirds (67.8 percent) of released prisoners were rearrested.
> - Within five years of release, about three-quarters (76.6 percent) of released prisoners were rearrested.
> - Of those prisoners who were rearrested, more than half (56.7 percent) were arrested by the end of the first year.
> - Property offenders were the most likely to be rearrested, with 82.1 percent of released property offenders arrested for a new crime compared with 76.9 percent of drug offenders, 73.6 percent of public order offenders and 71.3 percent of violent offenders.

The statistics speak (or I should say scream) for themselves. The few who do not misbehave again will live conflicted and repressed lives, as I explained. And just an insignificant, few of them genuinely transform into more positive states of being.

An Emotionally Archaic Civilization

In his book *Pre-parenting: Nurturing Your Child from Conception*,[52] Thomas R. Verny talks about how so many neurobiologists have tried to find a genetic marker in violent criminals. I quote directly from his book (emphasis added by me).[53]

> The search for this marker in blood, spinal fluid, and DNA has been thorough, but fruitless. While some violent criminals

---

[51] "Recidivism." *National Institute of Justice,* National Institute of Justice, June 17, 2014, https://nij.gov/topics/corrections/recidivism/Pages/welcome.aspx. Accessed August 4, 2016.
[52] Thomas R. Verny and Pamela Weintraub, *Pre-parenting: Nurturing Your Child from Conception*, New York: Simon & Schuster, 2002.
[53] Ibid., 195.

do suffer some abnormalities, scientists have never been able to detect a consistent difference in the genes. *Instead, the only reliable marker for violence in adulthood has turned out to be early exposure to violence and neglect.* Abused children often become abusers, and young victims of violence are at risk of becoming violent offenders themselves. In aggregate, data from hundreds of studies now solidly document the *intergenerational* transmission of violence and abuse.

Programs are being passed from generation to generation. You now have a very clear understanding of the unconscious mechanisms in our minds behind that transmission. We may have advanced technologically speaking, but our civilization is emotionally archaic. This circle of society's low emotional intelligence is completed by the victims of the crimes that these people commit. When a person gets robbed, or her children are attacked, or a friend or relative is killed, these events create traumas in them, programs with highly charged emotional batteries. More than anything, and understandably so, the only thing that people will want is that the perpetrators rot in jail, to say the least. These unprocessed programs will become the new filters through which they will see life and make decisions. Anyone who has suffered any negative significant emotional event needs to reprocess it with a pertinent support person. Otherwise, these programs will be making their own decisions for them.

As an example, we know that one of the hardest experiences for parents is to lose a child to murder. Most likely the parents will be the first ones to line up behind a government candidate whose agenda is to incarcerate anyone who breaks the law with maximum penalty times. Here you can see so clearly how these programs rob us from true free will. Instead of coming together and working constructively to find real solutions to our social problems, we keep making decisions based on vengeance, fear, or any other unprocessed emotion. With the added social stigma of doing emotional work, they remain hurt and reactive to these events for the rest of their lives. Do we need to limit the freedom of people who are doing harm? Yes, of course. However, that should only be the very first step of a whole process of re-empowering these individuals so that they can believe in their own abilities and be able to thrive in life. Plus, we need to have social programs that give them opportunities of reinsertion into society after they have served jail terms. If you take a look at the personal history of the jail population, what type of stories do you think you will hear? These people, in the inner reality of their minds, saw no other way to come ahead in life. Otherwise, they would have acted differently. I hope that with the information that I am giving in this book, not only will you have more understanding and empathy for these individuals, but you'll also have more wisdom to determine what to do with them as part of the society in which we live.

If you think that that is "their problem" and "Why should I have to pay for these social programs?" just look around how we live. Look at our society: everything is built based on fear and distrust. All our infrastructure, buildings, homes, and cars, are built with all kinds of security locks and alarms. There are security mechanisms for electronic accounts and identity protection. You are constantly making sure that your car is locked, that you are not going to be robbed, and that your children are safe. Our societal environment has created all these programs in each of us, and they generate stress in every aspect of our lives. For those living in conditions of abundance, be grateful, but also be consciously involved in contributing to the well-being of those who are not. They will affect your life one way or another, sooner or later. It is in your self-interest that everybody lives and grows in a harmonious environment. Even from a selfish perspective, there will be fewer chances that you will be robbed.

To close this section, let's talk about the few people who come from very negative environments but become great examples in our history. First of all, notice that they are few. But mind programs explain this as well. They had positive programs strong enough to pull them out of negative environments. Some of those programs may have come from a figure or event in their lives that gave them the critical support that they needed to come ahead. Or they were already born with these extra inner resources, as I will explain later. (Yes, there is justice in this universe, as you will see.) Notice that these are exceptional cases. By no means are they an excuse to consider the state of our civilization as acceptable and do nothing about the social environment that we have created.

Terrorists and Terrorism

Nowadays, the headlines in the media are full of terrorist attacks everywhere. Indeed, we do need to defend ourselves from people who want to harm us. Still, to think that the solution is to go out there and kill them is unrealistic. Let's say that we have this fictional group of terrorists. For my illustration, let's say that a particular terrorist individual has a little brother around five years old. We kill the terrorist. What programs are going to be created in the mind of the little boy as a result of that event? He certainly does not have a comprehension of the historic and political facts surrounding the conflict that he is going through. His brother has been killed. He loved him. All that he can feel is anger and hatred for whoever did such a terrible thing. This is now a program in his mind that is going to be amplified more and more by his family and friends, who most likely sympathized with the guy we killed. Here, you have the next generation of youngsters being programmed to be terrorists as well. Violence will always leave a trace of hurt and hatred. It may be a short-term solution to an immediate threat, but it's never a sustainable solution in the long term. For peace to have a chance to manifest and last, we need to build bridges of communication so that we can exchange points of view (which, by the way, are programs), and so that there be a chance to be able to comprehend where the other party is coming from. That little boy will only hate us more if he never gets to hear another point of view other than the story that his family and his society are giving him. They all will become solid (unquestioned) programs through which he sees life and the way he sees us: the enemy who killed his brother, the enemy that needs to be eradicated. Communication is critical for mutual understanding and tolerance.

To achieve harmony in our lives, we need to learn to communicate and connect with all others.

This principle is equally applicable to the individual as well as any societal level.

These programs can be so powerful that, with enough emotional charge, they can lead to acts that go even beyond the basic directive of the unconscious (survival). I am referring in this case to suicide bombers. As I wrote earlier, these are not mentally ill people (unless you simply want to define that behavior as such). These are people with programs whose emotional batteries are hyper-charged. They are the "best" example that illustrates how the unconscious is just a machine. During the last world war, the Japanese kamikazes were another example. It was societal programming about honor for the emperor and serving the country. To the Japanese of that time, they were heroes, and the pilots went willingly. Today, many suicide bombers are children. They are the easiest to recruit because they are ideal candidates for mind programming. Adults who become suicide bombers are individuals who become radicalized because of the unnurtured environment in which they grew. They already carry deep anger and frustration. The "benefit" of belonging to this type of terrorist group is the relief to express the anger while belonging to a "supportive environment." It's an environment that they have not experienced before. That is how these radical groups can recruit people into their ranks. It's emotional conflict easily redirected by the rationalization that the recruiting movement instilled in them. In their minds, it's a new coherent inner map of reality, which gives them purpose and expression to their inner conflicts. Very often it's young people from rich, developed countries. Having money does not compensate for the emotional vacuum that people carry inside themselves.

I know that this message has political consequences. I hope that you can see beyond that. It has nothing to do with one or another political party or system. Isolationism is not sustainable. Violence is not either. A beautiful example is that of Daryl Davis, a blues musician who, through having conversations with members of the KKK clan, changed their minds to the point that many of them (around two hundred) abandoned that group.[54] His main point was not to try to convince them, but instead to establish a conversation. He advocated giving the opposing party a platform—that is, the opportunity to express their point of view no matter how radical it is. Then he'd start exchanging while listening. This gives them opportunity to discover that there is a different reality from that one in which they believed.

The real solution is, ultimately, creating a nurturing and supportive environment for every human being on this planet.

This is what will avoid programs with highly charged emotional batteries that make individuals become radicalized in their behavior. This must be a global endeavor. To think that what is happening in another country is "their problem" does not work. Sooner or later, it will affect us. This is true today more than ever, not only because of the sheer numbers of people on this planet but also because our technology, which has created an inevitable interconnectedness among all of us.

---

[54] Dwane Brown, "How One Man Convinced 200 Ku Klux Klan Members to Give Up Their Robes." *NPR*, August 20, 2017, https://www.npr.org/2017/08/20/544861933/how-one-man-convinced-200-ku-klux-klan-members-to-give-up-their-robes. Accessed December 10, 2018.

Drugs, Alcoholism, and Addictions

One of the best examples of mind programming at a mass scale is the different standards that we keep between alcohol and other mind-altering drugs. It is truly amazing and stunning to me how incongruently we can live in this respect—with devastating effects. Whether someone is addicted to alcohol or any other mind-affecting drug, the root cause is ultimately the same: a need to escape a terrifying and unbearable inner emotional existence. That, in the vast majority of the cases, resulted from the unnurturing environments in which the addict grew up. Indeed, there are some chemicals (drugs) that have more addictive properties than others. Ultimately though, whether an individual falls into an addiction depends on how fulfilled he is living life. With strong, positive inner resources, a person who tries a hallucinogenic drug will not fall into an addiction. This is simply because to her, life is already an exhilarating adventure as it is in her everyday state of mind. All the same arguments that I already used when talking about criminals and terrorists apply to any type of drug addict.

Addictions are a mental health problem, not a criminal one.

A beautiful example of dealing with this social issue as a health problem instead of a criminal one is the case of Portugal. In the 1990s, 1 per cent of the population in Portugal was hooked on heroin.[55] The problem was so widespread that in 2001 the government decided to take action by decriminalizing drugs. There was not much of an opposition because almost every family had someone addicted. The results since then have been clear.56

- A 75 percent drop of drug cases since the 1990s.
- Drug-induced death rates five times below that of the European Union.
- A 95 per cent drop in drug-related HIV infections.

What is clear to most experts in this case is that the key to the success of this process was not the decriminalization of drugs but rather the aspect

---

[55] Lauren Frayer, "In Portugal. Drug Use Is Treated as a Medical Issue, Not a Crime." *NPR,* April 18, 2017, https://www.npr.org/sections/parallels/2017/04/18/524380027/in-portugal-drug-use-is-treated-as-a-medical-issue-not-a-crime. Accessed December 10, 2018.

of treating it as a health issue.[56] Once you understand this, it becomes quite absurd to incarcerate someone with this addiction. It's as absurd as it would be to incarcerate someone for having diabetes. And contrary to the common fears that people have about the decriminalization of drugs, the CATO Institute, a think tank based in Washington DC, released a report on this case.[57] Here are some of its conclusions.

- Fears of "drug tourism" turned out to be completely unfounded.[58]
- The most substantial barrier to offering treatment to the addict population was the addict's fear of arrest.[59]
- By and large, usage rates for each category of drugs continue to be lower in the European Union than in non-EU states with far more criminalized approaches to drug usage.[60]
- A 2008 survey of drug usage among Americans found that the United States has the highest level of illegal cocaine and cannabis use in the world.[61]

Any addiction that a person has is the result of a coping mechanism to an issue in his life, due to the fact that he has no effective and viable ways of resolving it. It's the result of a combination of negative limiting programs in his mind, and the lack of positive ones that would become the psychological resources to pull him through this particular challenge, from overeating all the way to any type of drugs. As a mind practitioner, it is painful to me to observe how society deals with this inner personal suffering in our "advanced" twenty-first century. It's a psychological inferno for them.

---

[56] Lecia Bushak, "Portugal's Drug Experiment: Tackling Heroin Addiction by Decriminalizing Drugs and Focusing on Health," *Medical Daily*, http://www.medicaldaily.com/portugal-drug-experiment-heroin-decriminalizing-drugs-382598. Accessed December 11, 2018.

[57] Glenn Greenwald, "Drug Decriminalization in Portugal: Lessons for Creating Fair and Successful Drug Policies." *CATO Institute*, April 2, 2009, https://object.cato.org/sites/cato.org/files/pubs/pdf/greenwald_whitepaper.pdf.

[58] Ibid., 6.

[59] Ibid., 8.

[60] Ibid., 24.

[61] Ibid., 25.

Resolutions, Positive Thinking

We know how so many people start the new year with great resolutions about healthier eating and exercising. Ironically, this "new year effect" is so well-known that before starting, many already say, "Yes, I know it probably won't last, but at least I will do it for some time." What is happening with all these resolutions? A resolution is a decision that you consciously make. This is the key here. This decision will not come to fruition if it is not in agreement with the programs that you have in your unconscious, because the unconscious is so much more powerful than the conscious. Then how do you want to approach this situation?

1. Set the goals that you want to achieve.
2. Start doing your activity.
3. If you see that you are not getting there, check what the possible stumbling blocks might be. They could be external (e.g., conflicts in your schedules) or internal (e.g., maybe you need to start at a slower pace or do it at a certain time of the day, when you are more energized for that particular activity).
4. If it still does not seem to be working well, then it is time to look deeper inside. There is a program in your unconscious that is sabotaging your goal. If this goal is important, then you need to do a mind transformation process. There is nothing wrong with you if you are facing this situation. It is part of the human experience, and we all have limiting programs.

Instead of sinking into lower self-esteem (negative programs created out of this experience), as often occurs, now you understand what is happening. It is up to you to decide what to do. There is nothing more to it. This applies to any decision that you make in your life. By understanding how your mind works, now you have a chance of becoming the master of your own life. You are no longer a victim of who you turned out to be.

Case 14: Weight Loss

Roberto Goltzman has his practice in Spain. He is a practitioner of emotional decoding[62] using NLP, Gestalt psychotherapy, hypnosis, and

---

[62] Which studies the relationship of emotions and illnesses.

psychodrama.[63] In one of his videos, "Sobrepeso y Obesidad" ("Overweight and Obesity"),[64] he illustrates this case, which is a great example about how the unconscious works. It is about a woman who comes to him because she feels that she is twenty kilos (about forty-four pounds) overweight. Nothing has worked for her to reduce that extra weight. In the sessions with Goltzman, the following story comes to light. Twenty years earlier, her father died, diagnosed with bone cancer. At the time of the diagnosis, the doctors told her that he would be gone very quickly. Given the circumstances, she decided to take him to her home and take care of him during those last moments of his life. As it turned out, he stayed alive for two more years. Her dad was a man who was physically strong, with a big body complexion. During these two years, he lost more and more weight. At his death, he was basically "skin and bones," in her own words. She took care of him during all this time. She bathed him and fed him, and she could see how he was getting thinner and thinner, weaker and weaker. As a result of these impressions, the association (i.e., program) that her unconscious made was that "thin people die." Understand that she, the conscious, did not make that decision. She simply took care of her dad. She saw how the illness was "eating his body away." Day after day, under those painful circumstances, that experience created this association in her unconscious.

Once she understood and processed this program in her mind, she started losing the weight that for so many years she was not able to do. This is a great example about how the unconscious works. She never knew, before the sessions with Goltzman, that she had such a belief in her mind. This case is also a great example of the control that the unconscious has over the body. As much as she did all kinds of different diets and procedures, she would not lose weight because to her unconscious, to be thin was to risk dying. Her unconscious regulated her metabolism and assimilation of foods in such a way as to ensure that she would not become thin.

---

[63] Gestalt psychotherapy and psychodrama are more examples of mind transformation processes. His website is http://www.sanatusolo.com/quienessomos.html.

[64] Roberto Goltzman, "Obesidad y Sobrepeso emocional PARTE 1." YouTube, September 13, 2018, https://www.youtube.com/watch?v=msJsnAm4WtY. Accessed December 11, 2018. Case starts at around 31:10 and continues in part 2.
Roberto Goltzman, "Obesidad y Sobrepeso emocional parte 2." YouTube, September 13, 2018, https://www.youtube.com/watch?v=uHutn1Rogrc&t=11s. Accessed December 11, 2018.

This example also explains why affirmations and positive thinking sometimes work, but some others don't. They are also decisions that the conscious makes. If the affirmation that the conscious is making goes against a program in the unconscious with a relatively small emotional charge, then it has a chance of overriding it (this is one way of reprogramming your mind—and the reason for doing it, as I will talk about this later). Otherwise, the unconscious will prevail. Do your affirmations, and do your positive thinking. If you are struggling to remain in that positive frame of mind, then it is time to go deeper inside and, if necessary, do a mind transformation process. That is what we as human beings need to do. There's nothing wrong with you, and now you understand.

Part 2

The Components
of the Personality

Mechanisms to Components

In the previous section, I presented to you a very detailed description about the mechanisms of the personality and how these mechanisms operate during the first years of our life to give shape to who we are today. Also, I showed how these mechanisms work and affect our behavior. Programs in our unconscious give us our identity and direct our responses to the environment. Through your body, you interact with this physical world, which is what you decided to do.

Now, new questions arise: Did I really decide that? When? How come I don't remember? Do newborn babies have personality? If so, where does it come from? How can it be that siblings from the same parents can have such different personalities? How come so many children have some amazing talents right from the beginning? Indeed, all these questions point at aspects in us that demand extra explanations. In this part of the book, we will fill in all those gaps.

From what we see in the fields of the mind, they strongly suggest that we are not just what we became in this life. While doing sessions with my clients and working on their own issues, their unconscious takes us to events that go beyond our present reality. It is important that you understand that these phenomena do happen in sessions. These are not bizarre cases that occur once in a lifetime. It is true that most of the issues with clients remain within the context of the present life. Still, transpersonal issues, as I call them, arise as well. That is when the practitioner and the methodologies that she is using are open to these outcomes. What I mean by that is that for a traditional psychologist, for example, if the client were to start talking about a previous life, the practitioner will discard or reinterpret that information and redirect the client to the "appropriate" explanation because her frame of mind and her framework do not offer space to that information as is. This has everything to do with what I talked earlier regarding the internal map of reality that a person has and how that map filters the information according to its own rules. Whether scientist or psychologist, these mechanisms of the mind affect everyone. In this case, the education that the practitioner received shapes how to interpret this type of phenomena. What I can tell you is that these cases occur, irrespective of the education or personal beliefs of the individuals in session. It's not just with my clients but with practitioners anywhere, as I will illustrate. It is true that different interpretations can be made about them. I will present these aspects of the personality as they show up in the sessions. In other words, if the client tells me that she is in another life, that is how I am presenting it here in this book. My aim here is to give you the components of your personality. How you interpret these components does not change the fact that they are a part of who you are as a human being.

Components of Our Personality

The human psycho-physical system

Not all of our programs originate from our early life experiences. Additionally, not all the behaviors that are the expression of our personality are the result of the programs that I explained in the first section of this book. The components that I am going to talk about in this second section are the different sources from where our programs come from, as well as the other mechanisms that regulate our behavior. Who you are is the sum of all these components—what I call the human psycho-physical system.

We can group the different components of our personality in two categories.

1. Intrapersonal components
2. Transpersonal components

Intrapersonal components refer to the components of the personality that originate from physical interactions in this particular insertion into the physical world. Transpersonal components are those that come from events that are beyond this particular insertion into the physical world. Each of these two has its own subset of components.

1. **Intrapersonal components:**
    a. Biology
    b. Prenatal experiences
    c. Childhood experiences (up to around ten years of age)
    d. Adolescence experiences (up to around twenty-five years of age)
    e. Adult experiences
2. **Transpersonal components:**
    a. Unit of Consciousness interventions
    b. Previous physical insertions
    c. Transgenerational effect

Most of these components generate, in their own particular way, programs with the same structure and functionality that I described in the previous section. However, biology and the Unit of Consciousness interventions, as well as biological factors in the prenatal experiences, are exceptions, as I will explain.

Intrapersonal Components

As I mentioned before, these are the components pertaining to your present life, from conception until the moment when your nonphysical Essence leaves the physical body behind. This section of the book will bring to light the enormous role that parents play in the shaping of the personalities of their children. Sounds obvious, right? After reading this material, it will be clear how much bigger it actually is compared to what most parents, and all of us in general, realize. When I explain all these concepts in my seminars, I see expressions of surprise, shock, and even tears in my audiences.

This brings me to a very important point that I want to make here: all parents are doing everything the best way they can. It has always been like that, including abusive parents. That is the best they can do, because of the very negative, limiting programming that they have in their unconscious. The information that I am about to present to you is not given here to create guilt and regret if you are a parent, or resentments toward your parents or caretakers. The purpose is that you take it and, through understanding, start using it to create the better world we are all searching for. It is never late to do it, whether you had children or not, or if your children are already adults. This information is relevant to you, even if you never had children (myself included) because, without exception, we were all children. It is crucial that you understand how you became who you are so that you can have the knowledge and the power to reshape yourself and our society while taking your life in the direction that you truly want.

The Biology Component

Your body is the vehicle that allows you to interact with this universe. We all know that no two bodies are exactly the same. As a biological machine, every single component exerts influence in your behavior. You can easily say that every single chemical reaction in each one of your cells is affecting you. True. However, there is no need to go to that level of detail to understand how our biology affects our personality. We can explain, at the level of our behavior as individuals, how our biology influences us, in these different ways.

1. Individual body characteristics (basic genetics)
2. Biological behaviors and tendencies

Individual Body Characteristics (Basic Genetics)

Genes are molecules within our cells that dictate the characteristics of our body. You have genes that determine the color of your eyes, other ones that determine your height, and others for the type of hair that you have. In general, these characteristics are transmitted from your parents' genes. The physicality of your body will affect your personality in two different ways.

1. **Mechanical characteristics:** All bodies are mechanically different. There are tall bodies, shorter ones, bigger frames, thin frames, ones with a propensity to obesity, and ones with higher metabolic rates. The perfect analogy here is that of the different car makes and models that manufacturers offer. Different cars will handle road conditions in their own unique way, independently of the driver's abilities. A van cannot handle the road in the same way that a sports car can simply because of its physical design. The same applies to our bodies. These characteristics affect our behavior in very significant ways. A person with a very energetic body will have behaviors that are very different to that of someone with a frail body or a body with a slow metabolic rate, simply because of its physicality and independently of whether the person is extroverted or introverted. I define personality as the sum of our behaviors, and our body mechanics must be considered a component of our personality.

2. **Brain architecture:** These differences in physicality include the brain and all its associated structures. Every individual has a unique brain, and no two brains are wired in exactly the same way.[65] This uniqueness of our brains also dictates differences in behavior. Notice that from what I am explaining here, you can see that there is a part of our personality that depends on the architecture of the brain, and thus some of its attributes are fixed. This points to the well-known paradigm of nurture versus nature that psychologists and neurologists debate so much. Nurture refers to how much influence the parents exert on the personality of kids, compared to nature, meaning whether it is already determined by genetic mechanisms. Let's talk about this under the model of the human

---

[65] At the level of single neuron connections.

consciousness and the components that I am presenting to you in this book.

Fixed Personality Attributes

One of the most shocking statements for parents is the fact that in study after study in psychology, the results show that their effect on the personality of their children is basically zero. This goes against everything that they believe, or want to believe, about them being significant factors in the end result of their children's upbringing. From the information that I have given you so far, and that I will give you next, it will be very clear to you my premise about how central parents are to the development of the personality of their children. Yet those psychological studies are correct. Let's piece together these seemingly incompatible concepts.

In psychology, depending on which model you choose to look at, you will find ones that talk about personality types and others that talk about personality traits.[66] To avoid getting bogged down with all these different definitions, I will simply talk about personality attributes. Let's take a specific personality attribute that we all can relate to and that is easy to understand: being extroverted. We can intuit that an extroverted child will remain extroverted, regardless of whether the parents instilled better or worse manners in her. There are well-mannered extroverted children and ill-mannered extroverted children. Still, both are extroverted, and in general you will easily detect that quality of their personality in them.

The parents (under normal circumstances) do not change the fact that they are extroverted; that is intrinsic to these children. What parents do shape is how that extroversion interacts with the rest of the world. The main mechanism in that shaping is the programs that I talked about in the first section of the book. To the point here, though: yes, there are personality attributes that do remain relatively constant throughout the life of the person. This explains the part of the personality that many of these psychological tests check and that show no influence from the parents, and correctly so. The confusion comes from the definitions of what personality is. All there is to this is the fact that these tests are based on narrower definitions. Yes,

---

[66] Very loosely explained, personality type refers to a more rigid classification, whereas personality trait refers to a more continuous scale. As an example, in personality type, you may be either extrovert or introvert (one or the other), but from a trait perspective, you may be anywhere in between.

there is usefulness and purpose in a more basic classification scheme. Still, my intention with this book is to give the main factors that affect our behavior *as individuals*. As I mentioned above, just because two people are extroverted, that does not mean that they are going to behave and react in the same way to different circumstances in life. Talking only about a personality type is not enough to explain why we behave the way we do on an individual basis. That is why I am presenting all these components to you. Thus, both nature and nurture dictate our personality. The brain architecture, dictated by genetics, sets the fixed personality attributes.

Coming back to our physicality, I want to emphasize about how you see yourself (with your body) and the implications in your interactions with others. In this case, the physicality of your body works in conjunction with the programs that I explained in the first section of the book. As an example, as a kid, if you had a big frame, you quickly learned that other children would be afraid of you if you threatened them physically. This may have given you a sense of power (that hopefully your parents and teachers guided you to use in a constructive manner). As such, this experience became part of your personality and how you felt about yourself.

Additionally, your physicality will also determine how you see yourself because of the implications that it has within the culture in which you live. As an example of this, in the West in particular, the shape of our bodies is strongly judged (implicitly and/or explicitly) by a culture that follows ideal models that are essentially impossible to match. This affects both men and women, but it is even more acute for women. I have met women who, under these arbitrary standards, are beautiful and have beautiful bodies, but they are not at peace with their appearance. How we see ourselves physically exerts a powerful influence on our self-esteem and thus our behavior. Genetics (i.e., our body's characteristics) combined with culture are a powerful force that shapes our personalities.

Biological Behaviors and Tendencies

As with all other animals, we have biological programs that need to be in place for our body's functionality and for the survival of us as a species. We are born with them. These are physical structures that control not only our biology but also many aspects of our behavior, profoundly in some cases and more subtly in others. An example of a biological program that profoundly affects our interactions is the survival of the body as the prime directive of our unconscious. Our unconscious structures of behavior are built, biologically speaking, with predetermined responses (fight, flight, freeze, faint) to the perception of danger. The whole first section was dedicated to explaining the consequences of this biological design.

Biological programs affect our behavior directly, without the use of the structures associated with the programs that I explained in that previous section. Another example of a biological program is our sociability. Human beings are, biologically speaking, social animals; just look at our cities. Another one is our sexuality. It includes the biological functionality for reproduction, and it also affects how we behave in order to accomplish that functionality. Major components of our civilization, like the cosmetic and fashion industries, are directly influenced by the consequences of us being sexual creatures. Yet the final behavior of a biological program is affected by the programs that we saw in the first section of the book. The ability to socialize changes quite a bit from an individual to another, for example. Even sexuality is shaped by the environment. In some cultures, certain parts of our bodies are considered erotic and others are not. Some societies are more sexually open, and others are very closed to the point of serious, life-threatening consequences if their particular rules of conduct in this respect are broken.

Besides these biological programs, there are also behavioral tendencies that are the target of the marketing departments of the major corporations. For example, the design of stores and the presentation of products are directly influenced by the knowledge that we have about these intrinsic tendencies that are part of the biological design of our bodies.[67] They affect our behavior in very subtle ways, which makes us vulnerable to manipulation (as I will explain next).

Implications

Hard-wired versus Soft-wired Programs

The mechanics of our bodies, the particular architecture of our brain that results in certain fixed attributes of our personality (personality type/trait in psychology), and the biological programs and tendencies of our bodies are, relatively speaking, constant in our lives. This can be viewed as a fixed functionality. As an electrical engineer, I am going to borrow terminology

---

[67] See Charles Duhigg's book, *The Power of Habit: Why We Do What We Do and How to Change*, London: Random House Books, 2013.

that is widely used in computer lingo because I believe it is very useful in the understanding of these concepts. This functionality can be thought of as fixed programs of behavior. As such, in my model of the human mind, I will call these programs hard-wired. Hard-wired programs are tied to fixed structures of the brain that control not only our biology but also many aspects of our behavior—profoundly in some cases (sociability and sexuality, for example), and more subtly in others (tendencies that marketing departments take advantage to sell their products). This terminology can also be applied to the fixed attributes of our personality, by calling them the hard-wired personality attributes.

Hard-wired programs:

- Mechanicals
- Hard-wired personality attributes
- Biological programs and tendencies

Hard-wired programs generally[68] do not change. That is in contrast to the programs that I explained in the first section of the book, which can change throughout the life of the individual. Because of this, I call these programs soft-wired.

Soft-wired programs: the structures in our minds designed to adapt to the specific environment we are in.

As an example, both an extroverted person and an introverted one (hard-wired programs) can adapt to the environment in which they live (soft-wired programs), without having to change their particular personality attributes. By borrowing these names from the engineering fields, I hope that they will give you a clearer description of these intrinsic qualities in them.

Notice that soft-wired programs "rest" on top of the inherent, biological hard-wired programs of our bodies.

---

[68] As I will be pointing out throughout the book, when talking about the human experience, there will always be exceptions to generalizations, typically in the extreme cases of abuse, neglect, etc.

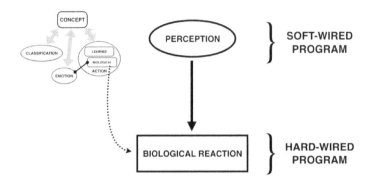

A lake may or may not be dangerous to someone, depending on the experiences that the individual has had with water. That is a soft-wired perception or program. If, for example, the concept of lake has been classified as dangerous by the unconscious of a person, the moment that the individual gets closer to it, the unconscious will automatically activate the biological stress response. This is the result of the hard-wired program for survival that will always respond this way to the perception of danger. Soft-wired programs are the result of interactions with the environment, which create associations that can be changed (for example, via a mind transformation process).

Hard-wired programs affect our behavior directly, without the use of the structures associated with soft-wired programs.

Mind-body Feedback Loop

The body provides a feedback that also dictates what the nonphysical structures in the unconscious are going to do. A very simple example of this is when you are feeling down but decide to go out for a run (assuming here that running is an activity you enjoy). Once you have done it, you now feel energized and in a good mood. Feeling down may have originated from challenging events that you had during the day that triggered negative programs. Through exercise, the chemistry and energies of the body change, triggering positive programs while putting back the negative ones into standby mode. (Notice that there was no transformation, just activation and deactivation of programs.) This is a powerful reason to maintain a healthy lifestyle: adequate sleep, the best natural foods at your disposal, exercise, rest, and a balance between work and leisure.

I do want to emphasize that these practices are not a replacement to the transformation of negative, limiting programs that we all have. As I already explained earlier, negative programs generate stress, which has direct implications on the health of the body. You can have the healthiest lifestyle, and yet if you have limiting programs that are impacting your behaviors and attitudes in life, they will affect your physical health. This is something that we hear about people who do their best to keep such a lifestyle and then, to their dismay, find out that they have a cancer or any other severe illness. That creates a double punch because not only they are confronted with the tragic news about their health, but also as a result of this shocking experience, their own unconscious will end up generating programs like "life is so unfair," "life is so unpredictable," and "Why me? There must be something wrong with me." It can have a direct impact on their self-esteem and outlook at life. This is yet another reason that I went through such a great extent to explain to you the power of the unconscious.

Detrimental Behaviors as a Result of Biological Inhibition

Soft-wired programs can be so powerful that they can radically affect the expression of the hard-wired programs of our bodies. What is crucial to know, when considering and questioning our society's rules of behavior, is that:

Societal programs that inhibit the expression of biological programs create, as an end result, detrimental behaviors.

A clear case is sexual repression, starting with milder consequences (like individual obsessions) and ending with extremely damaging ones (like that of sexual predators). This is a problem that affects not only our population in general but also the whole of public institutions. In the United States, according to the US Department of Justice, an estimated 80,600 inmates each year experience sexual violence while in prison or jail.[69] In jail, we traumatize even more those who already come from abusive environments. The point here is the urgency that we need to give to transforming and healing our society. On the opposite side of the institutional spectrum, a well-known public case is sex offenders within the Catholic Church because of the forced celibacy that the institution imposes on its members

---

[69] Allen Beck, "Sexual Victimization in Prisons and Jails Reported by Inmates, 2011–2012." May 2013, US Department of Justice, Office of Justice Programs, Bureau of Justice Statistics, page 8, https://www.bjs.gov/content/pub/pdf/svpjri1112.pdf. Accessed December 11, 2018.

(added to the personal problems that they bring from their personal lives). For 2016, the US Department of Justice reported 298,410 cases of rape or sexual assault.[70] This statistic results in an average of one assault every 105 seconds.[71] In other words, less than every two minutes, another person had been sexually assaulted in the United States for that year. Almost everywhere in the world, for most of the parents it is okay for their children to watch violent movies as long as the movie does not contain sexual material. The mind programming that this combination creates in the children is a negative double punch: it normalizes violence in their minds while making sex a taboo. Instead of making sexuality the natural human aspect that it is, they convert it into an abstract moralistic issue. We want children and adolescents to be at peace with this energy and be taught about how to take responsibility for it, so that they can enjoy it in a safe manner and without the guilt that society imposes on them.

Let's talk about our intrinsic sociability. We are a social species by design. Individuals who are not comfortable around people have limiting programs that need to be addressed. It is perfectly fine to have preferences, like loving the outdoors rather than sightseeing a big city. That is different than avoiding activities and opportunities that otherwise would be interesting to the person because they involve dealing with other people. This leads to unbalanced lives, and when they go to the extreme, they have the potential to generate dangerous antisocial behaviors (as we have read so many times about the disgruntled person who ends up causing physical harm to others). The limiting programs that the person has suppresses the biological urge that one has to socialize. This creates an inner frustration and resentment that needs to be processed in order to discharge and transform that emotional energy into a positive and constructive new force for behavior.

Manipulation through Biological Tendencies

The more limiting programs that we have, the easier it will be for external circumstances to manipulate us into the automatic tendencies of our bodies' biology.

---

[70] Rachel Morgan, et. al., "Criminal Victimization, 2016: Revised." US Department of Justice, Office of Justice Programs, Bureau of Justice Statistics, page 2, Table 1, https://www.bjs.gov/content/pub/pdf/cv16re.pdf. Accessed December 11, 2018.
[71] Dividing the total number of seconds per year (31,536,000) by 298,410 assaults results in 105.68 seconds/assault.

Marketing makes extensive use of this to entice us into buying particular products. We all know that sex sells. Just look at the advertisements everywhere full of "attractive" people, whether men or women. In Las Vegas, you find casinos where women, with costumes revealing much of their bodies, dance on top of some of their gambling tables. The casinos pay extra for the dancers because it pays off. It is easy to understand that the more repressed the sexual energy of an individual, the easier it will be to get him to play at one of those tables. (This applies equally to the other extreme, that of sexual addicts.) The more balanced the sexual energy of an individual, the less influence the dancers will have on him (or her, depending on the sexual orientation).

In the case of our inherent sociability, as an example, let's say we have a person who goes to the gym because his friends are there too. In principle, this is wonderful; this is making use of this biological tendency (the need to belong to a group) to give an extra motivation to accomplish his personal goals (in this case, maintain a healthy body). There is a problem, though. If this person is not be able to maintain these goals because he does this activity only when his friends are present, this points at a limiting program in himself. He depends on external circumstances. There is an inner emotional vacuum that takes advantage of this human tendency. In this case, he is not making the decision to go to the gym. It is his limiting programs that ask for the presence of others. Exercise is simply the means to accomplish this, but in itself it's irrelevant. In most of these cases, this is unconscious, and the problem aggravates if his friends decide not to go to the gym anymore. Now, he doesn't feel motivated to go there, and his self-esteem will hurt because he will not reach this goal that the conscious part of his personality set for himself. His conscious and unconscious are not congruent. It is part of our human experience, and there is nothing wrong with him; he simply needs to process the limiting program(s). He then will be able to do his physical exercise at the same time that he maintains a healthy social lifestyle. These are examples of reduced free will due to limiting programming.

Marketing departments of the different companies have a deep knowledge about our biological tendencies. Their advertisements and sales offers make use of them. As I mentioned already, the layouts of many stores are designed to take into consideration our intrinsic behaviors. It can be debated whether or not the use that they make of some of their techniques is ethical. However, from the perspective of you as an individual living your life, the more liberated you are from negative programming, the freer you are (even from your biological tendencies) to make decisions that are congruent with what you truly want for yourself. You will have an inner emotional peace that will give you the solidity and freedom to be able to say no, no matter how enticing the offer may be, if you know that it is not in your best interest. This applies to buying decisions as well as all others that you are making in your life.

Within companies, managers nowadays are generally encouraged to understand the psychology (including biological behavioral tendencies) of their staff. Because work issues are so directly connected to survival, the easiest trigger for both biological hard-wired and negative soft-wired programs is when people perceive the slightest threat to their jobs. The more empowered the employees are, the less reactive they will be to the different business conditions that any company must traverse. Also, the more self-initiative and creativity they will be willing to risk taking within their jobs—a direct, positive consequence on the productivity and success of any business. Everybody benefits when everybody is empowered.

Summary

As you will see, as we progress through the explanations of the different components of the personality, there will be more and more concepts coming into the picture that I am building here. In order to keep this progression as clear as possible, I will add a graphical summary in key places of the book. Here is what we have so far, with respect to the biology component of the personality.

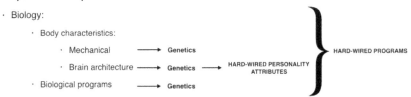

As expected, this component affects the personality through hard-wired programs. Soft-wired programs come into the picture next.

The Prenatal Experiences Component

I explained how the unconscious stores all that happens in your life. I illustrated this at the beginning of the book with a natal regression with one of my clients. Anyone can do a natal regression, as we all did in the academy where I got my certification. This is a regular course at the academy, repeated several times every year. None of us were specially gifted in this respect. (Ironically, I can tell you that I was the only one who could not do it in class because of other blockages—that is, programs in my unconscious—that I had to process. I needed some extra sessions with one of my teachers before I was able to do it.) This component is yet another example of the wisdom that nature applied to our design. The unconscious of the embryo in utero is already learning about the environment in which she will be born and is creating the corresponding programs to maximize her survival. It is another head-start mechanism for the new individual.

Case 15: Too Old to Be Pregnant

Here's a case from Juan José López Martinez, the Spanish medical doctor and hypnotherapist whom I mentioned earlier. This case is from his book *La Respuesta Está en el Alma*.[72] It is about a man who suffers from agoraphobia, or fear of open spaces. Since he was a little child, he always needed someone to accompany him whenever he went outside from his home—even now that he is married and with two children (he does not have to work because he had a big inheritance from his parents). This is obviously a big handicap in his life, and so he goes to López Martinez.

Once in the session, he regresses to when he was in his mother's womb. When his mother finds out that she is pregnant, she feels embarrassed because she is "too old to be pregnant." She is nervous about what people are going to think about her. The man reports how he, inside his mom at that moment, feels nervous and a huge pressure in the area of the stomach (which physically is just starting to form after four weeks). The situation gets even worse when his mom tells his dad about the pregnancy. He is shocked and tells her, "How can you do something like that, getting pregnant at your age?" Her mom feels even more embarrassment and guilt. The man, as the embryo in the womb, feels guilt and rejection. On top of that, his aunt tells her mom that she should abort. He feels anger. His mom resists all the pressure from the relatives and insists that she will keep the baby. Nevertheless, she is afraid of going out on the streets and being seen. Every time she goes out, she has the feeling that

---

[72] Juan José López Martinez, *La Respuesta Está en el Alma: Terapia de Vidas Pasadas*, Barcelona: Ediciones Indigo, 2006, 123–126. Translated to English, *The Answer Is in the Soul*.

people are looking at her and judging her. She wants to be back at home as soon as possible. The man, in trance as the baby inside his mom, can recall how she has tachycardia and how her hands are sweaty every time she goes out of the house. Her anguish is so big that many times she vomits because of the apprehension she feels before going out into the streets.

Later in the session, Lopez Martinez also asks him about the moment when he was being born. I transcribe here exactly how he described it.

> I don't want to go out, it's a hostile world. They are pushing from above so that I come out. I wrap myself with the cord around my neck and I feel pressure in my head and the neck. I don't want to be born, I am scared and embarrassed to come out.

After becoming conscious of all these circumstances and processing all this information in the session, he can now release these programs in his unconscious. For the first time in his life, he walks out on his own from Lopez Martinez's office without the need to have someone at his side. From then on, he can lead a normal life in this respect.

There are several important things to notice about this example.

1. Doesn't it become obvious how our social conditionings create so much emotional damage? Embarrassing to be pregnant at a certain age. The reaction of her husband and relatives. Ponder the absurdity of the mental structures behind that thinking, the damage that we inflict upon ourselves over and over again. These are arbitrary limiting programs that we implant on ourselves generation after generation, even before the next generation is out of the mother's womb. It's time to start questioning more about the basis on which we have built our civilization. Our suffering is self-imposed—it is not intrinsic to this reality.

2. You have another clear example about the unconscious knowing about everything that is happening in its surroundings. Look at the luxury of details in his narrative. He can recall exactly how his mother felt, including her physical symptoms (tachycardia, sweaty palms). It is as if an adult person was observing the scene.

3. Notice how this detailed narrative applies to when the mother just found out that she was pregnant. That means the embryo was around four to six weeks old. At that time, the embryo would have been less than half an

inch big (measure it with your fingers, so that you get an idea of what I am talking about here). There is no significant development in the brain that you could point to, to explain how this embryo could have captured this information. There is no support, at the physical layer, to explain this. Yes, the chemicals (amniotic liquid) that are shared with his mother do convey information. It is easy to understand that these molecules provide chemical information, like being in stress or not. Intuitively speaking, though, it seems difficult to explain how these molecules would encode all the details (conversations, events, etc.) of the circumstances that this person describes about his time in the pregnancy stage. This is why I suggest that there is a nonphysical layer that is the basis for this information transfer. This is yet another phenomenon that points at my premise about us not being just physical entities.

4. This embryo not only captured what was happening with the mother. It also knew what was happening with the father. Here, you cannot use the argument that there is some sort of communication via the chemicals that are exchanged between the mother and the new being inside of her. It would not explain how, at this stage of development, this clump of cells can detect the emotional state of the father. I want to emphasize that these are not weird, isolated cases. This is a relatively common occurrence in the world of hypnotherapy, and more specifically in natal regressions, that indicates the embryo knows about what is happening not just with the mother but also with the father and others (like the aunt in this particular instance). Current science has no way to explain this transmission of information under these circumstances. This is another example of phenomena that suggest that the unconscious operates beyond the known physical realm.

5. Observe what he, as a baby, was feeling at the moment of his birth. The decision that he took to wrap himself with the umbilical cord, to avoid as much as possible coming out to a world that he already knew was hostile. You can see very clearly that his unconscious already had programs, like any other child or adult. These programs were created by the events while in utero and were the basis for the perception of a hostile world, to be avoided at all cost. It's exactly the same process for this baby in the womb as that in children up to around ten years of age, as I described in the first part of this book. The response of these programs in this case was to flee (one of the four automatic unconscious reactions to danger), which manifested with the wrapping of the umbilical cord (trying to

avoid coming out; escape). This was a reaction, not a conscious decision. You know by know that there is no conscious at birth; this is simply the language that we adults use to describe events.

6. The programs created while in utero affected his future behavior exactly in the same way that any program during his childhood would have done, in this case with very dramatic consequences. This was the result of highly charged emotional batteries that controlled him in an extreme manner. There is no difference between the programs created before being born and those created afterward. The functioning of the unconscious, in this respect, is remarkably simple and consistent.

This case is a great example of two of the three key stages that happen up to the point when the baby starts her life as a separate entity from her mother.

1. Conception
2. Life in utero
3. Birth

Before we get into these topics here, just a note of perspective about this material. Because of the nature of these themes, I will be talking a lot about the role that parents play in shaping the personality of their children. It is important that you understand that even if you are not a parent, this section will give you a deeper understanding of yourself because you were the child of your parents; it applies equally to your primary caretakers if you were raised separated from your biological parents. Reflect on the circumstances in which you grew up, the situation at home, and your parents. Reading this material will help you, as a guidance system, to scan your early experiences in life and how they affected you then and today. Of course, if you are a parent right now, this material will apply to you two ways: you as an individual shaped by your own previous personal experiences, and you as the parent who, with this information, has the opportunity to raise your children with a new understanding and awareness. Whatever the personal situation, this material applies equally and centrally to you.

Conception

Within the context of the intrapersonal factors, nature starts the programming of the unconscious of the new human being right at its conception; with the transpersonal factors, it starts even earlier, as we will see. The mental and emotional state of the parents, at the moment of conception, will translate into programs that have the potential to influence how the new individual will see and act in life. Parents who did not want a child will create very negative programs right at the moment when the sperm fecundates the ovum. On the other hand, parents who truly wanted that child will induce healthy positive psychological resources right from the start of the life of this new creature. In the case of negative programs, how much they will affect the person in the future depends on the psychological resources (i.e., positive programming) that the person brings and receives while growing up. Remember, the beautiful aspect of all this information is that the negative programs can be transformed into positive resources. Let me give you generic cases that come out of mind transformation sessions with my clients, as well as those of other practitioners, so that you get the idea about how this works.

1. The father who has a business and wants to have a child to inherit it so that it stays within the family. That intention will be imprinted in the unconscious of the baby as a program ("my father expects me to be …"). The problem with this is that parents are imposing their emotional needs on their children. What is behind that desire? Now, this new individual will have a conflict between that program in her unconscious and what she really came to do in this physical world (I will talk more about this in the transpersonal factors). If she follows the parents' directives, she will not be happy because she will not be following her own path. On the other hand, if she decides to follow her path, there will be a constant guilt associated with it. Unless she transforms this program, she will be condemned to live a conflicted life in this respect.

2. Families who have a large number of children, with the implicit expectation that the older ones will take care of the younger ones. This is programming. Children have been preassigned roles in their early lives that do not correspond to them. Nature, in the case of humans, never intended this. Children are supposed to have a childhood. They should grow and learn while playing.

    Parents who transfer their responsibilities to their children are robbing them of their childhood.

    One thing is to teach them to take responsibilities gradually and according to their age. Another is to make them act like an adult. These children do not develop emotionally well. Typically, as adults they become the very "responsible" individuals as seen from the outside: rigorous and tied to all kinds of (social, moral) rules of behavior. These are demanding, rigid individuals with difficulty coping with the dynamism that life's changes require. On the inside, they cannot relax and enjoy life because everything is seen as a responsibility.

3. Parents who have the child because this one will be the one who will take care of them when they are older. This intentionality may be a conscious desire, but it can also be totally unconscious on their part. It does not matter. That intention programs the new embryo at conception the same way. The child, as an adult, will give precedence to taking care of the parents over his own personal life. It may very well happen that he cannot even have his own relationship or family because doing that would be in contradiction with this program. For these individuals, it is difficult to find the right person in their lives. They were programmed to take care of their parents, and this program in the unconscious will control their behavior. Even if they have their own families, there will be an emphasis on the part of that person to act that way.

    It is important that you understand that it is perfectly natural that sons and daughters take care of the well-being of their aging parents. That is different from the imprinting that occurs in this case, which interferes with what should be their lives as independent adults. This imprinting creates conflict.

4. Parents who decide to have another child because one of their children died. This becomes a "substitution child." Even worse in the case where the parents give the same name of the deceased child to the newborn. This strengthens this program. This child's unconscious will carry programs like "I came here to fill a need. I am just a substitution" or "I am second to someone." It is a feeling she carries all the time, even though she cannot pinpoint it to anything specific). Her feeling is a heavy emotional burden because there is a lack of intrinsic value. There are many well-known cases—for example, Salvador Dali. Salvador Dali was born nine months and ten days after his older brother died. His brother's name was also Salvador and died at less than two years old. Salvador Dali talked about him and how he felt the emotional burden of feeling that he was "a copy of his dead brother." He grew seeing his mother go to the cemetery twice a week to mourn him. Other famous cases of substitution children include Vincent van Gogh, who had a stillborn brother with the same

name precisely one year before his own birth,[73] and Beethoven, who had an older brother also called Ludwig, born one year earlier and who lived only for six days.[74] You may say that maybe that was the force behind their creativity. It could be. That is not a justification to impose such an emotional burden on anyone. These individuals do suffer. Let's be creative, coming from a positive place. That is how it is supposed to be. Thus, an important note about these cases. It is perfectly fine to want to have a child. It is another thing to want another one as a substitution for the lost one. Parents who lose a child must make sure they do a complete mourning for their loss. They need to emotionally close that experience before deciding to have another child. This needs to be done independently of whether or not they want more children.

5. A woman who is married but who doesn't really love her husband (and vice versa). From the unconscious point of view, this implies that she doesn't want him to be the father of her children. Children born from this type of relationships are undesired children. This translates into very limiting programs like "I am not a desired person" and "I feel like I am a bother to everybody." A clarification note: don't confuse this "not wanting to have children with this male" with not loving her children. This woman can very well love her children and take good care of them. That does not take away the fact that she would have preferred to have them with someone else. That will be imprinted in the embryo right at conception.

6. Single parents by choice. Here, let me reinstate that because of the very nature of the material that this book covers, it often touches very sensitive areas of our lives. I write the following fully aware that this could trigger strong reactions in many of my readers. All that I write about in this book comes from what we practitioners see in sessions with clients. It is important that we become aware of our behaviors and what is behind them. I am talking here about the case of single parents, most of them women. More and more women, after trying unsuccessfully to have a stable relationship and feeling that their time is running out, decide to get pregnant and raise a child by themselves.

---

[73] "Young Vincent." *Van Gogh Museum (Amsterdam),* Van Gogh Museum (Amsterdam), https://www.vangoghmuseum.nl/en/vincent-van-gogh-life-and-work/van-goghs-life-1853-1890/young-vincent. Accessed December 12, 2018.

[74] Alexander W. Thayer, "The Life of Ludwig van Beethoven," New York, G. Schirmer Inc., 1921.

Here is the delicate part: if someone is unsuccessful in creating a steady relationship, it is because there are limiting programs in the unconscious that are sabotaging the person's behavior with potential partners. (This is coming from someone who did not have children because of the load of limiting programs that I have carried in my life.) I invite you to explore this, whether you are thinking of becoming a single mom or are already one. Additionally, there will be an imprinting at conception. It will depend on the unconscious reason of why you are doing it. For instance, behind the desire of having a child, there could be the desire to have some company in life because you feel lonely now, or you're afraid of a future by yourself. The first imprint in that baby will be that he was conceived to "save" the mother. That imprinted mission will collide with the real reason that the Unit of Consciousness chose as the objective for coming into this physical world. The child will grow unconsciously feeling that obligation. It will also very likely translate into a behavior of pleasing others or saving others. This is just an example of a possible scenario. Thus, at conception there will be an imprint of why the single mother decided to have the child, and from then on, the limiting programs that sabotaged her relationships will be transferred as well. Additionally, children growing with single parents will have more challenges dealing with the energy and dynamics of the missing gender (even if it is simply having to explain to their peers the fact that they live with a single parent). You cannot possibly avoid this transfer of limiting programs. If you already had a child, I encourage you to explore and transform them. By doing that, you will automatically transform the life of your child by example and by your new attitude. The quality of your life will improve, as well your chances of finding the partner that you wanted in the first place. I hope this book helps to shed some light that it is not just "bad luck" in life that you couldn't find a partner. Of course, this applies to single men too. Today, we have the knowledge and the tools to change this type of situation. If your relationships are not working, the first course of action is to explore and transform the sabotaging programs. Going further into this delicate topic, if there is still the urgency to have a child, then I invite you to consider adoption. This option is always a win-win situation for all parties involved. Already born in difficult circumstances, children in orphanages will always be better off in a loving home. These children have an immense need to find nurturing in this world. Additionally, adoption is also an alternative that helps to address the serious problem of overpopulation that we face today. I will talk about this shortly, and you will see how it connects to the topics in this book.

7. Parents who wanted a boy and end up having a girl, or vice versa. This has the potential of creating sexual identity problems ("I am of the wrong gender"). Also, there will be a feeling of disappointment on the part of the child with respect to the parent who wanted the child of the opposite gender. This will translate either into a permanent conflict with that parent or a continuous pleasing in an unconscious effort to try to gain that parent's approval, which for obvious reasons can never be satisfied with respect to this particular aspect.

8. A situation that I think everybody hears about at one point or another in their life: couples who are having troubles with their relationship and decide to have the child, as motivation to solve their problems. You can see here how good intentions, coupled with a lack of knowledge, actually do harm. Couples with relationship troubles have limiting programs that create that situation. This becomes a very similar case to that of single mothers. Anything outside of the couple will be a patch that can never solve the situation. If they cannot solve their troubles, they need to go to a counselor in order to process their programs in their unconscious. Conceiving a child under these circumstances imprints the program of "I am here to save my parents." You already understand the consequences of this emotional burden.

This is just a sample of different scenarios of programming that occur right at fertilization. Understand that the intention of the parents for having a child, and the circumstances that they were living in before and around the conception time. have a direct impact in that new life. The conflicts that these programs create in the life of the person can be very strong, to the point that they may feel the need to go to a professional for help. All this is what comes out of these sessions. Everyone gets programmed at conception. It may affect you negatively or positively, or to a lesser or greater degree. The net effect of these programs will depend on the rest of the circumstances in which you grew up, as well as your own internal psychological resources.

Life in Utero

Everything that happens during the pregnancy creates programs in the fetus, in the same way that the environment affects a child while growing up. The attitude of the parents is being recorded with respect to everything. In López Martinez's previous case, you saw how the embryo took on the reaction of the mother when she discovered that she was pregnant. At that instant, a new program was imprinted. The program "the outside world is dangerous" was put in place. Parents, how did you react at the moment when you knew that you had a new child coming into your life? I am not speaking of the outside behavior but rather the true, inner, visceral reaction to this event. Your reaction created a program in that clump of cells that was to become your child (well, not in the clump of cells, but rather the unconscious behind those cells). I encourage you, the reader, to talk to your parents (if possible) about the circumstances of your conception, pregnancy, and birth. You may discover a lot about yourself simply by having this type of conversation with them. Do it *not* with an attitude of blame. Your parents did everything the best way they could, exactly the same way that you are doing with everything in your life today. Talk to them with the purpose of understanding and liberating yourself from programs from the past. Parents, you need to be honest with your children. Secrets need to be brought out to light and the conflict behind them resolved. As I will show soon, keeping secrets in the family is a mistake. The family unconscious picks them up and translates them into limiting patterns of behavior.

There are two aspects to consider about the influences that parents exert on the fetus while in the womb.

1. Architecture of the brain
2. Psychological

Architecture of the Brain

I include this aspect of life in utero here, instead of presenting it under the biology component, because this is a physical factor that affects the personality of the individual and that results from the parents' perception (how they see life), rather than just biological factors and nothing else.

If you go to the Internet and do a search with the words "prenatal stress and brain development," you will find many articles related to this topic. Nowadays, it is well understood and well accepted that the psychological state of the mother has a direct effect on the physical development of the fetus's brain. Traditionally, these studies have been done by taking a number of women during pregnancy, determining their stress levels during this period, and then doing anatomical measurements in the brain of their kids at different stages of their development.[75] Researchers are careful to take in consideration the post-birth factors that could affect the overall development of these children. What these studies reveal is that kids whose mothers where in a stressed state while pregnant with them are not only at an increased risk of having behavioral and cognitive problems later on in their lives, but they also show differences in their brain development.[73,76] Notice that this is an effect on the brain architecture that comes from the environment, in addition to that of the genes that we saw in the biology component. As such, this is yet another factor that also has an effect in the fixed characteristics of the personality of the individual. As I mentioned earlier, I will complete this effect in the transpersonal components. What is relevant here is that the in utero environment that the mother provides to the fetus affects brain architecture and thus the personality of the future individual. Simply put, stressed mothers provide an in utero environment that leads to kids being more reactive to the circumstances in their lives. This is congruent with nature increasing the chances of survival of the new individuals by adapting as early as possible to where they are going to be. A stressed mother is indicating to the fetus that her perception is that it will be born in a dangerous environment where reactivity (with its companion, constant high alertness) is key to survival.

For the sake of completeness, and to add weight to the implications that this entails, let me add the following. As careful and complete as the scientists can be in doing the analysis of these studies, there is always room for speculation about how much the results could have been influenced by the environment after the baby was born. From this, and thanks to advances

---

[75] See, for example:

C. Buss, E. P. Davis, L. T. Muftuler, K. Head, and C. A. Sandman, "High Pregnancy Anxiety during Mid-gestation Is Associated with Decreased Gray Matter Density in 6–9-year-old Children," *Psychoneuroendocrinology* 35, no. 1 (2010): 141–153.

M. Mennes, B. Van den Bergh, L. Lagae, and P. Stiers, "Developmental Brain Alterations in 17-year-old Boys Are Related to Antenatal Maternal Anxiety," *Clinical Neurophysiology* 120, no. 6 (2009): 1116–1122.

[76] Vivette Glover, "The Effects of Prenatal Stress on Child Behavioural and Cognitive Outcomes Start at the Beginning." *Encyclopedia on Early Childhood Development*, Institute of Reproductive and Developmental Biology, Imperial College London, January 2011, http://www.child-encyclopedia.com/stress-and-pregnancy-prenatal-and-perinatal/according-experts/effects-prenatal-stress-child. Accessed December 13, 2018.

in technology and the ingenuity of the researchers, today there are already studies that show, while the baby is still in the womb, how stress in pregnant women changes the developing brain of the fetus.[77] The results using these new methodologies continue to confirm what previous scientific studies indicated in this respect. Everything points at the importance of taking a deep look at our current approach (if there is any) to bringing a new life into this physical world. You must understand that even though the brain has the capacity to alter its neural connections (neuroplasticity), these hard-wired structures are, as their name implies, more difficult to change compared to the structures that hold the programs I talked about in the first part of the book.

Psychological

These are the programs that the unconscious creates as part of the adaptation to the environment, the soft-wired programs. Lopez Martinez's case at the beginning of this section is a clear example. To what extent? Consider this next case.

Case 16: Blind Baby

Christian Fleche is a registered nurse from France, psychobiotherapist, master neurolinguistic programming practitioner, and Ericksonian hypnotherapist. He created Biodecoding in 1993, a therapeutic approach that relates emotions and illnesses. (As I have already hinted earlier in this book, I firmly believe in the emotion-illness relationship.) Here is a case that he describes in his book *El Cuerpo como Herramienta de Curación*.[78] A baby boy was born blind. After a few months of consultation with doctors, the parents are starting to consider doing surgery on him. As a last resort, they come to Fleche. What comes out of the sessions is that his mother had to hide her pregnancy because she was so ashamed of it (Fleche, in his book, does not explain what the story was behind that feeling). What she lived

---

[77] Lisa Munoz, "Prenatal Stress Changes Brain Connectivity In-Utero: New Findings from Developmental Cognitive Neuroscience," *Cognitive Neuroscience Society*, March 26, 2018, https://www.cogneurosociety.org/prenatal-stress-changes-brain-connectivity-in-utero-new-findings-from-developmental-cognitive-neuroscience. Accessed December 13, 2018.

[78] Christian Fleche, *El Cuerpo como Herramienta de Curación, Descodificación Psicobiológica de las Enfermedades*, 4th ed., Barcelona: Ediciones Obelisco, 2013, 118. Translated as *The Body as a Tool for Healing, Psychobiological Decoding of Illnesses*

emotionally was that extreme urgency to "not see"; she did not want others to see her pregnancy. Emotionally, to her unconscious, "to see" equaled danger. That program was imprinted in the baby. And the unconscious, who is in charge of the biology of the body, translated this to negating that biological function. The child was born blind. During the therapy, the mother became conscious of her conflict. And once she understood and processed it, she explained everything to her little child, who recovered his sight without the need of surgery.

This is a very dramatic case in all respects. First, the somatization of the conflict resulted in the loss of vision in the newborn. It shows how big the conflict was for the mother. Her emotional message, that it is such a big danger to "be seen" (pregnant), made the unconscious of the little baby go to that extreme to protect the baby. Nature trusts the parents in their perception of life, and the unconscious executed as the machine that it is. Second, notice that when the sessions took place, the child was still a baby. The parents were considering surgery some months after he was born. Nevertheless, the mother was able to "explain to the baby" what had happened. You would think that this does not make sense, because the baby cannot understand what the mother is saying. The baby may not understand the verbal language, yet it does understand the emotional language—the language of the unconscious. That is, in fact, how these programs are being generated from conception and throughout the preverbal years. From all the examples that I have given you already, you can see that our unconscious minds communicate among themselves (in a way that science cannot yet explain) when we interact with each other. All mothers have an intuition about this. You see them talking to their babies, and they know that the baby is getting their message. This applies to fathers too.

Let me share with you this personal anecdote, so that you understand that this is happening all the time between parents and their young children. My wife and I were visiting a couple at the hospital because she had just given birth to a baby girl the day before. As expected, the conversation revolved around babies and children. While having this conversation, the baby was sound asleep right next to her mom's bed. At one point, the mom mentions that she would like to pierce the baby's ears (to wear earrings) as soon as possible, so that she can avoid the potential hassle of dealing with a rebelling daughter later. As soon as the conversation went on that topic, the baby started to cry. The new parents reacted with the traditional, "Oh, oh, time for her next meal." Because of this interruption, the conversation then went on to other themes. Without the parents doing anything, as soon as the conversation changed, the baby went back to sleep. Now, I am the first one to tell you that there is no way for me to prove to you that the baby cried because she understood what the conversation was about. From my experience as a practitioner, I have no doubt in my mind that that was the case. I see this type of event all the time without people realizing what is going on. Her parents had no clue of what had just happened. Nevertheless, the baby's unconscious knew very well what the conversation was about. In Fleche's case, the unconscious of the baby understood the new emotional language of the mother. And she healed.

This brings me to the third point to notice: how the unconscious controls the body. In the same way that the baby understood the conflict while in the womb, the baby also understood the new vision of reality that the mother had and changed the biological function to reflect it. That's the power of the unconscious, and the power of the parents in shaping the personalities of their children.

Here is another one, from one of my clients.

Case 17: In Charge of Her Mother

I have been working with this client on different issues. She is an attractive, successful businesswoman—what one would call in our Western society a successful person. Still, her relationships have not worked out. Out of all the siblings that she has, she is the one in charge of her mother. She always took it upon her to take care of her mom. That was the natural dynamic that run in her family. We start exploring this pattern in our session.

She regresses to this particular event, when she was in her mother's womb. Her mother at that time was having problems with her marriage. On one occasion, she sat in a cafe in complete anguish because of the situation with her husband. My client, as a baby in her womb, felt the anguish of her mom. The impact was so strong that at that point, she took on the responsibility to take care of her.

Haven't you heard of stories where children take it on themselves to take care of the parents in dire circumstances? It's exactly the same here. My client was even able to recall the exact place in her town where this happened. That became the program that ruled her life. As an adult, her home was next to hers. They shared the same cleaning service, and she was in charge of her mom's finances, bills, and appointments. Even though her siblings could have helped in all of this, it was "understood" among them that it was she who was in charge of all this. The weekends too, in great part, were spent looking after her mother.

Difficult to build a relationship under those circumstances, wouldn't you say? It is not just the physical aspect of this but the psychological state in which she lived her life. How can the unborn make such a decision? The unconscious works with impressions, emotions, and desires; there is no reasoning. The baby in the womb is feeling every single emotion that the mother feels. The suffering that the baby perceived from her mother created a desire that translated to the program, which later controlled the behavior in her life. These effects have the potential of affecting the life of the person in profound ways.

Birth

With all these examples and explanations so far, you come to understand that the events during the birth are not an accident. Look again at López Martinez's case in which the man experienced his birth. Because of his previous perceptions while in utero, he did not want to come out of it. He wrapped himself with the umbilical cord as a way to hold on staying inside because the message from his mom already created a perception of the world. From conception and all the way to birth, the baby has spent nine months of events seen through the perceptions of the mother (that is, the perceptions created by her own programs) via the chemicals of emotion, and also via the connection of their unconscious minds. There's also the unconscious connection with the father. Notice how all the sessions with different clients that I have shown here, under all types of different circumstances, confirm how the unconscious is capturing everything in our lives. The way that the unconscious is creating programs in the unborn is exactly the same way that it will do later on as a child.

At the moment of birth, depending on how the baby "sees" the outside world, she will be more or less willing to come out of the womb. The birth experience is the result of the mother's perception of life and the baby's interpretation of those perceptions. I say interpretation because, as we will see later, the baby also brings transpersonal factors already in her unconscious. These are simply more programs that are already acting as filters of the reality that she is living in utero.

The birth circumstances are the result of programs in the mother, the father, and those in the baby. Premature births (why the need to leave the womb early?), late births (why delaying coming out to this world?), breech babies (why not wanting to come out to this world? The need to emphasize the gender?)—the events during the birth itself leave in the baby an imprint in the form of new programs in the unconscious.

Case 18: I Don't Think He Is Worth Saving

David Chamberlain, in his book *The Mind of Your Newborn Baby*,[79] gives the case of a compulsive overachiever. As successful as he is in his life, he cannot get a sense of self-worth. At fifty-five, he finally finds resolution to his problem. In session, he regressed to his birth. It turned out that he was born prematurely, after seven and a half months; he weighed just three and a half pounds. After the birth, the doctor said to the nurse in charge, "Don't waste too much time on him. I don't think he is worth saving."

This case illustrates so many things that I have talked about earlier. Because our unconscious picks up what is going on in our surroundings, doctors need to be mindful about what they talk about while in the presence of their patients, even in the surgery room. With all the knowledge that we have about the mind, this needs to be considered nowadays as an ethical professional issue. It needs to be part of their curriculum, as an essential component in the treatment procedures that doctors have with their patients. Also, the case shows how the events of his birth created a program in this individual that profoundly affected how he lived his life. The reason for being an overachiever was simply that he was trying to prove to himself and to the world that "he is worth it." Because in his mind, he was not worth it, as programmed by the doctor's words. That is how this program affected his behavior. This case illustrates perfectly well what I talked about regarding free will. Look at how this program controlled this man's behavior for fifty-five years. Of course, during all those years, he was thinking that he was making his own choices. Not really. It was that program making the choices for him. Only after he processed that program did he acquire the freedom to choose what to do and to what extent to do anything. Perfectionists, take note. (I say this affectionately; I am a recovering one.)

---

[79] David Chamberlain, *The Mind of Your Newborn Baby*, Berkeley: North Atlantic Books, 1998, 94.

That is what negative programming does in our lives. You are thinking that you are the one choosing. Every human being in our civilization has them. We need to take responsibility for our behavior—not by blaming others or the system, but instead by taking action and transforming ourselves. Whatever feels right in your life, keep doing it. If something does not feel right, it is your unconscious giving you a signal that you have something that you need to take a look at. That is the purpose of our emotions. This is why categorizing them as good or bad is actually counterproductive. They are just signposts that feel negatively or positively to tell you where you are in your journey of personal evolution. Listen to them. Transform yourself upon them.

About C-section

I want to add some notes about cesarean procedures when it is done just as a convenient routine procedure. If it is done as a necessary medical emergency, by all means, it saves lives. More and more doctors and studies are showing the negative effects of this procedure. As an example, Thomas R. Verny, in his book *Pre-Parenting: Nurturing Your Child from Conception*, which I mentioned earlier, talks about the psychological profile of children born with this surgical procedure. Because they could not experience the contractions, they will tend to look more for physical contact. They tend to get themselves into difficult situations and then hope to find someone to rescue them. Third, they tend to have hyper sensibility on issues of abandonment and separation. What science is finding out gives more basis to these statements. Research[80] suggests that it is the baby who makes the decision to start the birth. This makes total sense, by the way, because it is the unconscious of the baby who is in charge of its body. The unconscious of the baby will know when its body is ready to take on its own its biological functions. When you program a C-section,[81] you rob the baby from a decision that was hers to make. The unconscious of the baby will interpret this as "my opinions/decisions are not relevant; they don't count" and "I am unable to complete something on my own," which explain the behaviors cited above.

---

[80] Jennifer Condon, et. al., "Surfactant protein secreted by the maturing mouse fetal lung acts as a hormone that signals initiation of parturition," *Proceedings of the National Academy of Sciences of the United States of America (PNAS),* April 6, 2004, http://www.pnas.org/content/101/14/4978.full. Accessed December 13, 2018.

[81] Cesarean procedure.

Besides all this, I also want to bring the perspective of negative programs affecting the decisions of parents. Most of the time when it is not dictated by an emergency, mothers and fathers choose C-section because it is supposedly less risky or more convenient. If it is because it is supposed to be less risky—I invite parents to do their homework; that's very debatable, to say the least—that means that they don't trust the innate body intelligence. They need to take a deeper look about what is behind these programs in their minds. It will branch to other programs that made them susceptible to take on that belief and that are likely affecting other areas in their lives. Dr. Verny talks about the cascade of hormonal reactions that occur in both of them during vaginal birth, which contributes to a deeper bonding between the two. That will not occur during a C-section. This is confirmed and reasserted by practitioners of the mind. In hypnosis, clients regressed as newborns express the anguish they feel if they were separated from the mother after birth for one reason or another. Because a C-section is a surgical procedure, in order to reduce the risk of infection, it often takes hours before the newborn is allowed to be in contact with the mom. This leaves a clear psychological scar. The baby needs to feel the mother's touch immediately after birth. I encourage parents to study the psychological effects that this procedure has on the baby and the mother. There is plenty of information available today in this respect.

If the parents are making that decision because it is more convenient for them, they are sending a very limiting message to their child: their other life activities are more important than him, or he is just one more item that needs to be accommodated within their busy schedule. There's an obvious impact that this type of messages will have on the self-esteem of the newborn.

Notice implicitly what I am saying here.

Children are beautiful, giant mirrors that reflect the parents' programs back at them.

Aware parents understand that they will learn as much from their children as their children learn from them. An example of this mirroring effect is the constant questioning from children about the why we do things the way we do. They have not yet been conditioned by society. I encourage parents to take this as an opportunity to revise their beliefs and behaviors. Children at a young age are the reformers that move our civilization into its next evolutionary step. And yes, they, in turn need the nurture, support, and education from their parents to be able to fully accomplish that.

Modern medicine has taken us to a new level of quality of life that our ancestors did not know. However, I hope that from all that I have been describing to you in this book, you can see that nature's designs are integrated systems in which each subsystem (stage, component, etc.) plays a specific, important role. Look again, for example, at how the events that occur during these early stages of our development are an integral part of us being prepared for the environment in which we will be born. We need to be careful when we attempt to change this human ecosystem.

Summary

Let's do another iteration of our graphical summary, this time including this prenatal experiences component.

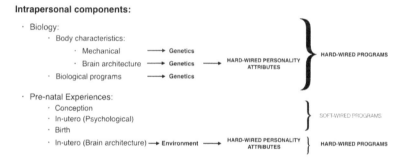

I differentiated the bold lettering in the hard-wired versus soft-wired programs to make it clearer in the diagram. Also, I moved the in utero brain architecture factor to the last position so that I can group better the different factors. The soft-wired programs that we went through in great detail in the first section of the book show up already, even before the baby is born. This is nature's "preparedness curriculum" so that the fetus in the womb is already adapting to the environment in which it will be. It's pure wisdom in this design. And again, more hard-wired programs are added at the prenatal stage: the brain architecture is additionally being shaped by the environment provided by the mother and the father, shown here as the physical in utero factor of this component.

The Childhood Experiences Component

This component of the personality is the one I covered in the first part of this book. It is, in general, the biggest factor that shapes who we are in our lives. As we saw, those early years in our lives are critical in the quality of the programs that will reside in our unconscious. The environment in which we grow is crucial. Within the environment, the variable that is central to our development is, not surprising, the parents. Because the whole first part of the book was dedicated to explain in detail the structures of the programs and how they work, what I will do in this section is focus on the role that parents play with their children, under the perspective of how they transfer their programs to them.

Parents' Influence on Their Children

I have stressed quite a bit how the unconscious has the ability to capture information about its surroundings. It's much more than the conscious can perceive. The same way that the baby in the womb was able to capture the emotional state of her dad, the unconscious of the parents captures information about their children. Mothers have a high sense about what is happening with their babies even when they are not in direct presence of each other. This is a well-known fact, as much as science may not have proven it yet. The unconscious of parents and children are highly attuned to each other. And from the perspective of the children, there are two reasons why this attunement is critical to them.

1. In contrast with many animals that populate this planet, the newborn humans are totally unprepared to survive on their own. A chicken comes out of the egg, ready to walk and pick the food from the ground. A human baby on its own will not survive. From the baby's unconscious perspective, the parents are the key component to survival.
2. As I mentioned before, to nature, parents are a successful model of survival for the particular environment in which they are. They have reached an age when they can already reproduce. They've made it. The parents' programs do succeed in this environment. Therefore, to increase their chances of survival, these programs need to be transmitted as soon as possible to their children.

Parents have an extraordinary influence in the unconscious of their children.

Think of it as a special, high-priority channel of communication between their unconscious minds. This does not invalidate anything that I mentioned previously. What it means is that if the father says "A" about something, and a stranger says "B" about that same something, what the father said will have more priority to the unconscious of his child. The child will create a program according to what the dad said rather than what the stranger said. The role that parents play is crucial. Ironically, this is also confirmed by the fact that by far, most of the session work that I do with my clients relates to traumatic programming that came from the family environment in which they grew up. I say ironically because isn't home where all the love and support is supposed to be coming, so that children become resourceful to fully live their lives?

We need to understand much better how parents affect their children. From what I explained above, nature wants to transfer the programs of the parents as soon as possible to their children. Here are the ways in which they do it.

1. **Explicit Transfer** (post-birth)
   a. Direct (during the programming event)
   b. Redirected (pre/post event programming)
2. **Implicit Transfer**
   a. Biology
   b. Prenatal
   c. Post-birth
   d. Parents' secrets

Explicit Transfer

Explicit transfer occurs when parents interact directly with their children. By definition, this happens after they are born (post-birth). There are two subcategories in which explicit transfer will occur.

Direct Transfer

In this case, the parents are programming their children directly. The best way to understand all these concepts is via examples. Let's say that we have a little boy who is playing with his dad. They are building a simple airplane model made out of wooden pieces.

Positive reaction to a positive event: Our boy takes a piece and puts it in the correct place. His dad responds by saying, "Great, Billy! You did very well. See? You can do things. You are so intelligent!" How is Billy's unconscious going to interpret this experience? It is going to create programs like "I am intelligent," "I am capable," "I feel supported," and "I feel loved." As you can see, these are powerful psychological resources that are going to give him a very strong base to succeed in life. And if the father is there playing with him and encouraging him as he builds the model, it is because the father has that type of programs in his unconscious. That is, he believes in giving support, he believes in expressing love, and he believes in the importance of being present while the children are growing. As trivial as all this may sound, this is exactly how programs are being transferred from the father to the son. Parents need to be aware and present in their interactions with their children. This power that they have on their child's unconscious implies responsibility. It goes both ways.

Negative reaction to a negative event: Let's say that our boy took a piece and put it in the wrong place. Here, the reaction of his father will be crucial. The father reacts by saying, "Hey! Pay attention! Can't you see that this piece does not fit there? You need to look more carefully." More than the words, it is the energy of how he is expressing that. It is the emotional language that the parent is transmitting to the child. It is well understood that when we talk, we transmit more information through nonverbal gestures than words themselves. The child's unconscious will get the impression according to how the father is reacting. If the father was irritated that his boy put the piece in the wrong place, the boy's unconscious is going to create programs like "I am not intelligent, because my father clearly expected me to be able to put it in the correct place the first time," "I don't feel supported," "I am not good enough," and "It's dangerous to make a mistake. People get upset with me." These are examples of what could be happening in the mind of the little child.

I need to make sure to remind you that there is no reasoning happening in the boy's mind. All the programs that his unconscious is creating come from direct impression—that's it. I have to academically explain it here, using our faculty of reasoning, because that is how we as adults communicate. You can see, from such a simple experience, how limiting programs are being installed by the boy's unconscious—programs that are going to have tremendous repercussions for the rest of his life. It's a direct impact to his self-esteem. Now he will start hesitating about taking the initiative when doing anything. "Am I going to be able to do this? What if I make a mistake?" Understand that he doesn't necessarily make these questions consciously (though he may). What the unconscious is doing is evaluating everything against the programs that it has. The actions of this boy are now regulated by these newly installed programs. In this second scenario, because the father reacted that way, what does it mean about the father's programs? That he believes Billy should not have made that mistake. That he should have been able to do it the first time.

That he'd better pay attention, because it's really a bad idea to make mistakes in life. The father must have had that type of programming, or else he would not have felt that irritation. That is how easily the programs get transferred.

Positive reaction to a negative event: Let's take the second case, where the boy put the piece in the wrong place. If his father would have reacted like, "Ah, Billy, let's see what happened here. Look here, this piece did not go there because … See? This here does not fit there. It's okay, let's look for another place where they will match. That is the fun in this. We'll figure it out together. You're doing good, you can do it," what programs are going to be created in the boy's unconscious? "It is okay to make mistakes; there are more chances," "I feel supported," and "I am okay, even if I make a mistake." These are positive psychological resources. These particular ones will help him directly when he confronts new experiences and projects. He will know that the result may not come exactly as expected the first time. Still, it's not the end of the world, and so he will give it a try. These are the individuals with initiative who are willing to take risks to start ventures that no one dared to do before. From here is where great things happen in our history. Notice that in this case, this type of program came from an event that one could have categorized as negative. The actual end result is in the attitude of the parent. If the father reacted in this way, that means that he has exactly that type of programs in his mind. It has to be that way. Our programs regulate our behavior.

We cannot cheat here. As a parent, you cannot stop being yourself for the eighteen-plus years that your children are going to be under your supervision. Besides, the unconscious of the child will capture the true essence of the parent's message, even if he is trying to cover up how he really feels.

Redirected Transfer

Here, parents transfer programs to their children before (pre), or after (post) another programming event in the child's environment. Examples.

Pre-event programming: Let's say that we have this little girl who tells her parents that she is going to have a math exam the next day. If the parents react by saying, "Wonderful, dear. You are going to do fine! Just be relaxed and enjoy the experience. If you don't know an answer, just stay calm, move on, and then come back to it. You are intelligent. If for some reason you don't know the answer to a question, you will be fine," how is this girl going to feel going into that exam? Her parents, with these comments, transferred programs like "I feel supported" and "No matter what the outcome, they believe in me." If they are saying that and honestly believe it, these are the type of programs that the girl's unconscious is going to create from that feedback. The girl is going to be in a positive mental state that will set her towards a positive outcome for that exam. It's a redirected explicit transfer, pre-event.

Compare that to a parent who says, "All right, Angie. We expect you to do well, and we assume you studied. If you get a bad grade, no friends and movie this weekend." For Angie, friends and movies that weekend is a big deal, and that is a big variable in the child's world at that age. That means she is going into that exam with a big weight on her shoulders because of the programs "It is a big deal if I don't perform well" and "It's dangerous to make a mistake." That was the message from the parents. Before the exam has begun, she will be in a mental state that will not help her think clearly. Her unconscious now has her in alert, in stress mode. Once in the exam, even if she studied, if for some reason there is a little difficulty with one of the math problems, she may not be able to resolve it because of the tension that she will feel. The parents' comments reflect their programs, and these programs will now affect her future experiences.

Post-event programming: We have this family where every evening (dinner is a great opportunity to do this), the parents sit down with their children to share what happened during the day. As a result of this sharing, the parents notice that their son had an experience that upset him. They react by saying, "Okay, you made a mistake, Mike. That's okay. That is exactly how we all learn in life. With this experience, now you learned something. This gives you new knowledge that you are going to use from now on." These parents, because of the power that they have over Mike's unconscious, will change his programming. (If it is a very traumatic event, then more attention will be needed.) Understand the example in the context of our routine, everyday experiences. Thus, an event that originally created negative programs in the child now gets transformed into new, positive psychological resources. From this example springs this very important point, which is so relevant nowadays in our stressed-out lifestyles.

It is crucial for children that their parents be present while they are growing up.

Ultimately, there is no substitution for this. Today, with our lifestyles, it is a huge factor related to the children's problematic behaviors. Notice in this example what would have happened if the parents had not sat with their children and shared. Mike would have stayed with the negative programming that came out of the experience he'd had. The opportunity that the parents had to give him positive psychological resources would have been lost. Parents who are not present in their children's lives not only miss opportunities to give them positive teachings, but they also leave an emotional vacuum. This is the classical situation where guilty parents give all kinds of presents to their children to compensate for their not being with them. You cannot trick their unconscious. The programs that these children will inevitably create in their unconscious will revolve around "I am not good enough for Dad/Mom to be with me," "I am not important if not even my dad/mom is willing to spend time with me," and "I don't count." These writings here are not just an opinion. They come directly from all that happens in the sessions with my clients. We do need to consider and understand the consequences of our lifestyles. If we want to create a better world for us, we need to be congruent with our actions. We all want peace and harmony, and yet we are not willing to invest the time and energy that children require and deserve. The future we talk so much about is these children.

To complete the illustration of the post-event case, for this example we have a girl who has a lot of initiative. At school during lunch time, she noticed how her classmates like the candies she brought with her lunch. It occurs to her that if she brings extra ones, she could sell them and make some money. Because she got this idea, she feels good about herself. "I am intelligent. I get great ideas." This type of inner event also creates programs. Excited about her new brilliant idea, she goes home later in the day and shares it with her parents. They respond, "Where did you get that idea? Do you think school is a market? No way you are doing that!"

Like a bucket of cold water thrown at her, her programs out of this experience become "I don't think things through very well," "I am stupid," and "It's dangerous to take initiative." A positive event is transformed into a negative experience. It's easy to see how this will affect her personality. The emotional energy that the parents express causes the impressions in the child, which in turn will generate the corresponding programs. It's redirected explicit transfer, post-event.

Strictly speaking, with any interactions that parents have with their children, you can categorize them as direct, explicit transfer. For academic purposes here, I created these extra categories to emphasize even more the consequences that parents' interactions (or lack thereof) with their children have over their personality.

Implicit Transfer

Implicit factors are those in which parents transfer programs through their actions and their attitudes by example and by how they behave in their own lives. They don't have to be explicitly interacting with their children. Because their children's unconscious is so attuned to them, everything they do has an influence on their young ones. I already explained the first two cases for implicit transfer, biology and prenatal, under the factors that affect our personality. As we saw, these programs are being transferred before the baby is born. They are great examples of how parents affect the child's personality implicitly. Certainly not at conception, and neither for the vast majority of the time while inside the mother, parents are not directly interacting with the new creature (I say the vast majority because you could say that when they talk to the baby through the mom's belly, that is an explicit communication). As we saw, all the programs created at that time come from the emotions and attitudes that the baby's unconscious perceives while in the mother's womb. For the sake of clarity and consistency, I will include the headings of the first two factors that I already explained so that you can follow with the original list at the beginning of this section.

Biology

Presented earlier as one of the components of our personality.

Prenatal

Presented earlier as one of the components of our personality.

Implicit Post-birth Transfer

This transfer occurs after the child is born and is living within the family dynamics. For example, little girl is walking on the street with her dad. As they are walking, the dad sees one of his friends, and they stop to talk. His friend tells him about an accident that another mutual friend had. His dad, surprised, reacts and says, "I feel so sorry for him. Life can be so unfair!" Her dad is talking to his friend, not to his daughter. That comment was directed at his friend. It does not matter. The girl's unconscious will pick upon that comment and will create the program "Life is unfair." This will start to become the lens through which she sees life. You may tell me, "Peter, that was just the expression he used." I will tell you:

Everything that you express—it does not matter how—reflects what you have stored in your unconscious.

In our example, because he made that comment, it necessarily means that there is a program in him that believes, to a lesser or greater degree, that life is unfair. Otherwise he would have reacted using a different expression. Well-trained practitioners, while doing sessions with their clients, are paying close attention to how the client expresses anything. And just by listening to how they talk, they can get a very good idea about how this person sees life or a specific situation. The language that she is using already tells a story beneath the story. Once more, you can't cheat your way out of this. Children know when what their parents are telling them does not match their actions. The classic example is when a parent who smokes tells his child not to smoke. If the child ended up not smoking, it was more because of other factors in the environment that led her not to smoke. In spite of what the parent is saying to the child, that child's unconscious will register the action, not the words.

Actions and attitudes are, more than words, the real expression of the programs in the unconscious of the person.

The more the little girl hears her dad use that expression, the more that program will be reinforced in her. Say that some other time, the dad is driving with the family, and the car gets a flat tire. He goes out of the car exclaiming how unfair life is. This is repetition reinforcing the program … and implicit transfer.

Parents' Secrets

This may be one of the most surprising factors for most people. Parents keep secrets with the best intentions of protecting their children from the possible negative effects they may have on them. Externally, it may look like secrets work. Not to the unconscious. Here you have some real-life examples.

Case 19: One-year-old with Bronchitis

Ruben García founded the Insituto Ruben Salud (Ruben Salud Institute) and the Instituto de Descodificación Natural (Natural Decoding Institute) in Spain. He uses hypnotherapy and neurolinguistic programming, among other techniques. He published a video called "Los Niños Expresan lo que los Padres Callan"[82] ("Children Express What Parents Silence"). It is a whole video about sessions related to secrets that parents keep from their children. This case is about a one-year-old girl who has bronchitis that does not want to heal. The parents have taken her to different medical doctors multiple times, she has gone through different treatments, and they have given her inhalers. Nothing seems to work. As a last resort, the parents go to him.

García understands the connection emotion-illness, which is part of his program called descodificación natural (natural decoding). Because he knows that the baby's and the parents' unconscious are so tightly coupled together, he works with the parents. At first, everything looks okay with them: they love each other, and their lives seem completely normal on the outside. He then works with them one at a time. Here is where the mother expresses a big conflict that she carries with her husband. He is a great guy, great husband, and great dad—except that he is extremely disorganized and leaves the house in a complete mess. She feels that she doesn't want to create problems at home, and so she doesn't say anything (which, by the way, is a limiting negative program in her: "I can't express what I feel. I don't give myself permission to express what I feel."). Of course, because she doesn't tell her husband about this, he has no idea of what is going on and that he would be doing anything to affect her. This situation is eating her alive.

So that you get the unconscious symbolism in this situation, she feels that she cannot "cough this up." As I have amply illustrated by now, the baby's unconscious is deeply connected to her mother's. The baby does not have the programs that her mother has and that inhibit her from expressing how she feels (the beauty of children, as we all know). The baby feels and expresses the conflict. In the sessions, once this situation comes to light and the parents sit down and resolve the conflict, the baby heals the bronchitis within three days.

Though doctors and medicines couldn't do it, in three days the healing occurs. (This is not a criticism of doctors; instead, it is a call to the medical

---

[82] Ruben García, "Los Niños expresan lo que los Padres callan—Descodificación Natural—Ruben Salud—Sevilla," *YouTube*, Ruben Salud, February 17, 2014, https://www.youtube.com/watch?v=smVNVm4OQnU. Accessed December 13, 2018. Starting at the 29:47 mark.

community to expand their approach to include how we see ourselves as human beings.) The mother, as all parents do, had the best intentions. She wanted to keep that apparent harmony at home, which everybody saw from the outside. Even so, in the family unconscious, the conflict was present.

Parents: you need to resolve your own conflicts.

In this case, the baby expressed the conflict with a physical illness. It won't always be like that, depending on the combination of programs of the parents and the children. You can see how easily we can explain the complexity of human behavior with this model. We are talking about millions of programs in each individual, and no two people are alike. Thus, the end result of our interactions with others will depend on the particular programs that the involved individuals have. A parent who lives in a conflicted environment will create programs in her children's unconscious minds like "Living in conflict is normal." These children will go through a double set of painful experiences. Not only will the children suffer while living with the conflicted parents, but these inherited programs will lead them into relationships that will have similar dynamics … with that same suffering once more. A secret is a conflict by definition; otherwise, there would not be a need to have it.

Case 20: Constant Vigilance

This case comes from the same video as the last case.[83] Here is a case that combines prenatal programming with family secrets. This is a woman who lives feeling threatened constantly. She admits that it is not based on anything real, but she can't help it. She lives in permanent fear and anxiety about anything bad happening to her. What comes out of the sessions is this: her mother, when she was pregnant with her, attempted an abortion because she felt already overwhelmed; she already had six children. Obviously, it failed. The mother did not tell anyone, not even to her husband; the event remained as a secret in her. You can see the impeccable logic in the program that this event generated: "Life is very dangerous—even my mother wanted to kill me." Thus, the woman's behavior. Her unconscious was executing the

---

[83] Ruben García, "Los Niños expresan lo que los Padres callan—Descodificación Natural—Ruben Salud—Sevilla," *YouTube*, Ruben Salud, February 17, 2014, https://www.youtube.com/watch?v=smVNVm4OQnU. Accessed December 13, 2018. Starting at the 43:20 mark.

program, trying to protect her. Once she understands this situation, she can let go and live life normally.

A secret is a program, and it will remain active as long as it is not liberated. It is important that parents understand this. Secrets do not work in the long run. They have direct consequences not only on their children but also in the family tree, as I will show in the transgenerational component. As long as these secrets remain in the unconscious, they will be transferred within the family.

The human psychophysical system was designed to encourage us to resolve our conflicts.

A more appropriate word would be *demand* than *encourage*. Nature wants us to be congruent. It's that simple. This does not mean that there isn't a better time to bring a secret out to light. As an example, if a child was adopted, the parents should use their intuition to decide when it is the best time and occasion to let her know about this. Eventually, though, this needs to be done. You would be shocked at the stories that come out in sessions, that people keep and carry inside themselves. These are psychological weights that wear down people. It's the weight that humanity is carrying today, and it is in our mass consciousness.

I want to finish this section with an important note. I have made it clear that parents are critical in the development of the child, and so is the rest of the environment in which the child is growing. School, teachers, and peers, and outside experiences exert powerful influences that create programs in the child's unconscious as well. Everything in these early years is creating programs, shaping personalities. Attentive parents will be aware of how the outside circumstances are shaping the child's vision of the world, and they will be there when they need to reframe or transform the negative programs that may have resulted from those experiences (more on this soon).

Foundational and Nonfoundational Programs

When a child grows in an abusive environment, he sees life through all the programs that were generated all those years. The only reality he knew is that life is dangerous. These programs become the foundation of the personality of the individual. As an adult, he will see life through these lenses. Everything will be colored by the concept of "Life is dangerous." This is in contrast to someone who was born in a home where there was love and support. This child grows and becomes an adult who is seeing life in a very different way as that of the abused one.

Let's say that someone breaks into the car of the person who grew in a supportive environment. Indeed, it is a negative experience that may create an associated program in her unconscious. Still, because of all the previous experiences that she has had in her life, it is very unlikely that she will change her whole life perspective to match the individual who grew up in the abusive environment. Her internal map of reality was built based on positive programs. Thus, when her unconscious evaluates this negative event against all the other experiences stored in its memory banks, that evidence overwhelmingly tells her that life is still an enjoyable journey. This is in contrast to the reaction of the person who grew up in the abusive environment: this event will become yet another experience that adds to all the previous evidences that his unconscious has and tells him that life is dangerous. These two people are seeing life's events through completely different lenses and acting accordingly.

Programs that are generated by events that don't have associations to other events and that become a reference for many other programs are foundational programs.

You can easily understand that for the most part, this type of programs is generated during the first years of our life because it is during this period that we don't have previous references to compare against, or the faculty of reasoning to discern about the events that are happening then.

Foundational programs are the base on which the personality rests.

So that you can see clearly the difference between foundational and nonfoundational programs, let's use an example. Take a person who, after having a serious accident while crossing an intersection, as a consequence is now afraid to cross any other intersection. From what you have read in this book, you understand that it is because his unconscious has classified, as a result of the accident, the concept of intersections as dangerous. That program now controls his behavior. It does that by activating its associated emotional battery. Every time he nears an intersection, the battery zaps the person with the emotion of fear. He will try to avoid this type of situations as much as possible.

If this individual transforms this program by working with a practitioner, he will not feel that fear anymore under these circumstances. He will be free to go where he decides to go, using the path he wants to take. This is a typical example of a nonfoundational program. Before the accident, he knew very well that with the proper precautions, intersections are nothing to be afraid of. While growing up, he learned to safely deal with them, and afterward he lived life crossing them without any problems. Then the accident happened, and in spite of knowing from previous experience that he should be able to easily navigate them, it became a struggle. After processing the trauma, he went back to the original behavior effortlessly. The key here is that he could do that because there was already a learned behavior (a previous frame of reference). Thus, there was nothing new to learn once the trauma had been processed. That is the big difference of this type of programs, when compared with a foundational program.

The Criticality of Our Early Environments

The person who grew up in an environment that taught him that life is dangerous does not know how to see life from a different perspective. There is nothing in his unconscious about how to live and behave in harmonious circumstances. He did not go through positive experiences that would have made his unconscious generate the corresponding programs of behavior. To change foundational programs requires more extensive transformative processing because they are such an integral part of the personality of the individual. Using an analogy, think of them as the foundation and weight-bearing structures of a house. They hold and support the whole building. Once people are living in there, they can change walls and rooms as long as they don't change those structures that are holding it. If they do want to change a weight-bearing wall, it will require more extensive work and calculations on how to do that without the house collapsing. I will talk more about this later, in the section about processes for mind transformation. For now, understand that because these programs were created early in your life, they became the foundation on which the personality was built. They are the basis of who you are as a person. They define your personality, and they give the support to all other programs. Because your interaction with the environment in which you are growing (family and external) takes many years, during that time, all its messages and attitudes will be repeated again and again, resulting in highly charged emotional batteries associated with all these programs. These foundational programs are core rules of survival to your unconscious.

Anything that attempts to change them will be taken as a severe threat (by the unconscious). This is the reason that politics and religion, for example, are topics that generate so much conflict among people: they reflect the very basic points of view that we have about us and life that were, by the most part, generated during our first years of existence. It is within our families that we were ingrained with the first principles of religion, spirituality, and morality. Also, in the attitude and teachings of your parents, you learned how to see the rich, the poor, social classes, money, justice and injustice, and more. This is how you were structured to see life, and generally speaking, it's the only one perspective you were shown. You did not live alternative infancies that you could compare and use as different frames of reference from which to choose.

It is also important that you understand that in the beginning, most of the programs created are foundational ones and that as the child grows, that rate diminishes. It is a gradual process. As the child keeps experiencing life, there will be more and more references that will affect how the new (nonfoundational) programs will be created. However, the subjective objectivity effect of the foundational programs will take place, and the new programs will be created based on the interpretation of events, as perceived through these foundational programs. This means that the few positive events that may occur to the youngsters going through rough childhoods may be reinterpreted, washed out by the perceptions that they already have of life ("That was just a one-time thing," "Life is just rough"). A double price to pay.

Another thing that I want to point out, which we see from our experience with natal regression sessions. They show us very clearly the importance that the father plays in the development of the child from conception. Logically, we emphasize the role of the mother as the one who physically bears the child in the baby's development during pregnancy and even for the first years of the newborn (many psychologists talk about up to three years of age. Certainly, the mother's physical and chemical connection with the baby in utero is the strongest connection that the baby has with the physical world in which she is now starting to participate. Even so, from the unconscious perspective, the attitude of the father is equally critical to the future personality of the baby. A father that is not emotionally present in one way or another, *starting from conception*, will cause deep (foundational) wounds in that child even if the mother was 100 percent emotionally engaged.

Once you understand the consequences of these foundational programs, it becomes clear how critical it is that we create a society where all the children are raised in a supportive and nurturing setting, and in which a critical factor is empowered, knowledgeable, and emotionally mature parents. Even though it is always possible to transform our minds, the early years mark us in profound ways that will require more effort if corrections are needed later on. This is accentuated even more if you consider the physical consequences in the development of the brain that I mentioned in the prenatal component of the mind. It is indeed much harder to reform criminals who come from abusive, violent childhoods. It is a heavy price that we all pay, as a society, for not taking the responsibility to ensure that everybody starts life harmoniously.

Babies are not born perpetrators. We shape them into perpetrators.

Perpetrators experience intense inner suffering from extremely limiting programs that manifest as hurtful behavior.

Summary

Adding this childhood experiences component, our summary looks as follows.

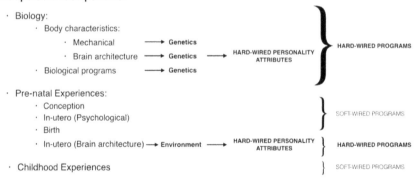

Childhood creates a slew of soft-wired programs, including those that are going to be the foundation of the personality. The environment (parents, teachers, peers, and the physical surroundings in which the kid is growing up) is critical. It is here that we form the deep-rooted beliefs and points of view about how life is, how life feels. Precisely because of this, it is here where children need to get the necessary positive psychological resources (programs) that will enable them to live the full lives that they came here to experience.

This is the period in our lives where the nurturing factor plays its role at a maximum in shaping who we will become.

The Adolescence Experiences Component

Adolescence is traditionally viewed as the parents' dreaded period when their children distance themselves from them, rebel against them, and immerse in new "risky" behaviors (including the world of sexuality). Indeed, this is a new stage in our development as human beings, marked by pronounced physical and behavioral changes. And it is true that for many parents, this stereotype will become a reality. Nevertheless, it doesn't have to be that way. Daniel Siegel is a clinical professor of psychiatry at the UCLA School of Medicine and is the founding co-director of the Mindful Awareness Research Center at UCLA. In his book *Brainstorm: The Power and Purpose of the Teenage Brain*,[84] he talks about the main behavioral changes that occur during adolescence. He describes and condenses them into four main aspects: "increased emotional intensity, social engagement, novelty seeking and creative exploration."[85] He explains that if properly channeled, these new energies and behaviors become a new positive platform that ought to remain as such throughout adulthood and for the rest of our lives.[86] I couldn't agree more with him. Most of the people recall their younger years as a time when they were full of energy and eager to convert their dreams in reality. Years later, they saw themselves as shadows of who they were back then. In my model, this is the result of not having enough psychological resources (positive programs) to sustain the challenges that those dreams implied, combined with the negative programs in them, and their limiting consequences. Thus, they end up settling under the weight of their life circumstances: "The economy is not good. There is too much competition. I am not good enough." As Dr. Siegel points out, the changes in this time of our lives, which extends all the way to around twenty-four years of age,[87] correspond to physical changes in our bodies, and in particular, in our brains. Yes, hormonal changes do occur, but are not as central in explaining the teenager's behavior as people think. As a result of these brain changes, new behaviors rise, marked by the four characteristics

---

[84] Daniel J. Siegel, *Brainstorm: The Power and Purpose of the Teenage Brain*, New York: Penguin Publishing Group, 2013.

[85] Ibid., 7.

[86] Ibid., 10.

[87] Ibid., 1.

that he mentions. I want to use my model to expand and complement on Dr. Siegel's model.

Problematic Parenting Aspects

As we saw, after around ten years of age (Dr. Siegel says around twelve years[88]), Nature assumes that the child has assimilated the core rules of survival for the environment in which he lives. In the meanwhile, his brain was building the structures that by this age will have the initial functionality of the conscious and its faculty of reasoning. With these two factors in place, now the child is ready to start becoming a new, independent human being. Understand that this is a long process in us, extending all the way to the age of about twenty-five. One of the aspects of seeking new independence manifests as the social engagement that Dr. Siegel talks about. Teenagers now want to engage more with their peers and less with their parents. This is a natural, biological behavior associated with the expansion of the species. This becoming more independent on their part can bring natural tensions that arise from the new, changing dynamic of that relationship with them. Change implies readjustment, and that is okay. However, there are problematic aspects in the education that parents give to their children and that unnecessarily aggravate and amplify this tension and distancing. Adolescence brings them up to the surface.

1. From what I have seen in sessions with my clients (plus those of other practitioners) and the directives that I still hear parents giving to their children nowadays, the distancing of teenagers is aggravated by the arbitrary, illogical "rules and regulations" that parents force on their children while growing up. Every single time a parent responds to a child's "Why?" with a "Because I say so" or "Because that's the way things are," they are giving the message, "This is an arbitrary world. Just cope with it." Simply reading that statement makes anyone feel uncomfortable. While children are growing and learning about this physical world, they are trying to make sense of it so that they can better navigate it. We all know that it is much easier to deal with something when you understand it. Nothing is more frustrating than when you have to do something that does not make sense to you. That is exactly the same for them. Even though their faculty of reasoning is not well formed, when they ask a why,

---

[88] Ibid., 1.

it is an indication that it is starting to develop. Of course, the answers need to be given according to their age, but it is crucial that the answer genuinely fulfills their questioning.

If you, as a parent, don't have a better answer than "Because I say so," then you need to question the beliefs that are behind the directive that you are giving to your child.

This is what I meant earlier about children also being teachers to their parents. They don't have all our social conditionings yet, and in this respect they are a blank slate, which they want to fill in with something that makes sense to them. While growing up, they are dependent on their parents, and so when a parent responds with a "Because everybody does it like that," children have no choice but to follow. (There may be some resistance, but at this stage in their development, parents rule.) This experience will create programs in their unconscious like "Life is weird," "Life does not make sense," "My own initiative does not count," "I need to follow, rather than being genuine," and "I cannot do or express what I truly feel," with the respective negatively charged emotional batteries. These programs were created as a result of this type of interaction with their parents, and thus these negative emotions will manifest themselves as resentment toward the parents in their adolescent years.

2. Incongruence. The stereotypical example here is a parent who smokes yet tells his children not to smoke. Another occurrence is the parent who is teaching her children to respect others, but later on when she gets upset, she screams at someone else. These inconsistent messages don't give a clear direction to the children about how to behave. This causes confusion and frustration at the beginning, until they somehow reconcile the parents' behavior with programs that tell them that being incongruent is okay. The problem with incongruence is that by definition, it is an unresolved conflict that you carry inside yourself. The more incongruence in the parents' behavior, especially while the children are growing up, the more conflicted the teenagers (and later on, the adults) will be, with the obvious implications in the relationship with their parents.

3. Education based on fear. This is the easiest route that parents use to make their children comply with their directives. They grow up behaving because otherwise they face the consequences of punishment from the parent, added later to that from the principal at school or from the police,

and even including the ultimate eternal punishment by the particular god that they were taught about. Fear is an unsustainable negative force. It may give short-term results, but it only does damage on the long term. When parents tell their children to do something "or else," without any explanations, they are forcing them to behave with no understanding of the why and irrespective of what they may be feeling at that moment. This creates programs that give a vision of life as scary, on top of "My feelings don't count" and "My opinion doesn't count." This includes imposed morals sustained by the concept of the dire consequences of sin against God, which I will talk about later.

Children need to grow into adults with an intrinsic respect for others, irrespective of the presence and pressure of a vigilant authority in their lives.

We naturally expect to be treated in a respectful manner by others, and this necessarily needs to apply in the same way to every single human being. This is an example of a universal principle that stands the test of time and space (i.e., geographical and cultural location). This makes them authentic, and it is sustainable because this behavior is aligned with the characteristics of our nonphysical Essence. With these individuals, there is no need to have a police force or a punishing God. These teachings require time, patience, and perseverance, especially when your directives go against what the children feel in the moment, which inevitably will happen at one point or another. Education based on fear creates negative, emotionally charged programs that will bring anger and resentment in the relationship with the parents.

4. Directly related to adolescence are parents who don't have the knowledge about the behavioral changes of this age. When their children change, parents feel left out, and they feel that children are ungrateful. All parents need to go beyond social stereotypes and instead educate themselves about their children's development. Some parents, in spite of having this knowledge, still feel offended or hurt by this new dynamic. If this is so, they need to look inside themselves. And I say this not just so that they transform the negative programs that are behind this response and thus increase their own quality of life. It's for the sake of their relationship with their young ones. If they don't transform these programs, they will become demanding of their children's attention and irritated with them,

to the further detriment of the relationship. Now the teenager will want to distance herself even more. It's a growing vicious circle.

An integral part of parenting is to fully allow their children to grow and become independent beings.

It is natural to love the company of your children, but not to the point where emotional needs interfere with their growth.

The Consequences on Their Adolescent Children

When children reach adolescence, they now face these situations.

1. Because their faculty of reasoning is truly starting to engage, they now can, via their own reasoning, see the arbitrariness of all these rules that were stuffed into them and that don't make sense. The credibility of the parents will be readjusted according to the new evaluations that they will make. The more arbitrariness that they see in what they had to comply with, the less credibility the parents will now have, with the implied detriment in the relationship. Now they have reasons to rebel against their parents.

2. Precisely because of the new independence that the teenager is feeling, now the parents are no longer on that pedestal of being the saviors with supreme authority, which he (that is, his unconscious) saw in them as he was growing up. These biological behavioral programs finish their function with the beginning of adolescence. They acted like a barrier that gave the parents the biggest precedence, for all the reasons that I have already explained earlier in the book. Without that barrier, they get to fully feel the accumulation of experiences from all those years. Now children are "on their own," and all the emotional batteries (positive and negative) will come up to the surface full force. The negative interactions with their parents will express themselves as resentment toward them.

3. This will happen to not just the programs related to the interactions with their parents that I am referring to in this section, but to all the experiences that they went through while growing up. As the new, independent entities that they are becoming during this period, they get to own all the programs and their emotional batteries that the unconscious created over the previous years. This emotional avalanche will indeed be amplified by the physical changes in the body. If the

teenager grew up in a non-nurturing environment, the resulting programs will generate a slew of negative emotions that can easily overwhelm her. Here is where drugs become an easy escape from this overbearing situation. On the other hand, an adolescent who grew up in a nurturing environment (emotionally, intellectually, etc.) will have all the inner resources to balance the new behavioral tendencies due to the physical changes in his body.

It is an irony that contrary to the belief that teenagers don't want to be with their parents, surveys about them show the opposite to be true: they want to have the company and support of their parents.[89] This is not incompatible with their new urge to be more independent, and it's easily explainable with the information that I have given you in this book. The biological urge to become more independent carries an implicit implication: they must go beyond the known mental territory in which they grew up. As I explained earlier, anything that is outside of the known mental territory is danger to the unconscious. As exciting as all the new social (and sexual) experiences are to the teenagers, they are caught in the middle of two opposite internal forces: the biological impulse to become independent, and the unconscious warnings of danger that tells them to stay where it knows what the rules of survival are. Here, you can see how crucial it is for them to have a solid psychological foundation and a supportive, nurturing relationship with the parents, who also understand and respect the changes that they need to go through in order to become successful adults. Having this type of parents gives them the support to immerse themselves into their new experiences in spite of the protective warnings of their unconscious.

Emotionality and New Experiences

With respect to the emotional spark and novelty-seeking characteristics of this age, Dr. Siegel writes about the tragic consequences that these new behaviors can have in adolescents. As one of many other examples that he gives in the book, he mentions how a teenager, driving more than ninety miles/hour in a residential street, killed one of his teachers at his psychiatry training program.

---

[89] Kristin A. Moore, "Parent-teen Relationships and Interactions: Far More Positive Than Not," *Child Trends*, Child Trends Research Brief, December 2004, https://www.childtrends.org/wp-content/uploads/2009/11/Child_Trends-2004 _12_01_RB_ParentTeen.pdf. Accessed December 13, 2018.

This child was driving a brand-new sports car that his parents gave him after he had been arrested for speeding and crashing another one against a tree two months earlier.[90] As Dr. Siegel correctly points out, adolescents need creative, safe outlets for their new behaviors. That brings us back to parenting.

More than the changes in the brain of the adolescents, their "crazy behavior" stems from the lack of true parenting that is so pervasive in our society today.

Until all children grow in nurturing and safe environments, at home and in their communities, we will not know how much the physical changes in their brains are truly to blame for these behaviors. I sustain my point that parenting is the root cause for the adolescent's behavior, more so than the physical changes. The changes in their bodies do amplify the psychological state of the teenager. I say this based on these three observations.

1. A key difference between adolescents and adults is the amount of experiences that they have had as independent human beings. In the same way that children are blank slates (relatively speaking, as we have already seen about newborns) entering this world, adolescents are blank slates as independent human beings. In other words, in the same way that children needed to learn the rules of survival during their first years of life, adolescents acquire wisdom through experiences as independent beings. This takes time, in conjunction with the proper parental guidance. Let's take the case of speeding with a car. For most of us, as adults we observe speed limits more carefully than in our teenage years. Why? Because of the experiences that we have had, or that we've observed in our peers. For example, we probably drove faster before that first unpleasant event of being caught by an officer and having to go through all the embarrassing and inconvenient consequences of getting a speeding ticket. As a result of that type of experiences, our unconscious created programs that now make us behave in more responsible ways. The adolescent does not have these programs yet. And as in an adult, it can very well happen that if an adolescent gets a fine for speeding, he will drive responsibly from then on, in spite of the changes that are still going on in his brain. When this does not happen, then it is because of negative programs that override the learning that should have come out of this event. Now he has a program

---

[90] Daniel J. Siegel, *Brainstorm*, 19.

in his unconscious that regulates his behavior. The natural curiosity and novelty seeking, combined with the lack of programs in their unconscious that would give them a frame of reference on how to behave under these circumstances, is what makes them drive faster.

Let me take advantage of this topic here, to talk about adults. That curiosity and novelty seeking needs to be equally present in all adults. What happens is, that life has "tamed" adults through their experiences against the rules of society and also through the weight of the responsibilities that come with age. Unfortunately for most adults, this taming goes to the point where novelty seeking dies too. This does not mean that it is a characteristic that belongs to adolescence. We want every single adult to carry that same adolescent spark throughout their entire lives. Of course, that spark will express itself according to all the experiences and wisdom that the individual has acquired in her life. That spark is part of being human, not of a certain age. Conversely, supporting this observation is the case of teenagers who, because of abusive authoritarian parents, or other challenging circumstances while growing up, behave as responsibly as, or even more so than, other mature adults. These cases are examples of negative programs dictating our behavior during adolescence, which is our particular topic here. This is not a healthy result in this case. Nevertheless, notice that these programs affect our behavior already at that age similarly to how they do in adulthood.

Case 21: My Programs and Adolescence

I'll continue with my story when I was one year old in Germany and was left alone in the dark. As a result of that experience, I could not sleep well at night, with the consequence that during the day I was tired and irritated all the time. My parents did not know what to do with me. The situation became so desperate to them that they decided to take me to an institute that dealt with "problematic infants." Here was their solution: my parents would leave me with them for one week, and they could go on visiting Germany as they had planned. The institute's treatment was very simple. Every night, they would leave me alone in a room and let me cry to exhaustion. It worked. When my parents picked me up one week later, they noticed the change in my personality. My mother told me how there were no more smiles, no direct looks in their eyes. Here are some of the highly charged programs that were created as a result of that experience. (This is not the result of an intellectual exercise that I did; these have come out of sessions, either with a practitioner or by myself.)

- Even my parents will abandon me. (I was one year old, and I had no comprehension of what was going on and that they would be back in one week.)
- Crying (and expressing any negative emotion) has severe consequences.
- Parents are a powerful authority to be feared.

There are more programs, but these ones are enough to illustrate the point I am trying to make here. As a result of this experience, which generated these programs, it became very clear to me that disobeying or displeasing my parents could have severe consequences. My unconscious survival strategy became very simple: be the perfect son. Here, you have the reason for my behavior during the next forty years of my life—as I talked about at the beginning of the book, the "glamorous years." I was always among the best students in my class all the way through college, I became a national champion in swimming, and I never did drugs, smoked, or drank alcohol. I never had a physical confrontation while growing up. Even though I do not advocate violence, this program of being the perfect son determined my passive-evasive solution to my friend's bullying. At the very least, a more assertive attitude would have probably stopped him. To my unconscious, that was not a possibility. My point is that I didn't do crazy things during my adolescence. I was a well-behaved, responsible boy in every single respect and in spite of all the physical changes during those years. With all these honors to brag about, they were simply a defense mechanism that my unconscious used to survive, to adapt to the perceived circumstances. The real Peter remained unexpressed. As such, it was an unsustainable situation, a mask that eventually started to crack.

My point in this discussion is that in the same way that negative programs can make an adolescent behave as a responsible adult, positive programs combined with knowledgeable and empathic guidance can equally take the teenager so that he can fully express his new behaviors without damaging consequences on anyone. Parenting is what determines this result.

2. In case you haven't noticed, adults can be as emotional and irrational as teenagers. You can go to the Internet and watch all kinds of videos about adults doing stupid, crazy things, putting themselves in dangerous situations. In general, this behavior is less frequent because of the "taming" that I alluded to before. You may argue that those videos tell the story of immature adults. That is also a confirmation of my point. In spite of the fact that adolescents' physical changes of their brains are complete, they still do crazy things because it is programs that ultimately regulate behavior. Even in the case of mature adults who behave accordingly, adolescent behaviors can happen. Many of us have had the experience that, when doing an activity or project that are new to us, because of the lack of experience we did something that later on we realized put us at risk. "Shoot! How come I did not think of that? I was lucky. I could have hurt myself badly." Even though we normally take precautions (because as adults, through our experiences, we already have generated enough programs to make us more cautious), in this case due to the lack of programs with respect to this particular experience, we became adolescents.

   Last, think about how we all get irritated or upset with our work peers, friends, family, and our intimate relationships. Simply look at the news and heads of state, politicians, and businesspeople. There's emotionality everywhere, every day in our lives, for the very vast majority of adults. For more extreme cases, we even have coined the phrase "drama queen," which applies to men and women at any age. There is no difference in this emotional behavior in adults than from adolescents. It is the same emotional immaturity. It is programs (or lack thereof). Once you process those programs, whether as a teenager or as an adult, they will change your behavior accordingly.

3. Peer pressure, which is often used to blame for teenager behavior, exists in adults (keeping up with the Joneses). This is part of the biological programs that make us intrinsically a social species. In their study about resistance to peer influence,[91] Steinberg and Monahan point out that the results suggest that peer resistance increases linearly from ages fourteen to eighteen, but not so from ages ten to fourteen—or from eighteen to thirty. In other words, the ability to resist peer pressure increases in the

---

[91] L. Steinberg and K. Monahan, "Age Difference in Resistance to Peer Influence," *Development Psychology* 43 no. 6 (2007), 1531–1543. MacArthur Juvenile Capacity Study, https://www.ncbi.nlm.nih.gov/pmc/articles/PMC2779518.

middle of adolescence but not significantly from then on, in spite of the fact that brain changes continue all the way to around twenty-five years of age. This is in parallel with what I suggest: that teenagers with robust inner psychological resources will have the capacity to make the right decisions when they encounter critical or dangerous situations. They will still do crazy things that would not have occurred to us. That is the natural, healthy richness that every new generation brings to us. I will talk more about this in the transpersonal components section. It is fantastic to see their new ideas and creations because this is how humanity evolves. How boring it would be otherwise!

Parents need to know the information that Dr. Siegel gives in his book. It is crucial for their understanding of their children. Hormonal changes and brain changes create new inner needs that result in behaviors that the parents want to understand so that these needs can be properly fulfilled. The end result in the adolescents' behavior is a consequence of the parenting that they received more than anything else. (Notice that I consider the quality of the external environment, like school and friends, under this umbrella that parents provide to their children.)

Adolescence is a big transitional development in us humans. This is truly the birth of adulthood. It's a new period of learning and adaptation that will demonstrate how well she has been prepared, psychologically speaking, by her parents. It is a period in which she will learn to use this ability to reason at the same time that she goes through a whole new set of experiences. As is the case in children, and also in adults (as I will explain soon), whenever you experience something new in your life, your unconscious creates new programs accordingly. Thus, this is a period in which there still will be a lot of new programs being created by the unconscious, mixed with the filtering effect that comes with the faculty of reasoning. This is a period of intense new experiences not just on the outside but also on the inside, which creates new vulnerabilities that now they need to learn to navigate on their own. When adolescents were children, parents were completely responsible for the well-being in everything they did. As adolescents, parents take a more sidelined support while the kids learn to truly stand on their own. The results of the first years of parenting will be put to the test, so to speak. The programs in their unconscious will determine how they tackle this period of all kinds of changes. It is a gigantic mirror that reflects to both the adolescent and the parents how well prepared she is to live a full life. It is not about being perfect.

The real power in human beings lies in having the knowledge and inner resources to change our limiting behaviors.

These resources will have come from the family environment for the most part. This is the foundation that will reverberate like a domino effect for the rest of the life of the individual.

Summary

Adolescence adds more soft-wired programs to our unconscious.

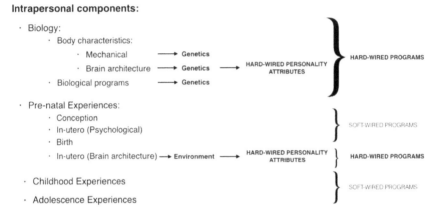

Childhood and adolescence are the periods of our lives where the most physical changes occur in our bodies as part of the process of growing up. These changes include the brain. In the brain, these changes occur not only because of natural biological processes but also as an adaptation to the events that the child is experiencing. That is what it is designed to do, as part of the adaptation to the environment. New experiences generate new programs that translate into new neuronal connections. You could argue that these changes in the brain architecture should be included in the description of these last two components. Yes, they could. However, the reason that I am not doing this is because it is the soft-wired programs that are driving the architecture of the neuronal connections. They are the true source behind these changes. Again, these changes are part of the normal, natural functionality of the brain.

Implications of These Last Three Components

Prenatal experiences, early life experiences, adolescence experiences. As you can see, the relationship between parents and children carry big implications, much more than people realize. That is why I want to present this section at this point. We live our lives on a very weak emotional foundation. Historically speaking, it had to be like that simply because we did not have the knowledge. And as a species, we had to keep on reproducing to continue to exist—a very basic biological law that applies equally today. Today, though, it is time that we start growing emotionally as much as we have been doing intellectually. There is a big gap between these two aspects in our current state of evolution.

Our Educational System

Look at our educational system. We give our children all kinds of wonderful knowledge: math, science, history, geography, and literature. Great intellectual knowledge. What about emotional knowledge? We give very little, if any at all. There are no courses on how our emotions work. No courses on how to build successful relationships. No courses on how to deal with conflict resolution. No courses to give us tools that we can use to help us through the emotional challenges that we all inevitably face in life. Don't you think that these topics should be taught as part of any school's curriculum? Everybody would gain from understanding how emotions work as well as math or any other subject. They are one of the most impacting variables in the lives of all of us, without exception. They are intrinsic to being human.

In spite of something that is so obvious, instead, we are all left on our own to deal with the emotional dimension of life. This means that we are left to deal with life at the hands of the programs that we inherited from the environment in which we grew, mostly from our parents—who in turn were taught by what their parents, inherited from the grandparents. These programs were mixed with the programs that were generated by their own personal experiences. Each set of parents is transmitting their learnings based on the subjective objectivity effect that makes them "know" what they are teaching to their children is the "right" way of doing it. In reality, it is simply the expression of what they went through in their lives. It's an unstructured, informal, and totally empirical way of preparing the next generation to take us to the next step in our evolution as a species. We excel in the comforts of the modern technologies that we have developed precisely because that is what we teach in schools: the intellectual side. We teach nothing about the emotional side, and so we live in this paradoxical civilization of high technology mixed with a disproportionate amount of unnecessary emotional suffering. As we can read every day in the media, not even the wealthiest and most famous people (they are just as human as any of us) can escape the suffering caused in big part because of this emotional knowledge vacuum in which we are left. There will always be challenges while experiencing this physical dimension. That is what we come to experience, so that we grow and empower ourselves. Still, our behavior as social entities lags far behind our material progress.

I hope this book will be a grain of sand in this mountain that we need to build, related to emotional development. I hope that the material that I am presenting here will inspire you, the readers, to address this urgent need in our education system. This needs to happen as much at the grassroots level as at the government level. We want all schools to include, as part of their required curriculum, classes on nonviolent conflict resolution, emotions, relationships, and tools for coping with emotional challenges. Not just at the theoretical level but also with practical exercises, where children learn through direct experience to better deal with their own inner experiences. This will help them not just in their private lives but also later in their professions and as members of society. Whether or not you are a parent, but particularly if you are one (or a teacher), our education system needs a radical review in this respect. As it is today, it is an unbalanced system that can produce only the unbalanced results that we see in our civilization.

The Ecology of Our Planet

In this section, I will make what may seem like a diversion from the topics of this book. You will see why I bring it up here and how it ties to this book's theme. It is a good example of how our emotional health has widespread repercussions in everything that we do on this planet—including the planet itself, our one and only home.

You may have heard this point before, and indeed it couldn't be a better example about our priorities: it is easier to have children than to get a driver's license. We like to think that we are so advanced and so above nature's laws, but when it comes to reproducing, we are as wild as any other animal species on this planet. And because we do not follow pre-established programs, like animals do, we are not subject (not in as an immediate form, as animals are) to the balancing forces of nature. In nature, as an example, when one species proliferates too much, its food source will become scarce (due to overconsumption by the trespassing species). Eventually, this will lead to a return to a balanced sustainable ecosystem. With us, technology allows us to break from these automatic mechanisms. Even so, in the end we cannot escape the consequences of creating such an imbalance on our planet.

In 2003, a group of researchers founded the Global Footprint Network, a nonprofit organization with the objective of providing tools and programs for a sustainable future for us on our planet.[92] The researchers in this organization created the metric called Earth Overshoot Day[93], previously known as Ecological Debt Day. What the researchers do is calculate the amount of resources that planet Earth can replenish every year and compare that with what we humans consume. Earth Overshoot Day corresponds to the day in the calendar year when we have already consumed all the resources that our planet can give us for that year. Ideally, we want that day to fall on the first of January of the next year, or even later. Let me give you a very simple analogy with money. Say that you have one hundred dollars in your bank account that gives ten dollars in interest every year, which you use as your sustenance. Ideally, what you want is to spend no more than ten dollars per year so that that you can keep on living from that bank account. By the end of the year, if you spent only nine dollars, you would have been able to save an extra dollar, and your bank account would have grown to $101. If you had spent ten, you keep things even. And, if you spent the ten dollars by July, you would have to withdraw more from the savings account to cover for the rest of the year than if you had spent the same ten dollars by, say, November. It's exactly the same way with the resources that our Earth can replenish every year—the ten dollars in our analogy. Until 1970, our planet was able to provide enough resources to meet our demands. From then on, we have been consuming resources at a faster rate than Earth can provide for us. Here is the graph provided on their sister website, www. overshootday.org.[94]

---

[92] See www.footprintnetwork.org.

[93] See www.overshootday.org.

[94] *Earth Overshoot Day*, Earth Overshoot Day, https://www.overshootday.org. Accessed December 13, 2018.

Earth Overshoot Day
1969-2018

1 Earth

1.7 Earths

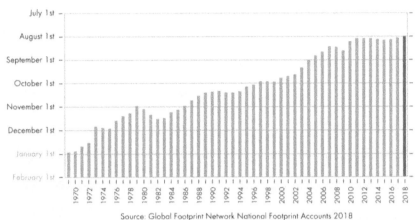

Source: Global Footprint Network National Footprint Accounts 2018

Because of the way in which the graph was generated, we want the overshoot day to fall in January or later of the next year, marked in lighter color at the bottom of the vertical axis—as it almost happened in 1969 and 1970. In 1971, we fell short because we consumed the renewable resources by December 21. From December 22 until the end of that year, we used extra resources that our planet Earth had. In 1972, we overconsumed another eleven days earlier, by December 10. In 2018, we consumed one year's worth of renewable Earth resources by August 1. By the end of 2018, we will have consumed the equivalent of 1.7 Earth years of resources. If the trend continues, in 2030, we'll consume two Earths in one year. What you need to understand for this case is that contrary to the games that we play with money (like printing more of it), there are no tricks that we can do here. At this rate, we will be depleting the resources of the Earth, and there will not be anything else to replace them. (We are not, in the current civilization in which we live, technologically speaking anywhere near bringing more from other planets to sustain the global population.) As you can see, this is unsustainable. We are walking directly into an abyss. What part of this, and so many other similar statistics, don't we understand? Among the four factors[95] that they mention on their website that

---

[95] *Earth Overshoot Day*, Earth Overshoot Day, https://www.overshootday.org/newsroom/media-backgrounder. Accessed December 13, 2018. The four factors are (1) how much we consume, (2) how efficiently products are made, (3) how many of us there are, and (4) how much nature's ecosystems are able to produce.

are contributing to this overconsumption, one of them is overpopulation. The fact is that we can implement changes in lifestyle and implement more efficient technologies. Yet we simply can't continue reproducing at the rate we are going. "We are using more ecological resources and services than nature can regenerate through overfishing, overharvesting forests, and emitting more carbon dioxide into the atmosphere than forests can sequester."[96] We are ravaging our planet, and overpopulation is a problem.[97] Nature solves overpopulation very quickly and efficiently. We have not.

How It Ties to the Topics of This Book

In the 1960s, psychiatrist John Bowlby developed what is known as attachment theory. Simply put, it tells us that children who receive consistent loving parenting develop secure relationships with them, which later become a successful model in their relationships with everyone else in their lives. Intuitively, it makes sense. There is much more to it, of course.[98] This model is still widely used today to assess how well a child is developing emotionally. The reason that I am bringing this up at this point is because as intuitive as the concept is, it entails more than meets the eye. In order to create a secure type of attachment with their children, parents need to have quality time with them. This means being present physically and emotionally while they are growing up, which means that they need to spend time with each one of their children and connect with them so that they can understand their physical, emotional, and mental needs. Then parents must be available to fulfill them. A parent who comes from work and starts to play with his child, but who is still thinking about his work issues, is not present. He might be in the same room, yet he will miss all the clues that his daughter is giving him. He will miss the different ways that she uses to communicate her needs and events. Ideally, for that period of time with each of their children, cell phones need to be turned off. With our current demanding lifestyles, how many parents are doing this? How many are willing to truly invest (i.e., give this type of

---

[96] "Ecological Footprint," Global Footprint Network, https://www.footprintnetwork.org/our-work/ecological-footprint/. Accessed December 13, 2018.

[97] As you can see, the argument that there is still a lot of physical space on our planet is simplistic and naïve.

[98] Later, it was enhanced by the work of psychologist Mary Ainsworth and her "strange situation" experiment. There is ample information about this theory and experiment in books and on the Internet.

necessary time) in this twenty-plus-year enterprise? On top of that, after reading about the information that I have given you about the impact that parents have from before conception, and the impact of the programs that they transfer to their children, how many children would you think a couple can responsibly bring into this world (i.e., create secure attachments in each of them) within the demands of our current pace of life? Maybe two or three? Of course, this is not about setting a fixed formula. I personally think that after three children, under any lifestyle the quality of parental education starts to diminish. This is independent of how much money parents may have (nannies may be a wonderful help, but they are not a replacement for the parents). It is simply too big an enterprise for a couple to still achieve good results. Let me point out that to be able to achieve this goal, parents must also attend to their very own needs (besides work and all the daily chores of our lives) for their sake and the sake of their children. Parents need to be fulfilled physically, emotionally, intellectually, and transcendentally in their own lives so that they can be the role models that we are talking about here. Even without children, maintaining our own needs as individuals is already a challenge.

No government can keep up with the demands of a nonstop growing population. We can easily see examples of this in our big cities. By the time a new freeway has been put in place to alleviate a past traffic congestion, there is already the need for more. This is simply talking about the physical demands of our society. Look also at the social implications of overpopulation, which comes down to the level of family and its members. High fertility rates (big families) are associated with lower levels of quality of life, which is a direct reflection of how (un)empowered parents are. From the perspective of the programs in our unconscious that we have been talking about in this book, unempowered parents will transmit unempowered programs to their children. Thus, for every two unempowered parents, there will be a new set of four or more unempowered individuals. Each of them will in turn generate new sets of families with most likely similar (unempowered) socioeconomic status. All of them require more social assistance in one way or another. As you can see, this becomes a problem that grows exponentially. From an economic point of view, no system of government can keep up with such a social burden. Then there are all the other implications on the quality of life for all these individuals and how it affects society emotionally (with yet another set of economic repercussions).

The imbalances that we see at all levels on our planet and our societies are a reflection of the imbalances that we carry as individuals. It is crucial that we become aware of the need of a more conscientious approach to the very core structure of our civilization: the family. With knowledge and understanding, while putting in place practices that enable individuals to live harmonious lives, we will be able to create the corresponding sustainable environment for our children with the added benefit of automatically becoming part of the solution to the social and ecological problems that we have created. A beautiful, immediate consequence is living in balance with our planet. Because everything is interrelated, everything starts to fall in place.

Our Family System

In order to drive a car, you must pass tests that demonstrate theoretical knowledge and practical abilities. To take on the responsibility of conceiving a new human being and providing him or her with the appropriate physical, emotional, intellectual, and transcendental needs during approximately twenty years so that he or she becomes an empowered, empathic individual, there is nothing that is required from the future parents. I understand it is an intrinsic right to have our own families. That is how it should be. Even so, we certainly have to become more aware of the need to properly prepare future parents for this major project in their lives. It's a project that will have repercussions not just for them but for the society in which they live and our civilization as a whole.

Nowadays, when future parents talk about having children, what comes to their minds is how well they are going to provide for them (that is, financially speaking), what schools they will go to, what extra activities (if any) they should do, and more. Of course, these are all part of the considerations that need to be thought out. And if one of them expresses nervousness about becoming a parent, then family and friends will step in encouragingly: "Don't worry. You'll do fine. Yeah, things happen, but you will figure out what to do. That is how we all did it, and here we are." Nice. But it reads more like, "Don't worry, (hopefully) you'll do fine. Yeah, things happen (we don't know why), but (somehow) you will figure out what to do. That is how we all did it (how else could we have done it?), and here we are (carrying our internal struggles, surprised by the unexpected turns that life gave us and still having no idea about why things happen the way they do)." We have no excuses today for this implicit behavior. We already have knowledge and tools to effect a major leap in how to better prepare for the journey of being future parents. I already talked about the emotional learning that needs to be an integral part of our educational system. That would give everybody a more solid base to understand and be more aware of their own behaviors. It's a great first step for everyone. For prospective parents, though, we need more. Governments, local communities, and private practices need to offer counseling workshops with, at a minimum, the following crucial objectives.

1. Today we don't include emotional education in our schools, and so this needs to be the basis on which these courses start: comprehensive education about how emotions work in them as adults. Also, how they work during the growing years of kids. This understanding is critical, as I have shown in this book.
2. Assess how solid the relationship is between the couple. In other words, this is not just about the emotional state of an individual anymore but also how these two in particular have bonded, as well as their capacity to confront and resolve conflicts as a team. Also, reassess how committed they are in the long run. They are going to embark (ideally together), on a twenty-year project.
3. Present them with a comprehensive set of different scenarios that they will have to confront with their children—a preview of things to come. Children introduce new dynamics that are different from those between the two adults. This will be a good way to evaluate how well prepared they are to deal with them. It will also bring to the surface the different parenting styles that each of them most likely has. It is quite common that couples with an otherwise good relationship go into conflict when dealing with how to parent their children, with the risk of causing serious damage to an otherwise healthy interaction between them. In this case, there would be a double negative effect inflicted on the children: two different parenting styles that cause confusion in them, plus the rift between the two adults who ideally would want to present a solid emotional base that their children need for healthy development.

These workshops need to be highly encouraged and known to everybody, like the concept of doing physical exercise in relationship to our health.

We want to change our current mode of becoming a parent, which nowadays is simply by default, into a mode of becoming a parent by design.

The design takes a conscious approach to deciding whether the couple is truly ready to have kids, how many kids to have, having the knowledge that this enterprise implies, and the tools for emotional growth and effective conflict resolution. These ideas could take some time to manifest as concrete actions, and you as a couple could start on your own initiative. I would suggest you first take a look at yourselves as individuals. Take a look at how you are doing in your own lives so far. If you feel negative or insecure about anything, transform that program (if necessary with a practitioner) so that your children will not inherit it or suffer from the limitations that it imposes on your behavior. These are unconscious processes, and you cannot cheat the system. The benefits of doing these processes are multiple.

1. By transforming your limitations, you are improving your own life, which automatically translates into giving your children a better one. You empower yourselves to live the life that you truly want. What an example for your young ones! It is a win-win situation for everybody in the family.
2. By doing these personal transformation processes, you will understand yourselves very well. You will see how these programs work, How powerful they are, and how challenging the transformation process can be some times. This is an amazing personal experience that will enrich how you see life—and equally important, how you see others. You will develop more empathy for every human being, including your own children, because you will know more than ever what they are going through internally. This will help you understand even your "enemies." You will know that their behavior is simply limiting programs, as all of us have. They are suffering too.
3. By doing these processes, you will perceive much more clearly how society has conditioned you to believe in so many things that are arbitrary and very limiting. Clear examples of this arbitrariness are the "boys don't cry" and "girls don't laugh" types of expressions that we still hear today everywhere. You will start to question our current paradigm more and more. When parents have the courage to question themselves and act upon honest answers, their interactions with their children will be more congruent with the positive consequences that I mentioned earlier.
    They will become living examples, showing us that in spite of any limitations that we may have, we are not condemned by them. We can transform ourselves. That's one of the most empowering messages that any child can have. It is not about being perfect; it is about our capacity to grow and live our dreams in the midst of challenges.

Parents are the biggest point of potential change in our civilization.

They are more so than politicians, more than any other influencers in our society. I am not discounting the work of these other groups of individuals. Nevertheless, conscious parents, by transforming themselves, automatically pass that transformation to their children. Just by doing that, they are already transforming our society.

Besides engaging in these personal transformations, parents want to keep studying and participating in courses and workshops about family dynamics, children's development, psychology, and more. Having children is a long-term enterprise. Similarly, when you start your own business, you keep investing in it—not just by showing up at work but also by studying the new related technologies, new strategies, and emerging markets, trends.

The Adult Experiences Component

For a person in her mid twenties the faculty of reasoning is fully developed, and the person has reached physical maturation. Now the filtering effect of this faculty is active in full capacity. Does this mean that there will not be any more new programs being created in her unconscious? Don't we as adults change anymore? Of course we do. In fact, we can change quite a bit. So, how does this happen? There are certain factors that, when one or more of them is present during an event that the person is going through, will create new programs or transform existing ones. Most of the factors that I will mention here were defined by Charles Tebbets in his book *Self-Hypnosis and Other Mind Expanding Techniques*.[99] I will further expand the list, marked with asterisks.[100]

1. **Conscious Initiated Factors**:
   a. First-time experiences*
   b. Explicit repetition*
   c. Willpower*
2. **Nonconscious Initiated Factors:**
   a. Implicit repetition*
   b. Authority
   c. Identification with your "tribe"
   d. Emotionally intense event
   e. Trance

Conscious Initiated Factors

These factors, as its name implies, are initiated by decisions made by you, the conscious. It's that simple.

First-time Experiences

Let's say that an adult man decides to try river rafting for the first time in his life. As much as he may have heard and read about it, he hasn't lived that adventure. There is nothing in his unconscious yet on how to classify that activity from a direct experience. Therefore the faculty of reasoning does not have anything to operate upon, except from associated learnings. If they allow him to go ahead, he will try it. Once he tries it, and if he enjoys it, his unconscious will create the program "river rafting: positive experience, fun, engage." This program will regulate his behavior from then on whenever he is offered the opportunity to go and do it again. He will want to go. Of course, he will reject future invitations if it turned out that he did not like it. Every time anyone (whether child or adult) has a brand-new experience, a new program is created in the unconscious. Children are just starting with physical life, and so essentially everything is new to them. What happens in the case of adults is that because of all the experiences that the person has had in her life,

---

[99] Charles Tebbets, *Self-Hypnosis and Other Mind Expanding Techniques*, London: Westwood Publishing Co., 1997, 20–22.
[100] Tebbets talks about repetition in general as one of the factors. I went further and divided this concept into explicit and implicit repetition.

1. The rate of truly new experiences diminishes as years pass.
2. New experiences are assessed, judged, and filtered by pre-existing programs.

In the case of this man, if he doesn't like physical activities at all, he may very well reject the first-time invitation to try it. In this case, a negative limiting program is precluding him from having new adventures in life. For most adults, as a result of what they have been through in life, they have more negative programs piled up that inhibit them from trying new things. This is the taming effect that I talked about earlier in the section about adolescents. When there are too many limiting programs, the novelty and creative spark that the person had in adolescence disappears. To be more precise, it is still there, but it is covered by the clouds of negativity. Unfortunately, this is so common in adults that it gives birth to expressions like "Old dogs don't learn new tricks." And in the case that this man is not too keen on physical activities but accepts to try it, there is already a predisposition to not liking river rafting. This is the information filtering effect.

Still, after having the experience, his unconscious will create the corresponding program, which could be one way or another. From then on, going river rafting adds new memories, not new programs. What can happen is a reclassification of the program if the experience of the activity radically changed. If he initially liked rafting, but on a subsequent trip he fell and hit a rock, the experience might have been so unpleasant that he will not do it anymore (river rafting = dangerous to his unconscious).

Another way in which preexisting programs filter new activities in adults is by prioritizing and categorizing. As an example, in my case I love hiking. Still, as much as I enjoy nature, I am not interested in doing, say, mountain climbing. Hiking fills in my "joy of nature and physical exercise" category. And, even though I would very likely enjoy mountain climbing, I also have other priorities in my life that make me decide to not take time to learn how to do it. In adolescents, they are just starting to fill in all these categories. Don't confuse this as not having spark as adults. Because of our previous experiences, we are more selective in what we do, yet that doesn't mean not having passion in what we pursue.

Explicit Repetition

When you are learning a new sport, what do you do? You go out and practice. Learning a new physical activity is also programming of the unconscious. As you practice, your unconscious learns the new patterns of movements, and your performance improves. You decided to learn that activity and take the time to practice—that is, repeat over and over each of the movements until you master them. You have programmed your unconscious as an adult or at whatever age you are doing this.

Another example that is a classic in behavioral change is affirmations; I touched upon them earlier. The idea behind this practice is that you write or mentally repeat a certain phrase (or phrases) that affirms what you want to accomplish. You do this every day for a minimum of three weeks, which is the time that it takes for the new neuronal circuit to take hold. There are certain rules about how these phrases need to be constructed so that they are more effective (always in the affirmative, in present tense, etc.). I personally use them and have for a long time. Affirmations do work. Just remember, this is the conscious affirming of something. If the unconscious has a program that strongly disagrees with that affirmation, it is going to be very difficult for you to achieve the results that you expect in a reasonable amount of time. Thus, you need to be very aware of how you use this technique. If you can feel how "impossible" that goal seems to be for you, then I suggest you consider two alternatives: (1) divide that goal into smaller, more reachable pieces, and (2) do a mind transformation process to eliminate the blocks that are in the way. An affirmation is also a resolution, like starting a diet or quitting a habit.

You may have heard about the movie *The Secret*,[101] which came out in 2006. The essence of this movie is that you need to keep mentally focusing on what you want in order to bring that into reality. Keep your thoughts in the direction of the goal—essentially, affirmations. The movie was an instant success because it seemed to offer the magic formula to achieve anything that we desire. *The Secret* is correct. What happened, though, was that as much as it was a huge success, after some time you started to hear disappointment in many people who tried to apply that "magic" formula. There were mainly two factors that contributed to this disappointment. The first one is what I have been talking about here. For example, you have been in a very tight financial situation most of your life, and you want to get out of it. You start to affirm (and visualize) "I am a millionaire." It is very unlikely that you will have a chance to convince your unconscious to cooperate because it has very strong limiting programs that are screaming that such a thing is never going to

---

[101]   *The Secret*, Rhonda Byrne executive producer, Drew Heriot director, Prime Time Productions, 2006.

happen. Your affirmations are going to have very little effect. People thought that simply by doing affirmations, it would get them there. It's not that simple, and now you understand better. Use them intelligently, with this knowledge that you have now. I do recommend watching that movie; it will inspire you to create the changes that you want in your life. It's a good starting point.

Regarding the second factor related to why so many people felt disappointed at the results of applying the movie's theme, I will talk about in the transpersonal factors of the personality. It has to do with how aligned your resolutions are with what you really came to do in this physical world. More on this later.

If this methodology is something that calls your attention, use it. The beauty of it is that it is very easy to apply (paper and pen is what you need, at the most), very convenient (do it whenever it is easiest for you in your daily schedule), and cheap (you do it yourself). What it does require is consistency. You need to do it daily—no exceptions. Otherwise, you need to restart your three-week cycle. Do it once a day at minimum, every single day. Nowadays, there are even apps that you can download that help you accomplish this. If you are going to do them, I do recommend that you learn about the best way to construct your phrases; it will make them more effective. As an adult, this is a technique that you can use to change the programming in your unconscious and therefore your personality.

Willpower

I mentioned this aspect when I introduced the concept of the conscious mind, and I am touching on it again under our current context. Notice how little children, in their early years before the programming of their parents start to take effect, don't exercise willpower. If they don't like something, they simply refuse it. They follow what they feel. The extensive use of willpower nowadays is more the result of programming than anything else—in fact negative, limiting programming. When you stay at a job that you don't like because it is the "responsible thing to do," you are applying a willpower that is the result of limiting programming. It is considered to be part of the conscious because it results from applying the faculty of reasoning to a concept that we have in our minds. Continuing with the example I just gave you, it is your reasoning that tells you that staying in that job is the most logical, sensible thing to do even though your heart clearly tells you otherwise. What you really want to do is follow your heart.

How can you apply willpower to change your personality? Let me give you examples where it is the main mechanism for transformation. Let's say that you know that you are very afraid of public speaking, and you have had this fear for a long time. Your boss asks you to give a public speech. Because it is your job, you go ahead and end up doing it. If you were able to give the speech and everything went well, then fantastic. Out of this experience, you showed your unconscious that public speaking is okay. You reprogrammed it, and thus as an adult, you changed your personality. Next time you have to do another one, you will feel more confident. You are on your way to liberation from that fear. On the other hand, if (precisely because you were so tense) your speech did not go well—you froze at one point, or you got confused in one of your topics—now you have retraumatized yourself even more. The next time is going to be even worse. This is the risk of applying willpower. In some way, it is a "brute force" method. You, the conscious, are fighting" against programs in your unconscious. Because of the power of the unconscious, this is not a good strategy. It may work, yet it may also leave you in worse shape than that you were before the event. Another similar situation could be a fear of heights. You could force yourself to get close to the edge on top of a building …

So, what to do in cases like this? I understand that there are times when we "have to do what we have to do." If your boss just asked you to do the speech with no previous warning, you have not even had time to prepare. Here is where, if you had a way to calm down your unconscious, you would be at a great advantage when facing challenges like this in life. This is what I will talk about later in the book, when I give you an example of a technique that you can use on your own to do this. You would go to your office (or conference room, or even the restroom if necessary), apply that technique, and in this way greatly increase your chances that the experience will be a positive one. If the speech is due in a couple of days or weeks, now you can make a decision. If you feel nervous, but because of the time that you have to prepare, you feel that you can handle it, then great. On the other hand, you may already know that public speaking put you in panic mode; no matter how well prepared you are, once you are in front of the audience, the world crumbles.

If this is the case, and once you have understood the information in this book, then do the following. First, you don't need to bring yourself further down by feeling terrible about this; you simply know that it is a program in your unconscious that you can change. That is all. Second, either you apply a personal transformation technique yourself, or if necessary, you make an appointment with a practitioner. One way or another, you transform that limitation. Out of this experience,4 you will be more empowered than ever because you will have proven yourself that not only there is ultimately nothing wrong with you, but also you have the power and the tools to face anything that comes across in your life. Beautiful! This is what life is about. Now you will feel empowered to live the life that you truly want.

If you have the option to transform a limiting program via a mind transformation process instead of applying willpower, always do it.

In general, I do not recommend willpower as the main way to transform your personality.

Nonconscious Initiated Factors

In these cases, the transformation is initiated by external circumstances that are beyond the decisions that you, the conscious, make.

Implicit Repetition

It's easy to understand through examples.

Blasting political propaganda: You may have seen old films that depicted totalitarian regimes blasting their political agendas through loudspeakers in the streets. Why were they doing that? Because it worked, and they knew it. The people in the streets, where the speakers where located, did not have to be consciously listening. That message, through repetition, got to their unconscious. If some of them really disliked the regime, then that propaganda probably had the opposite effect because it triggered their programs of disapproval. Still, for the majority of the population the message was implanted. It's a classical example of brainwashing.

Moving to new cultures: This mechanism is also in place when we adapt to new circumstances. This is indeed a very positive side of it. Say you move to a different country where the customs differ quite a bit from where you came from. At the beginning, everything seems strange to you. You feel awkward and uncomfortable. As time passes, you start to get used to the new environment. Things that were weird before may become enjoyable. To put it this way, you assimilate this new culture because by living in it, the culture repeats itself upon you. And you adapt, it becomes the new normal. This will happen not only with respect to their customs and behavior but also with your taste with respect to food and the new cultural aesthetics. As a personal anecdote, when we first moved to New Mexico, my wife found strange that the skull and horns of cows are used for ornamental purposes in so many places in the Southwest. One year later, she likes them so much that she is "threatening" to hang one above our bed headboard (which my own programming still resists, as much as I do like them otherwise). As you can see, our personal tastes have also been programmed by the environment. This occurs by itself, by living in it implicitly. Your unconscious creates new programs and also changes old ones as a result of this mechanism.

Religious/spiritual rituals: Take for example the strings with beads ("prayer beads") that you find in so many religions. How are they used? You use the beads to keep track of how many times you have repeated one or more prayers. You, the conscious, are simply thinking about praying to your particular god. You are not thinking about programming in any way when using this to practice your particular religion. Why do you think this is so prevalent in so many religions? Their leaders knew that this works. When you repeat and repeat those prayers, you are programming yourself. You will become more adept at that particular religion. From the particular religion logistics, this ensures that their followers will remain followers. To the person practicing that faith, it feels that he is more devoted. However, the real reason for that repetition is to ensure that the person will remain within that faith. This could be viewed as positive or negative, depending on your particular point of view. Simply understand that it is programming of your mind.

The media: TV, the radio, and public displays. The public displays that you pass on your way to work and back home. These leave an imprint in your unconscious. Remember that your unconscious is collecting an immense amount of data about your surroundings that you, the conscious, are not even aware of. If at one time you are considering buying a product related to one in a public display that you pass every day, your decision will be influenced by that display. It works because we are programmable machines. The big corporations know this very well. Their marketing departments are full of experts on the psychology of the mind. It is relatively easy for them to predict your behaviors once they get hold of your purchasing habits.

For instance, simply by noticing what a woman is buying, they can predict reasonably well whether she is pregnant, even if she is not buying anything related to pregnancy or babies. And many of them will customize the coupons that they send to their customers according to their shopping patterns. You think that they print coupons by the millions and send them to everyone all the same. Not necessarily. Without realizing it, you may be getting your own customized coupons. You can read about this in the book *The Power of Habit* by Charles Duhigg.[102] In the book, Charles mentions the case where a father complained to a company because they were sending his daughter, who was still in high school, all kinds of pregnancy product coupons. He went to the local store manager saying, "Are you trying to encourage her to get pregnant?" Afterward, he went back home and shared this with the rest of the family. The truth came out, and that was how he found out that his teenage daughter was actually pregnant.

This is not a criticism to companies, marketing, or sales. They are tapping into your habits. Today, with the added power of analytics that comes with the Internet, that increases sales. My point is to show you that we are indeed experiencing this physical universe through a biological programmable machine, our bodies. It is a machine. It is extremely easy for a company with a decent marketing department to predict your behavior. And as easy as it is to predict your patterns of behavior, it is even easier to manipulate you into believing or doing something. That is the power of the media. I want to make you aware of how your mind and body work so that you can really start to take control of your life. You have the capacity to master your behavior. First, you need to understand what is really going on within you. Then, you must increase your level of consciousness by transforming your limiting programs. This way, you will start to liberate yourself from your automatic, predictive behaviors that lead to easy manipulation. This is *your* responsibility.

Companies pay a lot of money to put ads through the media companies, especially TV, because of its added visual effect. They know that every time you watch or hear your favorite program, you will be exposed to their ads. Even if you stand up to go and get something from the fridge, that ad will go into your unconscious. Because of the unconscious's capacities and because of repetition, you are being programmed. This applies to not just ads. The type of programs that you watch, whether news or otherwise, also affect your mind. If you keep watching negative news day after day, you will inevitably come to the conclusion that this is a dangerous neighborhood, city, country, or world. From here you will make all kinds of decisions, from the personal (do I need to buy a gun?) to deciding who is going to be the next leader of your country. If you think that this is a dangerous world, the candidate for

---

[102] Charles Duhigg, *The Power of Habit: Why We Do What We Do And How to Change*, London: Random House Books, 2013, 196.

your country's leadership that will resonate with you will be the one who talks about creating a stronger army to destroy enemies. The negative events are happening, of course. Nevertheless, how balanced is the vision that you are getting from simply absorbing this type of news? The everyday newscasts do not give a balanced view of reality. Why? This is also related to the information in this book. Your unconscious's main concern is your survival. Anything that is perceived as threatening will call your attention. That is why the newscasts are, for the most part, about negative news and not positive ones. They grab your attention. They grab audiences that will watch the ads, which profit the company. It is a perfect socioeconomic machine, completely sustained by the natural inclinations of your mind. It is amplified by the fact that it is easier to manipulate you given the more negative programs you have. It becomes a self-sustaining circle, where negative newscasts generate more negative programs in your unconscious, which in turn make you pay more attention to them.

You need to transform yourself to have positive psychological resources. They give you the inner power to make your own decisions.

This is independent of what the rest of the world is saying.

Finally, naturally, the same goes for violence in the programs you watch. The more you watch violent programs, the more violence becomes normal to your unconscious, with all the consequences that that type of thinking entails.

Authority

Generally speaking, when you are ill, you go to the doctor. You do so because you believe that she knows something that you don't, and she can heal you. She is the authority in this topic. Once she has examined you, she will give you the results and consequences of your illness. You will accept what she says. Notice what happened in a situation like this. Because she is the one who knows and you don't, unconsciously you think, "I am not in a position to question what she is telling me."

When you interact with something or someone that you perceive as an authority, your faculty of reasoning stops working.

And this is the key here. If the faculty of reasoning stops working, then it means that it is not doing that filtering effect anymore. It is not discriminating about what or what not to let into your unconscious because it just turned off. Now your unconscious will install new programs according to the information that is freely flowing into it—exactly how it happened when you were a little child. As you can see, this is very easy to understand once you know how your mind works. With respect to our example with the doctor, there are several points to clarify here. A doctor has the legal and ethical obligation to tell you what the consequences of your illness are. You need to understand that not all of those consequences necessarily have to apply to you. You need to take responsibility about how to process the information that he is giving you. Get a second opinion and study your illness. Now your faculty of reasoning is functional. Then you will be in a better position to determine what to do about it and what attitude to take about its consequences. This applies not only to individuals but also to institutions, including the media, as I talked about earlier. The media has the power to influence (i.e., program) you not just because of repetition but also because of its intrinsic power as an authority figure in the minds of the people. When you watch the news from just one source, its anchors become gurus to your unconscious, and you will align more and more with their perspective that they inevitably bring to whatever it is that they are reporting.

Questioning is a basic practice that empowers us in life.

Question with an open mind, of course. Otherwise, questioning becomes a destructive practice that leads to paralysis. It is an art that requires balance.

Another very clear example of authority, as a mechanism of mental programming, is the so-called gurus and spiritual leaders. Today, besides the representatives of the different traditional religions, in our new age of spirituality there are lots of them. And people simply follow them with no questioning at all because these gurus are the ones "who know." That is how we have seen in the news when one of these gurus gives the order for mass suicide, and his followers comply. Their programming has become so strong that it even overrides the basic survival mechanism of the unconscious. Study with a lot of different teachers. Get the best out of them. Studying the different philosophies gives you a wider panorama of possibilities. My personal experience has been that no single teacher has all the answers.

Have the inner power to trust your own heart when it comes to deciding something that is as personal as the vision that you have of life and beyond.

This applies also to traditional religions. Have the courage to study several of them. Decide for yourself, not just because your parents told you so. And parents, do you have the courage and confidence in the guidance that you are providing to your children to show them some of the many options and then trust them to choose on their own?

In general, when you start to idolize anything or anybody, that should be a red flag. When you become a fan of anything or anyone, you need to become aware of why that is happening. Fan is the first stage to becoming a fanatic (as the word itself shows). It is wonderful to admire the great actions that other people take in their lives. That is, and should be, one of the many sources of inspiration that motivates us to do our own great things in turn. If this is the case, great; that means that you feel that you have the inner resources to express your own greatness. On the other hand, the fans that you see at concerts or at TV and movie awards, screaming and crying at the sight of their idols, are doing so because they see in them something that they believe they lack in themselves (recognition, money, talent). More important, they believe they don't have the capability of achieving that level. This is a limiting program.

Identification with Your "Tribe"

This factor explains why we are intrinsically a social species. Survival is the main objective of the unconscious, and belonging to a group has the added benefit of the extra protection that it entails. We had more chances to survive against predators because we formed groups. Also, grouping allowed a concerted effort for a more effective hunt. Living together increased our chances for survival. Our unconscious has an intrinsic, biological tendency to belong to a social group. As I mentioned, this is a biological program—hence our towns and (very big) cities. In our own personal lives, we have the need to have our groups of friends, and the need to belong to more or less well-defined organizations. This is natural in all of us. People who live isolated from others have very strong limiting programs ("people are dangerous/annoying," "you can't trust people," etc.) that make them live that way. It is by interacting with others that we experience the biggest growth in our lives not only as individuals but also as a society. To say, for example, that someone is shy because that is her personality may be true, but it reflects inner limiting programs that are the cause of that shyness. There is nothing wrong with being more introspective than extroverted. That is what brings diversity and richness for all of us. The point is that these tendencies do not need to be so extreme as to become limitations in our behavior. Even if you are more of the introspective type (I personally am), you want to be able to have a group of friends that you can relate to and also be able to comfortably interact with other human beings.

Because of this inner need to belong to a group, the more you identify with one, the more your unconscious will do whatever it takes to remain a part of it. It goes to the point where you will stop questioning the groups decisions and simply follow. The mechanism behind this factor is the same as the one for authority. Your faculty of reasoning will stop working when it comes to the decisions that the group makes.

One example is the youth gangs. These youngsters come from either very abusive home environments or places where there is no emotional nurturing at all. There is a huge emotional vacuum in these boys and girls, with very big limiting programs ("If I cannot get love at home, where else?" "If I cannot get love from my parents, then it must be because there is something really wrong with me."). When they find a group that they can relate with, which will be individuals of similar upbringing, this group will be the nurturing environment that they yearn for. In their own way, this is where they will find the love that they never had. And if the leader or the group makes a decision of getting involved in illegal activities (like drugs or robberies), they will follow. Think about it: What is their choice otherwise? To be left at the home where they are being abused? No. And the longer they stay in such a group, the more they will follow whatever the group does. Their faculty of reasoning shuts down in favor of belonging to the group. This factor of belonging to a group combines with the factor of authority that I just talked about, to create a powerful force behind these groups of individuals. It's the same with religious and spiritual groups. The followers (notice what they are called) will follow what the priest or guru says. And the more they identify with the group, the more readily available they will be to do whatever the leader says.

I remember when I was still living in Colombia, South America, in 1982, when Argentina's military junta decided to reclaim the Falklands (Malvinas) Islands. As much as Argentina always claimed the islands to be part of their territory, it was very clear that it was a political maneuver that the military did in order to distract the population from the serious inner political and economic problems that they had at the time. And it worked. Argentineans "forgot" about all the inner troubles and united for their newfound cause. They united as a tribe who identified very clearly and strongly in their cause.

Even the military gained a temporary boost in support. Here is another example of how easy it can be to manipulate groups of people. And so that you can see how far we go with this group identification, I remember reading in the newspapers how Colombians, residing in Argentina at that time, were attacked by who were their very own (Argentinean) friends because the Colombian government did not support that war. Friends you had now became enemies. Colombians became a symbol of an institution (the country) that decided not to be part of the tribe. This is a mild example compared to the genocide that occurred in Rwanda in 1994, when "approximately 800,000 Tutsis and Hutu moderates were slaughtered in a carefully organized program of genocide over 100 days, making history as the quickest killing spree the world has ever seen."[103] As if that were not enough, it is estimated that between 250,000 and 500,000 women were systematically raped.[104] Immaculée Ilibagiza survived that genocide and wrote the book *Left to Tell: Discovering God Amidst the Rwandan Holocaust*. She describes how, while hiding in a cramped bathroom with five other women, she could see the people outside the house who wanted to hunt and kill them.

> It wasn't the soldiers who were chanting, nor was it the trained militiamen who had been tormenting us for days. No, these were my neighbors, people I'd grown up and gone to school with—some had even been to our house for dinner.[105]

This is how we behave, all driven by the programs in our unconscious. This "belonging to your tribe" effect is extremely powerful and widely used by politicians, heads of state, and religious leaders to move the masses in the direction that they want. When combined with the information filtering effect that naturally takes place within groups' ideologies, it becomes the immense power behind the social changes in our societies, whether negative (Nazism, as yet another example), or positive (a very present-day example is the #MeToo movement). Whether positive or negative, be aware of this principle.

---

[103] "The Rwandan Genocide" *United to End Genocide*, http://endgenocide. org/learn/past-genocides/the-rwandan-genocide. Accessed December 13, 2018.
[104] "The Rwandan Genocide," *United to End Genocide*, http://endgenocide. org/learn/past-genocides/the-rwandan-genocide. Accessed December 13, 2018.
[105] Immaculee Ilibagiza, *Left to Tell: Discovering God Amidst the Rwandan Holocaust*, Carlsbad: Hay House, 2006, 77.

The more you identify with a group, the more vulnerable you are to its ideology.

Identification is simply programs with their associated emotional batteries. The more you identify with something, the more that these emotional batteries are charged. You already understand the consequences of this effect on your behavior. Be conscious about the decisions that you make when you identify with a group of any type. I encourage you to observe and question yourself in these situations. You will need strong inner resources to be able to stand on your own if you don't agree with the group's decisions.

Emotionally Intense Event

What happens when you go through an emotionally intense event? It shocks you. Do you reason while you are in shock? No, you don't. That means the faculty of reasoning shuts down—no filter between the unconscious and the external environment. The event will generate programs in you according to how you perceived it at that moment. It's exactly the same way as when you were a child. This will be true at any age. We all have heard or experienced cases that left us marked, even if it was just for a shorter while. My father died in Colombia while I was living in California. I got a call from my mother early in the morning. As a result of the emotional shock, it took me a while to receive a morning call without a jolt. Notice that the event does not need to be short and sudden, as we like to think about emotionally strong events. For example, someone goes through a very traumatic relationship breakup. After the process is finally finished, the person has no interest whatsoever in getting involved in another relationship. This is natural and equivalent to a mourning period that we all need to reintegrate emotionally. However, if the program is strong enough ("Can't trust men/women," "The pain of a relationship is not worth it"), it may very well happen that the person will never again have a relationship. Car accidents, bankruptcies, job losses—these are all kinds of events that occur as adults. This is also the explanation behind that case that I talked about earlier regarding the programs that get generated when a person gets the news about a serious illness in spite of following a healthy lifestyle. Irrespective of lifestyle, such news is a shock to us and puts us in this vulnerable position. If a strong negative event happens to you, notice how you change afterward. There is the potential of you being left with new limiting programs. You will know very quickly whether or not this happened.

Trance

Trance and hypnosis are the same: a single state of focus. There's nothing more to it. It's an example of programming in our daily routine under these circumstances. When you are completely focused on any project, you are so into it that the rest of the world disappears. Time even disappears. You may be reasoning through your project. Even so, because the focus is on that specific subject, the faculty of reasoning is not performing its filtering function on anything else. If you have the radio on while doing the project, the information that you are listening to will go directly into your unconscious (be it adds or news content). Another everyday example: you are watching a movie at the theater or on your TV set, and you really like it. You are totally into it. You are in hypnosis because you are watching only its contents. You are not thinking about anything else. Your faculty of reasoning is turned off. It's exactly the same as in the previous three factors that we just went through. Now you will understand even better why corporations pay the huge amounts of money to put their ads on TV. They know that while you are watching your favorite TV show, you are in hypnosis. Therefore when their ad comes to you, it will go directly to your unconscious, bypassing the faculty of reasoning. With the radio it's the same, but because of TV's visual component, it is even more effective. With the combined mechanism of repetition, the media is an extremely powerful and effective way to program the masses. When you spend your evenings, day after day, glued to all the negative news that the newscasts give, you are being hypnotized with that content. When you regularly watch violent content, you are being hypnotized into that type of realities. This content makes you see life accordingly, changes your behavior, and affects every single decision that you are making in your life.

That does not mean you cannot watch this type of programs for the rest of your life. In the news, I simply look at the main titles to see if there is something new happening (most of the time, the news is a continuous rehashing of the same main event). If there is something that I think is worth reading about, I read it. That is okay. If this becomes a bigger part of your daily routine, you will inevitably be programmed. It's the same as when you leave the news in the background while performing another activity. And let's not forget the hours and hours that children and adults spend on violent video games, in complete hypnosis. Become aware of the information that you consume and its effects on your mind.

On the other hand, precisely because when you are in single focus, your faculty of reasoning narrows down. In hypnotherapy, we take advantage of this to access the programs in the unconscious. In hypnotherapy, traditionally you take the client into trance by a process of relaxation not only physically but also mentally. The mind stops the chattering that it normally has during daily activities. With a quiet mind and the faculty of reasoning greatly reduced, it stops being a barrier between the unconscious and the external environment. The information that is stored there becomes accessible, including the programs that are limiting your behavior. Now you and your practitioner can process them directly. Understand that you are not unconscious. It's the same way that you were not unconscious while driving the car or watching a movie.

During a session, I need to talk to my client so that I can accompany her during the processing of the information that comes to the surface. The client is aware of what is happening. The client can reject my directions if she feels so inclined. Sometimes it does happen that she has difficulty, for one reason or another, to follow certain directions. She will let me know, and then we determine how to proceed. People have this misconception that once they go into hypnosis, they go unconscious, and then they magically wake up as a "new person." If that were really the case, we would have solved all the problems in this world, wouldn't you say? It's not so. Transformation occurs, and you take active part in its processing; you are aware of what is happening.

With this, we complete this section about all the factors that can create new programs in adults. These factors have the same effect on children.

Intrapersonal Components Summary

Here, we also complete the intrapersonal components of our personality. These are the factors that build your personality because of events that occur during the present insertion into the physical world that we call our lives. Here is how our summary looks now.

Intrapersonal components:

- Biology:
  - Body characteristics:
    - Mechanical → Genetics
    - Brain architecture → Genetics → HARD-WIRED PERSONALITY ATTRIBUTES
    - Biological programs → Genetics

    } HARD-WIRED PROGRAMS

- Pre-natal Experiences:
  - Conception
  - In-utero (Psychological)
  - Birth

    } SOFT-WIRED PROGRAMS

  - In-utero (Brain architecture) → Environment → HARD-WIRED PERSONALITY ATTRIBUTES } HARD-WIRED PROGRAMS

- Childhood Experiences
- Adolescence Experiences
- Adult Experiences

  } SOFT-WIRED PROGRAMS

As with the previous two components, soft-wired programs are the main mechanism behind any changes that occur at this stage in our lives, all the way to the end of it, when our Units of Consciousness separate from our bodies and move on to the next stage in their process of evolution. Notice the importance of a good understanding of how these soft-wired programs work (the whole first section of this book). They are a main driver of our behavior that explains most of the actions and reactions in our lives. By far these are the ones that mind transformation processes change.

Besides adding elements to the structures of our personality, transpersonal components also give us an idea of what happens when we are not experiencing a physical insertion. Let's immerse ourselves into their territory, where things get even more interesting because it is here where the nonphysical aspect of us really stands out.

Transpersonal Components

A fundamental premise in this book is that you are not just a physical entity. I talked about the NDE[106] phenomenon, which I encourage you to read about it. In this section, we will see more about why I sustain that premise. In the disciplines of the transformation of the mind, there are different phenomena that point out to components in our personality that seem to be beyond what we have experienced in this particular insertion into this physical world that we call our lives. Notice that I say *seem*. We don't have the capability to verify this scientifically today. Science simply has not advanced enough to be able to

---

[106] Near death experience.

apply in a consistent manner the scientific method to these phenomena. This is no reason to dismiss something that does happen in sessions, with people across all kinds of different cultures, spiritual beliefs, and socioeconomic levels. These type of events have also been recorded throughout the history of humanity. Even if these events do not correspond to the reality that they point to and were simply a construction of our mind, they need to be considered and studied scientifically because from the therapeutic point of view, they heal. That is already enough in itself to study them. Additionally, from the behavioral point of view, they affect how we are, how we see life, and how we respond to it. It's exactly the same as any other of the intrapersonal programs that we have been talking about so far. They are part of your personality. In sessions, these are repeatable, observable phenomena. This is a fact.

The Unit of Consciousness Interventions Component

As the core that the Individualized Consciousness is to all of us, it exerts powerful influences on who we are in a particular insertion. One of the main influences comes through the objectives of your life. I cannot overemphasize the importance of this factor. It is the whole reason that you are here.

The Present Life Objectives

> Every human is born an original, but sadly, most humans
> die copies.
> —Abraham Lincoln[107]

I already gave you an example of a natal regression, with the case of Juan Jose Lopez Martinez and the man who regressed to his mother's womb. I want to make a side point here that's important to this topic. You could say that these regressions are simply creations from the client's mind. Nevertheless, there have been occasions where these events were corroborated. It is common for mothers because of their protective nature to carry secrets about events related to the family, especially their children. Say a client brings up an event during a session where her mother was involved. The client later tells her mother about the session. The mother is astonished to hear about the event because it was something that she kept as a secret

---

[107] He used "men" instead of "humans" in his original quote. I changed it to be more gender encompassing.

all her life. Even though for now there is no way to prove for every single case that these regressions bring to the surface past events that did occur, there are very strong hints that this is the case. It's not just because of what I just mentioned, but also because these hidden events fit very well with the individual's behavior, the rest of his history, and the environment in which he grew up. Because of the logistical challenges, it may take a while before scientists may be willing to take on a methodical study of this phenomenon. I am hopeful it will eventually happen.

When I do a natal regression, I first guide the client to go into the trance state. Once the client is in a deep enough hypnotic state, I give the instructions to his unconscious to go to the time when he was in the mother's womb. In this state, I will be able to explore what happened during the pregnancy. As you saw in Lopez Martinez's case, his client was able to recall the reactions of his parents at the time when they found out that they were going to have another child. I pointed out to you that the fetus would not have been physically developed enough to be able to attribute this type of memories to his brain structures. In other words, at that point in the regression, the unconscious is accessing memories from information that was originally stored in a nonphysical field. Thus once in this deep trance, it is just another simple directive from the practitioner to the client's unconscious to go back to conception, when the client did not even have a body. And in turn, because the practitioner was able to take the client all the way to conception, it is simply one more directive to tell her unconscious to go before conception. There is no physical body to depend on for these memories in all these cases. The unconscious will make accessible the appropriate information according to how deep the trance is (a natal regression will require a deeper state of hypnosis than a regression to a post birth event in our early years). Before conception, what consistently comes out from these sessions is that:

1. We choose the parents that will be best suited to give us the next appropriate physical body and the experiences that we will be looking for in the next insertion into the physical world. Both the parents and their environment will be the perfect fit for the next set of learning that we seek in the next life.
2. We come into this physical life with very explicit objectives. Every one of us—no exceptions—has specific experiences that the unconscious wants to live. There are specific learning that we want to have.

Dr. Michael Newton held a doctorate degree in counseling psychology and was a certified master hypnotherapist. As a hypnotherapist, he regressed his clients to before they came to a physical insertion. Here is a quotation of just a part of what Michael labels Case 25 in his book *Journey of Souls*.[108] As you will read, even in trance, his client shows an easy attitude while explaining his selection of place, parents, and objectives. The Ring that Dr. Newton refers to is the name for the "place," in nonphysical reality, where this selection process occurs.

Case 22: Body and Parents' Selection

Dr. N: All right, move forward. As your time in the Ring draws to a close, give me the details of your probable life selection.

S: I am going to New York to be a musician. I'm still trying to make up my mind between a couple of people, but I think I will choose (stops to laugh) a dumpy child with a lot of talent. His body won't have the stamina of my last one, but I'll have the advantage of parents with some money who will encourage me to practice, practice, practice.

Dr. N: Money is important?

S: I know I sound … grasping … selfish … but there was no money in my last life. If I want to express the beauty of music and give pleasure to myself and others, I need proper training and supportive parents, otherwise I'll get sidetracked … I know myself.

This is just a segment of the whole case, as described in his book. I don't want you to be left with the impression that the only reason for his client to go into that physical insertion was to play the piano. It is all the experiences and challenges that will accompany that selection and that take part in that choice. Still, this is a lighthearted (yet real) example of why this person

---

[108] Michael Newton, *Journey of Souls: Case Studies of Life Between Lives*, St. Paul: Llewellyn Publications, 2003.

chose the place, the parents, and that future body. It will not always be that lighthearted, as I will show in a following case.

This first point that we choose our parents is something that is extremely difficult to accept for someone who grew up in an abusive home. It's even true for many who grew up in homes that were not necessarily "that abusive." We saw that in our class at the academy. This is also a big contention point in my seminars. When I get to this topic in my explanations, people have a very hard time accepting this. What an irony, right? This is how we react when I mention this factor about parents. It says a lot about our ways of raising our children. Nevertheless, for the people who do their homework and process the events that they lived at home (and life in general), they find the pearls of wisdom that were within those experiences. This wisdom is now theirs to take forever in their path of evolution as a Unit of Consciousness. It's a main reason why we come here.

Every single "negative" experience that you have had in your life contains wisdom that you need to learn.

Every single one of them. If you cannot say that from something that you experienced before, then you did not get the lessons from those experiences. It sounds harsh, but I know about this.

Case 23: The Son of a Holocaust Survivor

The programming that I got from my father, a holocaust survivor, is challenging to say the least. That type of traumatic experiences creates highly emotionally charged limiting programs. As a result of his experiences in the concentration camps, here are some of the heavy programs that I inherited and that I have had to process repeatedly in my life (because these are foundational programs).

- Life is dangerous
- People are dangerous
- You cannot trust people
- You have to be vigilant all the time
- It's extremely dangerous to make a mistake (making mistakes can be fatal)
- Everything is a big deal

Seeing and living life with these lenses is already a heavy emotional load. They keep us in a constant, hypervigilant state. It's exhausting and not how we want to be living our everyday lives. These are the programs that explained my mind's dramas that I referred to in the introduction of the book. On top of that, our home environment was one of strict discipline in which we children did not have much to say with respect to what we wanted. We simply did as we were told. Lots of emotions and personal expression were repressed. I could have stayed with the anger and fear in which I grew up and been scornful about their way of being and our upbringing. I could have lived the rest of my life being miserable "because of my fate." Nevertheless, since I was a little boy, I had a very clear feeling in me that this was not supposed to be like this. (This is the Essence's "whisperings," a component on its own of our personality, coming later in the book.) This feeling was the force behind the search for understanding the reality that I was confronting. Lots of studying and lots of transformation processes throughout my life, even during my years as an engineer. With the experiences and lessons that I had while living and seeing life through these lenses, I also learned to understand the pain in others. It taught me empathy and compassion. With my own pain came a deep desire to understand and do something about it, which has taught me about self-empowerment and transcendence. As I mentioned, both my parents were swimmers, and I followed that path for more than fifteen years. That experience taught me the value of consistency and persistency in achieving goals.

Also, I inherited (citing the most relevant one here) an amazing program from my father, which is "I will get ahead one way or another." This is the program that drove him to survive the concentration camps. That program has been within me during the hard times as well. That inner voice kept me going. Once I take a higher perspective, I can see that all my programs have been strategic for the path that I chose in this lifetime. The different components, positive and negative, have contributed to the point where I am today. All of them perfectly set up to push me into going deeper into the aspects of being human, one of the main purposes of my present insertion.

As a side note, this does not mean that I am out of the woods. These programs are foundational in my case, and challenging situations in my present life tend to push me to regress and react as I used to. The difference nowadays is that I have a better power within me to stop and reassess how I am interpreting and reacting to the triggering events. I don't do it perfectly every single time, but I am at a point where I can say that I am beginning to enjoy life in a deeper sense. Not so before. I have come to better understand myself, my parents (my father with his concentration camp experience; my mother, who grew up in Nazi Germany), and others. From this came the need to share my lessons, write this book, and transmit this message. Today, I am grateful to them because they provided the platform that I needed for my own growth in order to become a better person. It's a contract that we all agreed to in nonphysical reality. Thus, notice my perspective to this situation. I am not saying that I am grateful for the suffering I went through. That is not the point. And this does not mean condoning (as an example) abusive parents in any way. On the contrary. The purpose of this book is to eliminate suffering in our lives through understanding and transformation. We are all going through challenging situations because this is where we are in our paths of evolution. People who are born into abusive environments are messengers to all of us about the priorities and perspectives that we as human beings have made of this physical experience. They are doing their individual growth work, and at the same time they are calling on all of us to work together, as a collective, to focus our efforts into a harmonious life for everyone. Understand that this applies equally to the abusers. They are also messengers, and they too are suffering—and immensely. Think about the brutal inner conflicts that this type of parents must have to get to the point of abusing their own children. This goes against the most intrinsic biological programs that we have. Once you process your life experiences at a higher level than the personality (by connecting to your unconscious and your Essence), you get a more encompassing perspective of what it is that you are doing in your own path of evolution. Every situation becomes a platform to launch the positive change needed in this environment that we created for ourselves.

Finally, don't interpret all this as, "We should be looking for drama or pain in our lives, so that we can learn more." First of all, life is not supposed to be painful. Second, don't worry because you will have challenges of your own, and they are part of the current state in our evolution. Simply understand that when you are going through some sort of pain, it is simply because you still have something to learn about the particular situation. You will have learned the lesson when you transformed the negative energy (anger, resentment, hate, etc.) into a positive one (understanding, love).

Once we have learned our lessons, we will come to the point where there will not be suffering in our physical lives.

Evolution is inevitable and unstoppable.

The second aspect that we observe in sessions, when we get to that point when you are making the decision to come back to the physical world, is that you do it with a purpose. You don't show up here just because. Every human being, with no exception, is here to fulfill a set of goals that were determined earlier, in the nonphysical reality. These goals are concrete, as is the example with the client who wanted to be a piano player, and transcendental as well. The following case is from the book *Other Lives, Other Realms: Journeys of Transformation*,[109] written by Karen Joy. Joy was a counseling psychologist for twenty years before she got certified as a Life-Between-Lives^a regression practitioner at Dr. Newton's institute, the Newton Institute (TNI). I will quote this case from her book a little more extensively because it gives you an exquisite illustration of how this person came to choose his life body and circumstances according to his goals for the present insertion.

Case 24: Choosing a Weak Body to Know His True Power

Morris is a white English male who, even though still young in his thirties, has had a body prone to illness, including cancer. He wonders why he chose such a body. Joy regresses him to the point where he was making the body selection, according to his goals for the present insertion. Similar to the previous case (Dr. Newton's), in the regression he goes to the (nonphysical) "place" where this happens. Here you get a better sense of the elegance of this process. In this place, he will be shown four possible body selections and their most likely timelines. This will bring again the issue of free will, which I will address in a following section. Based on all these factors, Morris makes his final selection. Here is the direct transcript from her book.

> The first person he sees is a dark-skinned male of African ancestry. This man looks tall, broad, strong and robust. He will be born in Germany and adopted by white German parents. In addition to the challenges posed by his adoption, he will also be bullied when he goes to school. Because of his strength, he could overcome the challenge of being bullied. Due to his natural physical prowess, he is likely

[109] Karen Joy, *Other Lives, Other Realms: Journeys of Transformation*, Aspley: MediaLuna, 2015.

to become passionate about sport and find solace in his sporting abilities.

Next, Morris sees on the screen a white Caucasian male who will be born in Denmark. This man has a smaller body than the African. He will be very bright and intellectual and his family is very stable. Events will flow smoothly for most of his life. He will eventually face challenges, but these will come much later on.

Now there appears a Caucasian female who would be born in Greece. She is tall with thick, dark hair and a very beautiful face and body. Her father will pass away before she is born and the lack of this bond in her early life will greatly affect her. She will actively pursue intimacy while also fearing it. This will cause her to have many male and female relationships.

Finally, Morris sees a white English male. This man is small and slight. His parents will divorce early and he will not have a good relationship with his stepfather. This body is very sensitive and carries a high potential for illness. Morris sees that this would be a tough life.

Morris pauses, and reflects on the purpose of his life. He wants to create experiences that will enable him to realise his true power. His true power involves more than his physical body and more than his physical will. His true power is intuitive. It requires him to connect with his soul-self and allow this higher energy to shine through him. Once he has achieved a strong connection with his true power, he wants to use this loving light and wisdom to help others come into their true power.

Our lives are about learning and some souls like to proceed quickly in the classroom of Earth life. Morris is one of these souls. He does not choose easy lives. To accomplish his ambitions in this coming life, he needs a body and background that will provide significant challenges.

Morris now evaluates his different choices.

The African faces two significant challenges: being adopted by a white family, and later being bullied at school. However, with such a large powerful body, he might use his physicality to get through. For example, he might be tempted to stand up to people and intimidate them, rather than developing his compassion and wisdom. If he relied on his superior physical strength, he might never awaken to the fact that he is more than his physical body. This would mean that his intuitive abilities would be neither realized nor utilized.

Morris decides that the Danish life would not serve him, either. Being born into a stable family would allow him to easily succeed in the world. The opportunity to develop his intuitive abilities would not appear until late in his life. Morris does not want to waste time. He would prefer to meet some significant challenges earlier in life, and then move quickly towards his goals.

The Greek woman is too pretty. Lacking a strong male role model in her life, she will hide behind her beauty, hoping it will shield her from life's harsher lessons. As a result, she is destined to have many superficial relationships. Morris believes he will be better able to develop his intuitive abilities if he can forge a strong, steady relationship.

Morris chooses the slight English male, believing that a frail body and a fractured family will help him achieve his goals. His guide insists that it will be a very hard life. She asks him if he understands all the implications of this choice.

Morris reassures her that he is pleased with his choice, because he wants to learn quickly. Being sensitive to illness creates risks; it also presents Morris with opportunities to transcend his physical body. His sensitivity offers another advantage: it makes him more open to connecting with his higher soul-self. Morris wants to know his true power. True power is not physical.

After the session, Morris expressed to Joy how well he understood his choice. He was eager to pursue his goals for this physical insertion. And as part of the regression, he was given insights into how to heal his body. This is important because, as I already mentioned, we do not come here to suffer. His illness pushed him to this new understanding. That objective was then accomplished. Now there is no need to keep falling ill. His body does have a weaker structure than others, but with his new understanding and proper care, it will keep a healthy state.

Here you have a new understanding for people who are born with serious deceases or physical handicaps. These are powerful Units of Consciousness who insert themselves into these circumstances to do their own evolutionary work, and also to be messengers about the disharmony that we have created for ourselves on this planet. An inspiring example of this is the story of Lizzie Velazquez,[110] who was bullied as the "ugliest woman in the world." Born with a rare genetic disorder, Lizzie has become one of the great inspirational stories of today. I can only invite you to check her story through her books, videos, and public talks. Behind that persona is a nonphysical entity delivering a powerful message that could not be more relevant today, not just among the young ones but also to the leaders of the world. When we learn to see the entity that is behind the body that it chose to wear in a physical insertion, we will connect in a deeper way with each other. This applies equally to anyone whom the (arbitrary) social standards classify as "ugly," as well as those considered "beautiful." Look at the selection process in the previous case. Beauty was considered a handicap for the purposes of that Unit of Consciousness. Understand that all this is not about judging one condition or another. It is about being able to have a deeper, more meaningful perspective about all of us.

Your nonphysical Essence is interested in evolving, which means getting to the point of being so powerful as to be able to express only unconditional love.

---

[110] Lizzie Velasquez, https://www.lizzievelasquezofficial.com/about. Accessed December 14, 2018.

I can only encourage parents, family, friends, and people in general who are interacting with people with physical disabilities to look for the beauty and wisdom that is behind that interaction. If you can't see it, you have not gotten the message. We do want to help them in their limitations (which is part of the nonphysical contract for those directly involved with them), and science and society must strive to find solutions to our physical problems. This is part of us working together to create a better world for all of us, the individual and collective evolution.

Your life objectives are yours and only yours. It may happen that someone suggested an idea that completely resonated with your heart. That is perfectly fine. Yet you are the one who decides. They just happened to be a messenger.

The purpose of your insertion into the physical world is a major component of your personality.

This explains why there can be such big differences between siblings that come from the same parents. If you stick with just the intrapersonal components, you really don't have a good enough explanation for this. Even the environment cannot explain well enough the contrasting differences that one can see among siblings. What happens with this factor? It's very simple. Let's say that the first child (i.e., Unit of Consciousness) came to be a mountain climber because that is the setting that will provide the experiences and lessons that the Unit of Consciousness wants. This child will be one who, from the beginning, will be more interested in the outdoors and in nature. This child's interest will not be so much toward math, for example. Remember what I said earlier about the difference between preference and dislike. In this case, it is natural for this child not to be interested in math. Because of that, it may very well be that her grades in math will not be as good as, say, geography or physical education. If teachers and parents translate this to "she is not good at math," they implant a limiting program in her unconscious.

The same parents have a second child. This Unit of Consciousness came here to be a scientist working in a lab. How is the personality of this child going to be? Totally different from the first one. This one will prefer to stay indoors and will be more immersed in books of science. Understand that the goals a Unit of Consciousness sets have nothing to do with parents, siblings, or anyone. It is the Unit of Consciousness's decision, according to its own unique path of evolution that it is taking. There is nothing related to genetics or the environment that determines this aspect of the personality. That is what makes each one of us unique, which in turn is what makes invaluable our contribution to the evolution of this universe as a whole. As insignificant as we may feel, we are indispensable. I hope you can see the importance in doing what we came here to do. I cannot overemphasize this.

To live a full life, you have to follow what you set out to do for your physical insertion.

This is one of the great emotional epidemics in our society nowadays. I have done so many sessions on adults who are so frustrated with their jobs. How do you know if you are on the path that you set out to do? Do you have to do a regression? Not really.

You know that you are living your life if you feel passion about what you are doing.

It is that simple, conceptually speaking. I do understand the challenges that it may entail to find it, from my very own personal experience. Through passion and inspiration, your nonphysical Essence is communicating with you about the path that you set out to walk in this particular physical insertion. If you do not feel passion for what you are doing, you will be carrying a continuous inner frustration that affects everything in your life, and you will feel it every day, starting when you first wake up in the morning (because it is one of the moments when you are most connected to your nonphysical Essence). It will affect how you feel about yourself. If you are not following your passion, it is because you did not give yourself permission to do so due to a limiting program in your unconscious. That automatically translates into lower self-esteem. This in turn affects your relationships and whatever it is that you are doing professionally. Any challenge at work feels like a problem, another weight that you will carry on your shoulders. When you feel passion about something, you have challenges, not problems. Here in the United States, for example, we hear so much about how eager people are to retire. The implicit motto is sort of "Grow up, get married, have children, work for retirement, retire, and die." Think about it. Why would you want to retire if you are doing something that you feel passion about? On the contrary, you have to watch yourself so that you keep balance in your life and don't forget about all the other wonderful aspects of life. What does this mean about all the people who are dreaming about retirement, and what does it say about the lives they are living in the moment? They are not satisfied, and they will spend their youth and the prime years of their lives living a life that is not truly theirs. Still, there is no judgment. This is also part of their learning path until they get it and start listening to themselves.

Intuition, Imagination, and Gut Feelings

Contrary to what most people may believe, great ideas, scientific breakthroughs, inventions, and creations have come through anything but reasoning. They have come from those "Aha!" moments that everybody has experienced. Here is an example of Einstein describing one of these moments: "I was sitting in a chair at the patent office at Bern when all of a sudden a thought occurred to me: If a person falls freely he will not feel his own weight. I was startled. It impelled me toward a theory of gravitation."[111] The "all of a sudden" moment that Einstein refers to was not the result of reasoning. It simply "came to him."

Creative ideas may also come from dreams. Nobel Prize laureate Otto Loewi dreamed about the experiment which would prove his idea that nerve impulses are chemically transmitted.[112] The faculty of reasoning is a faculty of manipulation of ideas. Thus, it needs (existing) ideas to work with. Through rationalization, you may come to certain new conclusions, however they will be limited to the scope of the ideas being manipulated by the intellect. This process does not bring the major breakthroughs that we hear so much about in our history. Creativity, whether scientific, artistic, or any other kind, by definition refers to the inception of new ideas: intuition, imagination, gut feelings, dreams. It is intuitive to all of us that these processes do not belong to the conscious. You do not reason an intuition—you simply have it. Our language reflects this very clearly by giving this phenomenon its own name (intuition). This is another example of something that so clearly transcends our normal awareness, our personality. Everybody has had this type of experience and understands what it is about. Yet when we experience it, we have no explanations for it. These personality-transcendent experiences come directly from our nonphysical Essence. These are the different channels of communication that it uses to "talk" to us.

---

[111] Albert Einstein, *Quotable Einstein: An A to Z Glossary of Quotations*, Quotable Wisdom Books, 2015.

[112] Kristian Marlow, "Solving Problems in Your Dreams," *Psychology Today*, August 29, 2015, https://www.psychologytoday.com/blog/the-superhuman-mind/201508/solving-problems-in-your-dreams. Accessed December 14, 2018.

Why They May Turn Out Wrong

Now, sometimes our intuitions and gut feelings turn out to be wrong. There are two reasons for this.

1. The Unit of Consciousness is trying to send you a message, but it gets distorted by the structures (negative programs) in your unconscious. Whatever message the nonphysical Essence wants to communicate to us, it has to go through the structures of the mind. They may filter or distort it. An example is when you have a new idea (which comes from your Essence), and it turns out to go against a limiting program that you have. That idea will trigger the program, and what you will feel is the program's emotion. This process is so unconscious that you interpret it as a gut feeling or intuition.
2. An outside event triggered a limiting program that is so deep in your unconscious that you have a feeling without being able to verbalize it. This feels like an intuition, but it is not; it is simply a triggered unconscious program.

What to Do to Improve These Channels

The situations above are nothing strange in our lives. In fact, that is how we move through most of our everyday activities. We are making decisions through these unconscious processes all the time—thus the limited free will that I have talked about, as well as the important need to transform the negative programs in our minds. Here is yet another powerful reason to do it. Negative programs block or distort the messages that come from our Essence, which is where our true power resides. It's the power to live the lives that we truly want. When we connect to our Essence, we are able to connect with who we truly are and therefore know what we came here to do. What better incentive to understand that we all need to do mind transformation processes? The more you transform your negative programming, the more you will be able to make use of these direct channels of communication with your Essence.

Another way to activate these channels is through quiet time: meditation, trance, relaxation, going out for a walk, being in nature. If you are in an excited state, whether positive or negative, it is because of activation of programs in your unconscious. The activation of programs blocks these channels and take over your mind. It is important that you feel comfortable in your own silence.

It is there where you will hear yourself. These channels of communication are available to everyone, not just to what we refer as the brilliant minds in our history. Learn to listen to what you are feeling through your daily activities. Not all those sensations are necessarily intuitions, but nevertheless, that simple exercise of tuning in will help you connect with the messages that your Essence is sending to you.

Paranormal Experiences

Clairvoyance, clairaudience, and telepathy—these phenomena are outside our current scientific fields. Still, people have reported them throughout history, across all kinds of different cultures, socioeconomic levels, education levels, and religions. They are another way to communicate to and from dimensions other than the physical. Why some people have these abilities and others do not needs to be studied more. Besides the logical component of the genetics of a particular body type, there is also the factor about the Unit of Consciousness wiring the brain during its insertion process while the baby is still in the womb. This is something that you can read about in Dr. Newton's books and those of practitioners who regress their clients to states of the mind where they can recall their insertion into the new host (i.e., the baby developing inside its mother). In Case 29 in his book *Journey of Souls*,[113] Dr. Newton describes it this way.

> **Dr. N:** Okay, why don't you explain what you do with the mind of the baby.

> **S:** It's delicate and can't be hurried. I start with a gentle probe … defining connections … gaps … every mind is different.

Wiring the brain may include the activation of certain organs that seem to be associated with these faculties (like the pituitary and pineal glands). In my case, the only experience that I have had in this respect happened around forty years ago when I was still living in Colombia. I was driving and decided to take an illegal shortcut across a bridge. Before doing it, I "heard" a voice very clearly, as if coming from a person sitting beside me (I was driving alone), that

---

[113] Michael Newton, *Journey of Souls: Case Studies of Life Between Lives*, St. Paul: Llewellyn Publications, 2003.

said, "Don't do it." I did it, an officer saw me, and that is how I got my first ever traffic citation. I never heard that voice again or had any other similar experiences. What is interesting about this is that the voice was very distinct and different from my own. Also, it was a warning about the consequence of a decision that I made with immediate, tangible consequences. This was not a hallucination or dissociation of reality. You see, as much as any scientist may want to say to me that it is just fabrications of the mind or coincidences, the experience was so clear and real that their arguments are pointless because they are at the same level as denying any other "normal" experience that I have in my life. To those of you who have the privilege of having these abilities, there is a reason why you have them, enjoy them, and use them for your own growth and the growth of others.

Implications

This component is key to our lives and how it affects all of us, as we would expect it, because this is who we really are at our core. I will dedicate this whole section to writing about its consequences, and writing about a whole range of issues, just to give you a sample of how this component truly affects us as individuals and as a society.

The Role of Parents

Units of Consciousness choose the parents who will give them the bodies and the circumstances to accomplish the goals that they set out to do in this physical world. This is who our children are.

If parents keep this perspective while interacting with their children, their attitude toward them will be very different. They understand that behind that younger body is an entity that is as powerful as they are, equal to them. Therefore the child is not just a defenseless, ignorant creature that they have the right to shape in any way they want. There is a nonphysical entity within their child that deserves as much respect as any other adult. His new body needs to be programmed with the skills to survive and prosper on this planet. With every new generation, each of the Units of Consciousness brings new wisdom. They bring the new (re)evolutionary ideas designed to take humanity to its next iteration, higher up in its evolution. Think of them as a newer version of all of us. This is what parents need to see in every instant when they interact with them.

The parents' role is as follows.

1. Provide children with an appropriate physical environment
2. Raise the children so that they are emotionally connected with themselves (and others)
3. Guide the children to find what they came here to do.
4. Raise the children so that they are transcendentally connected with themselves

Point one is obvious and includes providing physical shelter, nutrition, a harmonious social environment, and a full education. As for point two, I have already talked about it extensively; it's a main point of this book. Point three implies that parents respect whatever it is that their children decide to do with their lives. I am aware that this could sound preposterous to many, however due to the tragic consequences that I see not only in sessions with my clients but also everywhere with friends and acquaintances, I have to state this:

It is outside the scope of parenting to tell their children what to do with their lives.

This is a very strong statement, yet it's completely justified because of the tragic consequences of telling them what to do with their lives, even with their best of intentions. Just because parents provide the physical vehicle to that Unit of Consciousness, it does not give them the right to determine what that entity will do with its life. That is beyond their responsibility. As we saw, the Unit of Consciousness already made that decision before getting into the body that the chosen parents would provide. The Unit of Consciousness chose the parents, and the parents agreed to this contract, executed at a nonphysical level. The corollary of this is as follows.

A core responsibility of being a parent consists of guiding their children to find out what it is that they came here to do.

Parents who push their children into a specific life path are curtailing them emotionally and transcendentally. That individual will not be able to genuinely express himself for the rest of his life. On top of that, they are robbing the world of the unique gift that that person came here to give. I know parents want what is "best" for their children. First of all, understand that what they perceive as best is based on their programming that they received decades ago, based on the circumstances that they grew up with way back when. Second, telling their children what career to choose already implies that they don't believe that their children have the capacity to discern on their own—a very limiting message (programming). That in turn reflects how confident they feel about how they brought up their own children. Third, most of the time parents who direct their children on how to make a career decision do so because of financial or other social status concerns. This is a reflection of their own programs that give them a very limited version of reality. The result of social conditioning. If the parents are doing this, it already reflects limited programming that does not allow them to be truly genuine in life. They are guided by what society has to say. They have put the power over their lives in the hands of others.

Social success, fame, wealth, and social status are irrelevant to living a satisfying life if you are not following your own true path.

Even if you are a billionaire, allow your child to be a world backpacker if that is what she wants. That is the most empowering statement that you can give her. The implicit message that it conveys is that she can be who she wants to be, which means that she counts and she is important as she is. It also conveys the message that whatever she does matters. That's it—no strings attached.

Regarding point four, which was about parents raising their children so that they are transcendentally connected with themselves, whether or not parents believe that there is more to this physical dimension, they should allow and encourage their children to explore and reach their own conclusions. This will also apply to what particular religious or spiritual belief they want to adhere to, if that ended up being the case. It is important to find purpose in life, even if you believe that you will become dust and no more. That purpose will guide you and give you coherence in all that you do.

The Scope of the Role of Parents

If you are a parent who keeps the perspective that your child is a Unit of Consciousness, equal to and as powerful as you are, you will also have a clearer vision about the scope of your role. Once you have given that Unit of Consciousness all the necessary skills to thrive in this physical world, your job as a parent is done. You do this until the time the children are finished with their education in their twenties. Yes, you are still the biological parent.

No, that does not mean that you are active in the parenting role for the rest of your life. As independent entities (the Units of Consciousness that your adult children have become), they deserve all the respect to make their own decisions and walk the lives that they came here to live. That is their responsibility, and it's no longer yours, in exactly the same way that you, as any other adult, are making your decisions without having other people be part of them (unless by choice). That is what you prepared them to do, right? If you are confident about the preparation that you gave them, then this should not be an issue. Understand my point: if your adult son or daughter comes to you asking for advice then, by all means share with them your wisdom. Simply have the very clear attitude that it is up to them to make the final decision. It's exactly like you would do with friends.

Parents who cannot let go of their influence over their children have unresolved emotional dependencies. Don't call this emotional dependency love and concern for your children. That is a mask covering this type of limiting programs. Your adult children are just that, adults. Treat them as such. And, on the other side of the coin, adults who let their parents intrude in their personal lives have limiting programs that need to be addressed. They need to transform these programs so that they empower themselves to be able to set healthy boundaries on their own.

Living a Full Life

When you follow your passion, you will not be thinking about retiring. Think about it. When you are enjoying something that you are doing (trip, party, hobby, etc.), do you want to stop doing it? Retirement is something that will no longer make sense to you. Can you see how different life looks from this perspective? It becomes a life lived in constant purpose and meaning. Now you have a chance to live a true, full life from beginning to end.

To live a full life requires that you walk your own path.

It is a first, baseline requirement.

It is very important that you realize that it may very well happen that you reach a point where you don't feel that passion anymore in whatever it is that you are doing. Yes, it also could be that you will be satisfied with one career path for your whole life, but not necessarily. That is perfectly normal. It is the expression "Been there, done that." When you feel that, it means that your Essence is telling you that you already got all the experiences, lessons, and learnings that you wanted from that particular activity. It's time to move on to the next chapter in your physical insertion. You want to recognize this as a crossroads point in your life, which takes us to the second crucial point to be able to live a full life.

To live a full life, you need to be empowered enough to follow your path.

Empowered means that you have the necessary inner emotional resources that make you feel confident about yourself and life in general. When you get to the point where there is no passion anymore, you need to be confident that you will be okay, wherever the new direction takes you. There are several traps that people fall into in this crossroads situation.

1. Identity with the activity they have been pursuing
2. Status that the activity has given them
3. Fear of the unknown

Point one refers to you making your activity part of your identity: "I am an engineer" or "I am a doctor."

You are not whatever activity it is that you do.

You are a Unit of Consciousness having experiences in this physical world. That's it. You are not an engineer, doctor, lawyer, servant, garbage collector, or whatever your job is. If you are tired of what you are doing, then change! They are simply activities, and they have nothing to do with you as a nonphysical entity. This is where point one works with points two and three, and as a result, people give all these justifications for not changing. All the years that you invested in your career, the great job that you have now that gives you the income to support your lifestyle and your family … what is your partner going to think? What about friends and professional colleagues? All the justifications keep you stuck in an activity that you no longer enjoy, and they will make ample use of the faculty of reasoning to justify their position. This is the unconscious doing its job of keeping consistency in its internal programs.

Points one and two are actually easier to surpass than point three, the fear of the unknown. What to do next? How to make the transition? This is why you need to have a very strong emotional foundation, so that you believe in yourself and trust life in order to take this step. Just be confident that all will be well. If you have family and other responsibilities, plan accordingly. That is okay. It does not mean that you have to make the transition the next day.

Case 25: Never Too Late to Find Your Passion

My client is a professional woman who has worked in marketing for many years. She has worked with big corporations, holding different positions in a very successful career. Even so, at this point she is running on empty. She is in her fifties. The spark is gone, and going to work is … well, work. She wants to feel that spark that she felt before. We do a session in which I use neurolinguistic programming to help her connect with herself and find out what it is that she would like to do now. Once we finish the process, I see tears in her eyes. I ask her about them. (It is rare, but sometimes during this particular process, negative memories may surface.) She says, "I am so happy. Once again I have found something that calls me!"

You can truly feel how people become alive after doing a process like this. Before doing it, they were living like machines, just going through the motions. What was it for her? Open a seafood delicatessen store. That had nothing at all to do with what she had been doing. Once she gave herself permission to honestly explore the different possibilities, anything could happen. And in her case, a new, very different path came to the surface. The added beauty of this was that it gave a new purpose to her current job. The new meaning of her current job was now to help her transition to that new activity, to give her the time and financial backing to study all that is related to starting a new business on her own, as well as the particulars of seafood delicatessen.

Everything falls in place when you follow your true path. Think about this from the perspective of your nonphysical Essence: why would it direct you to anything that had no purpose in its evolution? The insertion process is a privilege to the Unit of Consciousness, a process that requires energy and determination. The last thing that it wants is to waste such an opportunity. The other point to know about this is that your Essence would not direct you to this new change if you were not ready for it, as scary as it may feel to you, the personality. If you are in this situation, evaluate where you are in your life and your current circumstances. Make plans accordingly; that is fine. Still, sooner or later you will need to move in the new direction that your Essence is asking you to take. Otherwise, you will start feeling frustration every day that you postpone that move. That frustration will generate its corresponding dramas. This comes not only from my own experience, as you read in my introduction at the beginning of the book, but also from what I see in others under similar circumstances. Right away, the new lessons that you need to learn from your new path arise.

When you truly come to the realization that life is fluid and that you can do whatever it is that you want to do, whenever you want to do it, you will feel an amazing freedom: to be just you!

You need strong, positive inner psychological resources to do this without having the need for the approval of others to do so. Life lived as a constant adventure, from beginning to end. It is amazing to me to see how deep the societal programming is, where most of the people don't even see this as a possibility in their lives. I know that for many, this sounds not only scary but even irresponsible. They are condemned to continue doing what they are doing because that is what "they are supposed to do."

Implications to Society

The social implications on this topic are big, to say the least, and they are getting amplified more and more. Most people today live simply to make money or for retirement, to escape jobs that are meaningless and are a way to survive. Take for instance the situation that the European countries have faced with respect to their labor force. Because Europeans traditionally have had a very low rates of population growth (few children per family), their governments have faced serious financial challenges to maintain a system in which a shrinking young workforce has had to support a growing retiring population. So what is it that economists and sociologists warn about? The need to have more children in order to keep the economic numbers going. The economics of society pushing for more population growth. These policies are unsustainable and take us on a path of self-destruction. Here is my point. If you are passionate about your job, why would you quit? You are, by definition, having fun. You would live a full life contributing to society. It's full not only in the sense of completeness, satisfaction, and quality of life but also in the sense of time, meaning all the way to the end of your life. You're contributing financially to the system, contributing to the finances of the societies and countries where they belong, without the need to increase the population for the economic numbers' sake. On top of this, the problems of living life with unsatisfying jobs is amplified even more with automatization. This technological effect is unstoppable, and it will take more and more of the repetitive and mechanical jobs that human beings do nowadays. The fact is that we don't want people doing these types of jobs. They are precisely for robots. Automatization should be viewed as technology contributing to the liberation of humans. Instead, it is viewed as a threat. Our overpopulation now creates a competition for any job in order to survive, and then people look to their governments to save them. Automatization will amplify this social problem more and more, which will put governments into a very challenging situation where not even policies like protectionism will be a solution.

The New Role of Companies and Institutions

Silicon Valley is an area well-known for its dynamic environment where constant innovation takes place. It's innovation that literally reshapes our society. Companies strive to get the best individuals into their teams. And as part of that endeavor, they offer amazing working environments, with all kinds of sophisticated perks attached to them. Fantastic—that is what we want everywhere. While working as an engineer, I remember attending a class at a university about how to motivate people in their jobs. I remember the distinct feeling that the professor left in me about this struggle that companies have, to find the magic formula to keep people motivated. In spite of all the creativity in salaries, bonuses, and all kinds of other benefits, it is largely an unresolved issue in the professional world. Yes, companies need to keep their employees motivated, and it is in their own interest. Additionally, companies are social entities (societies within society) that shape the lives of many more than their employees. Having said that, and with the new understanding of this section, it is important to realize that no matter what great working environment you are in, if you are not on your own path, you will not be satisfied in that environment. In the beginning, that extra bonus you got, the nice cafeterias, and even recreation rooms and other fancy services surrounding you will pump you up. It will be temporary. That inner voice, that frustration that you feel, will always be there. And so will the tragedy that comes when, because of all those incentives, people are unable to take on their path. This is called the golden handcuffs: they might be golden, but you are still handcuffed. People are financially very successful (a common situation in Silicon Valley) but trapped in their jobs, unhappy. That will inevitably affect the individual's performance in his job, and then also that of the rest of the team.

We want companies to move to a new level of consciousness when creating and shaping their teams—one in which the focus is not just in the external achievements that the individual has accomplished (which is what you read in the resume). The hiring process must also focus on the individual as a congruent entity in her life. This is not just because of some ethical, societal principles but even because it is in companies' best interest to do so. If companies want truly satisfied, passionate, dedicated employees, then they must make sure that they hire people who are walking their life paths. It is actually very easy to notice when someone is or isn't. The language and energy are completely different from someone who is doing things because that is what they are supposed to do (or because of the money), compared with someone who is passionate about that career path. The added benefit to companies integrating this aspect in their hiring process is that they become a social catalyst that motivates people to be authentic. It is a win-win situation for the individual, the company, and society.

The same applies to promotions within the company. The classic example in Silicon Valley is engineers promoted to managers. What they actually like to do is engineering, but they will take the new job, for the money. It's a lose-lose situation for the individual and the company.

Walking your own path is nonnegotiable.

Notice that this requires solid psychological resources as well so that you stay loyal to yourself in spite of temptations that offer temporary gratification. We want companies to take part in this aspect as social entities. I talk here about Silicon Valley simply because that was my personal experience there. Of course, this applies to any professional environment, anywhere in the world. This single issue, if put into practice, would reshape our civilization in a significant, positive way.

Being of Service to Others

Today, with the weight of millennia in human history, being of service to others has become a mass consciousness guilt inflicted mainly by religions. Nowadays, it is being reenacted by the so-called New Age movement. By all means, being of service to others is wonderful—but not when it is done because it is something that "we should do." This is societal programming that translates into guilt, a very limiting program. When being of service to others, you want it to come from your heart. There will be a very tangible joy coming out of you while doing that service. You'll have a "can't wait to be there" attitude. Otherwise, it is not genuine, and as such you are not being congruent. There is a very easy way to erase this guilt that everybody carries in their unconscious

When you follow your path, you are automatically being of service to others.

Simply by the way you behave, by the way you express yourself through your activity, you are already inspiring others. Your energy is different and uplifting. You give the best service you can possibly do. You are uplifting the world. It will be tangible every day and everywhere. It's that powerful. People will look at you in awe and ask you how you found that passion. On top of that, whatever activity you are doing is automatically serving others. Think about it: what activity does not affect other people? We are social entities; whatever we do requires interaction. You are automatically and always serving others. It does not matter whether you sweep the streets or are a waiter, doctor, engineer, or CEO. If it is genuinely coming from your heart, you are already serving others. And if on top of you following your passion, you want to do extracurricular activities to help others because your heart truly calls you to it, then fantastic. Now we are talking about a win-win situation!

Recruiting Terrorists

I bring this up here once more, as a complement to what I already explained before in the first part of the book. We see how so many terrorist organizations are able to recruit people who come from developed countries. It is very clear that this is not simply just because of low standards of living. An added factor to the success of the recruiters is when they hit on someone who has not found a sense of purpose in life. Life simply does not make sense to them, and the recruiters give them a purpose. This factor, in conjunction with the emotional problems that they have, makes them an easy target. They did not have the opportunity to truly explore what their paths are. They are living like robots, going through the daily motions with no ultimate purpose. When a terrorist organization contacts them and, with a well-crafted discourse, offers them an ideology which promises a "better world," they easily embrace it. That ideology is a gate to release their frustrations because of the absurdity of life. Plus, add to this belonging to a tribe, where they will have a sense of belonging and protection, and you have the perfect formula for recruiting them. These recruited people have very limiting negative programs in their unconscious.

These programs could be transformed, and their life purpose can be found as well.

It Is Always Your Path

I know that I have been very clear and emphatic about the importance of living what you came here to do, if you want to have a chance to live a truly fulfilling life. This is what one would call the "right path." I put it in quotes because I want to point out that as much as you may call it the right path, there is no such a thing as being on a wrong path. If you are not following your passion, then you are walking the path that will give you the experiences and lessons that you need to get to the point where you have the power to be congruent with what you really want to do. You see, from a higher perspective, nothing is wrong. Everything has a purpose in your personal evolution. Simply understand this:

To make sense of what life is about, you need to raise your perspective beyond that of the personality.

The personality is extremely limited in its scope. In fact, that is why we suffer: because we stay at the level of the personality, which does not have the full picture of reality. Once you take into consideration the transpersonal factors, everything starts falling in place. So either way, whether or not you are feeling passion for what you do, know that that is your current path. Everybody has been in that situation at one point or another. There's no need to bring yourself down. Do be conscious about where you are, and if life does not make sense or does not feel great to you, do what you need do to change your limiting beliefs, one step at a time. Sooner or later, you are inevitably going to where you want to be. As I said earlier, evolution is inevitable.

Willpower Derivatives

I talked about operating in life from a place of inspired action. Inspired action has the direct backing of the power of your nonphysical Essence. This is the greatest power that you have at your disposal in your lifetime. In this physical world, we are required to do tasks that are generally not enjoyable. Doing your taxes, putting gas in your car, and paying bills are examples of tasks that we don't consider fun, but they need to be done to function in our lives. That is the place for willpower.

Willpower belongs to the small tasks that life on this planet requires us to do. Inspired action belongs to all the major projects that you embark in life.

Stretched Willpower

When willpower is being used for a major project in your life—what I call stretched willpower—you are using the faculty of reasoning in conjunction with the power of negative emotional batteries associated to the programs behind that project. This negative emotional energy will never be as powerful as that positive energy of our Essence because by definition, it is a subset of it. Our nonphysical Essence provides the life force to all these mechanisms, including the energy that becomes the negative charge for these emotional batteries. This seems to be a contradiction given that our Essence is supposed to be, and is, unconditional love.

One Vital Energy with Different Manifestations

Let me give you an analogy to help understand this. In a gasoline-powered car, the ultimate source of energy is the gas that you put in its tank. The chemical energy stored in this fuel is transformed mainly into mechanical movement, heat (that you feel when you open the hood), and electricity (to power all the electronics that today's vehicles have). These are very different forms of energy, compared to that in the gasoline. In an analogous fashion, the person (body plus personality) is a vehicle to the Unit of Consciousness. The Unit of Consciousness is the primary source that gives life to the body and all its mechanisms (physical and nonphysical). These mechanisms will transform that vital energy as needed. Some of that energy goes into the physical activity of each of its cells, and some of it is used as the emotional energy that gets stored in the emotional batteries that I have referred to all along in this book. Remember that these mechanisms were designed to protect us from the predators, as well as to adapt to the environment in which we live. As such, negative energy is not "bad" as we like to judge it. It is negative, simply a different facet in its manifestation. We call it negative because when it activates, it creates a sensation that leads us to avoid a certain circumstance. For example, the fear that you feel when you confront a lion, or that you feel when you have a close call with a car that you did not see is energy, is meant to keep you alive. As such, it is simply a different polarization with the same positive intentions. In a similar way that the car uses electric energy generated from the energy in the gasoline to keep the engine running, the body uses negative emotional energy to keep it alive in this physical world (survival). Unfortunately, nowadays in addition to these necessary uses of this negative energy, we also use it to hurt and kill each other. This is our own doing. Continuing with our analogy, a car is meant to be a positive instrument that allows us to more conveniently transport from one point to another. Nevertheless, we now hear in the news about individuals making use of cars to kill as many people in the streets as possible. That does not mean that a car is "bad." We have created unnurturing environments for ourselves that deviate from the original purpose of these energies, making them weapons that we use against each other. It's real proof that we do have free will within this paradigm—with the implication that it is also our responsibility to make use of that free will to change our actions and make the appropriate use of all these mechanisms to live harmoniously on this physical planet.

Stretched willpower makes use of negative emotional energy. Let's say that a parent is working on a job that he doesn't like. He does this because he sees no other option and wants to keep providing the same level of comforts to his family. There is a component of love for them that inspires him to stay at that job. That component provides energy in the form of inspired action. Yet even in this case, there is also a negative program that makes him believe that that is his only option, or that life is supposed to be sacrifice. This negative program is causing damage not only to him but also to others because of the inner frustration he carries. That frustration will come out, as much as he wants to present himself as a good-mannered, mature adult. He forces himself into that situation even though he is suffering. He can do that because of willpower. If you ask him why he keeps doing it, he will give you his reasons (faculty of reasoning, part of the conscious). As commendable as that father may seem to be, what we want is everybody to live a successful and satisfying life.

Negative Inspired Action

Negative inspired action results when willpower is taken to extremes. A clear example that I gave earlier was Hitler. He applied his willpower to be able to go through the routine whippings that his father inflicted on him. The frustration and anger repressed in him took such a magnitude that the energy now becomes a force that inspires action. Hitler was "inspired" to create a superior race but with total disregard to the basic elements of human dignity and respect. Stalin was also brutally beaten by his father. You will find similar stories in many of the despotic rulers that we find in history. Without having to go to such extreme examples, you see this type of action in the public arena nowadays, whether from government officials, other organizations, or individuals professing certain policies or doctrines that imply discrimination or division in one way or another. That is how you can differentiate true, positive, inspired action, which comes from our Essence, from the negative inspired action that is the result of heavy negative emotional batteries. Actions inspired by negative energies are not sustainable; the end result is either transformation or collapse. Often, people who went through traumatic experiences (war, rape, alcoholism, sexual abuse, etc.) become the voices behind the cause for change. We need them, and they become the best examples to create the better world that we all want. However, as long as they keep the powerful negative emotions unprocessed, these emotions will be part of the force asking for change. Because they are negative energies, they will "contaminate" the positive desired change. These unprocessed energies will seek revenge, punishment, and drastic measures and will cloud the individual to a more encompassing solution.

In order to be a force for positive change in a sustainable way, people must first process and heal the wounds of their traumatic experiences.

Once transformation has occurred, they will act from positive inspired action, backed up by the most powerful force that they have at their disposal, their Essence.

Summary (and Derived Concepts)

This aspect of our personality, which is actually what we truly are at our cores, brings a new dimension (literally and figuratively) to our graphical summary.

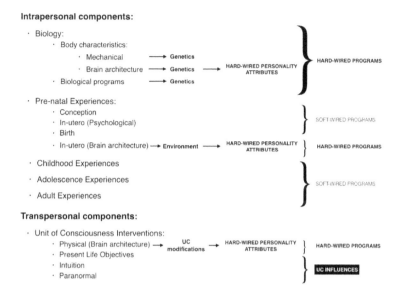

Intrapersonal components:

- Biology:
  - Body characteristics:
    - Mechanical → Genetics
    - Brain architecture → Genetics → HARD-WIRED PERSONALITY ATTRIBUTES
  - Biological programs → Genetics

  } HARD-WIRED PROGRAMS

- Pre-natal Experiences:
  - Conception
  - In-utero (Psychological)
  - Birth

  } SOFT-WIRED PROGRAMS

  - In-utero (Brain architecture) → Environment → HARD-WIRED PERSONALITY ATTRIBUTES } HARD-WIRED PROGRAMS

- Childhood Experiences
- Adolescence Experiences
- Adult Experiences

  } SOFT-WIRED PROGRAMS

Transpersonal components:

- Unit of Consciousness Interventions:
  - Physical (Brain architecture) → UC modifications → HARD-WIRED PERSONALITY ATTRIBUTES } HARD-WIRED PROGRAMS
  - Present Life Objectives
  - Intuition
  - Paranormal

  } UC INFLUENCES

The Unit of Consciousness interventions component shows up in the modifications that it does to the brain while in the womb, and as the influences that it exerts on us through the present life objectives, intuitions, and paranormal experiences. These influences are not programs, and neither are they hard-wired or soft-wired. They come directly from our nonphysical Essence. As such, they are an integral part of us, of our personality. These influences are not programs, and by definition they are nonphysical, so we are "forced" to create a higher-level classification.

Layers of the Personality

I will talk about layers of the personality. Under this perspective, our personalities are comprised of two layers.

- The core layer of the personality
- The adaptive layer of the personality

The Core Layer

The core layer is, under normal circumstances, relatively unchanged during the life of the individual. As always, there can be exceptions in extreme cases. As an example, an adolescent girl who was clearly extroverted may become more introverted after a very traumatic event, like a rape. Even after doing therapy and healing from such an event, she may not revert back to being the extroverted person that she was. Think of it as the scar that remains after a wound has healed. The structures of her personality were "repaired" through therapy, but that does not mean that they went back to what they were before.

With the exception of these types of extreme events, the core layer of the personality remains relatively unchanged during the lifetime of the individual. When considering only the intrapersonal components of the mind, the core layer would be comprised of just the hard-wired programs. The Unit of Consciousness interventions change this in different ways. To begin with, it has two facets.

1. Physical
2. Nonphysical

Physical Core Layer of the Personality

The physical core layer of the personality is simply the hard-wired programs that affect our behavior.

I defined them as follows (and also as shown in the summaries).

Hard-wired programs

- **Mechanical**
- **Hard-wired personality attributes**
- **Biological programs and tendencies**

If you look at the summary that I gave for the intrapersonal components, you will see that with them, there are two physical factors that shape the brain and thus the hard-wired personality attributes: genetics and the in utero environment that the mother and father provide to the fetus. In this section, we also saw that the Unit of Consciousness further customizes the body by actively participating in the wiring of the brain, while the baby is still in the mother's womb. This has a direct effect in the architecture of the brain. As such, we then need to add this factor (italicized) to the hard-wired personality attributes.

Hard-wired personality attributes:

- **Brain circuitry generated from genetics**
- **Brain circuitry generated from the in utero environment**
- *Brain circuitry generated from the in utero modifications by the Unit of Consciousness*

In other words, the physical core layer of the personality corresponds to the hard-wired programs, now including the expanded definition of the hard-wired personality attributes that added the Unit of Consciousness brain modifications while the baby is in the womb.

Nonphysical Core Layer of the Personality

The present life objectives are an inner influence that comes directly from your nonphysical Essence. As I explained, your passion about the activities that you do may shift according to the experiences that you have with them. Nevertheless, this force within you has a relatively constant direction in your life. Notice that this is a force that does not have anything to do with being extroverted or not. As such, it is a nonphysical aspect of the core layer of the personality. You can see this force in action in children with their innate inclinations, irrespective of their personality type or the environment in which they are growing up. It comes directly from their Essence.

Additionally, from Dr. Newton's books, an Individualized Consciousness has interests and inclinations of its own. For example, some of them are interested in evolving through teaching and others through energy or matter manipulation. These inclinations from our Essence filter through the mechanisms of our mind and influence our personalities in a very deep way. Therefore, they are also part of the core layer of the personality, but they are nonphysical. This applies equally to our intuition and any paranormal abilities that we may have. Taking this into consideration, we can now define the core layer as a whole as follows.

Core layer:

- **Hard-wired programs (physical)**
- **Unit of Consciousness influences (nonphysical)**

The Adaptive Layer

The adaptive layer consists of all the soft-wired programs. This layer is the result of the experiences that we have in the physical world, and thus academically speaking,[114] they are not part of this Unit of Consciousness interventions component that I am explaining in this section. These programs come from intrapersonal components as well as the other transpersonal ones, as I will show next. This is the layer where parents and the environment in general exert influence—and as we saw, it's a very powerful one. As a reminder, this layer is then comprised of the foundational and the nonfoundational programs, which are the two classifications within the soft-wired programs.

Layers of the Personality Summary

We can summarize these concepts in a more graphical format for easier visualization and grasping of the concepts:

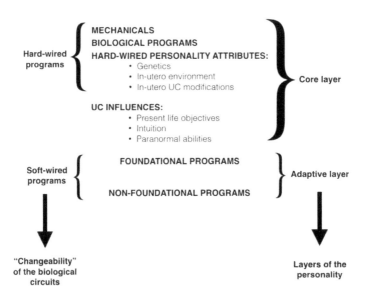

From this figure, it is easy to see why I was forced to create the concept of layers of the personality. Even though the adaptive layer is the same as soft-wired programs, in contrast, the core layer is not just the hard-wired

---

[114] A reminder that all these classifications are for the purpose of facilitating the understanding of all these concepts. We are a unified entity, and we are an interconnected whole. All these definitions are intellectual and nothing more.

programs. It also includes the influences that our nonphysical Essence exerts on our personality. As the name of this layer implies, these influences are at the very core of who we are. For this reason, it is very important that I point out I am not doing these extra classifications simply to do an academic exercise. By doing this exercise, I want to convey very explicitly how important these influences from the Unit of Consciousness are. They play a profound and active role in guiding us through our lives.

The quality of our lives is directly dependent on how in tune we are with these directives from our nonphysical Essence.

The Previous Physical Insertions Component

When I am talking to my audiences in my seminars, this section brings up the strongest reactions in them. Isn't it interesting? As much as I explain to them that this does not mean that they have to believe in this concept as a physical reality, it still poses great resistance on their part. Of course, this ties closely to religious beliefs, which are core (foundational) beliefs for everyone. To challenge them is to challenge the foundations through which we see and make sense of our lives. If you feel resistance to this topic, let me make it a little easier for you to read this section by stating this: The phenomenon, which is traditionally called reincarnation, could very well be just a construct of our minds. It could be explained, for example, as our minds filling in the gaps, or even as simple imagination. Simply stated, there is no scientific proof that backs up this concept at this point in time. Having said that, I do need to say that this is because science does not currently have the tools to study this. For now, we work with what the fields of the mind show us until science catches up.

It Does Not Matter if You Don't believe in It

The first thing to understand is this:

Whether real or not, this phenomenon of physical reinsertion shows up as part of the human psyche, even in individuals who do not believe in it.

In other words, even if you vehemently do not believe in reinsertion, I am suggesting that it is a component of our personality. I can state this from what I see in sessions with my clients, and it's repeated by other practitioners everywhere. This phenomenon will occur independently of whether or not the practitioner believes in it, and whether or not the client believes in it.

Case 26: Unexpected Past Life Regression

I have been working with this client already for some time. We are in the middle of the session processing some family issues that she has. As the session advances, her unconscious takes us into a particular issue about always being generous with other people but feeling guilty about it. While processing this information in a hypnotic state, she tells me, "This feels so old …" This is an indication of an event that is surfacing from her unconscious. At this point, I instruct her to keep tapping on her hand (this is just a part of the EFT technique) while she keeps her eyes closed. This takes her deeper into the hypnotic state. With some extra guidance, I then instruct her to go to the event that is giving her this feeling of "so old." After following my instructions, she starts talking about being somewhere in the west, at the time of horses and horse carriages. She is a little girl, a beggar in the streets. As we go through different scenes of that life, in one of them she is on a boat with other people. The boat sinks. She stays alive by holding to a wooden box. While holding to it, she starts to grab the hands of other people nearby and, as a result, saves other lives. This event is what created the program where she "feels the need to save" other people, but in this lifetime by means of her generosity. Once she understood this, she can let go of her guilt, and at the same time that she can keep being generous in a more balanced way. At the end of that life, she finds herself living well as a teacher for little children, and she's married. She dies giving birth to her son. She can see herself bleeding to death before she could even hold her baby.

Here is another example of how a past insertion was affecting her behavior (in a very clear way) in this lifetime. At the end of the session, while talking about all that came up, she tells me that she hadn't believed in reincarnation. Nevertheless, in one of the scenes during the regression, she saw herself in a mirror. Her comment about this particular scene was, "How strange. I was seeing myself in that mirror, and I knew it was me, but I had a different face." I restated to her that she did not have to change her beliefs. She replied, "I don't know yet what to think about it, however I cannot deny what just happened here."

During the session, I have no way of knowing whether the issue originated in a past life. Because of that, I never use language that may lead the client into that scenario. Furthermore, it is not a good idea in my case, because I normally don't ask my clients about their beliefs in this respect. Thus if I were to explicitly lead them to a past life, it could go against their beliefs, with the consequence that my clients may reject my directives. As you can see, there is no need for me to know whether the client believes in past reinsertions or not. Once someone has been working with me for some time and we have established good rapport, that person trusts my guidance. That opens the door for her unconscious to bring to the surface whatever it is that is relevant to the issue that we are dealing with independently of what she believes, which is what happened in this case. Because I respect my client's beliefs, I did not ask her about how she resolved what she experienced in that session. It could be that she still doesn't believe in this concept. As a mind transformation practitioner, what is ultimately relevant is the change of the limiting issues that are affecting her current life.

As I mentioned, even the practitioner does not have to believe in past reinsertions. As long as there is a good rapport between practitioner and client, the unconscious of the client will go to the source of the problem, whatever it is. Iconic past life practitioners were skeptics themselves. Psychiatrist Brian Weiss is well-known today as one of the main proponents of past lives. In his book *Many Lives, Many Masters*,[115] he tells how his life was straightforward from the beginning.[116] He was raised in a nurturing environment, was educated in great schools and with a great career, and was filled with professional accomplishments. Describing himself as a scientist in the full sense of the word, he was an automatic skeptic of anything that could not be proven scientifically, and this means that past lives were completely out of the question.

Until 1980, when a client whom he calls Catherine in his book comes to him because of anxiety, phobias, and panic attacks in her life. She has had these symptoms all her life. After trying conventional psychotherapy for months without success, he decides to use hypnosis. Catherine regresses to past lives, where they find the cause of her symptoms (and which he describes in his book). In the end, she heals as the result of these sessions. As Dr. Weiss says, it took him four years[117] before he had the courage to write about it because of his fears with respect to his professional reputation. Do you think

[115] Brian L. Weiss, *Many Lives, Many Masters: The True Story of a Prominent Psychiatrist, His Young Patient and the Past Life Therapy That Changed Both Their Lives*, New York: Touchstone, 1988.

[116] Brian L. Weiss, *Many Lives, Many Masters*, 9.

[117] Brian L. Weiss, *Many Lives, Many Masters*, 11.

his encounter with Catherine was a coincidence? I hope that you are starting to see how the events in our lives are anything but random. It is clear to me that part of Dr. Weiss's purpose for this lifetime was to build up the courage to speak his truth. It took him four years. Also, he then had to teach that truth to humanity. His client, Catherine, had contracted with him in the nonphysical realm for the occurrence of this event. In turn, it served perfectly well that Unit of Consciousness's objectives for this present insertion. This is how our lives mesh and intertwine with each other. Dr. Weiss's books have become bestsellers because people do resonate with this phenomenon. This is an intrinsic phenomenon of our mind. It has been part of human history across all kinds of different cultures, irrespective of social status, education, and other factors.

It Is Affecting Your Behavior in This Lifetime

That brings us to this important fact about the phenomenon.

An issue related to a past physical insertion, when properly processed, brings positive transformation to the current life of the person.

In other words, some of the limiting behaviors that you experience in your life may come from events that you lived in a past physical insertion. If these events were traumatic enough, they may affect in a significant way your behavior in this life. Irrespective of how significantly they are impacting you in your current life, because past physical insertions are a component of your personality, they influence your overall personality traits, such as liking the ocean or the mountains, cold foods versus warm foods, antiques, and certain historical periods. Many of our personal preferences and affinities that we so casually talk about come from experiences that we had in previous physical insertions. The well-known event of déjà vu is a classic effect in this respect. These are memories from other insertions that "percolate" into your present-day awareness.

Programs from previous physical insertions affect the personality of the newborn baby.

That is yet another reason why babies from the same parents can have such different personalities. Each one of the siblings (even identical twins) within a family is an independent Unit of Consciousness with its own unique history. Each child carries that history, which manifests in her behavior in this life.

There are a lot of books about this topic. Some go from anecdotes that children tell about remembrances of their past lives, all the way to university professors trying to be as scientific as possible in their analysis of this phenomenon. Notable among them are Ian Stevenson and Jim Tucker at the University of Virginia. Their work is remarkable, and their cases suggest, using common sense, that this phenomenon is real, and certainly that it is part of our human psyche. I do have to comment that many times, these scientists are not able to come to the conclusion (scientifically speaking) that a specific person was indeed talking about a past life, because a certain detail did not match their observations. I think we can all agree that something like this occurs even to most of us when someone reminds us about events that happened in our current lives. Yet of course we require no scientific proof that we are living this life. Ironically, we most likely would fail these scientist tests with respect to our present lives. It is remarkable that someone can talk with luxury of details about lives that happened decades, centuries, or even millennia ago.

How People Experience Past Insertions

Here is another point about how people can experience a past reinsertion, which is important for you to know if you happen to go through such an event. Depending on the programs that you have, you may regress more associated or dissociated. In my case, because of all the hyper-vigilant programs that I have had, going into a deep state of trance takes a long and deep hypnotic induction process. When I go through a past life, I experience it as a series of almost abstract images. I can easily identify with the information that I am getting, but I am very dissociated from it. On the other hand, I know a lot of people who fully associate in the regression. They not only feel a complete identification with that other personality (as being them), but they also feel the suffering, the pain, and the agony (as well as the happiness and joy) that it is going through in that life. They feel it as their own. It can go to such an extent that, in the case of very intense traumatic events, I have to guide them to dissociate from what they are reliving and instead watch them as if in a movie theater.

Case 27: Too Intense to Relive

This client is a professional, successful woman in her present life. Still, she has negative, limiting attitudes that affect her self-esteem, and she wants to transform them so that she can have a positive outlook about herself. At the beginning of our sessions, I always ask her about how she is continuing to feel as a result of our transformational work. As part of her answer, she tells me about the anguish that she has been going through during the past days because of a situation that a friend of hers experienced. Her friend (a woman) was exchanging e-mails with a someone (a man) with the serious prospect of becoming a committed relationship. As would be expected in this type of situation, she was excited about this new possibility in her life ... except that it turned out that the guy was completely dishonest with her. (I don't have the details about how her friend became aware of this, because this was not relevant for the session.) When my client heard about what happened to her friend, it affected her deeply. She felt it was a "deep treason," and it became very difficult for her to come to terms to what happened to her friend. I noticed how affected she was by this event, and I offered to her to explore what was behind this strong reaction. She accepted. We start processing this feeling of treason.

After a while in the session, she starts getting images of a past life in Germany during World War II. She is in a concentration camp with her daughter, waiting in line before they are sent to the gas chambers. Her pain and agony are so intense that not even dissociating is enough for her. We have been working in this session for some time, and given the intensity of her experience, I know that she has reached the maximum she can process at this point. I take her out of trance and reground her emotionally, and we agree to follow up with this. I want you to notice that during the session, she is interacting with me, and thus one part of her mind is still aware that she is in this present life and safe in my office. Nevertheless, her unconscious brings up that past physical insertion experience so vividly that for her, she is there again. She is once more standing in line in that concentration camp with all the emotions that she felt back then.

And so that you can see how our reactions to events that happen in our daily lives can have deeper roots than we may casually think, here is the rest of the story. In the next session, she regresses back to Nazi Germany. She was married with a daughter. She arrives home, her husband is there, and the house is mostly dark. She can tell that her husband is tense. He is reading a book, and she tries to get close to him, but he rejects her approach. The night comes, and someone knocks at the front door. Several men enter by force and ask her and her daughter to take their belongings. Then they take them both—but not her husband. The next scene takes her once more to the concentration camp. This time she can follow through all the way to their deaths. She could recall in all detail how the chambers looked, how they were directed to a previous room before the final step, and more. Her reaction to the original event related to her friend's e-mails was a reminder of how her husband had betrayed her (and her daughter) and the consequences that the betrayal had entailed. This e-mail event, which otherwise would cause a milder reaction in most of the people, triggered deep and painful memories from a past physical insertion.

In general, when you react to a particular event in a much stronger way than most people do, this is an indication of a program that has been triggered. If it is negative, you may want to explore what is behind it; it will be limiting you in some other ways. To people who can so vividly recall these past lives, it is as clear to them that this was a past physical insertion as it is to them that this life is simply another insertion. How would you feel if someone were to come to you and tell you that this present life is not real? That is how they feel when skeptics talk about this topic.

Why Not Remember Past Insertions?

The question that everybody asks is, "How come we don't remember those lives?" That's by design. Think about the emotional load that we carry with just the events and people with whom we have interacted in this current insertion—the pain, anger, and irritations that people have caused in our lives. Isn't that already enough emotional load to deal with? Many people still have this idealistic view about past insertions, where they think they were someone famous or royalty. Yes, this does happen, but for the most part, this is wishful thinking. There has been a lot of suffering in most of our past lives. Wanting to remember your past insertions carries the implication that they would come with all the feelings (of hatred, pain, suffering, etc.) that they created. For each one of the dozens or hundreds (or more?) that you have lived before, it would be overwhelming. Take the previous case, which was just about one single lifetime. We simply could not function. By coming back with a (relatively speaking) clean slate, we can focus on the specific issues that we want to transcend in this particular physical experience. It is a logical, coherent, and brilliant design. From what we see while doing deeper work with the mind, the Units of Consciousness do have the complete picture of their own journeys.

Even though it is very obvious that there is much more involved in this process of "forgetting," we can see physical changes that contribute to the dissociation from our Essence. When the conscious starts to show up, beta waves appear in the electrical activity of the brain. This conscious activity creates tremendous noise in the mind. Monitor your thoughts in your head and try to stop them. This is the biggest challenge that meditators face as soon as they sit down to practice. All this activity creates or adds a virtual barrier with our Essence. An analogy to this is when someone tries to whisper something to you while in a night club with music at full volume. You will not be able to hear them. To hear that whisper, you need to go out to a quiet place. That is what meditation is about. Notice also how congruent this is with the fact that so many children seem to have past life memories up until around six years of age. From then on, they "forget." If parents were more aware about this type of event, they would pay more attention to their children's stories. Most parents today think that it is their children's active imaginations. This attitude invalidates the children's experience, which in turn creates programs in their unconscious that accelerate the discarding of these memories. Of course, children do exercise imagination. Open-minded and observant parents will know right away the difference between the two.

And why does this noise in our minds form a barrier to these memories? After all, we remember in general most of the events of this life without having to go into a hypnotic state. The reason for this is simply that the memories of this life are being stored in conjunction with the physical structures of the brain of your current body. Your human apparatus has the physical links to these memories. For obvious reasons, it cannot have the links of the events experienced by other bodies. These memories are part of your nonphysical Essence, which has experienced all of them. You, the personality, are associated to this lifetime only. In order to access the memories of past reinsertions, you need to quiet your mind so that you can hear your Essence "whispering" them to you. That is what the state of hypnosis does, whether in a session with a practitioner, doing meditation, or performing deep states of prayer.

Physical Healings

What adds weight to this component of our minds is the fact that even physical healing can occur after a past life regression. Brian Weiss's daughter, at age twenty-five, healed from cataracts after she regressed to a past life.[118] Dr. Weiss presents lots of cases in the many books he has written on these topics. This happens in the realm of mind practitioners who do past life regressions.

Case 28: Rotated Hammer Toe

Ann C. Barham is a licensed marriage and family therapist (LMFT), as well as a certified past life therapist. In her book *The Past Life Perspective*, she explains how, during her counseling training, she experienced a powerful past life regression that resolved a long-standing physical issue.[119] She had a condition known as rotated hammer toe, and in spite of several medical treatments, it could not be resolved. It was a painful condition that affected her quality of life. In her training, she volunteered to do a past life regression in front of her classmates. She regressed to a time when she was an Asian girl whose parents wanted her to follow the tradition of foot binding.[120] She refused to go through the procedure and tried to escape from her home. Nevertheless, she was caught, and as a result of the dishonor that she brought to the family, she was sold as a servant. Eventually she took her own life. As the professor reviewed with her the life lessons from that physical insertion, Barham describes how her legs shook as if releasing some sort of stored energy. Since that session, the pain from Barham's condition disappeared; it's been over twenty years.

Another interesting aspect about these reinsertions is that they can explain certain birthmarks in newborns. Jim Tucker, in his book *Life before Life*,[121] gives examples of children who were born with birthmarks that corresponded

---

[118] Brian L. Weiss and Amy E. Weiss, *Miracles Happen: The Transformational Healing Power of Past-Life Memories*, New York: HarperCollins, 2012, 149–155.

[119] Ann C. Barham, *The Past Life Perspective: Discovering Your True Nature Across Multiple Lifetimes*, New York: Atria/Enliven Books, 2016, 7–9.

[120] This is a tradition that originated in China, in which the feet of young girls were tied and deformed. This was a status symbol and also considered a standard of beauty in the societies of the time. It's an extremely painful process for the young girls—another example of how extreme our norms of behavior can become.

[121] Jim Tucker, *Life before Life: A Scientific Investigation of Children's Memories of Previous Lives*, New York: St. Martin's Press, 2005.

to the wounds inflicted on them in a previous life, where they'd had violent deaths. In his particular cases, the children not only remembered their past lives on their own, but their marks confirmed their stories. Because of the intense emotional impact of the event of their previous death, it permeated to the unconscious of the new personality, which in turn expressed it as a physical somatization.

What Happens in between Insertions?

If you have a serious interest in the study of who we are and what human consciousness is about, the books of Michael Newton are a must read. I consider them an integral part of the complete picture that I am trying to show you here about us as human beings. Similar to Dr. Weiss, when people asked Michael about past life regression, he would tell them that he did not do that. To him, that was just "New Age stuff." Later (the "coincidences" in life), a man came to him about a pain that he had on his side. The doctors did their exams and took X-rays, and nothing came up. They told him that it must be psychosomatic. Michael asked him if he thought whether it could be because of something that happened in his childhood, to which the man answered that he believed it must have been so, as much as he could not remember the event.[122] I write about this detail because I want to convey to you that this individual believed, as most of the people do, that there must have been something in childhood that had created this condition. This individual did not hint about a past life. As Michael explained in his first book, *Journey of Souls*,[123] he approached the problem by using a technique of pain management, where he teaches the client to control the pain by teaching him to make it worse and then eventually learning to make it less intense. By using imagery, he instructed him to make it worse. The man "came up" with the imagery of being stabbed. Searching for the reason for this particular image, Michael's client ended up regressing to a previous life during World War I, where he was a British sergeant fighting in France. He was killed there by a bayonet stabbing. Once this new information was processed, the man's pain disappeared. Incidentally, Michael was very interested in history, and

---

[122] Tim Miejan, "Journey of Souls with Michael Newton." *The Edge,* July 1, 1997, http://www.edgemagazine.net/1997/07/journey-of-souls-with-michael-newton. Accessed December 14, 2018.
[123] Michael Newton, *Journey of Souls: Case Studies of Life between Lives*, St. Paul: Llewellyn Publications, 2003, 57.

while his client was in the regression, he asked him about details of the event, like the British unit he belonged to, the day of his death (July 1, 1916), and other data. Afterward, he contacted the British War Office and the Imperial Museum in London to find out if that British sergeant existed.[124] Indeed, they confirmed that he had died that date in 1916 during the events described by his client. It sure is a very compelling case, wouldn't you say? Notice how not only did Michael not believe in past lives, but also how his client believed that it must have been something from his early childhood. Independent of what either of them believed, this component of his personality affected his life in a very tangible way.

Dr. Newton wrote several books about Life Between Lives (LBL)—that is, what happens to us in our true state as nonphysical Units of Consciousness, before and after an insertion into this universe in which we live. He did all this work with hypnosis. The two basic books about this topic are *Journey of Souls* and *Destiny of Souls*.[125] They are the result of more than seen thousand life-between-life sessions that he performed during thirty-five years in his practice.[126] There are very consistent results from individuals of all different walks of life. He founded the Newton Institute, which trains practitioners to conduct these types of regressions. With his practitioners, more than thirty thousand regressions[127] have been done across more than forty countries[128] with the same consistent results. The books explain in detail what happens after you leave a particular life's body, what happens while you are in your true state as a Unit of Consciousness, and the process you undertake in selecting the body, family, times, and events that will be your next physical life experience. I cannot overemphasize recommending reading them. They

[124] Richard Martini, "It's a Wonderful Afterlife and Flipside." Blog, September 29, 2016, https://flipsidetouristguide.blogspot.com/2016/09/the-passing-of-michael-newton.html. Accessed December 14, 2018.

[125] Michael Newton, *Destiny of Souls: New Case Studies of Life between Lives*, St. Paul: Llewellyn Worldwide, 2001.

[126] "History of TNI." The Newton Insititute, https://www.newtoninstitute.org/about-tni/history-of-tni. Accessed December 14, 2018.

[127] Peter Smith, "A Tribute to Michael Newton." *YouTube*, TheNewtonInsitute, June 19, 2017, https://www.youtube.com/watch?time_continue=1281&v=p-jEsXbW2IQ. Accessed December 14, 2018. Statistic given at time mark 22:36

[128] Peter Smith, "President's Message." The Newton Institute, February 2017, http://newtoninstitute.org/wp-content/uploads/2017/02/Presidents-message-launch.pdf. Accessed December 14, 2018.

show a realm where there is only learning and evolution in a nurturing and supportive environment. They show how we come back into the physical world with very explicit intentions and objectives. It's the same way that we got to experience as students in the academy, during our certification as hypnotherapists. We all are on a journey where there is an explicit, intentional, inevitable continuous growth in true power and wisdom.

Case 29: A Life Lived to Learn about Questioning

As an engineer many years before I became a hypnotherapist and did any kind of regressions, I went to see the movie *The Mission*[129] with some friends of mine. The film devastated me. Here you have another example of a stronger reaction that I talked about in the earlier case. I came out from the theater feeling destroyed, hurt, and disoriented by what I felt was the human cruelty—and even more, that of an institution acting in the name of God. Interesting enough, one of my friends made the comment that to him, the movie felt almost like a documentary! How could he see something that horrific as a simple story of facts? How could he not be affected in the slightest by such a story? Notice how our internal map of reality (i.e., our programs) makes us see the same reality so differently. Obviously life went on, but more than twenty years later, while doing sessions with my teacher at the academy, I would obtain the answer to this event.

In that particular session, we decided to do a regression to the past life that has exerted the biggest influence on me in this present one. I regressed to when I was a priest during the time when Spain was colonizing the newly discovered territories in the Americas. I was sent by the Church to indoctrinate the natives to Catholicism. Once there, I realized how the Church was exploiting and treating the natives with total disrespect to their own culture, to the point that I ended up defending them, going against the directives from my superiors. Eventually, due to my subversive actions, I was imprisoned and then judged. The final sentence was death by hanging. This explained, among many other things, my reactions that day toward the movie decades earlier in my life. I think you will understand that at the time of the session, that movie was not at all on my radar. I was already living a totally different life under totally different circumstances. Still,

---

[129] *The Mission*, Warner Brothers, Goldcrest Films International, Kingsmere Productions Ltd., Enigma Productions, AMLF, 1986.

an event that was otherwise trivial in the context of a lifetime took special significance as the result of that session.

At the end of the regression, after you die in that life, it is very common to see yourself leaving that body and entering the nonphysical world (most of the time, people refer to it as the spirit world). This is the point where my teacher asked me, "What was the objective of that life?" The answer came to me very clearly: learn to question authority. In fact, this extended to simply "learn to question everything." This led me to further understanding so many other aspects of my life. This is the explanation behind the questioning that I referred to in the introduction of the book, where I was talking about my inner quest and referring to the story of me walking with my father in the streets with beggars. At school, in religion class, we were taught the concept of God as a being with infinite love for all of us. On the other hand, if we died in sin, we faced condemnation for eternity. There was something within me that couldn't accept what I felt was the absurdity of such a paradigm, and I questioned it immediately. It took me no time to reject religion as it was taught, and instead I decided to start my own quest in understanding what life is about. In my frustrations and anger while trying to understand my personal dramas, I screamed and cursed God for my sufferings. I had no fear of doing that; deep in me, I always believed in a universal consciousness that is all love, and thus there was no such thing as eternal damnation. This book is the manifestation of all these questionings.

Every piece of my life—the country in which I was born, the family I grew up with, the circumstances I have been through—fits perfectly well in that bigger picture that goes well beyond this present physical experience. And that is exactly the same for every single one of us.

Implications

Having the courage to confront our own beliefs gives us courage to confront any other challenges in life.

If you truly believe that this component of our minds is simply a creation of our brains, then you may want to skip this section. With this information, you have a deeper understanding of who you are. Use it to lead your life in the direction that you want.

As you can see from my case, the experiences of that past life, and the wisdom learned from those terrible events, became the basis for my objectives in this life. If you stay at the personality level, life is cruel and essentially nothing more. From a transpersonal point of view, there is purpose and wisdom in the process.

My Personal Take on This Phenomenon

I believe that this reinsertion process is a real mechanism of a bigger reality that still evades us. It gives the basis to a paradigm that is very consistent and congruent, and at the same time it is compassionate and evolving oriented (multiple opportunities, rather than a single merit and punishment result). I believe in it not only because of all the study and personal experiences that I have had in this respect, but also because of the way I experienced being introduced to it. Colombia is a Catholic country. While growing up there during the sixties and seventies, I'd never heard of anyone talking about other religions besides in an academic context. In high school, in my class we had one Jewish classmate, and that was quite an exception to be noticed. Reincarnation never showed up during any conversations that I had during all those years. I was, as I explained earlier, already reading lots books with different views of reality.

It was when I was around fifteen years old that I read about the concept of reincarnation. I still remember very clearly today how, as soon as I read that word, I had this feeling from every cell of my body that expressed itself as, "How come I forgot about it?" I cannot express to you how clear and deep that remembrance was. This was not an intellectual realization. It took me completely by surprise that I could have forgotten something like that. In the end, that was my personal experience. You need to do your own introspection.

I am going to talk about the implications of this phenomenon under the assumption that it reflects an actual reality. At this point, there is simply no logical reason to deny something that is so clearly an intrinsic part of our minds (if you take the time to seriously study it), and it also provides such a coherent, logical, and intelligent scheme of reality that matches the equally impressive intelligence we see in the design of this universe. There is no such a thing as randomness. Randomness is an abstract concept created by us to explain what we cannot explain. This component explains the inevitability of human evolution as we see it in our history, as well as giving us a deep support for all of us in our striving to create a better experience on this planet that we call Earth.

A Strong Pointing to Nonphysical Dimensions

We don't know what the exact mechanism is about how and what gets transferred to the current life. These sessions do indicate the ability, in this scheme, to choose certain past events with their associated memories and emotions, and to insert them as programs in the unconscious of the next personality. Notice that genetics as we understand it today doesn't explain this type of transmission of information of memories and emotions, and neither can it explain the particular previous-life-program selection process. What we see about past insertions is that they can go from just one generation to thousands of years back in time. In the case of hundreds or thousands of years back, the genetic mixture results in a complete washout of any genetic effects that a particular event could have had back then on an individual in our present times.

As I noted earlier, in this type of regression, clients describe how the nonphysical Essence, during the in utero time, is rewiring and programming the brain of the baby. This activity probably involves part of this previous-life-program insertion process. From what I am explaining here, and all that I have explained before, it is easy to understand that there is so much more happening during the pregnancy than people think. It is a magical time in the creation of new physical life, where parents and the incoming Unit of Consciousness are truly working as a team to prepare for the scenarios that they have decided to share as part of their own individual journeys. This is another angle that I believe should make parents see their children under a very different light. It is teamwork among equals more than anything else that we traditionally think about children.

All this brings us back, forced by the limitations of our current knowledge to consider the existence of a yet undetected field where these memories and emotions are stored and transmitted. You, as a Unit of Consciousness, are deciding about the next insertion's circumstances, which I call the reality set (the particular group of people/events/geographical locations/times), that best fits the goals and lessons that you want to experience. If, as part of the lessons that you want to master in the present insertion, you want to include a non-accomplished past insertion's goal, then you will plug in the generated programs from those (past life) experiences into your new personality's unconscious. The new baby will be born with them. This program will play a more active role in your behavior than other past life experiences. Other past life experiences do add color to your personality, but not as strongly as these particular selected past insertion events. These explain the exceptional traits that we see in children at an early age, whether positive (like an innate talent) or negative (like an unexplained phobia).

The Crazy (or Rather Creative) Behavior of Adolescents and the Evolution of Humanity

I am not talking here about the negative destructive behavior that they can have; that is the result of a lack of proper guidance, as I already explained earlier. What I am talking about are all the crazy, creative ideas that each new generation brings. Adults call them crazy because these ideas are so outside their thinking (programming). Every new insertion of nonphysical entities brings a new perspective that can express itself more and more because slowly but surely, we evolve. As an example, we can easily agree that humanity is more open-minded nowadays than we were in the Middle Ages. This brings a permissiveness that allows the expression of these new ideas. Our individual, internal maps of reality open up more and more to new possibilities with every new generation. Every time we experience a physical insertion, we acquire wisdom that is going to be applied to the next one. We are constantly recycling ourselves literally and figuratively. This gives you a very clear explanation of why we evolve and why the evolution of consciousness will always continue.

Similar to how we learn to do anything better with experience, humanity's consciousness inevitably increases with every new generation. This is the "craziness" that every new generation brings to us. They shake our foundations, which are nothing more than old programming received decades ago. Like the beautiful, new green leaves that you see sprouting every spring, they give us a new fresh perspective of our rich creativity and potentials. It is a necessary factor in our evolution, rightly balanced by the mature and exiting generations.

Your Very Vested Interest for a Better World for All of Us

If you understand the implications of the reality that this aspect of our mind points to, you see very clearly how crucial it is to create a better world for everyone because this is the world that most likely we will come back and revisit. In our next future re-insertion on this planet, we will live with the consequences of our present contributions to our civilization. They will have a direct impact in the quality of the experiences that we will have then. Think about this. Under this scheme, you have a very vested interest in making this world a better place for all of us. And when I say for all of us, I am not using clichéd wording here because your next reinsertion can be anywhere on this planet. From the personality perspective, it does not make sense to choose to live in challenging circumstances; we simply want the most comfortable path we can get for ourselves. Yet from the perspective of our nonphysical Essence, we are here to grow individually as well as collectively. Thus, you as a Unit of Consciousness may choose to insert yourself, as a messenger, in circumstances where there is still a lot of conflict and injustice. It could be in a troubled neighborhood next to where you live today, or in a region on the opposite side of the planet.

What people fail to see in Hitler, Stalin, a murderer, or a suicide bomber is the messenger trying to show us the consequences to ourselves of what we have created ourselves.

We are solely responsible for the present state of humanity. We brought ourselves here, and we are equally responsible to take ourselves to a better place. Historically, it happened in big part because of our ignorance, however that is an excuse that we can no longer use today. Our knowledge about us and this universe is already more than enough to give us the impulse and motivation to become more evolved human beings.

Free Will

The question comes again: If a Unit of Consciousness has chosen a life before insertion, where is the free will? The answer is simple: you, as a nonphysical entity, select a particular reality set of people, events, geographical locations, and times that you want to pursue as your individual goal for that physical insertion. If you are able to learn the lessons as expected, that set will manifest as the reality that you wanted to experience. On the other hand—and here is where the free will comes to play—if you, *as the personality,* do not allow the expression of your Essence, your manifested reality set will change. The set is not fixed; it is the most desired and highest probabilistic path for a specific mastery to be attained in that particular physical insertion. From what we see in the regressions, it often happens that a nonphysical Essence was not able to accomplish the goals that it set out to do in an insertion. This is not uncommon, and it does not mean failure. This is completely analogous to you starting a project. Along the project, you encounter challenges and setbacks. You confront and resolve each one of them, one at a time, until you complete what you wanted. It may happen in the time frame that you set out to do, or it may not.

On this planet, the instrument that we use, which we call the human body, is an instrument that, because of its design, generates extremely powerful behavioral forces via its intrinsic biological tendencies as well as its aspect that we call emotions.[130] It is the ultimate purpose of your nonphysical Essence to be able to master those forces, no matter what body it uses. At this point in our evolution, we still are at the mercy of our emotions (my continuous mantra to you: you cannot promise me that you will not get angry again). Do not judge either this body or any negative emotion. They are the means that we chose to make of us extremely powerful entities. I want to remind you that repression is not answer, and it will never be. Repressed emotions keep affecting behavior. That is what we do nowadays, with very explosive negative results. What we are looking for is transformation in order to transcend them. We do that by acquiring the wisdom that every positive and negative experience gives us. When you experience a negative emotion and you don't extract the wisdom from the event that generated it, you did not transcend it. You will go through a similar event until you get it. That connects us to the next topic.

Karma

This process of reinserting ourselves many times and into different bodies has been tied, from some old traditions, to the concept of karma. This concept existed before Buddhism, but it was Buddha who formulated the concept in a more complete way. For most of the people today, karma is understood as a law of punishment or reward. If you were "good" in a past life, you will get a better life next time. Otherwise, you will pay for your actions. Let me say it very clearly and emphatically: this is not at all what we observe in the fields of the mind.

Your nonphysical Essence knows very well what lessons have not been mastered. It will choose the ones that will be part of the next insertion's objectives and reality set selection process.

Case 30: A "Jewish Nazi"

Brian Weiss, in his book *Same Soul, Many Bodies*, gives a classic example in this respect. He talks about a Jewish woman who hated Arabs so much that

---

[130] I want you to notice that there could very well be physical bodies that do not produce emotions.

it was becoming an all-consuming experience. After exploring the events in this life without success, she agreed to explore past ones. You can imagine her surprise when she regresses to her previous life, where she was a cruel SS Nazi officer in charge of loading Jews into the cattle wagons to send them to their deaths in the concentration camps. What comes out of her sessions is that she came here to learn to overcome hatred to any particular group of people. We will always find "good reasons" to hate some people. Today, Arabs and Palestinians have their own reasons to hate Jews. Jews have equally "valid" reasons to hate them. In fact, notice that the vast majority of the people within these different groups stay in these negative emotions, which perpetuates the continuous cycle of violence that we see in that region. They have not gotten it despite that it is so historically obvious that that attitude has not helped to solve the situation in the least. Up to that point in her life, Dr. Weiss's client had not mastered that lesson and had not gotten it either. Nevertheless, by recognizing the effects of her hatred and taking action about it (going to Dr. Weiss for sessions),[131] she was on her way to moderating her views and better understanding the human experience. After a number of sessions with Dr. Weiss, she comes to this very clear understanding, which I quote from his book.[132]

> In her life review she recognized that there were and would always be people to hate, but now at last there was an epiphany. "Compassion and love are the antidotes to hatred and rage," she said, her voice full of wonder. "Violence only perpetuates the suffering."

Notice that in this case, both the client and the practitioner are Jewish, and so I would suggest to you that all this is very unlikely a result of imagination. These paradigms do occur in sessions. Once she transcended her personality, she could see very well a much higher scheme of wisdom taking place within her. In what otherwise would qualify her life as a very successful one, she did suffer as a consequence of that unlearned lesson. That was the reality set that her Essence chose as a way to transcend it. It is very important that you understand that this woman did not come here as a Jewish woman, as a

---

[131] Right there was an exercise of free will. Most of the people choose to live in hatred and suffer its consequences. That is a choice that goes against what their nonphysical Essence is, and therefore what it wants.

[132] Brian L. Weiss, *Same Soul, Many Bodies*, New York: Free Press, 2004, 44.

punishment for her previous life. It was actually more a strategic move from the part of her nonphysical Essence. By coming here as a Jewish person, hating the Arabs, and then confronting the fact that she was a Nazi in a previous life, that was the exact reality set to shake her out of that position. She came here to complete her new wisdom about respect and tolerance, and that is how she integrated it. Now that she completed that chapter in her evolution, she will not need to go through that type of experiences anymore. She now has become a new beacon of light for humanity.

As is very clear from Dr. Newton's books, there are master teachers and guides involved in our evolution. Even so, certainly there is not a god (or gods) of any kind administering justice and deciding whether you go to hell or heaven, or any other place that a particular religion professes. Neither are these guides punishing for incomplete learnings in a physical insertion. Practitioners simply don't see that in their sessions. There's a very consistent picture across thousands and thousands of sessions that have been done in this area.

The other aspect of karma that we don't see is this model where if you suffered in one life, then your next one will be "better." Qualifying physical insertions like that is shortsighted and a perspective from the level of personality. As I have just illustrated, your nonphysical Essence is choosing the objectives and reality sets of each insertion according to its goals. It can very well be that in a previous insertion, you lived a life of high social status and financial abundance, only to go to the next one with scarcities. You cannot judge evolution by simply looking at the different physical reality sets. Another example that I talked about earlier is very advanced Units of Consciousness who may choose a physical instrument with severe handicaps. You see, in this case it is exactly the opposite: it shows the tremendous power that they have when they seek mastery through these circumstances.

I also frequently hear how someone, when going through challenging life circumstances, exclaims, "It must be my karma." Again, that is not what we observe when we work with deep states of trance. You are simply learning; you are not paying debts under anyone (God) and to anyone. This type of mentality is a good example of how much this concept of punishment and reward has become a mass consciousness state in humanity. Even if you do not subscribe to traditional religions and their eternal punishment schemes, you still interpret different models of reality under that point of view and resign to your life circumstances as a victim, instead of being an active participant in a transformative process designed to empower and liberate you.

The law of karma, as it is understood nowadays, is still based on judgment and fear. If you look at human history, punishment may have worked in the short term, but never as a long-term solution. Take the Catholic Church and the Inquisition. As brutal as that method was, in the end it did not work. It did not deter people from seeking the truth, whether in science or in faith. Humans, even under the threat of eternal damnation, have continued to sin as seen in the eyes of religions that profess that type of destiny. These institutions were never able to stop them, and they will never be able to do so. Here, you can see how this aspect deep within our minds explains that resulting inefficacy, even under such dire threats.

When you go into the deepest recesses of our minds, you uncover a scheme in which there is only love, as well as evolution so that we can fully express it.

Remember, it is our unconscious that truly drives our behavior. In other words, deep in our minds we don't believe in those schemes. Whether you think this is a trick from the devil or that this aspect of our minds does not reflect a truly existent reality, this is the part of our psyche that drives our behavior against these suggestions of eternal consequences. These religious teachings then become nothing more than very negative, limiting programs with highly charged emotional batteries. As such, they are unsustainable. They are repressed emotions of fear, like any other resulting programming from any other life circumstance. They create inner conflicts that rob us from our inner peace and the full creative expression that is within all of us. From what I explained in the section of parents and the education of children, we need to behave respectfully toward everyone and everything because it is an intrinsic expression of who we are. We all want and expect to be respected equally by all others, and thus this has to be reciprocal. It is natural and logical. Yes, it is possible to accomplish that without the threat of punishment. This is a sustainable path. This is a solid basis from which we can build true harmony.

Morals

For exactly the same reasons that I have mentioned just previously, generation after generation, our young ones are abandoning more and more the arbitrary, moralistic judgments that we have created under the name of religion or any other authority. Deep inside, we don't believe those threats. Even the conservative minds of Western society would be considered sinners under the eyes of humans of one hundred or more years ago. As much as they complain about the moral liberalization of our youth, they themselves are part of it when compared to previous generations.

Sexuality has been the major target of our moral codes. So many parents insist on imposing moral codes on their children in spite of the fact that they themselves broke them in their youth. Behind such an incongruence is the thinking "If we did what we did, even with those moral codes, imagine how far we would have gone without them." There's fear and insecurity about how their children would handle such powerful forces without those threats. These parents did not have a role model on how to guide children so that they can take a more congruent and harmonious path in this respect, and they keep repeating the programming that they got while growing up. As I write this book, all kinds of sexual scandals, harassments, and abuses are making headlines in the media, whether from liberal or conservative institutions and individuals. It shows so clearly the power of our human nature, irrespective of particular beliefs, and that we try to tame and hide by using negative, conflictive programming. This programming tries to repress the natural forces within us with explosive and damaging behaviors to everyone involved. The perpetrators and abusers, as well as their victims, are messengers that tell us we need to change what we all have created. In spite of all the denouncements (and rightfully so), there will inevitably be more of them in our future unless we change our own paradigm. That's the reason for this book.

What we want is for adolescents and adults to be able to fully enjoy this beautiful life force that we have within us. They can take responsible use of it, with the proper understanding that it has on our emotional lives as well as the consequences that it has as the force that is behind the most powerful act that we can ever do as physical entities: the creation of life in this universe. We need to be able to have proper, open education in which children and adolescents learn, in a safe and constructive manner, how to deal with this intrinsic aspect of the human body.

Discrimination

Given that past insertions are a component of our personality, they are a relentless inner voice that guides us toward mutual respect irrespective of race, sexual orientation, social class, or any other characteristic that differentiates us from each other, as human beings. The more you become conscious about this aspect, the more you start seeing your fellow human beings under a different light. The beggar whom you see today in the street could have been a king or queen in a previous insertion. Following this logic, why would you look down at him if you also are conscious that you could have been a beggar in a past physical life? Under this paradigm, when you see a beggar in the street, what you see is a nonphysical entity that came here to experience what it decided as part of this life's goals, including being a messenger and a mirror that shows us what we have created, where we still have people dying in the streets while others could feed entire populations with their fortunes. We all deserve unlimited wealth in the full sense of the word. The message is a call to attention to the disparity that we have created for ourselves. Every human in suffering is a call to action to all of us. That Unit of Consciousness is as powerful as you are, despite what you may see on the surface. Any discrimination on the basis of social class, castes, or financial status not only doesn't make sense, but ultimately as we continue on our evolution, it will disappear. Under this scheme, social classes simply do not make sense.

And under this scheme, discriminating against women does not make sense either. Men were women before (and vice versa). Anyone doing this discrimination, as an individual or behind an institution, perpetuates a social state where they may find themselves on the other side of these circumstances in a future insertion (as so well exemplified in the last Dr. Weiss case). We are Units of Consciousness using an instrument designed, in a similar way to those of different species of beings[133] with which we share this particular planet, to express certain energies in two different ways: one that we chose to call male, the other that we call female. That expression results in slight variations in physical construction. Think of it as two models of the same product. All of us have made use of these two models in our different insertions and taken advantage of the particular experiences that each entail. On other planets, there may be more types of models for a design, whether sexual or any other type of differentiation. As I mentioned at the beginning of the book, there is no reason why we could not insert into an advanced enough machine that we create in the future. Your body is an astonishingly sophisticated machine to which you attach yourself to experience this universe. That is all.

The same logic applies to race. Think of all our different races as yet other models derived from the original design. Discriminating because of race is an absurdity. Sessions show us that we all have experienced this physical dimension via a body of a different race.

---

[133] Plants and animals.

Discriminating because of sexual orientation is equally absurd because it is another variation that is part of the diversity through which we can experience this planet. The Unit of Consciousness that selects the body and circumstances that manifest as a different sexual orientation from the norm is doing that because of the particular experiences and learnings that It wants to have through that type of life. That is all, with no more to it. Why can't we let them be? Different sexual orientations are not "aberrations" of human behavior; they also exist in other animal species as well, and not as an isolated phenomenon.[134] People who judge this diversity in the name of a particular religious belief are judging what the particular god in which they believe created. This diversity of nature is another mirror that shows us the artificial fears that we created. It shows us the need to look deeper into ourselves and (re)discover what we really are. The norms of behavior that we have created in our civilization have no relevance in the nonphysical realm. The only relevance is unconditional love, which implies full respect for the diversity that is part of our creative expression.

Evolution Is Inevitable

In spite of all the negative news and impressions that we get from the media, it is very clear that our level of consciousness has increased. Slavery and discrimination, though not yet a thing of the past, are aspects of us that we agree more and more need to disappear from our societies. Our awareness of the consequences of our actions on our planet is increasing at a global level. There is an evolutionary process that plays in our minds.

Past Life Insertions Explain It Very Well

Even if you think that they are simply a creation of our brains, it still explains this direction of movement in our behavior. It is a component of our psyche. We are all carrying deep memories of past life experiences that are unconsciously guiding us in the decisions that we make today. The lives that we lived (real or not, but that reside in our unconscious) when we were discriminated against leave an imprint that makes us rebel against any discrimination that we see today. As time passes, more and more nonphysical entities will have had these experiences in the physical world. When they come back, they become part of a psychological mass that, when it reaches a critical point, creates the change that we see. We know that discrimination is wrong at a gut level. If

---

[134] You can easily find abundant information on this topic on the Internet.

this component were not present in our psyche, we would remain static within the programming that our parents and society instilled in us. Instead, every single new generation questions and rejects outdated beliefs (to the dismay of the adults of the time). In the same way that you learn from your experiences in your current life, we carry the lessons from past ones. This is the reason and mechanism behind the unstoppable current of human evolution.

Interaction Accelerates Evolution

How fast or how slow a society changes depends on how tightly coupled the community's lives are and how closed it is to external influences. We can see this in the isolated tribes that remain in the Amazon. Because of their isolation, combined with their relatively small numbers of individuals of their communities, it is easy for their figures of authority to keep a tight grip on their beliefs and traditions; they don't have to be imposed by force. The programming of the community is so strong that without any external references to other possibilities, it silences the voice of this component of the personality that they also have in them. Once they get in contact with individuals coming from other societies (like when scientists visit them to study their culture), they start to realize that there are different ways. The process is irreversible. That inner voice will start to take a stronger stance in their new generations. This is a process that takes their cultures into a deep crisis of identity that they need to resolve by moving forward with new changes, discarding outdated beliefs and rituals, and keeping that which is truly in resonance with the emerging consciousness that they are going through. As an example, many of them have brutal rituals like that of the Satere-Mawe,[135] where twenty times in men's lives, they have to wear gloves full of bullet ants (named for their incredibly painful sting from a single one of them). Eventually, these rituals will become a part of their past as their new generations start to question the validity of the beliefs behind these activities. As is shown in that video, the chief of the tribe explains that life would not be valuable if you don't suffer or put effort into it. Putting effort under the proper motivation is great. Nevertheless, life is already challenging as it is, and there is no need to add extra suffering to make it worthwhile. Their new generations will question this thinking in a similar way that women did with

---

[135] National Geographic. "Initiation with Ants." *YouTube*, National Geographic, December 21, 2007, https://www.youtube.com/watch?v=ZGIZ-zUvotM. Accessed December 14, 2018.

the rules that were imposed on them about swimming suits. It is important to note that it is up to them to decide their destiny. In the same way that we decide ours, we must respect their ways. On the other hand, their deep connection with nature is something that they will hopefully carry into their future. They will need to come to peace with the inevitability of this process. In the case of societies that are not so tightly coupled, like Western civilization, change occurs much faster (as we all are experiencing it within our own lifetimes). In the tribes, their elders or priests can exert their authority over the whole community very easily, but in our larger groupings of people, authority is further removed from each of us. This automatically allows for more variability in individual expression.

Our Inevitable Evolution Colliding with Obsolete Dynamics

That brings us to the events that we are witnessing today. There is a deeper trouble brewing underneath the conflicts that we see every day in the news. On one hand, we see the waves of terrorism and violence that are gripping the world. New terrorist organizations and ideologies that did not exist in the past are sprouting and causing chaos in the middle of Europe and the United States—events that would have been unheard off just a couple of decades ago. All this violence is the result of an emotionally immature civilization, as I explained earlier. The new trouble with this is that more and more democratic systems are being forced to intrude into the personal lives of their citizens. It is coming to the point where everyone is essentially a potential suspect. This will inevitably lead to suspicion and restriction of liberties, which goes directly against of our intrinsic nature of seeking expansion and freedom of expression. This is not just an opinion—this is what we observe when working in the fields of the transformation of the mind. This is an integral part of our psyche. This is what drives our history.

Any form of authority, whether religious, governmental, or otherwise, that attempts to restrict the free flow of human expression inevitably collapses.

A few examples are the failure of the Inquisition and the disintegration of the Soviet Union and all its Iron Curtain countries, which exerted a brutal control over their citizens. The Chinese took note and allowed for economic liberties that its revolutionary leader, Mao Zedong, would have been dismayed to see. Without those freedoms, China would have never become the economic power that it is today. This force of our inner psyche is what drives these types of global events, and governments need to understand this intrinsic human force. This is the force that also drives the smaller ones that are truly revolutionary in their own way, like women now being allowed to drive and participate in running races in Saudi Arabia—something unthinkable just a few years ago. Deep in our unconscious, we know we are nonphysical entities who are wearing these instruments that we call bodies, and we use them to accomplish goals that may even lead to putting ourselves in harm's way. This is the influence of the Unit of Consciousness that has the power to override the survival mechanisms of the unconscious in the name of the ideals that we pursue. Rosa Parks, Martin Luther King, Nelson Mandela, the student who stood in front of a tank in Tiananmen Square, Malala—they were and are catalysts of change in our societies. And they will keep coming until we achieve the intrinsic freedoms that we know that we have the right to experience. This is part of our core unconscious structures, whether or not you think they represent an actual reality, that drives our behavior. Governments need to understand this force because they cannot keep going against it. In the same way that China took the "risk" of allowing economic freedoms, it needs to realize that it is in its best interest to allow personal freedoms. The way to do it is through emotional education and empowerment of the individuals. An empowered individual has no need to break any laws as long as he has the freedom to express himself in a manner that is constructive, creative, and respectful of the others. Indeed, it's a much more challenging process than installing cameras in every corner of their city streets, as is the new trend around the world. This applies equally to the United States, where we see how the government is penetrating more and more into our private lives, even if it is under the banner of keeping us safe from terrorism. Indeed, this applies to any country and authority anywhere. This is coming from the perspective of the human consciousness (and I write this to emphasize that I am *not* saying it from a political perspective). Restricting human expression may work for some time, yet it is unsustainable in the long term.

Today we have a dangerous, vicious cycle where terrorism is fueling government control, which in turn ends up fueling violence. This cycle can only be broken when we start confronting our problems at the root level. Right away, that brings us back to each one of us. In order to see the change that we want to see in the world, we need to change ourselves. Each of us needs to transform our minds so that we can move to a different level of consciousness. Once we are there, we will make very different decisions in our lives than we are making today. We will transform our family dynamics, our relationships, our education system, and our governments. We cannot expect to see changes in the government if we don't change ourselves. Government is nothing more than individuals like you and me. That's what this book is about.

Summary

This component of our personality adds soft-wired programs only. Thus, our summary looks like this.

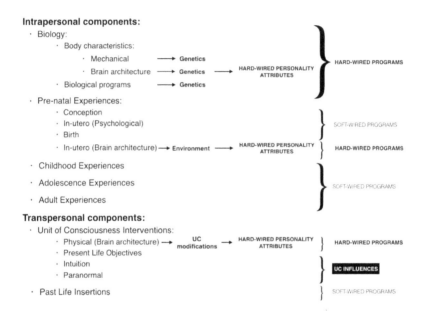

The Transgenerational Effect Component

In general, we all understand how each country has its own culture. That culture translates into behavior, customs, and ways of thinking that vary from one country to the next. Even within one country, it is easy to identify different customs in different geographical areas. When groups of people gather and interact in a consistent manner, a group culture emerges. Implicit and explicit rules of interaction and behavior start to show up, to which the individuals within the group adhere. Individuals comply with those rules in order to satisfy their need to belong. The stronger the ties between the individuals, the stronger the influence of that culture in the unconscious programs in each of them. In our societies, the most nuclear association of individuals is generally the family. Precisely because the ties of the individuals that form part of a family are so strong, from the unconscious point of view, the family clan exerts a powerful influence in each one of its members. There is a family unconscious. We all can relate to it. When we talk about our families among friends, we often state how in our family certain things are done a certain way (compared to theirs). We talk about family traditions. Indeed, we can see and feel this difference in family cultures when two individuals come together to become a couple.

This family unconscious plays a bigger role than most people realize. In the first part of the book, I showed you how the mind mechanisms are designed in such a way that it makes it imperative that we solve our limiting beliefs in order to live life to the fullest potential. The family unconscious is another mechanism nature uses to make sure we clear out our limitations. This mechanism within the family makes perfect sense because learning to solve our conflicts at this micro-society level prepares and enables us to solve them at the macro level—that is, at the level of society and ultimately at the level of civilization as a whole. It is crucial our understanding of it. This mechanism affects directly our lives by means of programs in the unconscious that we inherit from our ancestors. By ancestors, I mean up to your great-grandparents from both sides, including aunts and uncles from both sides and their relationships. These programs have the same structure and work exactly in the same way as any other program that your unconscious created in your present life. The difference is that your unconscious takes and creates these programs from the family unconscious rather than from direct, personal experiences. In contrast to the programs that parents transmit to their children consciously or unconsciously, transgenerational programs skip generations as well as direct links between the family members. Their effects can be observed very clearly.

Case 31: (Transgenerational) Hobbies

This is another case that Christian Fleche gives in his book *The Body as a Healing Tool*.[136] It is about a man who has two hobbies, collecting rocks and collecting butterflies. He goes to therapy because he feels "bad about himself" and "uncomfortable in his own skin." He has done extensive therapy with no success. Then this therapist tells him to inquire about his family history. As it turns out, he discovers a grandfather about whom he was never told anything.

---

[136] Christian Fleche, *El Cuerpo como Herramienta de Curación, Descodificación Psicobiológica de las Enfermedades*, Barcelona: Ediciones Obelisco, 2013, 193.

He was a fugitive who was sent to Africa to do hard labor, splitting rocks. In the end, he dies, executed in a gas chamber. Nobody in this family talked about this grandfather because they were ashamed of his history; he remained a family secret. Not so in the family unconscious. This secret expressed itself in this individual doing the session. You can see how his collecting hobbies were actually an expression of this unconscious memory (part of the method of collecting butterflies is killing them in a jar with a lethal gas). The sensation of feeling bad about himself was the expression of the family shame.

This example shows so eloquently how it is we humans who judge. Nature doesn't. With the material that I have already presented to you in this book, you now understand that this grandfather was a product of the environment in which he grew. Trying to hide this person is not the way to resolve the conflicts that we have created. We need to bring them to light and resolve them. This case is another clear illustration of the limited free will that we have in our present state of consciousness. This person genuinely liked to collect stones and butterflies; these were his hobbies. Nevertheless, as long as that family secret remained as such, these hobbies were more an unconscious expression of the unexpressed history than a true expression of that individual. Once this secret was brought out to light, he may or may not have felt compelled to collect these items. If he did, now it became true free will. It is now his free choice, not just an expression of a program that runs in his unconscious.

Case 32: Binge Spending

This is a case presented by Angeles Wolder in her video *Deudas Económicas (Financial Debts)*.[137] Angeles Wolder is the director of the Escuela de Descodificación Biológica Original[138] (School of Original Biological Decoding) in Barcelona, Spain. She has degrees in social and cultural anthropology, among others, as well as certifications in neurolinguistic programming and hypnotherapy. In this case, she talks about a man who comes to her because he finds himself in a repetitive pattern of binge spending, to the point where he gets into financial debts and must ask for help to other

---

[137] Angeles Wolder, "Transgeneracional: 'Deudas Económicas.'" *YouTube*, Instituto Ángeles Wolder, August 26, 2015, https://www.youtube.com/watch?v=5vu-xnv2v-Y. Accessed December 14, 2018.

[138] https://www.descodificacionbiologica.es. Accessed December 14, 2018.

members of the family to resolve the situation. Normally, he has a good job and earns enough to even save money. He simply falls into this behavior again and again.

Logically, the sessions first focus on finding relevant events in his life, including birth, in utero, and conception. Nothing shows up. After these series of searches with no significant results, it is time to look at the family history. Thanks to his aunt, who opens up the untold family history of his grandfather, he gets to understand where his behavior comes from. His grandfather died young, at age forty-one, due to liver complications because of his drinking. He was an individual who ruined the family because of his gambling. His son (the father of the client), was fourteen years-old when he died. The grandfather left his fourteen-year-old son, his wife, and his eight-year-old daughter to fend for themselves. As a result of that, this fourteen-year-old boy was forced to take on the responsibilities of an adult at an early age. As a consequence of that situation, the client's father becomes a "very, very responsible" person (using Wolder's words; she corroborates what I talked about earlier in the book: this is not normal in the development of a youngster). The history of the grandfather was forgotten not only because it was shameful but also because the family was left in a dire situation that forced them to focus on rebuilding life. The client's father did so.

The client tells how he never felt a lack of money at home while growing up. Nevertheless, because his father was so rigorous (i.e., "life needs to be taken very seriously"), he received very little personal allowance. As it turns out, he had his first girlfriend when he was fourteen years old. This was the first time in his life that he felt that he did not have enough money. Because his allowance was so small, and he wanted to invite her out, he started to find ways to get the money, even if it meant procuring it in dishonest ways (like stealing money from his sister or others). Here is where this behavior of mismanaging money begins in his life. This is the result of the unconscious transmission of unresolved conflicts within the family. Notice the repetition of the number fourteen in the history of the family. This is an unconscious trigger point to these programs. Not only did the family not mourn his grandfather, but they were ashamed of him. The client's unconscious expressed this situation through this behavior. As much as we want to hide our programs, their hidden emotional batteries affect how we interact in our lives, and he could not help but fall into this irresponsible binge of money spending. Once he understood and processed this situation, he liberated himself from these programs and thus the binges.

As I mentioned above, these programs are exactly the same as any other program generated in your lifetime. It is the way these programs get installed in our unconscious where the difference lies. In this component of our personality, it makes sense to consider the role of epigenetics.[139] At the physical layer, it seems plausible that it plays some role in this mechanism. For example, the repetition of significant events at age fourteen in the last case (I want to emphasize that this is not just this particular example that I am showing here; this is, relatively speaking, a common occurrence in transgenerational programs). It is easy to see that this time information could be epigenetically encoded, yet there are many questions that remain unresolved. Epigenetically speaking, why did this particular individual pick certain programs from a certain member of the family? Why not the others? The many cases of this transgenerational component show us that different unresolved family conflicts may be picked by different individuals within that clan. Then who or what is "assigning" these unresolved conflicts? It is very difficult to explain this from the perspective of the (epi)genes. We can clearly see this type of programs, their effects, and the fact that the affected individuals transcend their limiting behaviors once the information is processed from this transgenerational perspective. As with the case of those coming from previous physical insertions, we simply don't know how they are plugged in. As a possible explanation, it makes sense to make use of that yet undetected field that would explain memories and programs from past lives, as well as the in utero customization of the brain of the baby by the Unit of Consciousness. It is a very congruent picture. The question that remains is why. Why does someone else in the family have to "pay" for the actions of previous generations of the clan?

1. This point is the same as that of past physical insertions. Nobody is paying for anything. The Unit of Consciousness chose a life (i.e., its particular reality set) because this type of events matches exactly what it is looking to master in this insertion into the physical world. These events are concerned specifically to the path of evolution of that Unit of Consciousness. If there would have been another family with the same

---

[139] The body's characteristics have been traditionally viewed as dictated by the molecular structure of the genes (gene's coding). Now we understand that a certain gene may be turned on or not depending on different factors, including the environment. Epigenetics studies how these other factors (which are different than a change in the genetic code itself) affect our bodies, including the heritability of this activation/deactivation of genes.

opportunities to learn, the individuated consciousness could have chosen that one instead. Understand very clearly that there is no victimization here. It is a chosen process for mastery from your Essence, in which that clan provides the perfect environment to fulfill it.

2. Nature is ensuring, through this mechanism, that we clear our conflicts at the personal level and at the group level. Because if we cannot even resolve conflicts at the family level (our loved ones), how do we expect to do it at the societal level? Look at all the wars in our history and still going on today. Isn't it time that with all the violent history that we have behind us, and the knowledge that we have acquired, we pause and understand that we need a new way of interacting? We all have personal roles, simultaneous with social roles, that we came here to play. The social role starts with the community of family.

On the practical side of things, the tricky aspect of these transgenerational programs is that because they were not created by events that you experienced, they create behaviors that seem odd when looked at only within the context of your life. (This equally applies to past insertions' programs.) Take the last case, where this man has this irresponsible behavior even though he comes from a father who was very responsible. If you stay within this scope, you cannot explain that behavior, and now you become a victim—the classic "bad luck" we resort to, with victims of a universe whose understanding seem to be beyond us. Now you have a better understanding of the whys in your life.

This transgenerational aspect of our personality is under the umbrella of what is called psychogenealogy. It had its beginnings in Europe[140] and is still a relatively unknown branch of psychology in the United States. It is impossible for me to give a complete picture of this field. What I want you to take away from here is that your family history is also a part of you—literally. You inherit positive traits but also negative ones. Unresolved conflicts within the clan will affect its members, whatever the conflict is. As a guide, let me give you a partial list so that you have an idea of the extent of the territory to search for when considering sources for negative patterns of behavior.

1. Family secrets. This is the direct extension of the parent's secrets that I talked about earlier in the book. We extend this aspect to the whole family clan. Any secret kept in the clan is potential for limiting manifestation

---

[140] Anne Ancelin Schützenberger, Jacob Levy Moreno, etc.

in the personality of one or more of its members. Here are some of the events that tend to be kept away from public view.

- o Abortions, whether induced or natural
- o Unrecognized or illegitimate children from outside the formal relationships
- o Secret relationships
- o Abuses within the family (physical, sexual, emotional)
- o Illnesses with a social stigma, like sexually transmitted diseases
- o Suicides
- o Members with mental illnesses (who many times are sent away to a mental institution and disappear from family history)
- o Members who were fugitives or had stories outside the law (killings, robberies, etc.)
- o Financial ruin, bankruptcies

2. Unresolved family disputes that leave a rift within the clan. Included in this point are any of the cases above, even if they are not kept as a secret. If they still cause conflict, they will linger in the family unconscious. An example under this category would be the infighting that occurs due to inheritances or businesses, which often cause deep divisions among the relatives involved.
3. Death of a family member who was not recognized or not properly mourned. As I showed with the two previous cases, sooner or later, this member needs to be recognized and fully accepted as part of the family history if we want to clear the unconscious from the hidden charge.

Let me give another case that illustrates so well how this clan's unconscious hovers over its members.

Case 33: The Effects of the "Erased" Family Member

Jean Guillaume Salles, who is a teacher at the Christian Fleche School of Biodecoding, presents this case.[141] The title of the video is *El*

---

[141] Jean Guillaume, "Conferencia: El Transgeneracional—Herencias familiares por Amor hacia vosotros por Jean Guillaume." *YouTube*, La Caja de Pandora, July 20, 2015, https://www.youtube.com/watch?v=gykm8TlRLNE. Accessed December 14, 2018. At around 37:15 mark.

Transgeneracional, Las Herencias Familiares, Por Amor a Vosotros (The Transgenerational, Family Inheritances, for the Love for Yourselves). It is about a woman who comes to him because she feels that she cannot have a successful long-term relationship. What comes out of the sessions is as follows. Her paternal grandfather had a lover who was a married woman. He has a child with her. Even though this is an illegitimate son, this man decides to recognize him and take him under his care. This is an example of a conflict that was resolved (from the father's side; Salles doesn't talk about what happened on the lover's side of the story). Later, this man marries another woman, and from that union they have a daughter. World War II erupts, and he is called to service. When the war is over and he returns, he arrives home to find out that not only had his wife had a child with another man, but even worse, the other man turned out to be a German officer. From his perspective, this is the worst treason there can be (he fought against the Germans). He separates from her and later marries another woman. From this last union, the father of the client is born. The woman who had the child with the German officer is "erased" from the family history. Nevertheless, as Salles says, those who have been erased or forgotten will show up in the descendants. The information remains in the unconscious. Information that is repressed always wants to express itself, which is what happening to his client, manifested in that feeling that she cannot have a long-term relationship. This information will become accessible when the client is set in the proper state of mind by a well-trained practitioner.

Salles describes how he processed this case, which I include here so that you can get an idea of how this happens in a therapeutic setting. Because the people involved in this case, the grandfather and the "erased" woman, are no longer available for questioning, Salles tells his client (who will be in hypnotic state at this point) to imagine having his grandfather and this woman in a room. The client sees her grandfather in front of her, and the woman is standing at the exit of the room (her unconscious symbolically expresses the family situation: that woman is "out"). The client feels the excruciating pain that her grandfather felt for the treason inflicted on him. She then projects a negative judgment over the woman at the door. Next, Salles asks his client to "bring into the room" the German officer. As soon as she does that, she feels that the man who appears in the room is a cold, cruel person. It becomes obvious to her that the woman did not love that man—she was raped. Her negative judgment starts to dissipate with this new understanding. Salles now instructs her to tell that woman that she now recognizes and accepts her as part of the family. Once she does this, the client feels an enormous weight taken off her shoulders.

This case is a great example for multiple reasons.

1. From the transgenerational point of view, notice that the woman who was "erased" genetically speaking (in the traditional sense) did not have a connection with Salles' client. Her grandmother was the last woman her grandfather married. Still, even though there was not that physical connection, this woman took the unresolved conflict between her grandfather and her previous wife. That is because from the unconscious point of view, the woman who was "erased" still is part of the family. It doesn't matter how much the "new" family may want to forget about her. Reality cannot be erased simply because we don't like it. We cannot cheat our unconscious.

2. This unresolved family conflict created a program in her along the lines of "I cannot trust men; they are dangerous, because they will erase me, even if I were confronted with a situation about which I could not do anything." You can see how such a program in her unconscious would sabotage any relationship that she would have. It becomes a filter through which she looks at life. She is not conscious about it, yet it is there regulating her relationships. Even though she wants to have a long-term relationship and start a family, this program won't allow it. Going back to the first section of this book, this program only wants to protect her. It is very easy to understand the danger of being erased from a survival point of view. That's exactly what the unconscious is designed to protect us from. The problem is that this program is already obsolete and out of context. Nevertheless, because the unconscious is mechanical, it simply executes what it has stored in its memory banks whenever an associated event triggers that particular program. In her case, whenever she got into a relationship that may have had a long-term potential, her unconscious activated this program to come to her rescue.

3. Notice that even though the original people involved were not available anymore (they were already dead), this fact did not prevent the healing from occurring. The client's unconscious had all the necessary information. Under Salles' guidance, her unconscious presented it perfectly well. To her unconscious, these scenes are as real as our everyday external reality.

She felt all the associated emotions. And because of that, when Salles tells her client to tell this woman that she recognizes and accepts her, the healing occurs. She feels it when she expresses how that enormous weight was taken off her shoulders. That was the weight of the hidden conflict within the family, and her inner conflict about wanting a stable relationship and not being able to have it. This type of transgenerational healing often benefits not just the person doing the transformation but also the whole clan, though unconsciously. It is not unusual for these clients to comment about how family dynamics shift as a result of that transformation.

4. I want to emphasize that this is not an intellectual process. Neither is it imagination. When Salles tells her to imagine them in a room, he is actually guiding her unconscious to pull that information and present it to her. It is the symbolic language of the unconscious. It's also a smart way from the mind practitioner side, with the objective of keeping the rational mind relaxed in dealing with this irrational situation. His client is feeling all the associated emotions. This is an internal experiential process; it is not intellectual.

5. Think about the transgenerational consequences that traumas have in us. Family violence of any kind has ripple effects that can go down two, three, or even four generations. All that conflicted energy is in the way of these individuals reaching the full potential in their own lives. It's wasted energy that could have been used to create and expand our lives for the better. Think about the devastating effects that wars have on all of us. A great number of individuals (the armies) participate in them and come back to their societies with an enormously conflicted legacy. This will have a direct effect in the relationships with their families. More than that, these conflicts go well beyond the immediate relatives. They will be transmitted to the future generations as well. Because of their numbers, this has implications that go far beyond the family level. It creates mental illness at the societal level.

As you can see, this transgenerational factor can affect us in profound ways. Talk with your family members, bring the hidden histories to light, and reconcile with whatever happened. After all, it did happen, so come to peace with it. Those who have secrets may have them because they believe they are protecting the rest of the clan from the negative impact of those events. There are good intentions at the personality level, however in the end, they are incongruent and in judgment about the humanity in all of us. Your unconscious knows. As well intentioned as this might be, it does not serve anyone. It may be painful to bring up the memories, but in the long run, it is liberating for everyone.

With this component, we complete the picture of our personality. I will present the final summary at the end of the implications of this second section of the book, coming next.

Part 2 Conclusions and Implications

The Critical Nurture Assumption

The theme of how much we are shaped (personality and behavior) by nature (genes, biological tendencies, etc.) or nurture (parents and the environment in which we grow and live) always shows up in sociology, anthropology, psychology, and any other branch of science that studies the behavior of humans. I hope I have not left any doubts about how critical I consider the nurturing factor to be.

You can imagine the interest I took in reading and studying the book *The Nurture Assumption* by Judith Harris. In her book, she presents a strong case for discounting the nurturing factor in a big way. In her case, nurturing refers to the influence of the parents. Instead, she puts most of the weight on how we turn out to be as adults on what she calls socialization with peers. In other words, children are molded mainly by their interactions with their peers. The book became a (controversial) bestseller because it shook the foundations that everybody had about how important parents are as an influence on their children. It is very well researched, and she makes a compelling case.

I want to give you a different perspective, coming from the model of the mind and all the related concepts that I have presented to you. I want to comment about some small pieces from her book—not only to show how her cases can be interpreted in different ways but also because I believe that with these explanations, they will give you an even deeper understanding about the topics that I presented in this book.

It Is about Constructive Exchanges

From the beginning, the first thing that I want you to see is how this is a great example of the two effects of the human mind that I talked about: the subjective objectivity and the information filtering effects. Both Harris and I believe that we are objective in the assessments that we present to the world. This is the subjective objectivity effect of our minds. The programs and data stored in our unconscious minds, working in conjunction with the faculty of reasoning, form a completely congruent picture in each of us. In our case, it's to such a convincing point that we are willing to make the effort to publish this information for the rest of the world to see. Based on our personal experiences (programs), we have created our own inner maps of reality, and it is through them that we see life. This is happening to every single human being on this planet. I will say it one more time because even though I talked extensively about this earlier, it is such a crucial point that everybody needs to understand: in our current state of evolution, this subjective objectivity effect comes with the unfortunate consequence that we kill each other for our views. Violence rages on our planet, starting at the level of our personal relationships. If we were to understand this, we would rather focus on building bridges of communication for mutual understandings, which is what is needed.

Coming back to Harris and me, once we both had a "critical mass" of programs in our unconscious to see the world in our own different ways, then the information filtering effect started to play its role. We both immersed ourselves in the study of material that would corroborate our points of view. Our books are a good testament to this. Even though in our case it manifested into this very explicit activity, every single human being is doing this in his or her own way. It is an automatic unconscious process to keep your mental structures stable, which is important to be able to function in our lives—even though it can easily propel us into closing our minds to new possibilities. The antidote to this is a strong awareness and intention about keeping an open attitude about anything. It is a continuous exercise to practice in our lives.

This brings me to the point here: that this discussion be viewed as just another building block in the process of understanding ourselves, which is what really matters. It's constructive cooperation.

At the beginning of her book, Harris writes about how she used to believe in the nurture assumption (i.e., that parents are the key shapers of the personality of the children) and how she ended up changing her opinion about it. Among other facts, she mentions three things that "bothered her."[142] These three observations were an important basis for the change of opinion. They are a good starting point for our exchange of ideas here.

First Observation

In her first observation, she writes about how she saw the young children of Russian parents living in Cambridge and speaking English more fluently than Russian and without an accent. In spite of their parents only speaking in Russian to them, since these parents did not know English very well. In other

---

[142] Judith Rich Harris, *The Nurture Assumption: Why Children Turn Out the Way They Do*, New York: Free Press, 2009, 9.

words, in spite of Russian being the home language.[143] This observation is a clear demonstration of the superb adaptability of the human mind and how well the mechanisms that I described in the book work in that respect. As we saw, in children before about ten years of age, their unconscious is generally open and absorbing everything that is happening in their environment. Also, as I explained, the unconscious is a machine that does not judge or reason. The implications here are that with respect to assimilation of rules of the environment, the unconscious does not differentiate or have favorites between the environment at home or outside of it. It will go ahead and assimilate everything as it is experienced. In this respect, the environment at home creates its own set of associated programs, at the same time that the external environments are creating their own sets. As we saw, the unconscious will create them with the proper associations. You can think of these associations as "if-then" conditions (if at home, then … if at school, then …) that determine how the child will behave wherever he is. The unconscious of the child will trigger the appropriate programs according to where she is at any moment in her life. It also implies that the more time the child spends in a certain environment, the more his unconscious will create programs associated with it, and the more these programs will be triggered and exercised. For children from immigrants who are going to the local schools, they are already spending at least five of the seven days of the week outside home. That means that the programs in the unconscious and the areas of the brain that are related to the local language will be exercised much more than those of the language of the parents (where they are different). It is then a matter of what programs are being triggered the most.

To further clarify this, let's take the example of a new immigrant Chinese couple who decides to settle in Chinatown in San Francisco. Chinatown is a very big community that you can think of as a mini culture within the American culture. This couple has a child, whom they decide to homeschool. The child plays during the weekend with the Chinese children of the community. In other words, this child, in her first years, has relatively few interactions with American children and English as a language. Because of that, she will indeed be more fluent in her parents' language than in English, at least during the first years, despite living in the United States. In reality, the local culture (in this example the American culture) is so pervasive that she most likely will

---

[143] Judith Rich Harris, *The Nurture Assumption: Why Children Turn Out the Way They Do*, New York: Free Press, 2009, 9.

have more and more interactions with it, and her unconscious will adapt accordingly, to the point that she may end up speaking English as fluently as her original Chinese (whatever version her parents had). In this case, this child at age of five will speak and behave closer to her parents' culture rather than the American one. Her process of adaptation will be gradual according to how she is interacting with environments as she grows up.

This is not just with children. In my own personal case, I immigrated to the United States when I was twenty-four. After living here for a certain amount of time, I felt much more comfortable expressing myself in English than in Spanish (the first language I learned). Then I went to Mexico for four years with my new partner (and now wife), and Spanish became again the most comfortable medium of expression. Now that I am back in the United States, English is taking a stronger stance. You get the idea. With respect to rules of behavior, the environment at home is just one more from which to learn. In the case that Harris talks about, it is obvious that the children spent most of their time outside home. Those programs are going to be exercised the most. That is why they learn the local language better than their parents'. The unconscious of the child will adapt to all the environments in which he is. That is all there is to this. In this respect, if you interpret the nurture factor to mean that parents are the main and basically only factor in shaping children behavior for all environments, then Harris is right: that is not the case. Our unconscious was designed to survive in whatever environment we are at a given moment. Behaving with our peers as we behave at home is not non-adaptive—in fact, it is dysfunctional.

Parents Are Still Key

Where I present a different view from that of Harris's is in the importance that parents are to their children. She states,

> The idea is that ordinary, run-of-the-mill parents like you and me don't have any distinctive effects on our children: we are interchangeable, like factory workers.[144]

There are two aspects to this.

---

[144] Judith Rich Harris, *The Nurture Assumption: Why Children Turn Out the Way They Do*, New York: Free Press, 2009, 335.

1. One thing is learning rules of behavior, and another is providing the children with the emotional resources to best deal with any environment in which they are. Take the case where someone was adopted by foster parents who provided a positive, constructive, nurturing environment. Indeed, it is true that the adoptive parents provided all the emotional resources in a similar way as the biological parents could have done. Harris is right in this respect. The point here is that children do need someone, whether from their biological parents or otherwise, to build in them those critical resources. That is the nurturing factor and is of critical importance. Our modern-day civilization is built on the basic social structure of the nuclear family (father, mother, children), and within that structure, this factor is a key responsibility of the parents.

2. The second aspect is one that I illustrated in the section about family secrets. The unconscious of a person knows whether or not the person was adopted. There is an unconscious connection with the biological parents. Thus, even though a child can grow as normally as another child with biological parents, this does not mean that there is no difference between the two scenarios. Growing without biological parents will translate into programs that will depend on what happened with the biological parents and how it is handled afterward. A child who was "given away" by parents is more likely to have a stronger negative program ("Not even my parents wanted me") than someone whose parents died tragically ("Why did this happen to me?" "How come I was not as lucky as all the other ones?"). When combined with the programs from the other intrapersonal and transpersonal components of that particular child, there is a whole spectrum of behaviors that can result from these situations. This explains why, even if the foster parents were as nurturing as I described above, their adopted child may turn out very well, or he may turn out a criminal, in an extreme case. These situations happen with biological parents as well, with children who bring heavy transpersonal programs with them. The reason why this positive, nurturing upbringing fails is because our ignorance in this respect, which I have talked about in this book. If a child is being raised in a positive environment but brings with her powerful negatively charged programs from a previous physical insertion (for example), today's parents (whether biological or not) face a losing battle. The negative transpersonal programs will create inner conflicts that will come out as problematic behavior. The parents will try their best to provide love and

understanding. Still, without this knowledge, they will not be able to go to the root of the problem. What happens then is that the child feels completely misunderstood, feels that there is something wrong with her, and feels guilty because she knows that she is hurting the people that she loves the most—and still she cannot control the problematic behavior. It is a downhill path for her that easily heads into drugs and addictions in an effort to alleviate the weight of all those negative feelings. In the end, everyone is hurt and scrambling for explanations about what went wrong. True nurturing requires knowledge about these factors and the presence of the parents, so that they intelligently guide their children to explore and resolve their inner conflicts (whether it may require the help of a practitioner or not).

We all have a unique combination of programs that produce our unique individuality. Generic psychological studies fail to detect this. These are the psychological studies that Harris heavily relies for her conclusions (and logically so).

Therapists versus Parents

Our individuality expresses itself fully in a session with a practitioner. To make this clearer, let's go to another quote in which Harris expresses her skepticism about the therapist knowing that a certain trauma was the "parents' fault."

> Why is the therapist so convinced it's the parents' fault?
> What does he see that makes him so sure?[145]

There are three themes that I want to address with respect to the therapists, parents, and generic scientific studies.

1. First, let's address her question. To do that, let me give you an example of a hypothetical but realistic scenario of a client who comes to see me because she wants to resolve a conflict that she has. Let's say that she has this behavior where she feels compelled to help other people but at her own expense. In other words, she feels obligated to help even if it will cause a significant inconvenience in

---

[145] Judith Rich Harris, *The Nurture Assumption: Why Children Turn Out the Way They Do*, New York: Free Press, 2009, 305–306.

her life, and she does this repeatedly. It is normal that something like this happen under extraordinary circumstances, it is not normal when it is a continuous pattern of behavior in a person. I will illustrate how a session develops. It is important to understand that every single session is different and that I have oversimplified how it actually progresses. Nevertheless, there are certain basic patterns that I can use to explain what goes on. In EFT, there is the concept of rounds. You take a scenario and do a round of tapping around it (do not be concerned about the details of this right now). Then you check what came out of it. Now you take this new information and do another round, and so on. Continuing with our hypothetical illustration, I ask her about the last time she experienced that type of situation. She comes up with the scenario. We use that scenario and the sensation of feeling obligated to help in our first round of tapping. What this technique does is trigger associated memories and emotions (programs) to this event. After I finish this round, I ask her about what new memories, images, and feelings came out of it. She tells me that she went back to when she was a teenager and was with some friends of her. As a result of that event (whatever it was), she felt scared of being left alone. This is what she is feeling now; because tapping resurfaced the event, she is reliving it. With this new information, I start another round using this last scenario and the feeling of the possibility of being left alone. This process can take more rounds, depending on the complexity of the issue. For our illustration, let's say that after another round she finds herself when she was six years old. She is playing with her younger sister in their room, and their mother shows up and makes a comment directed at her sister: "You look so beautiful in that dress, sweetie." Because of that compliment, which was directed only at her sister, my client did not get one at all, and the six-year-old girl feels left out with a deep sadness. In fact, her perception from that event is that her mother loves her sister more than her. And out of this, now she feels that to "deserve" her mother's love (in an equal amount as her sister), she needs to make an extra effort to please her. As an adult, that translates into making extra effort to gain the approval of others, even at the cost of her own well-being. It's because of the program that her unconscious created at that moment, which will be along the lines of "If I was not good enough for my mother, who is supposed to love me unconditionally, then I will have to work to gain approval from others."[146] How do we know that this was the originating event? Because when we do another round of tapping, no new events surface. It is the end of the chain of associated events in the unconscious of the person. Also, to the client it is very clear that we arrived at the root of this feeling or behavior. It is something that she knows. Now the work focuses on clearing the emotion, reframing the event, and adding positive psychological resources. Do you think this is a silly example? Think again. These situations are extremely common; we saw them at the academy, and they show up with my clients all the time. Events like this one may originate from something that a parent said, or it may also have been something from a teacher, friend, or anyone else who turned out to be relevant in the programming event. Unfortunately, most of my sessions are related to negative programs generated within the family. That brings me to the second theme that I want to address from the quotation.

2. Let's discuss blaming the parents. Not only it is useless and harmful to blame the parents, but it also shows a lack of understanding of us as human beings. Let's go over the possible scenarios in the programming event of my hypothetical client.

    a. The mother did love the younger sister more than my client. If this is the case, then it is the result of limiting programs in the mother. Parents and children feel different affinities between them, yet that is different than loving one more than another. Children know the difference. One explanation for the mother's preference is that my client, as the little girl with her own personality, triggered more negative programs in her. In other words, my client, as a little girl, did things that irritated, frustrated, and angered her mother more than her sister (who had a different personality). In this case, a nearsighted explanation is to blame her mother for her different ways to feel about her daughters. I say nearsighted because my next question will be, "How come the mother is reacting that way? How come she gets so triggered by her daughter?" Because of the programs that she acquired while growing up with her parents. It's the start of this endless regression from parents to

---

[146] A quick reminder that this is not the result of reasoning. In our early life, all these programs are the result of perceptions, of impressions.

grandparents, which is pointless. We as a species are responsible for what we have created. Notice that I am not using the words *blame* or *fault*; instead, I am talking about responsibility. We are learning from our experiences, and where we are today is simply a mirror of what we have gained and what we still need to do to improve the state of our civilization. The mother was doing the best she could with whatever understanding she had of what it is to be a child, or a human being for that matter. Notice that this applies all the way to abusive parents. No mind practitioner should ever blame the parents for the repercussions that they had on their children. That would still leave their clients as victims in a life that automatically becomes unfair. This book shows you a whole scheme that gives you explanations about why things happen the way they do in our lives. It is not something that came out of wishful thinking but instead from thousands and thousands of mind transformation sessions that give us a very consistent picture. As I mentioned before, these sessions show us that you chose your parents. I am very aware of the difficulty of even coming close to accepting something like this for many of you. If you take the time and effort to process the experiences that you had with them, you will discover what was behind making such a choice.

b. The mother loved both daughters the same, but it was my client's perception, her interpretation of the event, that led her to believe something else. Notice that it has the same consequences as if it would have been in (a). This happens as often, or even more often, than the previous scenario. As I showed in this book, children are not blank slates (which Harris correctly points out in her book).[147] They have their own personalities, which means their own programs. These programs are filtering the perceptions of their experiences and thus creating new programs according to the interpretation of their existing ones. In this client's case, it could be that she really had low self-esteem, or it could be that she was in a low mood (which otherwise she normally did not experience) that day, and it made her

---

[147] Judith Rich Harris, *The Nurture Assumption: Why Children Turn Out the Way They Do*, New York: Free Press, 2009, 308.

vulnerable to this interpretation of reality. What matters at this point in the session is how her unconscious interpreted the event. It is very clear that her mother cannot be blamed for her misinterpretation of her mother's comment. Even if she is at the root event of this trauma, it certainly was not her fault. It is impossible for any parent to know the inner state of their children at all possible instances of their lives. Neither is it necessary. We have enormous resources to come ahead in life, which is how we have made it throughout our history. Here is where the nurturing factor becomes key. If the parents of this girl are truly present in their interactions with her (playing with the children while checking a cell phone does not qualify as being present), then they will tune into her behaviors. They will notice the subtle change in her behavior and attitudes. They will make sure that they keep the communication channel open. If this is the case, and the unconscious of the child knows it, the child will open up. Because of the tremendous power that they have, the parents will be able to transform the programs in them. There's no need to go to a practitioner for cases like this; this is what parenting should be about. Notice that I have never said anywhere in the book that any of this is easy. It requires commitment, attention, and presence, and with our lifestyle of constant rush today, that is simply not possible. I go back to what I mentioned about how many children you can have while being able to keep that deep presence for all of them. This is not about imposing rules; it is about understanding and making choices accordingly.

That is how we know that a certain behavior came from the interaction with the parents. The sessions are crystal clear about how this happens. I really hope that we take the blame from the parents and start looking at ourselves and the consequences of the society that we have created. They are nothing more than the result of it.

In all the sessions that I have done, and in all the cases that I have studied, I have never found anything that could not have been avoided if the parents had more knowledge and tools to deal with their own limiting behaviors and those of their children.

Until we truly give this a try, we cannot know what else might be missing in creating harmony in our lives. This is the necessary first step.

3. The third theme related to the quote and the studies that I mentioned is what I just illustrated with this hypothetical client. In spite of this inner conflict that she had, for all practical purposes, her life is "normal." In fact, she could be an extremely successful person (I had clients who fit this exact profile). She is responsible in her job and in her family duties, and she pays the bills. She does not suffer from depression or from any other debilitating mental illness. If this woman were to be part of any of the myriad of psychological studies that Harris mentions in her book to support the fact that children turn out okay in spite of what parents do, this person would not only come out as okay but would do so with flying colors. My point here is that all those generic studies are fine with respect to understanding tendencies in human behavior, whether biological or not. Nevertheless, they are highly irrelevant when reflecting about a particular decision that a person is making in his life, as well as the true inner state of her mind. Even though my client had that inner conflict, otherwise she is fine (according to what we all have come to accept: that conflicts are just part of life), and that is how she would present her answers in these studies. That brings me to the next point.

We have brainwashed ourselves into very low standards of what it is to be okay in our lives.

We think that living with conflicts is normal. Yes, it is normal in our current state of evolution. Even so, life sure is not supposed to be this way. What we want are challenges that help us grow. Even though it is nice and necessary to take rests regularly in our life, if all of it were to be just that, we would get bored. To evolve, to grow, is intrinsic to us not just as humans but as nonphysical entities, and my sessions show that. Growing implies expanding and getting out of the zone of comfort—in other words, having challenges. When you start a new project that excites you (whether business or personal), you look forward to accomplishing your new goals and conquering the challenges that it will bring to you. That is different than living life with inner conflicts, which is how all human beings on this planet live today—in spite of what all these studies are saying: that a person is okay.

Let me clarify here that these studies are important. They do teach us about tendencies and characteristics of our behavior, and they do help us understand the mechanisms of the mind. For example, some of them show how subjective our perceptions are about events that occur in our lives. This is science that has important implications, for instance, in the credibility of witnesses in a court of law. However, when it comes to depicting an accurate image of our inner state, they come short. To do that, you have to go inside the mind of the individual to know what caused him to make a certain decision in his life, or how he really feels about it. This is because of the millions of different programs that each of us has, and which create the unique individual that each of us is. Generic studies then become a statistical collection of these programs. Their conclusions apply to certain contexts, but they will not be relevant to explaining the client's behavior that I illustrated in this case.

Second Observation

Up to this point, all these comments came from Harris's first observation, which is where we started. Let's continue with the second observation that Harris mentions and that also played a big role for her change of opinion about the nurturing factor.

She talks about how traditionally, upper-class male children in England were reared by nannies during their first eight years of life and then sent to boarding schools. In spite of that, at the end of their studies, they came out ready to join the world of adults as English gentlemen, with great resemblance to their fathers, whom they barely saw while growing up. She emphasizes how they did not take on the behaviors of their nannies or teachers of their boarding schools, who were the ones they spent most of their time during their growing years.[148] (According to her, because they were the nurturers of these children, the children should have taken on their behaviors rather than their fathers.) Once more, what a wonderful example of the adaptability of our unconscious. And it's precisely, the tremendous influence of our home environment in us. This is a great illustration of a case of implicit transfer of programs from parents to children.[149] During the first eight years, while

---

[148] Judith Rich Harris, *The Nurture Assumption: Why Children Turn Out the Way They Do*, New York: Free Press, 2009, 10.

[149] As I explained in the section, "Parents' influences on their children," under "The childhood experiences" component of the personality.

growing up at home, the unconscious of the child was capturing the dynamic of the family environment in which he was growing up. Afterward, while in boarding school, every single vacation year after year, and every time he went back home, his unconscious was once more taking notice of how things worked there. This is exactly what it is designed to do. No need for parents, nannies, or teachers to say anything in this respect. I doubt very much that in those boarding schools, children were explicitly trained so that as parents, especially as a father, they were to ignore their children. At that time, parenting would not have been even close to being considered as school material. We don't do that in our schools even today, which is one of my main points in this book. This behavior was learned, more than anything, from what they observed in their homes. I am quite sure that as an exception to these scenarios, there were also elite-class parents back then who interacted more with their children, who in turn would do the same as parents. Nowadays, we can see the influence of the environment in our homes while growing up as children, and in our homes as adults.

Here is where you can see how we bring our family customs into our adult life. When a young couple decides to live together, they have to negotiate the two different family cultures they came from ("We celebrated Christmas at home this way," etc.) in addition to their own personal lifestyles that were mostly molded in their respective parents' home. That is exactly where this type of programs needs to be applied. The unconscious executes the programs associated with home and at home. These programs were originally generated by the parents, explicitly and implicitly. Ultimately, how much all of our behaviors come from parents or the other environments is irrelevant; it is simply different environments to the unconscious (and there are associations that overlap between environments) where parents are critical is in the emotional building of their children. That is their most important role within the nurturing factor (which, of course, includes providing physical subsistence and education).

A Note about the "Elite"

Because we are talking about the elite social classes, there's a note to emphasize. The elite, with all its glamorous lifestyles that we see so much in the media, is not exempt from any of the consequences of the mechanisms of the mind. No human is exempt from the consequences of being a human being, not even a king. By far, the biggest difference between a king (or a genius in any field) and a beggar is in the content of the programs in their minds (which illustrates so well the huge loss of human potential in every single individual who lives in such impoverished conditions). Yet the mechanisms that operate on these programs are exactly the same on both of them. The beggar is living a life that is the product of highly negative, limited programming, which results in a deep unempowerment. The kings, queens, and elite classes, in spite of the power that they have in certain aspects of their lives (monetary, political), are living in an environment of deep social regulations and appearances that become an emotional jail to them. If you take the time to study the lives of these families, you will find deep conflicts and suffering. The enormous incongruence between the external image of perfection and their inner personal realities is unsustainable, and that is what we observe more and more in the media as well—the best example of a "civilization of masks" that we have created. Nevertheless, progression to congruence is inevitable.

Third Observation

Harris's third observation is, "Many developmental psychologists assume that children learn how they are expected to behave by observing and imitating their parents, particularly the parent of the same sex."[150] She challenges this conclusion that these developmental psychologists arrive at, and in general terms, I agree with her. I include her third observation for the sake of completeness because the answers to the first two pretty much give the explanations to this one. Children are learning from all the environments in which they are. I have never heard a generalized impression on anyone about this theme. With respect to parents, children will have more affinity with one or another. Even considering this, it is more relevant how the personalities of the parent and the child interact, because this is what is going to determine what programs are going to be created in the child that will exert the most influence in his or her life. It really comes down to the interaction of the individual combination of programs of the parent and those in the child that will determine the outcome.

The Powerful Nurturing Factor

A permanent theme through my book is how our unconscious defines us and our behavior. Related to this, I want to add the following quotation about

---

[150] Judith Rich Harris, *The Nurture Assumption: Why Children Turn Out the Way They Do*, New York: Free Press, 2009, 10.

the experience that Harris had when she left her daughter for the first time in the day care center.

> One of my most painful memories of motherhood concerns something that happened when my older daughter was three. It was her first day of nursery school. She was a quiet, somewhat timid child with no experience of being away from home unaccompanied by a parent. I brought her into the nursery school classroom and, after a while, she got interested in what the other children were doing and wandered away from me. Almost at once, a teacher came over to me and asked me to leave. "She'll be all right," the teacher said. So I left, and they closed the door behind me. Then I heard my child throw herself against the door, hammering on it and screaming. I heard the teacher talking to her but the hammering and screaming continued. I wanted to go back in but the teacher had told me not to, so I didn't. I stood there listening to my child's outraged screams, suffering as much as she was.
>
> My daughter did okay in nursery school, but I never forgot how I listened to the teacher—a woman only a little older than myself—instead of yielding to my very strong desire to go back in, pick up my child, hold her until she stopped crying, and remain there until she was ready to have me leave. I listened to the teacher because she was an authority and she made me feel that she knew more than I did about what was best for my child.[151]

What a powerful example, to say the least.

This experience that she had illustrates these points, which I have gone through in great extent in this book.

1. How the unconscious programs control our behavior. Even though Harris could very clearly feel that her daughter needed her emotionally when she was crying, she obeyed the teacher. Because Harris is in the

---

[151] Judith Rich Harris, *The Nurture Assumption: Why Children Turn Out the Way They Do*, New York: Free Press, 2009, 89–90.

teacher's territory, the nursery school, Harris is simply supposed to follow her indications. Societal programming. This is how it has to be for us to function as groups of individuals living together, and that is fine. I am simply pointing out to you how our behaviors are the result of programming.

2. This is related to point 1, but I want to differentiate the concept of authority, which I alluded in the adult experiences component. It comes out explicitly in Harris's last sentence. It was not only that Harris was supposed to follow the instructions of the teachers at the nursery school, as is expected of anyone who walks in there. Harris felt that the teacher knew more than her, and so she obeyed.

3. This is an example of exactly what the nurturing factor is to be: the emotional support that parents (primary caretakers) need to give to their children, especially and precisely while they are going through new challenging experiences. This is what builds a healthy emotional foundation on which the child will be able to live a more balanced and harmonious life as an adult.

4. Not only did Harris simply obey because of societal programming and the authority symbol that the teacher represented to her, but she did it even though it was very clear to her that her daughter was in a situation where she needed emotional support. In other words, her programming overrode what her gut feeling was telling her. That feeling was her unconscious talking to her. Her unconscious knows very well how it felt when parents were not available to a child's needs. We all had that experience because it is impossible, even for the best parents, to be 100 percent available and attuned to their children. When she heard her daughter cry, it triggered programs in her unconscious that gave her that strong desire to attend to her daughter emotional need. If you want to look at it this way, it is the remembrance of those memories that her unconscious (and ours in all of us) has. The need for nurture is intrinsic in all of us, and that is what her unconscious was expressing during that event. It's another very real-life example of how our programs control our behavior, depending on the strength of the emotional batteries associated with them.

Let me be very clear to my readers: this is not about Harris. If you are emitting judgment to her because of how she reacted to this situation, you are entirely missing my point: this is a societal problem, and all parents everywhere on this planet are taking similar actions.

What Parents Truly Need to Do to Lighten Up

I want to finish this section about Harris's book with a comment about something that she mentions at the end of her introduction to the second edition.[152] She expresses how she was hoping that her book would take away some of the stress that parents feel about rearing their children. She continues by saying that not only has she not seen that effect in others, but even her daughters have not relaxed a little more with their own children. This is ironic because in a certain way, Harris and I are going to agree. The reason her book has not helped parents lighten up is because of what I mentioned earlier. It does not matter how many truckloads of scientific studies anyone comes up against the relevance of parents in the child's upbringing, because all of us have an unconscious that, in its subtle but very strong way, tells us that it is not so. Harris, you illustrated it so well with your daughter's experience at the nursery school. Unconsciously, we all know how crucial parents were to our well-being as children. In humans, this is biological and psychological; it is an integral part of the overall design of this instrument that we call our bodies. There are two reasons parents stress out about parenting.

1. The first one is that they know that they will be central to their child's life.
2. The second one is that they know that they don't truly know about parenting.
   Let me highlight it one more time:

   Nowhere in our civilization have we created a structured, systematic way to transfer our current knowledge about parenting and emotional intelligence to future generations.

We don't do it in the way that we currently transfer our knowledge of the sciences. So what is the best advice that parents and friends can give to the future parents? "Oh, you will figure it out." On top of that, people had adverse experiences with their parents that reside in their unconscious, and those become a part of their anxiety with their future children. They want to spare their children from that suffering, but more than anything, they are left with wishful thinking. I said it earlier: I have not found any negative parenting

---

[152] Judith Rich Harris, *The Nurture Assumption: Why Children Turn Out the Way They Do*, New York: Free Press, 2009.

dynamics that could not have been avoided if the parents knew better. It's not their fault, and no one told them how. Under these circumstances, there is no way future parents can relax. Their unconscious knows the reality of things, and it will keep the alarms on.

The irony that I refer to comes in the fact that this very book, as a result of what I show and explain, may stress out parents even more. I highlight the profound and subtle ways in which they affect their children, and the tendency will be to worry even more about how they are performing. Adding to this irony, their worrying and stressing about how they are doing with their children is the result of limiting programs that in turn are going to be transferred to their children through implicit transference. The child's unconscious will capture that attitude and convert it into limiting programs ("My dad/mom is stressed out; life must be difficult," "It is stressful to be a parent"). Besides knowing all this information, parents need to transform their limiting programs. This is not just for their children but is as important for their own lives so that they can reach a place of trust in life and what they do.

There is no such a thing as a perfect parent, and neither is there a need to be one.

We have immense psychological resources, and the fact that we are here after thousands of years of emotional darkness is testament to that. As human beings, we come here to learn, which directly implies making mistakes during that process. It is an intrinsic part of the human experience. This book is about you having positive emotional resources to accept and understand that fact, while striving in a harmonious way to become a better human being. Welcome to the complexities of the human condition. Another very important consideration to keep in mind is that the nonphysical entities that come into the bodies that the parents provide know very well the state of evolution in which we are. That is also part of the reason they come to this planet under these circumstances: they want to participate in the challenge that we have set up for ourselves, they want to be part of the solution, and they want to contribute. They know that their parents will make mistakes that will hurt them. That is all included in the package. It's not an excuse to not do anything about it.

This is the paradox: we need to understand and accept where we are as the current stage of our evolution, at the same time that we also understand that it is our responsibility to clear the suffering that we impose on ourselves so that we can grow to the more harmonious next stage. When we and parents truly embrace this understanding and take action into transforming ourselves into better human beings, then we are on our way. You are right, Judith: parents need to relax about their role. But this requires knowledge and action on their part to clear their limiting programs.

Social Networks

We are a social species, and it is biological. There's no need to reference scientific studies; simply look at our conglomerations that we call cities. As such, being socially connected and having deep, fulfilling relationships are two of the most basic needs that all of us have. Having these relationships give us a sense of support and connection, and they become one of the most solid foundations in our lives. Technology has given us another tool that we can use to fulfill that deep inner need: what we call social networks on the Internet. They are a great way to reach out to our current family, friends, and acquaintances, as well as to those from our past or in distant locations. It's a wonderful way to supplement our need to connect. Notice I say *supplement*, meaning "adding to," as opposed to *replace*, which is the role that these networks are starting to take more and more in people's lives. They give an easy, yet illusory, sense of connection ("Look, I have 754 friends") that people are using to fill in the void that they experience in their person-to-person relationships. People are unable to navigate the social waters in a satisfactory manner and so resort to the virtual social waters. This happens because of two main factors.

1. We fail to connect with others because of limiting programming about ourselves, others, or life in general. These programs sabotage our interactions.
2. We fail to resolve our interpersonal conflicts because of our lack of knowledge and tools in this area of our lives (as I talked about our educational system).

The reason why I am writing about this here is because when you have the information that I have given you about the mechanisms of the personality, it becomes very clear that we need to deal person to person with the challenges that relationships bring with them. The unconscious mechanisms require us to do so. Even if we keep conflicts under the rug, we see that our unconscious minds will pick them through implicit transmissions of information from parents to children (and vice versa) and, as we saw in the transgenerational component, from within the members of a family clan. All the implicit needs should be made explicit. You will not be able to accomplish this on a consistent basis through your smart phone or by having thousands of virtual friends. Social networks are a great resource for our need to connect, but they also amplify our inner voids. It is not about discarding them; that not going to happen. It is about addressing the real cause of the addiction that they are bringing in people's lives. As with anything else in life, social networks are simply mirroring the problems in us. Nowadays, the challenges of personal relationships are being amplified by this technological society, where virtual networking is taking a bigger role in our lives. We are losing social skills. Direct personal interaction is what makes us grow in our own personal evolution, and it is irreplaceable.

Your "Personality Selfie" Completed

With this section, we complete the description of the different components of your personality. They are what make you who you are in this life. These components are interacting seamlessly, creating the amazing human being that you are. It is my deepest desire that you understand that these are simply mechanisms within this cosmological paradigm in which we take part. What I mean is that this is all that they are: mechanisms. These mechanisms are part of the package of this marvelous biological suit (the body) that you wear every time you decide to insert yourself into this physical universe and, more specifically, on this particular planet that we chose to name Earth. The body is not you. You are the nonphysical, Individualized Consciousness that is making use of it.

Here is a summary of all the components of the personality and their different facets.

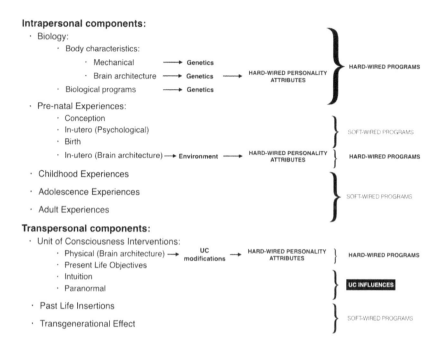

Regrouping them gives us a different angle that also helps to have a clearer vision about these components.

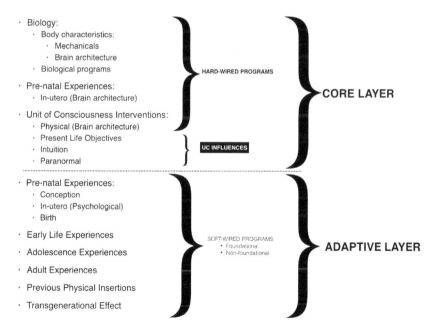

A you can see, and as I mentioned at the beginning of the book, we started with very basic concepts in order to arrive to this more complex picture of who and what we are.

Are there more components to our mind? Certainly. Universal unconscious, archetypes, and more are examples of other factors that also play within us. The ones that I have mentioned in this section of the book are the most prominent ones from what we see in the fields of the mind. As you can see, as a human being, you are so much more than you think you are. You carry an immense amount of information that transcends by far what you have experienced in this lifetime. You are a big mosaic of different aspects that become a unity that make you an individual. And you have the whole of that information within. If people would realize how little awareness that our conscious minds have about the other facets of who we are (which truly control our behavior), we would behave very differently. True understanding of this fact is a deeply humbling experience.

Soft-wired programs have a tremendous influence on all others, including biological ones. Once we understand the mechanics of these programs, we can also find ways to access them, process their information, and change them. That translates into new, more positive behaviors that help us accomplish what we set out to do in this iteration in the physical world. Thus, now that we have all this information about our mind's inner workings, let's go into how we can change it.

Part 3

Mind Transformations

Transformation

This section is relatively short compared to the others in the book, but I want to give you the basics about mind transformation processes. As I will show you, you have hundreds if not thousands of different alternatives from which to choose. Since the beginning of mankind, we have felt the need to find inner harmony, which has led us to search through a myriad of different ways to try to achieve it. As science has advanced, our knowledge about the mind has too. Nowadays, we have processes that have been methodically tested and have a solid foundation. As is always with human nature, you may feel more comfortable working with more empirical ones, and they may produce the results that you are looking for. I will try to give you a short guideline to get you started. From here, you need to study and make your own decisions about how to proceed.

Important: if you are experiencing issues that are a significant handicap in your life, you need to go to a professional practitioner to clear these first. Do not attempt to do this by yourself. The human mind is complex, and when you start working with it on serious issues, it may open up other ones that need to be handled as well. Or you may feel your emotions amplified, which could destabilize you even more. If you have persistent thoughts about hurting yourself or others in any way (physical, emotional, etc.), it is imperative that you go to a professional. If you have any doubts about what I am explaining here, that is a sign that you need to see a professional. Once you have cleared the major issues, and with the permission of your practitioner, you can start applying these processes to the everyday upsets that we all have in our lives.

Mind Transformation Processes (MTPs)

What Are Mind Transformation Processes?

As you live your life, you learn, you change, and you grow. Simply by living life, you are transforming yourself and your mind. You will evolve this way. However, when you start to pay attention to your limiting patterns of behavior and take action to change them, you enter into an accelerated path of empowerment and expansion.

A mind transformation process is a tool that you intentionally use to change limiting patterns of behavior into positive ones.

The big distinction that I want to emphasize here is that in my definition, it is an *intentional* event. It is a procedure that you willingly and by your own motivation undertake in order to effect positive change in your life. The MTP can be done on your own or via a practitioner, and privately or in a group setting.

What Are the Advantages of Doing MTPs?

1. By doing MTPs, you take more control of your life. Once you embark on this path, you start to observe yourself more carefully. You pay attention to how you behave. You tune in into your fears and negative behaviors. Once you have identified them, you take action to change them for the better. This transforms your life from a series of unfortunate events to a series of constructive events that build one after another. Whenever you see a new negative pattern arise, you correct it. Now you become the captain of your boat, taking it in the direction that you truly want.
2. Because of that awareness that you develop by watching your own behavior, you automatically live life much more consciously. Instead of going through the mechanics of it, you live it with full presence. By doing this exercise, you step up one notch your level of consciousness.
3. By doing these processes, you alleviate the suffering that limiting programs impose on you.
4. As you liberate yourself from limiting behaviors, you automatically empower yourself more and more to accomplish what you want to do

in your life. Your self-esteem grows, and you feel better in general. Life starts to become an adventure to be lived rather than an obligation to go through.

5. By processing your own limiting behaviors, you acquire an experiential understanding of how it is that we humans behave. You acquire the perspective of observing how you behaved before the transformation, as well as how you are doing it after the transformation. You now have the wisdom of seeing how you saw life before and after that personal change. This grows your compassion and empathy toward yourself and toward everyone else. When you see people doing something "stupid" or harmful, you understand them better. You understand that they are behaving according to their own programs, and you understand firsthand where the programs come from. You understand how it is that people become "bad." (This does not mean that we do not take action or condone their behavior!) Their actions follow, in a similar way, a negative behavior that you had because of a limiting program that you transformed. And because of the transformation, you can now see very clearly how these limiting programs make us interpret reality in a certain way, to which we react accordingly. We see how powerful they are: they control our behavior.

6. By understanding yourself and others, you now have an inner wisdom that allows you to make better decisions on how to help yourself, others, and society in general. You are going to make very different decisions at the personal level, and also all the way to the societal and political levels. What happens today in our democratic societies is that people make decisions based mostly on fear. There is an automatic pattern of classifying the others into "good/bad" or "friend/enemy" placeholders and then making the corresponding defensive decisions. From what I explained, these defensive reactions are very limited in their effectiveness. They are mechanical and very shortsighted. To be able to accomplish long-term solutions, you need to be able to get out of the sphere of fear. The more empowered you are, the more you will be able to see and strive for those long-term solutions.

7. The more empowered, compassionate, and empathic you are, the more you will be an inspiration for others. They will want to know how you do it. They will learn by example that they can accomplish what they want. This is an automatic, positive ripple effect in which you don't even have to make an extra effort. This is a service to others that always comes as

a secondary effect of doing these processes. It happens simply by being who you are.

What an MTP Must Accomplish to Effect the Positive Changes You Want

Mind transformation processes have been with us throughout our history. In old times, the shamans and priests of the tribes administered physical, emotional, and spiritual healing to their members. In those simpler societies, they were the central figures with the power to heal their peoples. From these societies, we evolved into the complex civilization in which we live today. It's a civilization big not only in numbers but also with a great cultural diversity. Many of the different cultures developed their own ways of healing. Because technology has given us an enormous interconnectedness, today we have an exchange of healing modalities that we have not seen before. Although this has brought a new richness of choices in our lives, it has also brought a lot of confusion about what is "real" and what not. Some people swear about one given technique, but others classify it as sham.

The first thing that I would like to do here is give you the conditions that are required for any transformational process to be effective. This is valid no matter how old the procedure is, what culture it comes from, or whether or not it has gone through the lens of scientific proof. I give you this information so that you, on your own, can discern whether a process that someone is offering could be effective or not. This is very important today, when so many people claim healings and transformations that do not always occur. There are two cases to consider here.

1. Conditions applicable to both foundational and nonfoundational programs
2. Conditions critical to foundational programs

Conditions Applicable to Both Foundational and Nonfoundational Programs

For a transformation to occur on any program in the unconscious, its associated emotional battery needs to be discharged.

This goes all the way back to the first part of this book. Remember that the power that a program stored in your unconscious has over your behavior is directly proportional to the intensity of the emotion associated with it (its emotional battery). As long as you keep feeling the same emotion under a particular circumstance, you will react accordingly. The more powerful the emotion, the less free will you have. You react instead of making a decision. You need to free yourself of that emotion in order to be able to decide on your own. The emotional battery must be discharged. How you do it and what method you use to accomplish it is irrelevant. In other words, if you were able to discharge that emotional battery through a given ritual you performed, or because you went to a psychologist, or because you did some chanting, you indeed transformed yourself. Here is where we can see the richness of being human.

Let's take the example where a person accomplished a big personal transformation by doing a particular ritual, as instructed by a certain spiritual guru. If that person follows the guru, it is because the programs in her unconscious resonate with the guru's teachings. That person's unconscious feels rapport with that environment. Thus, through that ritual, in this example, the unconscious will open up and allow the processing of the program. If the processing discharged the emotional battery, the guru was as effective as any traditional psychologist could have been. In fact, if the person's programs make her a skeptic of traditional therapy, the guru will indeed have better results than the psychologist. In the same way that our unconscious controls our behavior according to the programs that we have, it also controls whether or not to allow access to them. If the unconscious feels safe to open them up, transformation can occur. This is a key element that has to be present between any type of practitioner (guru, psychologist, etc.) and the client. It is crucial that the client feel trust in her practitioner, or else it will be very difficult for transformation to take place. The programs in our mind will determine the optimal environment for emotional healing to occur.

As a personal anecdote, in case that you haven't noticed yet, I am a highly analytical person. Even though I studied shamanism and obtained wonderful results through its practices, I resonate more with science. My sister, on the other hand, is a highly intuitive person and thrives with shamanism. I took some shamanic courses and then moved on, whereas she embraced it completely and followed that path. She obtained deeper results than I did because her mental structures and abilities are better suited for that particular practice. This is one explanation behind why some people heal with some practices, but others do not. For those where a given practice did not produce the expected results, their conclusion about that process not working is correct (for them). The mistake that they make is the generalization that they come to. The process does not work for them because of their own particular programs in their unconscious. For others, that same process is the perfect match for transformation to happen. It is very important to understand this before emitting any type of judgments or conclusions about a particular practice, even if that practice has not been scientifically tested in its efficacy. The power of our unconscious is enough to affect any type of healing under the appropriate circumstances. When this happens at the physical level, we call it a miracle, yet it is nothing more than the power of the inner mind.

There is another point that must be considered when talking about whether a process worked in a particular case. More often than not, a limiting program has a lot of different associations to other programs and/or highly charged emotional batteries. Writing from the perspective of the traditional therapy setting, even though the desired transformation could happen in just one session, it is more likely that it will require several of them to accomplish the desired results. Think of it as a big knot that needs to be untangled one step at a time. In this case, working with a certified practitioner may have the advantage of her experience and the more structured approach that this professional brings to the sessions. For those who go to retreats and workshops with different teachers, this may be their case too. It could be that by working with a certain teacher, they did not obtain the result that they expected. Later, when they go to a different one, they experience a wonderful transformation. It could very well be that doing the work with the first teacher may have been the necessary step to reach the breakthrough with the second one. It was a necessary step in the untangling of the knot; more simply needed to be done. They needed to process other associated programs to that limiting behavior before the unconscious would allow them to get to this final one.

Ultimately, any process has the potential to do transformation if it presents an environment that resonates with the programs that reside in the unconscious of the person who wants to go through it. Under these circumstances, the unconscious will open up and allow the access and processing of its internal programs.

A Point about Gurus, Spiritual Teachers, Priests, Ministers, Etc.

As I have mentioned before, the influence that a spiritual teacher has over a person can be very strong, to the point that he becomes the catalyst for personal transformation. This is the concept of authority that I talked about earlier in the book. This is a desirable, positive effect that goes along with being a teacher. Still, you want to be aware of your attachments to anyone with authority. The more attached and admiration you start giving to your teacher, the more you are giving your personal power away to her. This is an internal yellow flag that you need to pay attention to. Extract all the positive teachings and experiences you can from a certain teacher, but make sure you are always discerning for yourself on every single word you hear from him. It does not matter how famous that teacher is. In fact, I do not recommend following only one teacher (minister, guru, etc.). You put yourself in a very vulnerable situation (programming through authority and repetition) and enclose yourself into a single point of view of reality. It is important that you study with all kinds of different teachers. What you want is a studying, not a following. Different teachers give you different perspectives that will help you exercise your own discernment about what to embrace and what to discard. That is what personal power is about: to have the confidence to be able to come to your own conclusions about anything and, in this particular case, about your own spiritual life beliefs. An additional advantage of having different perspectives is that right away, it opens you up to be more tolerant. You learn to see through different points of view and appreciate the new learnings and experiences that each one of them provide. It enriches your life.

Religious and spiritual beliefs are one of the main influencers in our lives at all levels. They affect us at the personal level all the way to decisions that we make at the societal level. They are one of the main factors that determine the direction of our civilization, even today in this technological world. Learn to be an independent thinker. Study with different masters, transform, and enrich yourself with them while keeping your life and personal power in your own hands (or more appropriately, in your own mind).

Recognizing the Effects of Discharging the Emotional Battery

How do you know when the emotional battery has been discharged? Usually there are several effects that take place when this happens.

1. You feel the emotion. Ultimately, it should reach the original emotion you felt during the event that generated the limiting program you want to transform. Notice that I say should reach, because there can be different associated aspects to a given past situation. As an example, say a woman was sexually abused by her father during her childhood. One

of the first emotions that will come out in the session is anger toward her father. Anger may come out, but after processing this aspect, it could be that the woman still does not feel completely liberated from her past. Why? Because behind that anger toward her father, there might be an even bigger resentment toward her mother because she knew what was happening and did nothing to prevent or change the situation. This creates an enormous frustration and resentment that she will carry against her, on top of the more obvious emotion against her father. This is the case, for instance, when a woman talks a lot about such a situation in her past, but in spite of her expressing so much about it, you can tell that there is anger left in her. That is the indication that either this emotion has not been completely processed, or there is still at least one other emotion that needs to be worked on. Until all emotions associated with the event have been processed, there will not be a complete liberation from that past. I mention this particular example because this "emotion behind another emotion" is common in these cases. The resentment toward the mother gets covered not only by the anger towards the father, but also because socially speaking, it would be "unfair" or "appropriate" to blame the mother (who most likely also suffered abuse from him). Not so to our unconscious. Biologically speaking, it does not know about social rules. It does know, from its hard-wired biological programs, that parents are supposed to protect us as little children. This social programming can make it very difficult to process the anger toward the mother, and understandably so. I experienced this with my clients, with whom it could take several sessions before they were able to voice that resentment without feeling guilty about it. You can see how entangled programs can get. When there are too many of them, or with extremely highly charged batteries, then is when the person starts having problems that seriously affect his capacity to constructively interact in society.

The release of the emotion during the transformation process often occurs in a cathartic way because of its magnitude, and because it has been repressed for so long. It will come out with tears or with anger, sometimes expressed through screaming or even punching a pillow (as I had to do several times when I was going through these processes).

Emotions were never meant to be repressed.

Emotions are meant to be signals from our unconscious that give us feedback about a particular circumstance that we are experiencing. As such, their expression is an integral part of an experience. This does not mean that if you feel anger toward someone, you give yourself permission to punch that person. There are constructive ways to express what we feel. It is important that knowing about them be part of the emotional aspect that is so missing in our educational system.

2. When you discharge an emotional battery, there is a deep sense of relief, of feeling lighter. This has to do with what I mentioned earlier about emotions not meant to be repressed. Think of it as if you were constantly holding a balloon underwater. It requires great effort and energy to keep it down. As with the balloon, that emotion is trying to surface, and it is trying to express itself simply because that is its whole purpose. When you liberate that emotion, it is the equivalent to letting that balloon come to the surface. There is no more need to exert energy to try to keep it down. This is the wear and tear that we do ourselves when we don't know how to handle them. It takes big amounts of energy to maintain repressed emotions in our unconscious (and they still affect our behavior). That energy used to repress our emotions is energy that the unconscious also takes away from the body. In other words, that feeling lighter, that relief, is not just psychological but also physical. I always tell my clients, after doing transformations that were intense, to rest during the next days following the session. Many times they tell me that they feel as if they have run a marathon. When you transform a program, you are changing the energetic balance of your body. The body needs to readjust to the new levels of energy, and the person may very well feel that readjustment. This is also a reason to allow time to integrate the transformation, and it's why I normally would not recommend doing more than one session per week. This integration is both psychological as well as physical.

3. There is a new perspective about the event. This is the essence of the liberation process. The emotion is what pulls you to come to the same conclusion about that event. It triggers the same neurological path over and over. Because you are no longer feeling that emotion, you are now free to contemplate other possibilities, other perspectives about the event itself and also about life, depending on how profound the change was. Continuing with the previous example about the woman and her father, once she has freed herself from all emotions associated with those events, she will be able to see and understand how ill her father was, and how much suffering he must have gone through in his own life to get to the point of doing

something that terrible to her own daughter. She will also understand that it was not because it was her fault, or because "there is something wrong with me," as so many people think after these experiences. (Those were the programs created in their unconscious as little girls, because "What else could be the reason for my father doing this to me?" The faculty of reasoning was not fully developed, and so whatever the impression was at that time, that is the program that the unconscious created.) This does not mean that she will approve of what he did. Now that the emotion has been taken away, she has the capability to fathom why her father acted that way. It's important to note that this new understanding is not an intellectual experience. It is something deeper that the person feels integral to her being. The woman may have known her father's background and intellectually understood him before the transformation, yet the anger was still there. After the transformation, she is free.

True personal transformation is an emotional experience, not just an intellectual one.

Conditions Critical to Foundational Programs

As a reminder, this is the second point to consider about getting the positive effects that you want from an MTP. In a nonfoundational program, there was already a neural network already established before the incident occurred. Once the program has been processed, there is no need to learn a new behavior. That is the big difference of these types of programs when compared with a foundational program. A person who grew up in an environment that taught him "life is dangerous" does not know how to see life from a different perspective. There are no neural connections (or very few, and with little emotional weight compared to the other ones) in her brain that could give her a different perspective. In this case, discharging the emotional batteries associated to the main events that generated this perspective is necessary, but it's not enough. There is more to do.

For a complete transformation to occur, in the case of foundational programs in the unconscious, the new desired behavior needs to be learned,

In exactly the same way that the person was trained by the circumstances in which he grew up to see life as dangerous, now he must relearn to see the new evidence that will slowly give him the new perspective that life can be a positive experience overall. This new training, like any other, is what will create new neural networks that will enable this perspective to take place. Understand that what enables the possibility of this new learning is the fact that the emotional batteries have been discharged. That step is still necessary. Otherwise, they will not let the person contemplate new perspectives. From then on, the more the new neural networks are used, the stronger and richer their connections will be ("neurons that fire together, wire together," according to Donald Hebb) to the point where eventually the new perspective becomes the default way of seeing life. It's exactly like when you learn a new physical activity. The more you practice, the better you become at it, and the more automatically you eventually end up executing it.

This is a crucial point that must be understood. Just discharging the emotional batteries of these programs, and not doing anything else, will leave the person in a behavioral void. The person will not know how to behave or what to do differently. He simply does not know. Because foundational programs are so integral to the identity of the individual, they require careful and more extensive processing. They are the deep-rooted beliefs that form the foundation of our personality. It is important that you become aware of this whenever you intend to change a behavior that you have had had since the beginning of your life. In these cases, as much as anything is possible in the realm of the unconscious, it is more realistic to expect a gradual process of transformation rather than an overnight change. Some of these foundational programs are the target of the transformational courses that you hear so much today everywhere, such as how to get rich and how to find your ideal partner. This is a rich market, precisely because it takes time and commitment to change these basic structures in our minds. Now you understand the why of this phenomenon. This is not a criticism to all these courses. On the contrary, as part of the transformation process in an individual that is set on changing a foundational program, you need repetition and persistence. One way of doing that is through participating in courses and programs that emphasize the behaviors that the individual is looking for. Simply be conscious and aware of your process, as well as how you are executing it and evaluating it.

Choosing an MTP

As I mentioned earlier, any method can have transformative effects on an individual if the unconscious of that person resonates with the guide, the technique, or ideally both. The problem with a particular transformation technique that a certain teacher is imparting, and that is of his own invention, is that the method will not work for people whose beliefs are outside of the teacher's. As an example, a certain spiritual teacher may offer a technique, but if you are not a follower of that spiritual teaching or tradition, then you are not going to be a willing participant in that process. Your mental structures are not a match, and therefore your unconscious will not cooperate. These empirical methods are heavily dependent on the particular beliefs of the people involved, which restrict their applicability to just a particular spectrum of the population.

There is another aspect that also needs to be carefully considered here. A follower of a certain teacher or guru may have obtained wonderful transformative results with his practices. Nevertheless, it may also happen that the person reverts back to old patterns of behavior once he is out of the sphere of the influence (physical, emotional, or intellectual) of the teacher. The explanation for this is that because the teacher was such a symbol of authority to that person, it activates programs in the unconscious of the follower that override the programs that are the reason for the negative pattern of behavior. The admiration and devotion to the teacher are part of these sets of programs. However, once the influence of the teacher has diminished, the "devotional" programs deactivate, and now the negative ones reactivate (or are simply no longer covered by the other ones). If this happens, what it means is that there was no real emotional healing; the negative programs where simply covered up. The technique used did not accomplish true (permanent) transformation. This is just an example of these types of situations that are more likely to occur with empirical therapeutic methodologies (I say more likely because this could occur also with more science-based methodologies). Be aware of that. The advantages of techniques that have been evaluated more systematically are as follows.

1. They provide a more neutral intellectual setting that is more acceptable to a wider range of people, independent of their particular beliefs (at least to a greater point).
2. They provide a more solid background about their efficacy. Because they have gone through multiple trials, they can show results in a more convincing way. This is crucial for you as a client. You have to trust, or at the very least have a positive attitude about, the process into which you are going to immerse yourself.

3. They provide a structure that has been built before and through all the trials, which gives the practitioner a concrete path to complete the transformation in a more solid way. Let me explain. In the case of a nonfoundational program, by discharging the emotional battery, you transform yourself. Strictly speaking that is enough, and you are now free to make your own decisions. As it happens with the more systematic therapies, the practitioner adds to the transformation positive psychological resources for a more stable base, giving the client an extra layer of protection from falling back into old limiting programs. With empirical methods, many times after the emotional catharsis, the guide is satisfied with the result of the process, and that is it. This is fine, except that we have an extraordinary mix of programs that influence one another. It could happen that some other limiting program that has not been processed yet could be easily transformed by the individual by herself, thanks to these extra positive resources that she gained at the end of her session.

The human mind, as I have extensively shown in this book, operates following certain mechanisms. The better we understand them, the better we can make use of them, and with the appropriately derived techniques, the more effectively we can change our limiting behaviors. The more empirical techniques do work on the individuals who deeply resonate with them because of the power of our unconscious. Ultimately, it is up to you to decide which method you want to use to transform your limiting behaviors.

Lists of MTPs

There are innumerable mind transformation processes. If you search the Internet for "therapy types," you will find numerous sites with extensive lists. The lists can change dramatically depending on where you go to find this information, but as you will see, this is a testament to our incessant quest for a more fulfilling life. Also, it's a testament to the diversity of the human mind. The infinite combinations of programs in our unconscious make us see and interpret life in a particular way and then come to a particular solution for our problems and challenges.

How do you decide on a particular therapy? First of all, by studying, and second, by observing what resonates the most with you. If you are a person who resonates with science in its strict sense, the APA[153] is probably

---

[153] American Psychological Association.

your best bet. As they write it in their website, "Our strategic goals include expanding psychology's role in advancing health and increasing recognition of psychology as a science."[154] In other words, one of their goals is to be compliant with science and its methods. In this respect, if your preference is to stick to science, this is the safest approach you can take to transforming your mind.

The next category of therapies is those that produce consistent results in trials, but because of the foundation on which they rest, they still are not considered scientific. The example of this is emotional freedom techniques. EFT has been researched in more than ten countries by more than sixty investigators, whose results have been published in more than twenty different peer-reviewed journals.[155] The studies include randomized control trials, which are the gold standard in science. However, because EFT rests on concepts of what is called energy psychology, which works with the Chinese meridians and acupuncture points, which have not been proven (strictly speaking) scientifically to exist, EFT is not yet considered an evidence-based approach. Until science finds a way to prove these energetic channels, the APA will have difficulty approving this type of therapy. The reason I bring this up here is because there are trade-offs: some of the new techniques may show more effective results, yet they will not have the official endorsement of science. That is why you do need to study and make an educated decision about what therapy to use. That is your responsibility.

Last, in this very broad categorization, there are all the other empirical methodologies that I talked about. You decide—it's your life!

Your Role as a Participant in an MTP

My goal, by giving you all this information, is that you will be able to discern and place realistic expectations on the changes that you want to make in your life, and that you understand the different aspects of the transformation process. Irrespective of the particular technique that you (or your practitioner) are going to use, there are certain requirements that must be met. They have to do with how the unconscious works. The first one is:

---

[154] "Who We Are," American Psychological Association, http://www.apa.org/about/apa/index.aspx. Accessed December 14, 2018.
[155] "EFT Tapping Research." EFTUniverse, http://www.eftuniverse.com/research-studies/eft-research#clinical. Accessed December 14, 2018.

Truly want it: transform that limiting behavior.

This is, by all means, the first prerequisite that you need to change. It has to be a want that comes from your heart, from every cell of your body telling you to do it. It's not a rationalization. A typical example is someone who wants to quit smoking because "it is not good for my health," or because family or friends are putting so much pressure to do it. In reality, the person truly enjoys smoking. It is going to be very difficult leaving that habit behind. This has to be an *inner* motivation, a voice or (even better put) a feeling that comes from inside of you. If you truly feel the need to change, you will have the motivation to make it happen. You are ready to go through the process.

There are techniques that can effect change without having to go to the event that generated the limiting program, but in general they work with programs that have a very small emotional charge. Programs with significant emotional charge require processing of the originating event. This is yet another reason that people cannot be coerced into changing. There has to be a sufficient inner motivation to do this personal work, which can be challenging in itself. One of the goals that I have for my first session with my clients is to calibrate how motivated they are to do the work. If, for example, a person were to tell me that she is in my office because her partner told her to do the sessions, then I would tell her that she is not ready. Understand that it is you, as the client, who is doing the transformation, not the practitioner. An analogy of this is an orchestra director: he can move his baton as much as he wants, but if his musicians don't play the instruments, no music will come out no matter how brilliant he may be. The most prestigious practitioner will not get results from someone who is not willing to cooperate in the process. If the unconscious is not aligned with the transformation, it will not occur.

The second one is:

It is crucial that you feel that you can trust your guide.

This is the responsibility of the practitioner to instill that trust and rapport in you. This professional will accompany you in your journey through your unconscious. This is your inner world with all its most intimate and personal details about you. Your deepest secrets may surface during the sessions. You need to be willing to put yourself in that place of vulnerability. The only way that something like that has a chance of happening is because of trust. Otherwise, when reaching that vulnerable place, you (that is, your unconscious) will shut down, will close, and no more processing will ensue. This is a critical aspect in your relationship with your practitioner. If you don't feel that trust from your guide, you need to find someone else.

The Role of the Practitioner

Once you are ready to do a transformation process, doing it with a well-trained and experienced practitioner is key to its success. There are two main reasons for this.

1. Precisely because of the challenge of revisiting the original event, and its associated emotions, a well-trained practitioner will be able to gently and effectively guide the person through that work. Going back to traumatic events is a delicate process that, when done with an unqualified guide, could lead to leaving old psychological wounds now open again, with all the pain and incapacitating consequences. In a worst-case scenario, an inept practitioner may leave the client even more traumatized than the original event did.
2. I mentioned earlier that one of the effects of discharging the emotional battery of a program is that you gain a new perspective about the event that originated the limiting program because now you don't have emotions clouding your perceptions. To get the full potential of that opening, the role of the guide is crucial. With a practitioner who is truly proficient in guiding his client, you will not only process the past event successfully, but you'll also be able to fully comprehend the new perspectives that you were missing. Think of it like connecting new dots, the new possibilities that emerge from this change. These are new, positive ways to look at yourself, people, and life that you could not see before. This is where you extract true wisdom from the challenges that you went through in your life—which is, by the way, the reason for them: to learn. These are the experiences that your Essence goes through in order to evolve. This wisdom is what your Unit of Consciousness truly values and takes with it to eternity. Material things are inconsequential and irrelevant, and as such their only relevance is with respect to the experiences that they give to the individual. There

is nothing wrong with having material possessions; we want everybody to have wonderful, comfortable lives. What you need to understand is that a Unit of Consciousness elects whatever lifestyle according to the lessons and experiences that it wants and feels that it needs to have. When you go through an MTP, you are at one of the core reasons for having all these experiences in this physical universe: gaining wisdom. Having a proficient guide will be critical to helping you get the most out of the transformation.

You as a client need to do your homework when finding the person who you are going to trust to change your personality. That is what a personal transformation process does! In the same way that I believe you carefully choose your doctor, so should you carefully choose the practitioner of your mind. Nowadays, you can go to the Internet and read about the general guidelines that you want to follow in order to find the right guide for you. One thing that I do want to point out about the training of a practitioner. If you are going to a psychologist, for example, there is a body that dictates the requirements in their training to become one, the APA.[153] This is a modality that has matured over time and that also has a centralized institution providing such guidelines. Unfortunately, with emerging new therapies, this is not necessarily the case, which can be quite confusing. As an example, in hypnotherapy there are numerous associations to which different schools adhere. That is just part of the process of reaching that maturity. Eventually they all will come together and form one organization that provides unified standards for everyone. This doesn't detract from the effectiveness of the therapy. If you are going to go to a practitioner of one of these newer therapy modalities, you need to make sure that she has solid theoretical and practical training—at the very least, two hundred hours, but ideally more (four to five hundred). A weekend course does not make a mind practitioner.

Continuing with the example of hypnotherapy, anyone can learn in a matter of hours how to induce a hypnotic state on someone else. That is technique. Technique and mind transformation process (therapy) are two different things. Now that a person is in hypnosis, then what? The unconscious of the person is open at this point—what do you do with this state? Then is when the transformational process actually begins. Navigating the unconscious, and processing the events and programs in it, requires much more training and experience than just a weekend. The unconscious is a very different world (associative and symbolic) in which logic and rationale do not play. Make sure about the background of the practitioner you intend to use.

Leading Life with MTPs

At this point in our evolution, pain and suffering are still inevitable. The way we live life nowadays is punch through it, fighting through our inner pains and external dramas. We need better ways to deal with this dynamic. MTPs help us deal with life in a much smoother way as they soften the sharp edges on our path. Additionally, we want tools that help us reach new levels of accomplishments as we walk this journey in the physical world. It does not matter how successful you are at something; eventually you will want to explore new territories in your life. You need inner resources to be able to do these transitions. MTPs are one of the different tools that can help you build them. Best of all, there are already many of them that you can apply yourself without the need to go to a professional every single time you are dealing with a challenging emotional situation.

A Scenario

What I am suggesting here is that you learn a technique that you will be able to use on your own when facing routine emotional challenges. Understand that as an adult, every time you get upset in a certain situation (that does not include an attack to your physical integrity, like an assault), it is because that situation triggered a negative (limiting) program that you have stored in your unconscious. Whether because you are stuck in traffic or you had a confrontation with someone, if you feel that negative emotion, it is because it is being released by its associated program.

A point to clarify here. Let's say you moved to a different part in town, and now you are trying new routes to decide which is the best one to go to work. Say one of the routes was really congested. You feel the negative emotion that tells you that this experience is not agreeable with you. In this case, the emotion is giving you feedback about this new experience. That is what it is supposed to do. That is not a negative program; the emotion is simply giving you guidance in your life. You then look for another route, until you find the one that feels best to you. This is a very different situation to where every time you get in a traffic jam, you get upset. If this is a regular pattern in you, then you now have one or more limiting programs. If you want to improve your quality of life in this aspect, then you need to change this repetitive reaction to this circumstance. You need to explore what is behind that negative pattern. For example:

1. If this is truly, for the time being, the only way to go to work, then why don't you adapt to it? Why not have an audiobook or podcast that you can listen to and make you feel good and productive in your life? Instead, you remain in a mode of continuous resistance to life. You are not flowing with it, and you do not adapt. That is a limiting program: "There is nothing I can do about this."

2. If this is a situation that is intolerable to you, then why not change work, move your home closer to it, or move to a different town? Whatever the answer you give to this question, it will reveal a similar limiting program that makes you conclude that there is "nothing you can do" about your situation. You may believe that it is difficult to get a job in a more convenient location, or that with "this bad economy" you'd better stay put where you are. These are all limiting programs. And if you say, "Peter, that is the reality of life," well, that is another limiting program. These types of programs tend to be foundational ones, which require work and persistence to change. Understand that they are just programs, and they make you see life as such.

When you keep an attitude of openness to possibilities, the Unit of Consciousness (through your unconscious) will present them to you.

This takes practice. Notice that I do not claim that this is easy to do. Nevertheless, you will see the results and will be amazed how differently life can work. That is when magic starts to happen. As I have shown extensively before, the personality has an extremely small scope. It does not have the ability to see all the alternatives and ways to accomplish something. The Unit of Consciousness does.

What you as the personality want is to be a vehicle that allows all the life possibilities to come through you.

Living Life with MTPs

This can only happen when there are no limiting programs that block other possible solutions. We come back to the need to do MTPs. The dynamic for life that I propose to you is as follows.

1. When you become aware of a deep negative pattern (including trauma, of course) that you have had in your life, go to a practitioner to free yourself of the behavior that it imposes on you. You need to do this; otherwise you will live your life enslaved by that program. This is similar to when you go to your doctor because of a more serious physical illness.

2. Learn an MTP (or more, if that is what your heart tells you to do) that you can apply on yourself, on your own. Do not just read a book. Take a workshop where you have a professionally guided experience about the technique. Besides, you will find like-minded people who will support you in your endeavors.

3. Start paying attention to how you are living your life. Pay attention to your responses. This demands awareness, and it is a practice. This is your first step to get out of the mechanical, robotic way into which humanity has sunk. Just by doing this, you are already contributing to the transformation that we all want to see in our societies. It really starts right here, with you as an individual.

4. Whenever you notice a negative reaction on your part to anything, set a time to revisit the event while doing your MTP. It should take you to the originating event that created the program that made you react that way. If this event feels overwhelming, consider processing it with a practitioner. Otherwise, by doing the MTP, besides the emotional relief that it will give you, it will also transform how you see the originating event and give you a certainty that you will react differently, and in a more positive way, the next time you go through those same circumstances.

5. Move on with your life, living it with a renewed awareness and empowered by the knowledge and tools that you have. Because you yourself are transforming your own limiting programs, you now know that you can reach whatever it is that you want to do with your life. And that is what you came here to do in this physical universe.

I am not giving you a magic formula here or an "overnight results" one. If we had such a thing, we would all be enlightened by now, wouldn't we? What I am offering here is a method by which you will be able to improve the quality of your life one step at a time. It requires motivation, commitment, and persistence. If you follow it, your life will improve. If there are serious traumas in your life, you must address these first by going to a practitioner. Otherwise, they will keep sabotaging your life and also any efforts that you make on your own to improve your behavior. That does not mean that you have to do sessions with a professional guide for the rest of your life. Once the major issues are out of the way, with the permission of your practitioner, you can start to take care of yourself on your own as needed by using an MTP. Even better is if you can do it with a group of people where there is mutual practice and support. Out of the many techniques that you can use— and that I encourage you to research—I will talk about two of them that I have experience with and that I know produce wonderful results: emotional freedom techniques and meditation.

Emotional Freedom Techniques

Emotional freedom techniques (EFT), also known as tapping, is a therapeutic technique developed by Gary Craig, which he in turn derived from another technique known as thought field therapy (TFT).[156] These therapies are relatively new compared with traditional psychology, and therefore there is still the need for a wider acceptance among many conservative practitioners. This is in spite of the scientific controlled studies already done (and with significant positive results, as I already mentioned earlier). I am confident that EFT will be recognized as evidence based in the years to come.

My experience with this technique has been superb. With my clients, mixing with hypnosis, I have done past-life regressions and natal regressions, which are traditionally more of the realm of hypnotherapy. Included are the cases of past life regressions where my clients did not even believe in such a phenomenon. This is on top of the "traditional" processing of traumatic current life situations. Besides using this technique in my sessions, I apply it routinely to deal with challenging emotional situations that I may go through in my daily life (on average at least once a week, and often more than once). I hope you realize that there is no single week in your life where absolutely nothing upsets you. Remember, any upset is a triggered negative program, and it is controlling your behavior.

It is beyond the scope of this book to explain here how the technique works and how to apply it. I invite you to research it; nowadays, it is easy with the Internet.[157] I can give you a simple introduction here. The technique is based on stimulating certain points in the body through pressure. These points in the body coincide with some of the points used in acupuncture (which is where the idea for these techniques came from). Instead of using

---

[156] Developed by Roger Callahan.

[157] One site that I can recommend for you to start with is https://www.eftuniverse.com.

needles, you tap on them with your fingers (hence the name tapping). When you stimulate these points in a certain format, as described by the technique, it triggers a response from your unconscious, bringing to the surface (i.e., to the conscious level) emotions, sensations, and images associated with the negative behavior that you want to transform. Once these memories are brought up to the conscious, you can process them. The technique is so simple that you could probably read the manual in a couple of hours. Nevertheless, I strongly urge you to take, at the very least, a full weekend course before you apply this method to yourself. And again, deeper traumas should be processed with a competent trained professional. Otherwise, once you are familiar with the technique, you will be able to apply it to yourself on an as needed basis.

As an example, let's say you had a heated discussion with someone at your workplace. It left you upset. You can go to a place where you have some privacy and do the EFT sequence. At the end of the day, I also encourage you to find a space and time at home where you can sit down undisturbed and revisit the conflicting situation to go to the source of the upset (not the reason for the conflict with your co-worker, but rather the originating event in your early life that created the program that was triggered by the situation at work). If you got upset, irrespective of whether you were right, then you have a limiting program that you need to process. This way, the next time a similar situation occurs, you will be able to interact with your co-worker with more calm and ease. That is how, by using an MTP, the quality of your life will improve. Doing the technique at work will help you to get back to a more relaxed state so that you can continue with your job. It gives you a pause that enables you to decouple from the conflict. This decoupling is crucial for you to be able to restore your full intellectual capacities, which are greatly reduced as a result from the stress induced by the conflict. So, you see, now you have tools that help you deal with the challenging situations that life brings to you. Just by knowing this and having them, you live life with higher self-esteem and more confidence about achieving what you set out to do.

Mindfulness and Meditation

Mindfulness is the skill of being aware, present, in whatever it is that you are doing. This is closely related to what I talked earlier, about you paying attention to your reactions as you go along in your daily life as part of your personal work with MTPs. Meditation is just one specific practice in which you sit (or lie) down and keep your mind in a single focus, be it blank or a specific mantra. The point is to stop the erratic behavior of our minds and allow them to enter a quiet zone. When the mind enters into this zone, lots of interesting things happen. For instance, in hypnotherapy, this is the state that allows access to the unconscious and its programs. Also, in a beautiful example of science corroborating the positive effects of old, traditional disciplines, regular practice of meditation causes positive physical changes in your brain.[158]

- Studies suggest that the prefrontal cortex and the insula, key parts of the brain in higher intellect functionality, preserve their thickness better in longtime meditators than in non-meditators. As you age, the prefrontal cortex tends to shrink in thickness, and you lose intellectual capacity. These findings suggest that meditation helps preserve your intellect.
- The hippocampus, which assists in learning and memory as well as emotion regulation, thickens after an eight-week meditation-based program.
- The temporoparietal junction in your brain, in charge of perspective taking and empathy and compassion, thickened after the eight-week program.
- The amygdala, responsible for our reactions to stress, reduced in size in the participants of that program.

This practice does not have anything to do with any spiritual belief. You do not have to become a Buddhist to do it. Independently of what your beliefs are, you can simply take your mind to that quiet zone and reach its benefits, which as you can see are quite tangible. The same way that physical exercise shapes your body, mindfulness shapes your brain. Why would you want to let your prefrontal cortex thin out with age? Why wouldn't you be interested in reducing your emotional reactivity by reducing the size of the amygdala as a result of this practice? "Peter, my life is already too busy as it is, and now you are asking me to do all this stuff?" Yes, and that question points to what is one of the core problems in our lifestyles: that incessant race in which we live, which is the antithesis of mindfulness. What do you think are its effects on our brains? It makes us robots. There is no time for pause, for true decision

---

[158] Sara Lazar, "Welcome to the Lazar Lab." Harvard University, https://scholar. harvard.edu/sara_lazar. Accessed December 14, 2018. Check as well her presentations on YouTube.

making on how to live life. You think that you are making decisions, but it is simply your programs taking you from one place to another. On top of that, the irony is that by doing these practices, you will actually end up being more efficient in everything that you do. You will better prioritize what you really want to do in your life and execute your tasks with more harmony.

MTP and Meditation, the Push-Pull Effect

The reason I encourage you to incorporate these two practices into your life is because they complement each other in a superb way. That is the reason why I borrow the term "push-pull effect" (also used in business models and in electrical engineering). When you try to move a heavy object from one place to another, instead of you simply pushing on your own, you can get someone else to pull the object in the desired direction, making the job much more effective. When you do an MTP, your initial focus is on a negative limiting behavior that you have and would like to transform. When you do meditation, you aim at finding that inner quiet place, which is intrinsically a positive experience. They are complementary. When you transform a limiting behavior, you diminish your reactivity to external events, and you free yourself from the emotional chain that stops you from accomplishing what you want. When you meditate, you diminish your reactivity to external events by changing the structures of your brain. Also, if you agree with the model of the human mind that I presented in this book by practicing being in that quiet zone, you build a channel of communication with your Essence. By establishing better contact with your Essence, you enable yourself as a better receptor to Its messages, which are the true beacon that you want to have in your life. You will have a more developed intuition, better gut feelings, which will give you the direction that you need when making decisions in your life. And the less limiting programs you have (MTPs), the clearer this channel will be—two practices that complement each other very well. The time that you spend practicing them will more than compensate for the time "lost" in not doing "productive work." This is something that you will be able to corroborate only after you experience it. Experiment including these practices in your daily life, and then you can decide the optimal way to mix them with your lifestyle.

Part 4

Final Thoughts

Summaries

Even though we started with a very simple model of the human consciousness, as we went along, I introduced more and more concepts that gradually added complexity to it. I am aware that all these definitions and concepts can become overwhelming. To that end, in this section I will give you summaries, mostly in a graphical format, with the intent to make all these clearer to you.

Physical and Nonphysical

The original model of the human consciousness introduced the basic concept that a human being includes two very distinct aspects.

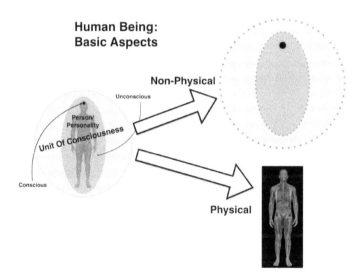

There is a physical part, which consists of the body that we use in an insertion into this universe, and there is a nonphysical aspect that includes the Essence of what we are and all the nontangible mind processes that we have talked about in this book.[159] We observe their actions and effects in the fields

---

[159] As a personal opinion, most likely the whole body has a nonphysical counterpart. In other literature, one reads about the etheric or subtle body. I do not talk about it in this book because I want to remain focused reporting what we observe in sessions of the transformation of the mind, repeatedly and consistently.

of the transformation of the mind (transpersonal components) even though science today cannot yet detect or explain them.

In this model, our true Essence is not physical.

This physical universe is not our native environment.

This implies that the root of all actions that we take as human beings is in the nonphysical. The ultimate control is at that level. It has to be because the body is simply an instrument that we use to interface to this universe. Because the control ultimately comes from our nonphysical aspect, this means that there has to be a mapping from nonphysical to physical.

Both the conscious and the unconscious have physical counterparts in the body, across different organic structures.

Some of these counterparts are the reptilian brain, the limbic system, and the cortex. This is what I mentioned earlier in the book about the fact that a surgeon can touch a certain region of the brain and trigger emotions, images, sounds, and memories. That does not mean that the physical layer is all there is.

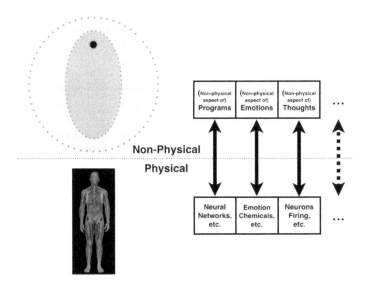

The previous figure illustrates, in a generic way, these two fundamental aspects of a human being. The blocks in the figure are simply examples of counterparts of some of the concepts that we have touched in this book. This graphic does not differentiate between conscious or unconscious. It is generic. Also, notice that I cannot be exact in the definitions of the blocks (hence the "etc." in them), precisely because the nonphysical aspect is still beyond the reach of the studies of our sciences.

The Design of the Body

Continuing with our review, we saw that for a successful insertion into this physical world, the unconscious (nonphysical, but acting through the corresponding physical structures of the body) must provide three basic functionalities.

1. Support and maintain the inner functionality of the whole body
2. Process the data that the receptors of the body provide about the environment in which it is
3. Interact with the environment accordingly

Points two and three are the most interesting to us. As I mentioned in that section, we really don't want to be paying attention to when our hearts are supposed to beat again. We came here to interact, and that is where we like to put our focus in life. To that end, notice how the body has been designed.

a. Input: The sensory systems (sight, hearing, olfactory, taste, and all the different skin receptors) provide input about the environment. Remember that they do not provide a complete picture of reality; they simply give you just a very small amount of information about it.
b. Output: With the feedback of the senses, the skeleton and muscles provide the additional mechanisms to interact with the environment. Examples are movement, speech, and facial expressions.
c. Support: The whole central part of the body contains the organs and systems that keep it going. Because of its physicality, the body requires maintenance and fuel to function properly, as well as discarding the no longer needed by-products of its internal activity. These requirements are fulfilled, for the most part, by the organs situated between the pelvis and the shoulders. All this is done automatically by the unconscious for us. You can view this part of the body as the one that supports the receptors and mechanisms for interaction, which are the relevant ones to experience the physical world.

Additionally, notice that points two and three refer to more than just the reception of data and the resulting interaction. In between these two physical processes, there are two corresponding key factors.

- Interpreting the received data (perception)
- Deciding how to act (determining interaction)

This is the core of what determines our behavior. Here is where the key organ, the brain (and all its associated structures), comes into play. Because of the brain's central role, in the following figures I am going to show it separately from the rest of the body's biology that I talked about in points (a) through (c). This will allow me to dissect it more and connect with all the concepts that I want summarize here for you.

Functional Blocks for Behavior

I will divide the internal processing of our behavior, in the brain, into five physical functional blocks.

I. **The virtual reality functional block:** Once the signals from the body's receptors arrive to the corresponding processing centers of the brain, it is then that this mysterious and fascinating phenomenon, the creation of a virtual reality, occurs. This virtual reality consists of a four-dimensional representation (three dimensions in space, plus time) of the physical reality that surrounds the body. Additionally, it creates qualities like color, smell, and taste that simply do not exist. To those who are still doubting or taking this as an exaggeration, here is another beautiful example. Take the case of a meal that you just cooked. That food is composed of molecules that, when inserted in your mouth and upon entering in contact with your tongue (where the taste buds are), send nerve impulses to the brain, which in turn translate them into the experience that we call taste. Realize that molecules are just molecules—they don't have taste. On the other hand, as you are eating that food, those same molecules that it emanates and that make it to your nose also trigger impulses to the brain, but they now get translated into the sensation of smell. They're exactly the same molecules. Your brain is giving you two totally different interpretations of the same reality. Molecules do not have taste or smell. It is 100 percent a creation of this particular apparatus that we call the human body. You are moving and interacting within this virtual reality that this body generates. When you wear the virtual reality headsets that I alluded earlier, you are adding another layer of separation from the actual reality to which you belong. I am interested in knowing about that primary reality more than generating tertiary ones (secondary being the one we are in). Do not get me wrong about the headsets; they are actually a lot of fun. I simply want you to understand my point here.

II. **The biological programs functional block:** They are common to all humans. They are biological tendencies that affect our behavior in a constant and similar way. As biological characteristics of our species, these correspond to hard-wired structures in the brain that normally do not change. We all are sexual creatures. Throughout your life, you are behaving as the male or female that you are (or the gender you identify yourself with). Even though society influences these behaviors, there are intrinsic actions that come to light when we are sexually interested in someone else. We are also social. That automatically makes us behave differently than if we were solitary creatures (people who are solitary have limiting programs that are repressing this biological behavior in them). Of course, included here is our instinct of survival that I have referred to throughout this book. There are many other biological tendencies that the marketing departments of the corporations take advantage to increase the likelihood that you will buy their products. Because these biological tendencies are intrinsic and do not normally change, these fall under the category of hard-wired programs.

III. **The hard-wired personality attributes functional block:** These are the attributes of the personality that normally do not change throughout the lifetime of the individual. From the perspective of how you see the environment, if you are an extrovert, you will describe a place with a lot of people very differently than an introvert, and you will also act very differently. This layer is already a filter of perception and interaction.

IV. **The foundational programs functional block:** As we saw, these have a wider effect on our behavior. If you believe that "life is difficult," this belief will color a great number of your perceptions and interactions in life.

V. **The nonfoundational programs functional block:** This tends to be more reduced in scope, like not liking a specific activity because of a previous negative experience associated with it.

The role of the virtual reality functional block is more that of a translator (receptor signals → "a virtual reality"), rather than a program that affects behavior. It corresponds to a hard-wired structure in the brain that normally does not change throughout the life of the individual.

Blocks II and III also correspond to hard-wired structures in the brain, but these ones take a more active role in dictating our behavior—thus the name hard-wired programs.[160] They correspond to the physical part of the core layer of the personality.

The last two blocks, IV and V, correspond to soft-wired programs. These are the programs designed to allow us to adapt to the environment. These correspond to the adaptive layer of the personality.

For better visualization, we can present these physical blocks in a more graphic way.

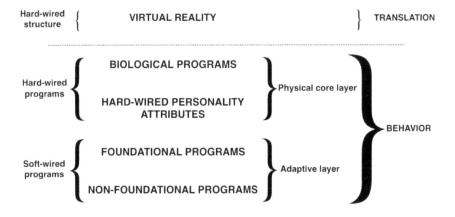

Because these are the physical blocks of behavior, notice that the nonphysical core layer (the UC influences) is not depicted here. I will introduce that factor soon. Now, let's use a less abstract illustration (notice that due to space constraints, I labeled the hard-wired personality attributes as "hardwired personality").

---

[160] Notice that I am not mentioning the body mechanics, because here I am talking about the functional blocks of behavior within the brain.

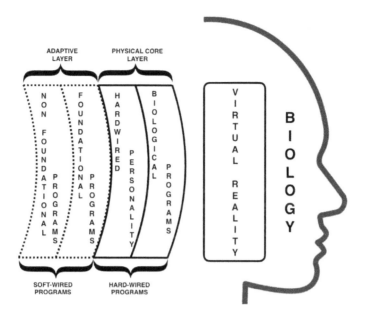

This illustration will be the basis for my next explanations. Here are some notes about it.

- Biology refers to the body, besides these physical structures that represent the five functional blocks.
- I put the functional blocks one after another. I have done this for the purpose of explaining these concepts to you. As we saw, the unconscious is a massive parallel processing engine (remember the number of chemical reactions that are occurring in your body every second). As such, it may be that this is also how it processes at least some, if not most, of the information that it receives from the body.[161] For our purposes here, exactly what the order is and how all this is executed is not relevant. What matters is that you understand how environmental information is interpreted and handled in the mind.
- With respect to the shape of the different blocks depicted, the idea is that they act as lenses that change the incoming information one way or another.[162] That is the reason why I present them as curved

---

[161] Certainly, a combination of serial and parallel processing of information.

[162] For the scientific-oriented readers: most of the lenses are either convex or concave, and the ones I depict are neither. I simply drew them like that for pure convenience of space.

instead of simple rectangles. This way, it will help remind you that the information from the virtual reality module is being reshaped by all these functional blocks of perception. These are the subjective objectivity and the information filtering effects.

- I draw the soft-wired program blocks with dotted lines, the hardwired programs with solid lines.
- Reminder: these structures are the physical counterpart of the nonphysical unconscious.

Now we are ready to describe the perception and interaction processes.

Perception Process

Using the previous illustration as a base, perception can be presented as follows.

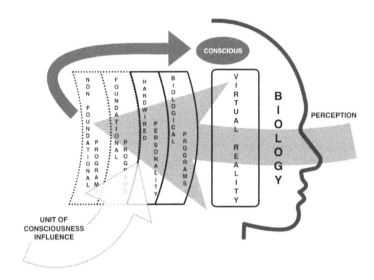

The graph flows from right to left. The information that comes from your senses (BIOLOGY in the picture) is transmitted to the brain to be processed and translated into a virtual reality. Once this is done (constantly happening while awake), the translated information goes through the functional blocks for further interpretation.

- The programs in these blocks will act as lenses that will filter out unnecessary information (which would otherwise overwhelm the extremely limited capacity of the conscious).

- The relevant information is then compared against all the concepts and their associations stored in the unconscious. The most important ones are stored as foundational and nonfoundational programs. These may have come from present life experiences or from transpersonal factors.
- The appropriate programs are then triggered, coloring the perceived events accordingly.
- Notice the "Unit of Consciousness Influence," represented with a dotted arrow and pointing to the line that belongs to both the soft- and hard-wired programs. It may affect the output of any of all these modules. Also, because we don't know exactly how it operates with the structures of the brain, this is where the concept of lenses comes in handy. The more negative programs you have, the darker these lenses will be. As such, they will let in less light (positive influence) from your nonphysical Essence, and your interpretation of reality will be just the darkness of the negative programming. For example, say that you were raised in a racist environment. Your programs (most likely foundational) will not allow the message of your nonphysical Essence, which is telling you that race is irrelevant with respect to how we see others, to come through and be part of the processing of what you are experiencing. The lens of your programs is too dark to let that light (i.e., message) come through.

After all this processing is done, only then is the information transmitted to the conscious, the "you" that you perceive you are as a human being, in your everyday experiences. This will take place even in the simplest of settings, such as observing a car. You think you are objectively seeing just a car. First of all, you don't see its atoms and molecules because your receptors are not designed to do so (i.e., your receptors have given you an interpretation of reality). Also, your unconscious is taking every single characteristic of the car that you are seeing and passing it through its programs. Just because at that point you are not interested in the color, brand, or shape and their associations, that does not mean your unconscious did not process them. It processed that information according to your own unique programs stored in your mind. You cannot escape this. There's no such a thing as being objective. Everything is subjected to your programs of perception.

Interaction Process

Once you receive and interpret information from the environment in which you are, now you will interact accordingly. You are going to decide what to do—except that it is not as simple as that. There are two basic cases to check: one when you are (relatively) calm, the other one when you are reacting due to a strong emotional trigger. Let's start with what hopefully is the more common scenario in your life, which is you making a decision under calmer circumstances.

Decided Interaction

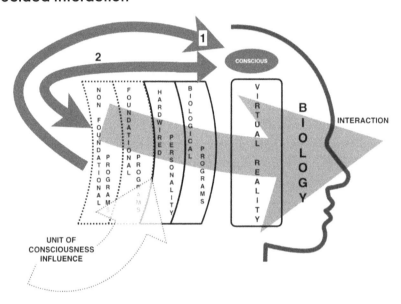

Arrow 1 in the figure refers to the fact that in order to make a decision, you must have had an input to trigger that process.[163] That input may have come from the external environment, as I explained in the description of the process of perception, but it may also come from your mind. For example, you sit down to decide about this business opportunity that was given to you days ago. Once you decided to think about this, typically you will go through the different scenarios that such an event would entail. Here is where bidirectional

---

[163] I am talking here about decisions that you are making while going through your daily life. There is another way, in which you enter an altered state of mind (like meditation) and let the answer come to you. This answer is coming directly from your Essence, assuming that it was not distorted by the programs in your mind.

arrow 2 comes to play. As you go through the different scenarios related to making such a decision (faculty of reasoning), every single time you think of something, the unconscious processes that idea and gives you feedback based on the consequences that the programs in your mind predict. You will feel it and then move through that process accordingly.

Continuing with the business opportunity example, say one option would be that you put some of your own personal money into it. Based on the programs that your unconscious has, this idea may be considered dangerous because of the negative associated programs that get triggered by it. Of course, you will not hear a voice saying dangerous; instead, you will think, "Nah! That is a bad idea," or, "I don't want to do that." If that is the case, you will search for another possibility, and so on. Notice that as much as you like to say that you made a decision, that decision was in reality completely guided by your unconscious. It is the programs in your unconscious that take you to the final choice that you make. The more negative programs you have, the more influence they will exert on your decisions, and thus the less free will. The more there are positive ones, the more possibilities you will contemplate (or rather, your unconscious will allow you to contemplate).

And here is once more where our analogy with lenses applies. Let's say that this business proposition entails some risks. You can see that, and the programs in your unconscious are giving you clear feedback about it. These programs tend to darken these lenses of our mind. On the other hand, you do have enough positive programs that give you confidence in yourself and life. These programs will allow the light (message) of the Unit of Consciousness to come through and guide you about this decision. If this business proposition is what your nonphysical Essence wants to use as part of its learnings and experiences, it will give you that feeling that tells you to take it, in spite of the risks. The positive programs will make the lenses transparent enough for that message to be able to go through, even while the negative programs are raising their concerns about it. You will follow that gut feeling, that intuition. Now you have enough free will to be able to lead your life in the direction that you, as a nonphysical entity, made. You are becoming the master of your life. That's it!

Reactive Interaction

The second scenario that I mentioned was that of a clearly reactive behavior. Someone said something that irritated you and "made you" say something that you ended up regretting later, once you calmed down. Here is graphically what happened.

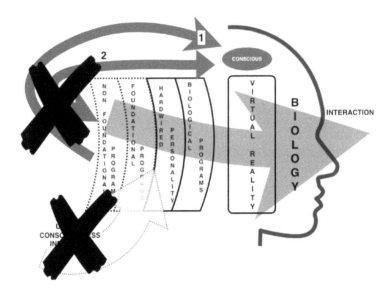

What that person said triggered a negative program with a big emotional battery associated with it. That program activates and takes control of you. The conscious (you do not decide whether to be irritated or not) and the Unit of Consciousness are shut out of the process altogether. It's 100 percent robotic behavior. Depending on how big the emotional battery is, this program will override the social programs that normally restrict your behavior within the accepted parameters. If you felt irritated, then you may have said something that you regretted later. If the emotion was more intense (strong anger), then you may have even screamed at the person, overriding more social programs (like "you do not scream at people"). Once you calm down, the negative programs that triggered during the event return to standby (after the activation and fight response in this case).[164] Now you will hear the alarms of the social programs because you broke rules of behavior, and you start feeling the regret. Like a machine, you go from one state to another, determined by which programs are active at any given moment.

True free will comes from our Essence, not from the personality.

---

[164] Remember the fight, flight, freeze, and faint automatic unconscious responses to danger.

Ideal Perception/Behavior Process

The body and its personality were meant to be the instruments that the Individualized Consciousness uses to experience the physical universe. Instead, they have taken control on their own—something that was never meant to be because they simply do not have the ability to do so. The analogy here can be that of the traditional cruise control that cars have.[165] This feature is supposed to ease driving by maintaining the speed that you selected. You still have to steer and determine where to go; otherwise, the car will crash at the slightest turn of the road. We are essentially in cruise mode in our current state of evolution. We, as personalities, have taken control away from the Individualized Consciousness, and that is why we are constantly crashing in our lives. The dramas, fears, and conflicts are the crashes in this analogy. The virtual reality that our brains create is an extremely small representation of the total reality that science already shows us and that we are just beginning to explore—and even smaller, if you are willing to consider the realities that deeper states of consciousness show us (and which this book is all about). It is our nonphysical Essence (the driver in our analogy) who has the more encompassing view needed to live a more harmonious life in this particular universe and planet that we chose to experience. What we want is to become the vehicles through which it can express itself.

Here it is graphically; I've removed the labels for clarity.

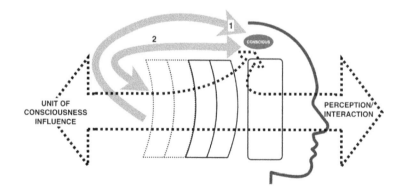

You want your programming to not interfere with your nonphysical Essence's guidance. That means no negative programs, except those needed for the physical survival of the body. That means no negative programs like "I

---

[165] Not the smarter ones in self-driving cars.

am not good enough," "life is hard," and others that we inflict upon ourselves. Notice that I still include arrows 1 and 2. The reason for this is that a human being that has reached enlightenment still needs to learn the behaviors and customs of the environment in which she or he is. You do need programs while in a human body, but your identity and self-esteem are not tied to them, and your behavior is a free choice within the culture.

The Deeper Reality That We Need to Connect With

Our history shows us how painful our path has been. We have not had a single period of global peace during our presence on this planet. Humanity has suffered a lot, and it still does today in spite of all the scientific and technological advances. What we refer to as humanity's suffering starts with the individual pain of the dramas in our lives. For millennia, men and women have lived at the mercy of the psychological forces in their unconscious without the least understanding of what was going on in their minds. Still, very slowly, in a combination of trials and experiences plus an increased knowledge of how the universe works, our standard of living has increased. However, in spite of the great comforts that we have achieved today, our emotional dramas continue. We watch, hear, and read about them every day in the media. They spare no one. From the impoverished masses to the "stars" of our society, we all hear their stories of pain. And in between, all of us are included.

This attests to the power of the programs that I have emphasized throughout this book. The good thing, as history has shown us, is that we will eventually transcend these limitations. The question now becomes: at what cost? Evolution will happen; it is inevitable. But do we really want to keep going through so much suffering to be able to get more harmony in our lives? In the earlier times in our history, we had the excuse of not having enough knowledge. What is our excuse today? It is not the lack of knowledge. It still is our dogmatic beliefs. It will take an enormous amount of time and energy before humanity recognizes the importance of emotional health at the level it deserves.

The Case of Scarlett Lewis

The wonderful thing is that we are starting to see the first shifts in that direction. At this point in our evolution, more often than not these shifts come as a result of traumatic experiences that shake people's foundations (that is, their programming, as you well understand now). It is these pioneers who move the world in the direction needed to get to the point where this dynamic will not be needed. One courageous and beautiful example of this shift is exemplified in the transformation that Scarlett Lewis experienced as a result of the death of her son Jesse, in one of the deadliest school shootings in US history. As a result of her journey through grief and through the anger that comes with the personal loss in this type of circumstances, she ended up writing the book *Nurturing Healing Love*.[166] In the book, she describes the mind transformation processes that she used (hypnotherapy, EFT, EMDR[167]) to transcend the trauma that she experienced. It was a deep transformation that included forgiving the twenty-year-old shooter and coming to the understanding that there is a deeper cause behind this type of tragic event. In a video presented on Uplift.tv,[168] "Every School Shooting Is Preventable,"[169] she comments,

> Why is this happening? The cause of this violence is the anger and disconnection of our youth. They face more trauma, less interpersonal connection and report more stress and anxiety than ever before.

She continues, in a testament to her true transformation.

> The solution is teaching them how to have positive and healthy relationships, deep and meaningful connections, skills and tools for resilience and how to manage their emotions.

She couldn't have expressed it in a better way. Notice that I said "in a testament to her true transformation," because it is this attitude and direction of action that shows true healing. Someone who went through a similar traumatic experience, but who did not transform the resulting programs and emotions that naturally arise from such events (your unconscious protecting you), will take action only in the direction that these programs dictate. In this particular example, it could be more (or less) gun control, how to capture

---

[166] Scarlett Lewis, *Nurturing Healing Love: A Mother's Journey of Hope and Forgiveness*, Carslbad: Hay House, 2013.

[167] EMDR: Eye Movement Desensitization and Reprocessing, another type of mind transformation process.

[168] https://uplift.tv.

[169] Scarlett Lewis, "Every School Shooting Is Preventable." UpliftTV, https://uplift.tv/2018/every-school-shooting-preventable. Accessed December 14, 2018.

these individuals faster, more severe punishment for them, et cetera. These are reactive responses that simply do not address the root cause of violence. As long as that person has these negative programs active in her unconscious, she will not have the free will to be able to discern the real solution. By going through a true healing process, Scarlett Lewis liberated herself from the darkness of those programs and as a result attained a higher consciousness that allows her to see what really needs to change to avoid these scenarios. This is free will. Free will takes action in a positive direction, congruent with what we are at our Essence: unconditional love.

She is not the only one in that path, more and more are embarking in this direction. There is so much more to do nowadays, especially given the magnitude of the impact that this human civilization has taken on this planet, with all its social and ecological consequences.

Jesse

I chose the case of Scarlett Lewis and her son Jesse because this is also an example that gives clear confirmation to what I wrote about us being nonphysical entities who come here with a purpose. Jesse was six years old when the shooting occurred. Days before that event, he wrote on a blackboard that they had at home the words "Norurting helin love."[170] He meant "nurturing healing love" and was just learning to write as a first grader. As Lewis points out, that's not the typical language of a six-year old. The last morning that she saw him was when his dad, Neil, picked him up to take him to school. On the way out, Jesse wrote in her frost-covered car, "I love you," and stood there smiling at his mom. Jesse spent that night at his dad's home. The next day was the day of the shooting. As his dad was taking him to school, Lewis narrates in her book,

> Although Neil and I had finalized the plans to meet at Jesse's classroom later that day, Jesse was worried about what was going to happen. He was certain that it wasn't going to work out, and he was uncharacteristically melancholy.
>
> "Don't worry, Jess, Mom and I will be there," Neil said.
>
> "No," Jesse answered, "it's not going to happen."

---

[170] Scarlett Lewis, *Nurturing Healing Love: A Mother's Journey of Hope and Forgiveness*, Carslbad: Hay House, 2013, 72.

Neil was surprised by Jesse's reaction—it was an odd way for Jesse to talk.

"Of course it is going to happen, Jess. It's all arranged."

"No," Jesse repeated, shaking his head. "It's not going to happen, Dad."

When they got to the school, Neil parked the car and walked with Jesse through the front doors and into the main hallway, where they hugged goodbye as usual. "Dad?" Jesse said, putting his hands on Neil's shoulders as they came out of the hug. "I just want you to know … it's going to be okay. And that I love you and Mom."

Then Jesse turned and walked away down the hall toward his first-grade classroom.[171]

If you recall, I mentioned how children at an early age are more connected to their Essence. Here is a clear example of how Jesse knew, in an intuitive way, that something was going to happen. That was his purpose in this physical insertion. Lewis writes in her book,

The kids who survived reported that even with this head wound, Jesse stayed on his feet and faced the gunman. And it was then that Jesse did what I am now certain he was put on this earth to do: he saved lives. When something happened to the shooter's gun and he was forced to stop for a moment, either to fix it or to reload, Jesse yelled to his classmates that this was their chance to escape. He shouted for them to run, to run as fast as they could, to run now! And they did. They listened to Jesse and ran for their lives. Nine terrified first graders managed to run from the classroom to safety as the gunman took aim at Jesse.[172]

---

[171] Scarlett Lewis, *Nurturing Healing Love: A Mother's Journey of Hope and Forgiveness*, Carslbad: Hay House, 2013, 13–14.

[172] Scarlett Lewis, *Nurturing Healing Love: A Mother's Journey of Hope and Forgiveness*, Carslbad: Hay House, 2013.

Truly take in what Lewis is describing here. I have emphasized over and over that the main priority of the unconscious is our survival in this physical world. I also explained that the automatic reactions to danger are fight, flight, freeze, or faint. Jesse did something here that transcended all of that. And he did it as a six-year old. What I mean by that is that even as an adult, this would have been a heroic, extraordinary action. Here is a very powerful Unit of Consciousness that was able to override all the survival mechanisms of the body and take action in the direction that it truly wanted. So that you can fathom the magnitude of what trying to tell you here, I will ask you, one last time, can you promise that you will not ever get irritated again? You cannot. Irritation is a very small survival response of the unconscious, compared to the forces that it would exert under Jesse's circumstances. The power that overrode Jesse's survival instinct is the power that all of us have inside ourselves.

Anything that you want to accomplish, your nonphysical Essence has the power to convert into reality.

Ramifications toward Our Evolution

Jesse's mission for his physical insertion was more than saving lives at that tragic moment (a heroic act in itself). Out of this tragedy, Lewis transformed herself and found a new purpose in life. She created the Jesse Lewis Choose Love Movement, a foundation whose mission is "to ensure that every child has access to Social and Emotional Learning (SEL)," as she explains on her website.[173] Out of that tragedy, Jesse's brother, J. T., connected with Rwandan survivors (from the genocide that I mentioned earlier) and started a campaign to help them. These are global reaching actions. They are the reason and purpose of Jesse's life. These are evolved nonphysical entities that come here to exert the powerful impacts that humanity needs if we are to move toward the harmony that we want for all of us. Lewis understood this too when she went to Boston a day after the bomb explosion during the Boston Marathon. That explosion killed three people, and an eight-year-old boy was among them. As she then narrates, she saw a photo of the boy in a newspaper where he was holding a blue cardboard sign on which he had written, "No more hurting people. Peace."[174]

---

[173] www.jesselewischooselove.org. Accessed December 14, 2018.
[174] Scarlett Lewis, *Nurturing Healing Love: A Mother's Journey of Hope and Forgiveness*, Carslbad: Hay House, 2013, 141.

Out of that experience, she wrote, "I wonder if the boys are in on this together."[175] Yes, as we all are, in the end. These are not accidental events or random coincidences. If you start paying a deeper attention to the events that occur in your life, you will find very clear evidence that there is a higher intelligence that transcends this physicality. Lewis writes about when Jesse was born.

> I must have sensed that as well. On the day he was born, I held Jesse in my arms and said this prayer:
>
>> Dear Jesus, thank you so much for Jesse. I know that he is a gift, and I know that you could take him from me at any time, but please don't.
>
> I don't know where that prayer came from or why I said it."[176]

Her Essence knew about the contract that it had with Jesse's, and that is where this prayer came from. This illustrates so well what I have mentioned before about the imperative of connecting to our Essence, to transcend the personality. We, as a personality, are instruments that simply do not have the reach in perspective of the totality of our reality.

Yes, we are all connected at a much deeper level. The nonphysical entities behind the eight-year old boy, behind Jesse, behind Lewis, and behind all those involved in these tragedies knew that these events were going to happen.[177] They took it on themselves to be part of these events because of a much, much greater purpose.

Deeper Realities

That brings me to this, which I write with the full understanding of the gravity that it implies.

> To the Hitlers, the mass murderers, terrorists, assassins, rapists, and school shooters ... I hear the outcry that you,

---

[175] Ibid., 141.

[176] Ibid., 2.

[177] These are probabilistic timelines, each with greater or lesser chances of occurring. In the case of these particular events, they became essentially certainty when these units of consciousness chose to be participants in them. More about this in book two.

as nonphysical entities, are trying to convey to us. You, as a Unit of Consciousness, chose a body that you knew would be subjected to one of the many brutal, unnurturing environments that humanity has created for itself. An environment that would create such powerful negative psychological forces in that mind that the scream of that internal agony would completely overrun your whisperings of unconditional love. Your outcry is trying to convey to us that our current way is not the way to the harmony that we so much desire in this physical universe. And with the double irony that humanity, in its emotional ignorance, not only will blame you for what it created but will also make you the perfect example of (a nonexistent) "evil" in this world. What an irony, indeed.

If you read this book, you will understand where I am coming from. Notice that I am not talking about the hurtful actions that they did. I am talking about what is behind those actions. As I wrote earlier, people who are hurting others in these ways need to have their freedoms taken away. Still, we need to come to the point of seeing what is behind these tragedies. If Lewis was able to do it when confronted with probably one of the biggest pains that we can experience as humans, that of a mother losing her child to our self-inflicted violence, then that is living proof that we all can.

Leading Life

Enough said. This book is about knowledge and also about action. When you learn to truly lead your life, you automatically become a life leader. As I have showed you here, your actions have direct repercussions at a global level. Always.

What I recommend to you, the reader, is that once you read it, let time pass to integrate all this information. Live your life with the new awareness and see what you discover. Then let your intuition tell you when you are ready for the next pass. Every time you read it, you will peel through new layers of understanding.

Besides the intellectual knowledge that it contains, the main points for you to take and process on your own are as follows.

At a personal level:

- Find your true purpose for this physical insertion. It is your most fundamental obligation to yourself.
- Understand yourself as a human being, how your mind works.
- Learn how to transform your mind in the direction that you want.
- Make use of the tools and techniques that are available.
- Learn tools for conflict resolution and how to put them to practical use in all your everyday relationships.
  At the community level:
- Organize groups of discussion about the topics of this book or related books. It's not just for better intellectual understanding. Even better, these groups can become safe environments for their participants to share their conflicts, fears, and secrets. One of the most basic tools for healing is sharing. It's that simple. Use the available tools for transformation.[178] This requires a deep commitment to mutual respect within the group.
  At a more global level:
- The urgent need to include emotional education in the curriculum of our schools, starting from kindergarten to high school. These courses should not be electives—they should be required at every single level of the education process.

---

[178] A reminder that deeper traumas must be consulted with a professional practitioner.

- Create structured, comprehensive programs for future and current parents who, because of a better emotional education, will know the importance of taking them on under their own will. They are responsible for guiding humanity to its next expression in this physical world.
- Currently, people are educated in such a compartmentalized manner that they can only see a one-sighted solution to our challenges. When economists, with their best intentions, suggest having more children to solve economic numbers, they put us in a path of self-destruction. Encourage schools, universities, and other educational institutions to create interdisciplinary courses required to complete an academic degree so that people understand the ramifications of their decisions at a more encompassing, global level.

May this book be of
support in your journey.

Glossary of Terms

APA: American Psychological Association.

conscious mind: The part of the mind that gives you the awareness of you as an individual. In simple terms, this part of the mind uses the senses to interact with the environment through the decisions that it makes.

EFT (emotional freedom techniques): A mind transformation technique based on acupressure (in this case through tapping) on certain points of the body.

epigenetics: The body's characteristics have been traditionally viewed as dictated by the molecular structure of the genes (gene's coding). Now we understand that a certain gene may be turned on or not depending on different factors, including the environment. Epigenetics studies how these other factors (that are different than a change in the genetic code itself) affect our bodies, including the heritability of this activation or deactivation of genes.

Essence: Another name for the Unit of Consciousness, when capitalized within the text of the book.

explicit transfer: The transfer of programs from parents to kids as a result of the parents' explicit interactions with them. See *implicit transfer* for a better contrasting understanding.

foundational programs: Programs that are generated by events that don't have associations to other events and that become a reference for many other programs.

genetics: The study of heredity in living organisms. In general, based on the study of genes, the molecules inside of our cells that determine the physical characteristics of our bodies.

hard-wired programs: Programs of behavior that, relatively speaking, change very little (or not at all) during the lifetime of the individual.

hypnotherapy: A therapeutic approach that takes explicit advantage of a single state of focus of the mind, which allows access to and processing of the unconscious structures of behavior.

implicit transfer: The transfer of programs from parents to kids as a result of the parents' implicit messages to their kids, either by interacting with them or by their attitudes and comments in general. These are the "hidden" messages behind their actions that get translated into programs of behavior in their kids.

Individualized Consciousness: Another name for Unit of Consciousness, the real essence of who you are as a nonphysical entity.

information filtering effect: The effect of the unconscious in trying to keep its programs stable. Once you have been programmed in a certain way, you will tend to filter your perceptions so that they reinforce your programs.

inspired action: Action congruent with your Essence.

intrapersonal component of the personality: A component of the personality that was generated as a result of experiences in the present physical insertion (life) of the person.

mind: The internal, nonphysical processes that result from consciousness manifesting through a human body.

MTP (mind transformation process): A structured process intended to bring a positive change to a limiting behavior in the person doing it.

MTG (mind transformation guide): A practitioner of MTPs.

NLP (neurolinguistic programming): A psychological approach that makes use of neurology, language, and programming to effect positive changes in our behavior.

nonfoundational programs: Programs that affect our behavior in a more "localized" manner. Their scope is narrower than that of foundational programs.

person: The particular combination of mind and body.

personality: The external manifestation of the mind and the physical structures of the body; in other words, the total sum of our behaviors.

program: As related to the topics of this book, this concept refers to the basic structure for behavior in our minds. It is the structure that the unconscious uses to determine how to (re)act within the environment.

reality set: The particular set of people, events, geographical locations, and times that comprise a particular physical insertion in this universe.

reasoning: A faculty of the mind for manipulation of ideas that seems to follow a logical path to the person making use of it.

soft-wired programs: Programs of behavior that are designed for us to be able to adapt to the environment.

stretched willpower: Extended use of willpower. As presented in this book, this is an undesired life dynamic. Rather, you want to operate under the motivation of inspired action.

subjective objectivity effect: The result of our body/mind combination that makes us believe our perception of reality as an objective experience, when in fact it is just one of the many possible interpretations of the physical world.

transpersonal component of the personality: A component of the personality that was generated as a result of events beyond the present physical insertion (life) of the person.

unconscious: The part of the mind that includes all the processes that you are not normally aware of in your daily activities. This includes the inner functionality of your body, as well as the hidden mechanisms behind your behaviors.

UC: Unit of Consciousness.

Unit of Consciousness: The real essence of who you are as a nonphysical entity.

willpower: The faculty of the mind that allows you to execute tasks without feeling motivation to do them. Also, to restrain a behavior that you would otherwise want to engage in. In essence, it's a faculty that allows to exert control over your behavior.

Appendix A: Main Summary Figures

- Model of the human consciousness:

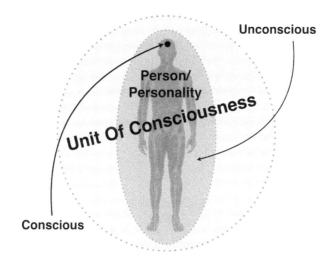

- Structure of the programs in the unconscious:

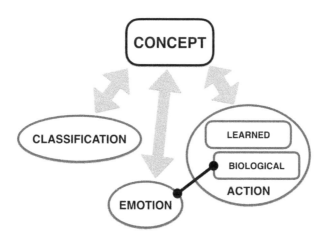

- **Layers of the personality and changeability of biological circuits:**

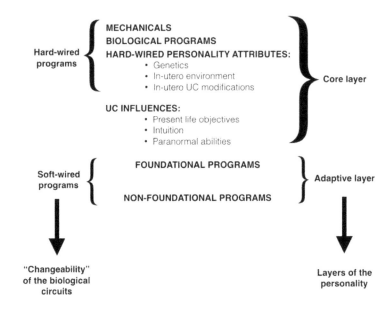

- **Components of the personality and their mechanisms:**

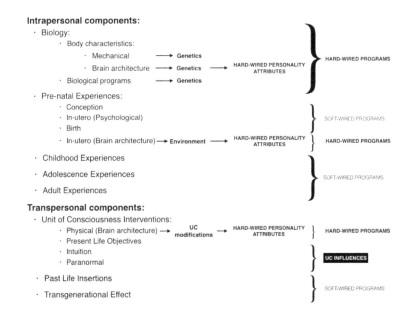

- **Components, mechanisms, and layers of the personality:**

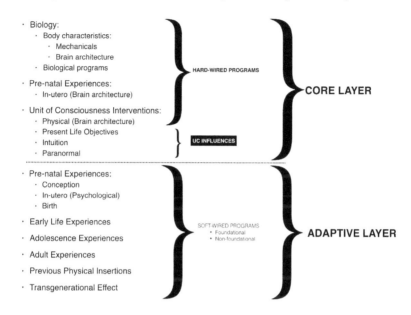

- **Physical functional blocks of behavior:**

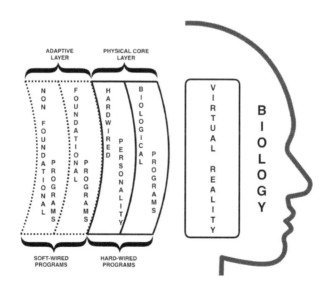

Index

A

Abraham 216

Action xxvi, xxx, xxxi, 7, 19, 22, 28, 29, 37, 54, 55, 58, 59, 61, 62, 63, 64, 72, 73, 81, 84, 96, 97, 105, 112, 113, 121, 150, 159, 164, 167, 168, 169, 197, 209, 215, 241, 242, 243, 244, 247, 260, 266, 267, 271, 272, 280, 302, 305, 312, 313, 337, 338, 341, 352, 353, 355, 357, 358, 362, 363

Adapt 44, 65, 71, 85, 111, 137, 185, 204, 242, 290, 329, 342, 363

Adaptive 86, 245, 248, 290, 342

Addict 121, 122, 141

Addiction 121, 122, 292, 306

Addictions 121, 122, 292, 306

Adolescence 46, 51, 80, 131, 177, 178, 180, 181, 184, 185, 187, 188, 189, 200

Adolescent 140, 179, 181, 182, 183, 184, 185, 186, 187, 200, 245, 264, 270

Adolescents 140, 179, 181, 182, 183, 184, 185, 186, 187, 200, 245, 264, 270

Adopt 82, 83

Adoption 6, 7, 83, 150, 222

Adult 3, 5, 45, 46, 47, 48, 65, 67, 75, 77, 82, 92, 99, 119, 131, 132, 144, 145, 146, 147, 148, 156, 164, 172, 173, 179, 180, 182, 183, 184, 185, 186, 187, 196, 198, 199, 200, 201, 202, 203, 212, 213, 214, 227, 231, 234, 243, 264, 270, 273, 279, 287, 293, 298, 299, 302, 328, 355

Adults 3, 5, 45, 46, 47, 48, 65, 67, 75, 77, 82, 92, 99, 119, 131, 132, 144, 145, 146, 147, 148, 156, 164, 172, 173, 179, 180, 182, 183, 184, 185, 186, 187, 196, 198, 199, 200, 201, 202, 203, 212, 213, 214, 227, 231, 234, 243, 264, 270, 273, 279, 287, 293, 298, 299, 302, 328, 355

Affirmation 125, 201, 202

Affirmations 125, 201, 202

AHEFT xix

Alcoholism 121, 244

Angeles xix, 278

Ann xix, 257

Annette 103

Apple 39, 40, 54

Archaic 116, 117

Architecture 133, 135, 136, 152, 153, 161, 188, 246

Assassins 15, 111, 356

Association 28, 39, 40, 41, 42, 43, 50, 56, 74, 83, 92, 124, 138, 173, 276, 289, 299, 316, 323, 324, 327, 345, 361

Associatively 32, 39

Assumption 12, 262, 287, 288, 289, 290, 292, 295, 298, 300, 301, 303

Attributes 37, 93, 133, 134, 135, 136, 137, 217, 246, 247, 341, 342

Authority 73, 86, 180, 181, 185, 199, 207, 208, 210, 261, 269, 273, 274, 275, 301, 302, 316, 317, 322

F

G

M

Machine 8, 11, 16, 17, 32, 34, 38, 57,
    64, 67, 71, 84, 90, 91, 92, 94,
    119, 132, 155, 205, 206, 207,
    236, 271, 289, 348
Malala 275
Mandela 275
Manifestation 20, 242, 261, 281, 363
Manifestations 20, 242, 261, 281, 363
Manipulation 47, 95, 136, 140, 206,
    228, 247, 363
Mapping 338
Marketing 136, 137, 141, 205, 206,
    236, 341
Marriage xxiv, 6, 7, 82, 105, 156, 257
Marrying 105
Martin 257, 275
Martinez xix, 37, 143, 144, 152, 154,
    157, 216, 217
Mass 111, 121, 172, 208, 211, 213,
    239, 268, 272, 288, 351, 356
Massacre 113, 114
Maximize 25, 31, 38, 60, 61, 143
Mechanic 133, 136, 308, 312, 342
Mechanical 47, 71, 84, 102, 133, 137,
    238, 242, 246, 284, 313, 330
Mechanism xxix, xxx, 1, 7, 13, 15, 16,
    22, 23, 25, 26, 31, 32, 43, 44,
    50, 52, 56, 57, 61, 72, 76, 90,
    113, 117, 118, 122, 129, 131,
    133, 134, 143, 185, 191, 203,
    204, 205, 208, 210, 213, 215,
    242, 243, 247, 262, 263, 273,
    275, 277, 280, 281, 289, 298,
    299, 300, 305, 306, 307, 323,
    339, 355, 363, 366, 367
Mechanisms xxix, xxx, 1, 7, 13, 15,
    16, 22, 23, 25, 26, 31, 32, 43,
    44, 50, 52, 56, 57, 61, 72, 76,
    90, 113, 117, 118, 122, 129, 131,
    133, 134, 143, 185, 191, 203,
    204, 205, 208, 210, 213, 215,
    242, 243, 247, 262, 263, 273,
    275, 277, 280, 281, 289, 298,
    299, 300, 305, 306, 307, 323,
    339, 355, 363, 366, 367
Medical 5, 6, 7, 13, 22, 37, 46, 68, 84,
    121, 122, 143, 159, 170, 257
Meditation 47, 48, 92, 110, 114, 229,
    256, 331, 332, 333, 334, 346
Member xxi, 29, 105, 120, 139, 190,
    194, 277, 279, 280, 281, 282,
    285, 306, 314
Memories 20, 21, 25, 37, 200, 217,
    236, 252, 255, 256, 257, 263,
    272, 280, 286, 293, 301, 302,
    332, 338
Memory 20, 21, 25, 36, 37, 173, 200,
    217, 236, 252, 255, 256, 257,
    263, 272, 278, 280, 284, 286,
    293, 301, 302, 332, 333, 338
Mental xxxiii, 49, 72, 93, 97, 99,
    100, 102, 106, 107, 109, 110,
    112, 121, 144, 146, 166, 182,
    193, 208, 282, 285, 288, 297,
    315, 322
Merriam-Webster 28
Michael 7, 14, 218, 230, 258, 259
Mind-body 5, 138
Mindfulness 22, 332, 333
Minimize 29
Mode xxv, 51, 81, 83, 109, 110, 138,
    166, 196, 203, 329, 349
Model xx, xxix, xxx, xxxiv, 11, 12, 13,
    14, 15, 16, 18, 19, 21, 23, 24, 25,
    26, 29, 42, 46, 47, 53, 78, 133,
    134, 135, 137, 162, 163, 164,
    171, 177, 178, 193, 194, 224,
    268, 270, 271, 287, 334, 337,
    338, 365

O

P

S

V

W